GOD'S LIFE IN
TRINITY

GOD's LIFE IN TRINITY

Miroslav Volf and Michael Welker, editors

FORTRESS PRESS
MINNEAPOLIS

GOD'S LIFE IN TRINITY

Sponsoring Editor: J. Michael West
Production Editor: James Korsmo
Copyeditor: Emily Cheney
Proofreader: Laura Weller
Design and typesetting: James Korsmo
Cover art: Half Shield of Triangles from an Apse. Musee Archeologique, El Jemm (Thysdrus), Tunisia. © Gilles Mermet / Art Resource, NY
Cover design: Ann Delgehausen

Library of Congress Cataloging-in-Publication Data

God's life in Trinity / edited by Miroslav Volf and Michael Welker.
    p. cm.
  Includes index.
  ISBN 0-8006-3823-9 (alk. paper)
  1. Trinity.   I. Volf, Miroslav. II. Welker, Michael.
BT113.G595 2006
231'.044—dc22
                                                                2006003301

10   09   08   07   06   2   3   4   5   6   7   8   9   10

CONTENTS

Contents

CONTRIBUTORS

NANCY ELIZABETH BEDFORD was born in Comodoro Rivadavia, Argentina. She studied in Tübingen from 1989 to 1994, where she obtained her doctorate in theology under the supervision of Jürgen Moltmann. Her most recent book is *Puntos de Encuentro* (Buenos Aires: ISEDET, 2005), co-edited with Mercedes García Bachmann and Marisa Strizzi. It explores feminist theory and theology from a multidisciplinary Latin American perspective. She is Georgia Harkness Professor of Applied Theology at Garrett-Evangelical Theological Seminary, Evanston, and Profesora Extraordinaria No Residente at the Instituto Universitario ISEDET, Buenos Aires.

SARAH A. COAKLEY is Edward Mallinckrodt Professor of Divinity at Harvard Divinity School, where she teaches systematic theology, philosophy of religion, gender theory and feminist theology, and the history of Christian spirituality. Before coming to Harvard in 1993 she held posts at Lancaster University and Oriel College, Oxford. Her books include *Christ without Absolutes: A Study of the Christology of Ernst Troeltsch* (1988), *Powers and Submissions: Spirituality, Philosophy and Gender* (2002), and *Re-Thinking Gregory of Nyssa* (editor, 2003). She is at work on a systematic theology, the first volume of which will appear as *God, Sexuality and the Self: An Essay 'On the Trinity'* (2006). She is the recent recipient of a $2 million Templeton Foundation grant to develop, with Professor Martin Nowak, the discussion of theology and evolutionary biology at Harvard.

NICHOLAS CONSTAS holds a doctorate in patristics from the Catholic University of America in Washington, D.C. He has taught graduate courses in patristics and Orthodox theology at Holy Cross Greek Orthodox School of Theology (1993–98) and at Harvard Divinity School (1998–2004). He is the author of *Proclus of Constantinople and the Cult of the Virgin in Late Antiquity* (2003), as well as numerous studies and articles in journals, including *Harvard Theological Review*, *The Journal of Early Christian Studies*, and the *Dumbarton Oaks Papers*. He is currently living in Greece.

HARVEY G. COX JR. is the Hollis Professor of Divinity, the oldest endowed professorship in America. He has been teaching at Harvard since 1965, when his book *The Secular City* became an international bestseller. His *Feast of Fools* (1969) was nominated for the National Book Prize. Among his other books are *Many Mansions: A Christian's Encounters with Other Faiths* (1998), and *Fire from Heaven* (1995), which traces the worldwide growth of Pentecostalism. Among his interests are urbanization, theological developments in world Christianity, Jewish-Christian relations, and current spiritual movements (especially in Latin America and Asia). His current research project is the history of Christian interpretations of Islam. His latest book is *When Jesus Came to Harvard: Making Moral Choices Today* (2004).

DAVID FERGUSSON is Professor of Divinity in the University of Edinburgh, having previously held the Chair of Systematic Theology in the University of Aberdeen (1990–2000). He is the author of several books, including *The Cosmos and the Creator* (1998) and *Church, State and Civil Society* (2004). From 2000 to 2002 he served as President of the Society for the Study of Theology.

DAVID H. KELSEY is a graduate of Haverford College, Yale Divinity School, and Yale Graduate School. He has taught at Dartmouth College and Yale Divinity School, where he is the Luther Weigle Professor Emeritus of Theology. Along with influential books on theological education, he has authored several theological works: *The Fabric of Paul Tillich's Theology* (1967), *Proving Doctrine: Uses of Scripture in Recent Theology* (2d ed. 1999), and most recently *Imagining Redemption* (2005). He is completing a book on theological anthropology.

M. DOUGLAS MEEKS is the Cal Turner Chancellor Professor of Theology and Wesleyan Studies at Vanderbilt University Divinity School, Nashville, and former Dean of Wesley Theological Seminary in Washington, D.C. From his earliest work, *Origins of the Theology of Hope* (1974), through *God the Economist: The Doctrine of God and Political Economy* (1989), to *Trinity, Community and Power: Mapping Trajectories in Wesleyan Theology* (ed., 2004), he has explored issues in systematic theology, Wesleyan theology, and the intersection of religion with contemporary life.

DANIEL L. MIGLIORE is the Charles Hodge Professor of Systematic Theology at Princeton Theological Seminary. Among his several books are *Called to Freedom: Liberation Theology and the Future of Christian Doctrine* (1980); *Faith Seeking Understanding: An Introduction to Christian Theology* (2d ed., 2004); and *Rachel's Cry: Prayer of Lament and Rebirth of Hope* (with Kathleen D. Billman, 1999).

GERALD O'COLLINS, SJ, was born in Melbourne, Australia, and received his doctorate at Cambridge University in 1968. Since 1974 he has been teaching at the Pontifical Gregorian University, Rome, where he was dean of the theology faculty (1985–91). Alone or with others, he has published hundreds of articles and forty-four books. His recent books include a series of interdisciplinary symposia (edited with Stephen T. Davis and Daniel Kendall): *Resurrection* (1997), *Trinity* (1999), *Incarnation* (2002), and *Redemption* (2004), as well as *Catholicism: The Story of Catholic Christianity* (with Mario Farrugia, 2003).

JOHN POLKINGHORNE is past President and now Fellow of Queen's College, Cambridge, and a Fellow of the Royal Society. A former Professor of Mathematical Physics, he is also an ordained priest in the Church of England. He was knighted in 1997. Among his many pioneering works in the area of religion and science are *The Quantum World* (1985), *Reason and Reality* (1991), *The Faith of a Physicist* (1996), and *Science and Theology: An Introduction* (1998). His latest work is *Exploring Reality: The Intertwining of Science and Religion* (2006).

PHILIP J. ROSATO was born in Philadelphia, studied classical languages and philosophy at Fordham University, and pursued his doctorate under the direction of Walter Kasper at Eberhard-Karls University in Tübingen. From 1979 to 2004, he lectured in systematic theology at the Pontifical Gregorian University in Rome. At present he is a member of the Department of Theology at St. Joseph University in Philadelphia. His books include *The Spirit as Lord: The Pneumatology of Karl Barth* (1981), *Introduction to the Theology of the Sacraments* (1992), and *The Lord's Supper and Social Love* (1994).

WILLIAM SCHWEIKER is Professor of Theological Ethics at the University of Chicago. He is the author of several books, most recently *Theological Ethics and Global Dynamics: In the Time of Many Worlds* (2004) and is also editor of the monumental *Blackwell Companion to Religious Ethics* (2005). His work engages theological and ethical questions attentive to global dynamics, comparative ethics, and the possibilities of a robust religious humanism. An award-winning essayist and popular lecturer, Professor Schweiker is an ordained minister in the United Methodist Church.

DIRK J. SMIT is Professor of Systematic Theology and Ethics in the Faculty of Theology at Stellenbosch University in South Africa. A prolific author, he has written more than 80 articles for journals and chapters for books, and he has been a Visiting Professor at the Graduate Theological Union, Berkeley; Duke University; Princeton Theological Seminary; and Heidelberg University, Germany. He is from the Reformed tradition and involved in local and ecumenical church activities, and his current research involves ecclesiology and globalization.

BRYAN D. SPINKS is Professor of Liturgical Studies and Chair of the Liturgy Program at Yale Institute of Sacred Music and Yale Divinity School. A priest of the Church of England, before coming to Yale he taught liturgy in the Divinity Faculty of Cambridge University. From 1986 until 2000 he served on the Church of England Liturgical Commission and was involved in the compilation of the new Church of England liturgy, *Common Worship 2000*. His work on baptismal rituals and theologies is to be published in two volumes in 2006. He is currently working on worship and sacramental theology in the Age of Reason.

Contributors

RONALD F. THIEMANN, Professor of Theology and of Religion and Society, has been at Harvard since 1986, first as Dean of the Divinity School (1986-98) and then in his current professorial position. He also is a Faculty Fellow at the John F. Kennedy School's Center for Public Leadership. An ordained Lutheran and a specialist on the role of religion in public life, Thiemann is the author of *Revelation and Theology: The Gospel as Narrated Promise* (1985), *Constructing a Public Theology: The Church in a Pluralistic Culture* (1991), and *Religion in Public Life: A Dilemma for Democracy* (1996); he is also an editor of *Who Will Provide? The Changing Role of Religion in American Social Welfare* (2000). He is currently working on a book-length project entitled *Prisoners of Conscience: Public Intellectuals in a Time of Crisis*. Before coming to Harvard, Thiemann taught for ten years at Haverford College, where he also served as acting provost and acting president.

MIROSLAV VOLF is Henry B. Wright Professor of Systematic Theology at Yale Divinity School. A native of Croatia, he is a member of the Presbyterian Church U.S.A. and the Evangelical Church in Croatia, and he was involved for a decade in international ecumenical dialogues, especially with the Vatican Council for Promotion of Christian Unity. Among his many book publications are *Work in the Spirit: Toward a Theology of Work* (1991), *Exclusion and Embrace: A Theological Exploration of Identity, Otherness, and Reconciliation* (1996), *After Our Likeness: The Church as the Image of the Trinity* (1998), and most recently *Free of Charge: Giving and Forgiving in a Culture Stripped of Grace* (2005).

JOHN WEBSTER is Professor of Systematic Theology at the University of Aberdeen. After theological studies in Cambridge, he taught at the Universities of Durham, Toronto, and Oxford before taking up his present post. He has written extensively on modern German theology, especially the work of Karl Barth and Eberhard Jüngel, and on topics in Christian dogmatics and ethics. His recent books include *Word and Church* (2001), *Holy Scripture* (2003), *Confessing God* (2005), and *Barth's Earlier Theology* (2005). He is editor of the *International Journal of Systematic Theology* and a Fellow of the Royal Society of Edinburgh.

MICHAEL WELKER is Professor of Systematic Theology and Director of the Internationales Wissenschaftsforum at the University of Heidelberg, Germany. His work in systematic theology also incorporates insights from biblical theology and reflection on contemporary science and culture. He is a frequent lecturer in North America, and he has taught at Princeton Theological Seminary, McMaster Unviersity, Harvard University, and the University of Chicago. His chief works in English include *God the Spirit* (1994), *Creation and Reality* (1999), *What Happens in Holy Communion?* (2000), and two works with John Polkinghorne: *The End of the World and the Ends of God* (2000) and *Faith in the Living God* (2001).

Nicholas Wolterstorff is Noah Porter Professor Emeritus of Philosophical Theology, and Fellow of Berkeley College, at Yale University. He is a graduate of Calvin College, and received his doctorate in philosophy from Harvard in 1956. After teaching for thirty years at Calvin College, he joined the Divinity School at Yale. He has been president of the American Philosophical Association (Central Division) and of the Society of Christian Philosophers. He has given the Wilde Lectures at Oxford, the Gifford Lectures at St. Andrews, and the Stone Lectures at Princeton Theological Seminary. His most recent publications are *Divine Discourse* (1995), *John Locke and the Ethics of Belief* (1996), *Thomas Reid and the Story of Epistemology* (2001), *Education for Life* (2002), and *Education for Shalom* (2004). He is currently working on a project about justice.

PREFACE

Perhaps no area of Christian theology has received such intense and fruitful work in the last century as our understanding of the Trinity. In this volume theologians from the entire world seek to advance our understandings of God's triune life, especially by engaging and extending the signal contributions of Jürgen Moltmann on the occasion of his eightieth birthday on April 8, 2006.

Jürgen Moltmann has shaped the international theological conversation in the twentieth century more than any other Protestant theologian since Karl Barth, Dietrich Bonhoeffer, and Paul Tillich. In the last decades, the power and attraction of his thought have been recognized throughout the world with more than two hundred dissertations written on his theology and with eleven honorary doctorates and countless other honors and prizes conferred upon him.

Moltmann's *Theology of Hope* (1965, English translation 1967), now in its fifteenth printing in 2005 in Germany, had an effect in the second half of the twentieth century comparable to that of Karl Barth's commentary on Romans in the first half: It was a passionate attempt at a new form of theological thought that was received with both enthusiasm and controversy. Works of "political theology," a field that Moltmann developed with Johann Baptist Metz and others, resulted and gave occasion for many-sided exchanges across the Iron Curtain. Moltmann, at the time energized by left-Hegelian and neo-Marxist thought, was criticized by Schwabian pietists as a theologian loyal to Moscow. Ironically, he was even forbidden to speak in some Eastern Bloc countries. In retrospect it is clear that this form of theology was an effective critique of orthodox Marxism and contributed more to the fall of the Berlin Wall than to the polarizing warriors of the Cold War.

The next significant theological impulse came from Moltmann's book *The Crucified God* (1973, English translation 1974), which—along with the *Theology of Hope*—influenced liberation theology in Latin America and elsewhere in multiple ways. The reception of this book also required the author to confront and respond to varying reactions. His attempts to promote a contextual theology of liberation met with both friendly reception and unfriendly distancing on the part of other theologians. Theology in critical engagement with contemporary trends was for some not sufficiently theological, for others not sufficiently critical, and for yet others not sufficiently timely.

Jürgen Moltmann's theological passion and delight in discovery nonetheless were not dampened, even in the midst of controversy and opposition. His next important achievement came in his trinitarian works, particularly his book *The Trinity and the Kingdom* (1980, English translation 1981). Here Moltmann searched for new insights in the doctrine of God in an attempt to intensify dialogue with Orthodox theologians, especially those in Greece and Romania.

The contributions in this volume are based on this last strand of his thought: almost all the articles are devoted to trinitarian theology and the doctrine of God. The volume is divided into four major parts. The first, "Trinity and Humanity," explores intersections between the triune life of God and some thought patterns and practices of modernity. The second part, "Trinity and Religious Traditions," examines the bearing of the doctrine of the Trinity for some central ecclesial and interreligious problems of today. The third part, "Trinity and God-Talk," contains dogmatic reflections on the intradivine life and its bearing on the life of the world. Finally, the last part, "Trinity and Historical Theology," is devoted to a critical exploration of the resources offered by the Christian tradition for Trinitarian thinking today.

At the same time as this book is being published, a similar one is appearing in Germany, published by Gütersloher Verlagshaus. The German volume, *Der lebendige Gott als Trinität*, first offers contributions on the theme of "God's self-revelation and the doctrine of the Trinity" from the perspectives of classical dogmatics, biblical theology, theological ethics, and comparative religions. The second section offers contributions from systematic and biblical theology to the theme "the doctrine of the Trinity in Scripture, creeds, and doctrinal development." These articles throw light on certain developments in the recent history of theology in exemplary fashion. The third section examines the bases for and contemporary challenges of the conversation between the church and Israel about the doctrine of God under the title "Jewish theology and the Christian doctrine of the Trinity." The fourth section considers the challenges for the "Trinity in ecumenical and interreligious conversations," with particular emphasis on conversations with Orthodox theology and with Islam. The last section ("Trinity, ecclesiology, and spirituality") contains contributions from systematic and practical theology on the subject of worship and the communal spirit in postmodern societies and on the relevance of the doctrine of the Trinity in the theology of baptism, spirituality, and preaching. Further information appears on the final page of this volume.

We heartily thank Tobias Hanel and Wolfram Langpape on the German side. Particular thanks goes to Heike Springhart for her intensive support during the preparation of the contributions for publication. On the American side, special thanks goes to Rose-Anne Moore for preparation of the manuscripts for publication.

A good relationship with Gütersloher Verlagshaus and Fortress Press, especially with Dietrich Steen and Michael West, has enabled not only pleasant cooperation with the publishing houses, but also the aesthetic and thematic affinities between both volumes of this *Festschrift*. For that we are also thankful.

Part ONE

TRINITY
AND HUMANITY

CHAPTER 1

BEING AS GOD IS

Trinity and Generosity

Miroslav Volf

AFFINITY

It is obvious but not trite to state that the triune God stands at the beginning and at the end of the Christian pilgrimage and, therefore, at the center of Christian faith. Christians are born as they come out of the baptismal waters into which they were submerged in the name of the Holy Three. After crossing the ultimate threshold of the resurrection and the final judgment where their pilgrimage ends, "in the deep and bright essence" of the exalted divine being, they will behold and recognize, in the words of Dante's *Divine Comedy*, three spinning circles of "different colors" but of "the same dimensions."[1]

The way the triune God is related to the beginning and the end of the Christian pilgrimage and, therefore, to the whole course of it, might be imagined skeletally something like this: God sets up a race course, gives humans a set of rules, and then commands them to run the course. God waits at the finish line and evaluates how well they performed. In this scenario, the nature of God would be more or less irrelevant to the character of the Christian pilgrimage. Not who God is but what God demands is what would matter; or rather, who God is would matter only to the extent that it informed what God demands. Whether God is triune or not would be of no direct consequence.

Christians, however, have not thought of God as the beginning and the end of their pilgrimage in this way. The nature of God's being, not just God's commands, is integral to the character of Christian beginnings and ends. As baptism *into* the triune name attests, beginning the Christian pilgrimage does not mean simply to respond to God's summons but to enter into communion with the triune God; to end the Christian pilgrimage does not mean simply to have accomplished an earthly task but to enter perfect communion with the triune God.

Unlike simple conjunction, communion presupposes a certain degree of likeness. There is an *affinity* between human beings and God and, therefore, between the way Christians—and by extension all human beings—ought to live and the way God is. The nature of God, therefore, fundamentally determines the character of the Christian life. It is because of such affinity between God and human beings that in the Sermon on the Mount Jesus could issue what can surely sound like an impossible and strange command: "Be . . . as your heavenly Father is"—and, therefore, act as God does (Matt. 5:48).

The injunction "Be as God is!" and the affinity between God and human beings that it presupposes form the most basic topic of my chapter. What could such an injunction mean? How should we understand this "being *as* God" by those who are manifestly *not* God? How does the nature of the triune God impinge upon the character of the Christian life? I will address these questions from only one angle in this chapter, that of gift giving. Examination of the topic from other perspectives—such as creativity, reconciliation, or identity—could supplement and complete the exploration; but here I will focus on gift giving and begin by addressing possible objections to this way of formulating the task.

ANALOGIES

The first and most fundamental objection could be that I build my view of giving on what human beings in principle cannot adequately know—the character of the triune God. God dwells in an unapproachable light. We can draw no conclusions from the divine life about the shape of human living for the simple reason that we do not know enough about divine life to draw any such conclusions, or at least no conclusions of significance.[2] If true, the argument would apply no less to divine attributes than to Trinitarian persons and their relations.[3] For we know no more and no less what divine love is than what divine personhood is. If we cannot speak of either, God would remain radically unknowable and would concern us only marginally.

My assumption, however, is that we *can* know God on the only basis on which God is knowable: God's self-revelation. In God's self-revelation, we are by definition dealing with God as God is in relation to creation (the so-called *economic Trinity*), not with God apart from creation (the so-called *immanent Trinity*). As we explore the relation between the Trinity and the shape of human living, we should primarily build on the claims about the economic Trinity and venture into the territory of the immanent Trinity more tentatively and only as necessary—a procedure I will follow below. But venture into the territory of the immanent Trinity we must. If we were not entitled to make claims about the immanent Trinity on the basis of the economic Trinity's engagement with the world, then in the encounter with the economic Trinity, we would not be dealing with who God truly is.[4] Appealing to divine mystery to forestall the movement of thought from economic to immanent Trinity amounts to a denial of the divine revelation's actuality; claims about the immanent Trinity are inescapable if we are to speak about the economic Trinity adequately.

As we venture into claims about God as Trinity, it is important to keep in mind that the terms *immanent Trinity* and *economic Trinity* do not designate two related but different aspects of a statically conceived divine being. Rather, their unity in itself comprises a movement—from *immanent Trinity* to *economic Trinity* and finally to the *Trinity in glory*, that is, the Trinity in the world to come when the economy of salvation will have been completed and human beings' participation in God perfected.[5]

Someone may grant that we are entitled to make claims about the *immanent Trinity* but still argue that God is nonetheless so different from human beings that we do well *not* to draw inferences about the character of human living from the nature of the triune God.[6] What this second objection rightly underscores is that the parallels between the life of God and the life of humanity cannot be exact or, in some respects, even close. For at least two reasons, all attempts at connecting the Trinity with the character of human life that operate with one-to-one correspondences are false. First, human beings are manifestly not God. As created beings, we can correspond to the uncreated God only in *creaturely* appropriate ways. Second, as long as we are on the Christian pilgrimage, we are inescapably marred by sin and cannot be fully adequate creaturely images of the triune God, which is what we are destined to become. As fleshly beings, we can correspond to God only in *historically* appropriate ways.[7]

These limits notwithstanding, correspondences between God and human beings can be sought on the basis of the affinity between the two. Because of the limits of analogies, as we develop the correspondences, we cannot simply proceed from the divine to the human, saying, "This is how God is; therefore, this is how humans should be." We must proceed *also* from the human to the divine, as in, "This is who human beings are as distinct from God; therefore, this is how they can correspond to God."[8]

MODELS

I operate here with what is sometimes called *social trinitarianism*, although not with the kind often contrasted sharply with a psychological model.[9] Though important, the debate between the advocates of the two models, the one allegedly Eastern and the other Western, is often unproductive because it tends to disregard a rather obvious fact: Each model is inadequate to the extent to which it fails to accommodate the truth of the other.

The most important early advocates of these models, Gregory of Nyssa and Augustine, were aware of their inadequacies. Gregory of Nyssa is well-known for employing social images for the Trinity (e.g., individual human beings as belonging to one human nature reflect divine persons as belonging to one divine nature). Yet he not only qualified this model significantly in order to guard the unity of God but also argued in *Contra Eunomium* that a social model, though essential, needs to be supplemented by other models.[10] Augustine clearly preferred a psychological model (Trinitarian persons are related to the one God and to each other as memory, intellect, and will are related to the human mind) and developed it with great power. But he was cognizant of the limits of this model and qualified it in important ways precisely by giving significant room to sociality within the Trinity. His understanding of persons as relations notwithstanding, he asserted that the Father "is also something with reference to himself"—a claim that likewise holds true for the Son and the Spirit.[11] In his account, the disanalogy between memory, understanding, and will on the one hand, and divine persons on the other, lies precisely in the fact that in the one God "there are three persons" and not one, as in one human being, and that therefore the Son, for instance, does his own remembering, his own understanding, and his own loving, even if his whole being "comes to him from the Father."[12]

The position developed below is *social Trinitarian* in the weak sense of that term, a sense that with some important adjustments might arguably fit not only Gregory of Nyssa but also Augustine. Moreover, along with most *social Trinitarians*, I think that we should not root the doctrine of the Trinity in the character of divine self-revelation[13] or self-communication[14]—a move that owes too much to the metaphysics of subjectivity—but in the history of mutual engagement of the *persons* of the Trinity in the economy of salvation.[15] Although we know God only on the basis of God's self-revelation, it is not the inner logic of divine self-revelation that demands that we think in Trinitarian terms (identity-in-difference of the communicator and the communicated) but the specific character of each actor in the drama of divine self-revelation and the nature of their relations.

I have entitled my chapter "Being as God Is." Is our being like the triune God a result of our efforts? It is—but only because God who works in us does not work without us, as Martin Luther famously put it in his *Bondage of the Will*.[16] So when I speak about human *imaging* of the Trinity, I mean that human beings receive themselves as created in the image of the Trinity by the power of the Spirit. Their *imaging* of the Trinity is the gift of God's movement out of the circumference of the Trinitarian life to create human beings and, after they have sinned, to restore them by dwelling within them and taking them into the perfect communion of love, which God is. The simple command "Be as God is!" would be oppressive and empty moralizing. If the best Christian traditions have not cured us of a moralizing predicated on the fallacious principle "You can because you ought,"[17] then Karl Marx's powerful critique of utopian socialism should have.[18] Because God has made us to reflect God's own triune being, our human tasks are not first of all to *do* as God does—and certainly not to make ourselves as God is—but to let ourselves be indwelled by God and to celebrate and proclaim what God has done, is doing, and will do. As we shall see below, this itself is one of the ways in which we imitate the Trinity—because something analogous is what the three persons of the Trinity do for and with one another in the economy of salvation and, somewhat differently, apart from it.

What is the content of *imitatio Trinitatis* that is made possible as the triune God draws us by the Spirit into communion with the divine three who are the holy one? As I have suggested earlier, we could explore the content of *imitatio Trinitatis* under at least four rubrics: creativity, generosity, reconciliation, and identity.[19] Here, I will limit myself to generosity, focusing only on certain aspects of it.[20]

In exploring the relationship between God's giving and ours, a crucial conceptual distinction needs to be made between giving and forgiving. Here and elsewhere I distinguish rather sharply between them; and as I write here about generosity, I will not address the issue of forgiveness. In this essay, I employ *giving* in a narrower though more basic sense. In its broader sense, of course, *giving* includes forgiving. When I forgive, I give—I give people who have transgressed against me the gift of releasing them from their genuine debt to me. Yet there is something unique about the gift of forgiveness. Forgiveness presupposes wrongdoing against givers, whereas other kinds of gifts presuppose simple need on the part of receivers (as when I help someone whose life has been made impossible by natural disaster) or the givers' delight in those to whom they give (as when I give my child a present upon returning from a trip). The dynamic of gift giving changes when wrongdoing is involved. Hence it is important to keep *giving* and *forgiving* conceptually distinct, while at the same time not lose sight of the fact that *forgiving*, as the English word implies, is also a form of *giving*. When it comes to *giving*, as distinct from *forgiving*, what then might it mean to "be as God is"?

FREEDOM

God gives freely. Take creation, viewed under the aspect of God's gift giving, as an example.[21] As a creative giver, God is under no compulsion to create. The compulsion does not come from outside; apart from God's creating, nothing exists but God. Neither does the compulsion come from inside, from God's own nature. Unlike Plotinus's One, which "is what he has to be" and which "acts as he has to act on account [of] what he necessarily is,"[22] God wills and decides and is free in the narrow but important sense of being self-determined. At the same time, creation is not a divine whim.[23] God gives as creator when the plenitude of divine love turns away from itself toward the nothingness of nonbeing. To be moved by oneself in love is to be divinely free.

Since God gives freely, we should too. That is how the apostle Paul thought of gift giving as he urged the Corinthians to provide financial assistance for the Jerusalem poor. It should be "a voluntary gift and not . . . an extortion" (2 Cor. 9:5). The apostle's thought was not far in this regard from that of Seneca, who said: "He who by his very hesitation has shown that he made his bestowal unwillingly has not 'given,' but has failed to withstand the effort to extract it."[24] To give properly is to give freely.

True, we are not divinely free when we give freely. First, we are human and not divine. God gives out of God's own proper resources; we can give only because we have been given to by God from whom, through whom, and for whom we exist. Fundamentally, we are not self-moved; but in our very being and activity, we are borne by God. When we give freely, it is God who gives through us. Second, we are sinners living in a sinful world. We are reluctant givers and need to be urged, even commanded, to give and to do it freely. If it feels to us as if the command to give is a constraint, it is because those who are captive to sin spontaneously *resist* giving. The command to give freely is part of a sketch of the character of life freed from sin. It nudges us to live as who we truly are as creatures redeemed by God. To the extent that we do so, the command is not a constraint but a portrayal of what we, indwelled by God, spontaneously do: give for the benefit of another.

THE GOOD OF ANOTHER

When God gives, God seeks the good of another. Consider again creation. God does not give in order to get something, unless what God "gets" is the delight in creatures. God does not need anything. That is partly what it means to be God—to lack nothing. If giving were a way of getting, God would not give at all. Not lacking anything, God would not need to get anything and so would not give anything. God gives without self-seeking and for the benefit of others. That kind of giving is at the heart of who God is.

We too should give for others' benefit. Indeed, to actively promote others' benefit is what it means to give. When we buy or sell, we give money or goods in order to receive one or the other. We engage in the transaction for our own sake. Our own good drives the whole process. The same is true when we lend. Givers, on the other hand, renounce gain for themselves and bestow it on others. Seneca put the connection between divine and human giving for the benefit of others well: "He who gives benefits imitates the gods, he who seeks a return [imitates] money-lenders."[25]

Of course, just as we often give reluctantly rather than freely, so we often give to get something for ourselves rather than to benefit others. We may give in order to receive something similar in return; we may give in order to receive honor and praise; or we may give to pay off a debt to our bad conscience or to stockpile moral capital that we intend to spend later as we see fit. Whether we give in order to extract goods from others, win praise for magnanimity, or put a fig leaf over our moral nakedness, in one way or another our generosity often proves either counterfeit or impure. We give to ourselves, in whole or in part.[26] But that is not how God gives. True, unlike God, in relation to others we cannot be *only* givers—at least, not as long as others fail to care for us. To survive and thrive and to have anything to give, for the most part we cooperate with one another by exchanging goods and services for their rough equivalents. Unlike God, we are traders, and legitimately so; but like God, we are also givers. We are good givers to the extent that we give for others' benefit.

There are two typical occasions on which we give for others' benefit: first, our delight in them and, second, their need.

Delight

God gives because God delights. It is not in relation to creation that God is first and foremost a giver. The gifts are most originally given among the three divine persons. Some theologians think of the three divine persons in the way some ancients thought about the Three Graces of Greco-Roman antiquity—"one for bestowing a benefit, one for receiving it, and a third for returning it."[27] According to this pattern, the Father would give, the Son would receive, and the Holy Spirit would return. But, as the honoree of this volume has argued, this pattern is one-sided and unfaithful to biblical salvation history.[28] It must also be said that each divine person gives, receives, and returns. Each loves and glorifies the other two, and each receives love and glory from them. One does not give first, with the result that the others would be indebted, but all give in the eternally moving circle of exchanges. Because they give in this way, they have all things in common except that which distinguishes them from each other. Their eternal bliss is the delight of this loving gift exchange.

Occasionally, something of the wonder of the perfect circular movement of gifts happens in the here and now, between human beings deeply marred by sin. Lovers can experience this wonder in their amorous embraces. Sexual union is then a sacrament of love—not just a sacrament of human love, but also a means of expressing and mediating divine love.[29] Pleasure—pleasure of the soul no less than of the body—given to the other and for the other's sake *is* then a pleasure received. A pleasure received by the other is, almost paradoxically, a pleasure returned to the giver.

Christmas gift giving at its best can be such an exchange, although it often is not. Each person gives, and each receives. No one gives first so that others feel obliged to reciprocate. All give and receive at the same time; or rather, each receives in turn so that all can rejoice with one another. Each is grateful, each generous, and all are rejoicing in each other's joy. Gifts themselves are no longer just things that people need, like, or desire. They are sacraments of love, both divine and human. The whole ritual is a feast of delight—delight in things given, delight in acts of giving and receiving, delight in persons giving and receiving, and delight in the community enacted by the whole process.

Need

Need is another reason why God gives, although not God's need. God does not have any, unless you want to call the fully and eternally satisfied divine desire to love and to delight in the flourishing of the beloved a need. It is to satisfy creatures' needs that God gives. Love spills over the rim of the Trinitarian circle of reciprocity, and gifts flow to creatures. Naked need is the reason for God's giving, not a need adorned with the clean, elegant robes of respectability and good works. In the latter case, God would be giving on account of merit; and gifts would become rewards. God, however, does not cease giving when our need is clad with the frayed and filthy rags of demerit.

Like God, we should give to the needy without any distinction—to stranger and to kin, to undeserving and to deserving. Where the needy come from, what the color of their skin is, or how they behave does not matter. Their needs and their incapacities matter, and they matter not simply as defined by us but as informed by the needy themselves When the need is present, a gift should be given, irrespective of whose need it is.

Then must we, like God, give to everyone? If so, our responsibility could never be fulfilled; and the choice to give to one person would be a choice to sacrifice all others.[30] We are finite beings who cannot meet all the needs of a single person, let alone all the needs of all people. There is only "one man," God-man, whose gift is meant for all—Jesus Christ (Rom. 5:15-21). My gifts are meant for only some people. Since God is the primordial and infinite giver, it is not a responsibility of any single individual to give to everyone. Giving to everyone is the responsibility of God and all human beings collectively.

If we must not give to all, must we give everything? Must we, like the Incarnate, give our very life or the "gift of death"?[31] In a fragile and sinful world, we may sometimes be required to give a gift of death as Christ died for our salvation; but we do not need to give our lives to give truly, for we are recipients as well as channels of God's gifts. It suffices to impart to others more than we owe them without expecting return or basking in our moral rectitude. That is a gift—an ordinary gift but a perfectly good one, even with all the ambiguities that attend gift giving. Nobody has a right to complain when we give such ordinary gifts—not philosophers of the impossible gift and certainly not recipients.

EQUALITY

When we give, we often engage in rivalries and set up hierarchies. But when gifts circulate within the Godhead, no rivalry happens; and hierarchy is not reaffirmed. The one who gives is not greater than the one who receives, for all give and all receive. Each gives glory to the other with each gift given.

What happens, though, to the equality of givers and receivers when God's gift giving turns toward the world? There is no equality between God and creature;

yet, paradoxically, God gives so that the relation between God and humans can be brought to greater parity. Martin Luther made the point by talking of the "wonderful exchange" between Christ and the soul on account of their unity.[32] Christ enters the poverty of our self-enclosed selves, indwells us, and makes his divine life to be our own. Christ's gift makes each of us a "Christ." When Christ gives to us, inequality remains—categorical inequality—yet we become, in some regard, Christ's equal.

Like gifts among divine persons, human gifts should express and foster equality. Between lovers, there is no first and last, no greater and smaller. Lovers give because they delight and adore. When they aim to outdo each other, it is not to get honor, whether by giving gifts or any other means, but to *bestow* honor (see Rom. 12:10). Good givers do not give gifts to recipients and honor to themselves. They give both gifts and honor to the recipients even if they, as a result, end up being honored as good givers. Then as the circle moves, they get both gifts and honor in return.

Like Christ's gifts to humanity, our gifts to one another should aim at establishing parity in the midst of drastic and pervasive inequality. When giving to those in need, wrote the apostle Paul, it ought to be like food given from heaven: "The one who had much did not have too much, and the one who had little did not have too little" (2 Cor. 8:15). The immediate goal is not uniformity. It is equality of satisfied needs, precisely those needs that motivated the gift giving in the first place.

COMMUNION

The one God is a communion of three persons in that each dwells in the others and is indwelled by them. Because the Godhead is a perfect communion of love, divine persons exchange gifts—the gifts of themselves and the gift of the others' glorification. The inverse is also true: Because they exchange such gifts, they are called a divine communion of love. So it is in God's eternal life, apart from God's relation to the world.

When God turns toward the world, the circle of exchanges within the divine communion begins its outbound flow. God gives to creatures because God delights in them and because they are needy. That delighting is part of God's more encompassing relation with human beings, and the name of that relation is communion. It is a different sort of communion than communion among divine persons. Still, it is a communion across the chasm that divides humanity from divinity.

We were created for communion with one another, not just with God. Christ came not just to live in us, or even just to live through us. He came to make us into one body—his body, the church. Each member of the body is endowed with what the apostle Paul called "spiritual gifts"—roles and abilities that the Holy Spirit gives to each for the benefit of others (1 Cor. 12:1-30; 14:1-40). Each one, gifted to give, now gives to others. The reciprocal exchange of gifts expresses and nourishes a community of love.

If reciprocity is taken out of gift giving, community disintegrates into discrete individuals. Without any reciprocity, the best-case scenario would be that we all live on our individual islands and send and receive packages anonymously to help those who cannot help themselves, or—amounting to nearly the same (though minus the voluntariness of gift giving!)—we all send our contributions to the government for distribution to the needy. Clearly, in the complex societies of today, the government has an important role in tending to social needs; but neither the governmental institutions nor our unidirectional gifts to those in need can replace reciprocal gift giving. Without reciprocal giving and receiving—giving and receiving not just of material things but of time and attention—we would at best inhabit a world of lonely altruists.

Or we would inhabit a world of collaborating egoists! If gift giving is taken out of reciprocity, community degenerates into individuals who will cooperate and split apart when it suits their interests. You have a good I want? I'll persuade you that I have a good you need, we will swap our wares, and then we will be on our merry ways. This is the exchange mode of human relations, and there is a place for it. We have the right to exchange goods for their rough equivalents. In a world organized in complex systems and populated by selfish people, we would languish and suffer oppression without such exchanges, since we would depend on large bureaucratic structures of distribution run by fallible and failing human beings. To transmute most reciprocal relations into self-serving exchanges would rob us of what is essential to our very humanity.

Often we do not give as God does and as we should. Selfishness, pride, and indolence overwhelm us and collude with ungenerous social environments to make us reluctant to give at all, let alone to give the way we should. How can we counter the effects of selfishness, pride, and sloth on our giving? The answer would take us back once again to the triune God, this time less as a model to emulate and more as a source of that very emulation. But that is an exploration for another occasion.

CHAPTER 2

THE SOCIAL TRINITY AND PROPERTY

M. Douglas Meeks

Jürgen Moltmann's most enduring contribution to Christian theology is arguably his doctrine of the Trinity. Following Barth and Rahner, he made the Trinity the central doctrine, not just serving the integration of the other loci but also constituting the cutting edge that opened up Christian engagement with the modern world. A significant output of trinitarian literature during the last thirty years has been a development of or reaction to Moltmann's doctrine of the Trinity. The fruitfulness for theology of Moltmann's view of the Trinity is unmistakable, although some critics see theological risks in his trinitarian thought.

Perhaps most contested is Moltmann's claim that the Trinity is social or communal. Critics have charged that this claim has resulted in tritheism, pantheism, or an instrumentalism that merely serves a modern social program for the church and the world. These criticisms usually cohere around two endeavors: to deny the implications of Moltmann's eschatological thought for a new theological ontology or to question Moltmann's conception of the church and its life in the world. Almost invariably, these critics are seeking to protect an ontology that preserves traditional views of God's sovereignty and freedom[1] or to question Moltmann's view of the church's relation to the world. While recognizing some valid cautions about relating the Trinity to socioeconomic and political questions, I want this chapter to show the import of the social Trinity for revising theories and practices of property, which I take to be the thorniest question of political economy in our time. It is precisely Moltmann's revision of divine power and freedom that opens up the possibility of the church's contribution to the enormous array of global quandaries centering on property, such as poverty, hunger, unemployment, enormous discrepancy in wealth, and destruction of the ecosphere. These problems seem insuperable because it is so difficult to imagine property in ways different from what have become sacred assumptions about property. The social Trinity makes possible the criticism and reconstruction of basic assumptions about property.

At stake is the question whether we can properly speak of analogies of the Trinity with the church and the world, but other crucial questions also arise. Does the ancient notion of vestiges of the Trinity in the world necessarily imply a natural theology that purports to prove the Trinity from the world or conceptualize God from social reality? Can we indeed think from the Trinity to human identity and action in the world? Or does the Trinity (especially the immanent Trinity) serve merely to distinguish God from the world in order to protect God's perfections?[2] For Moltmann, the social doctrine of the Trinity is not a reflection of or the epitome of human sociality but rather the font of our attempt to comprehend rightly the social way of being human desired by God.[3] "Making rational sense of the world doesn't require faith in the Trinity," affirms Bruce Marshall, who also adds, "but faith in the Trinity yields an immeasurable difference in the rational sense we make of it."[4]

For Moltmann, the Trinity serves as the primary criticism of all sub-Christian conceptions of God but is simultaneously the theory of the practice of the church's life and mission to the world. He has steadfastly insisted that the Trinity is not a speculative doctrine but contributes substantively to solving practical problems of Christian living as a function of the worship of the triune God and life *coram Deo* (before the face of God) in the world. An open doctrine of the Trinity means a church open to the world and to God's redemption of the world.[5] But the Trinity would be neither critical nor practical were it not also doxological.[6] As the name of God, God's narrative description, the Trinity is the central reality of the worshipping Christian community. The Trinity is preeminently about the church's participation in the Triune Community, and this participation takes place in the ultimate horizon of God's history with the whole creation. Thus, the rational sense we make of the church according to the life and logic of the Trinity is always set in first order acts of worship in the widest horizon of God's life with the creation.

FROM ESCHATOLOGY TO THE TRINITY

The development of the Trinity was in process *in nuce* (in a nutshell) from the beginning of Moltmann's theology. In *Theology of Hope*, Moltmann set out to develop a theology of God's reconciliation with the world and was immediately challenged to rethink traditional ontologies. The first phase was a critical doctrine that arose from his eschatological theology of the cross and the resurrection. The dialectic of the cross and the resurrection that takes place within God and in God's relation to the world has remained the ferment of his thinking. The resurrection means that practically all of theology is eschatological. The cross means that the power by which God redeems the world and by which the church engages its mission in the world is the power of God's suffering love.

These early theological moves entailed the criticism of monotheistic conceptions of God and their ontologies. The original attempt was to think of God's being as coming presence and present coming (*parousia*) that required a hopeful knowing of God.[7] If we know God historically and history eschatologically, then God cannot be construed as simple substance or absolute subject. Rather, God is God as God uncovers Godself in the narratives of Israel and of the Son of Israel's God through the Holy Spirit. Following Barth's emphasis on historicity and his theme of "God's being for the world," Moltmann attempted to ponder the Trinity from the economy to the internal life of God.[8] We know the immanent Trinity from God's self-uncovering in God's economy with the creation.[9] Moltmann connects with the Pauline way of thinking of the church arising out of the work of the Spirit in baptism and in the Eucharist. The Trinity is the primary way of reflecting the church's living *in* the Triune Community.

Moltmann's criticism of traditional ontologies led to his political theology and his new perspective on God's lordship and freedom as God's love led in turn to the development of the social doctrine of the Trinity.[10] At its best the doctrine of the Trinity has been a sustained criticism of the dominative concepts of God's power and human power. Moltmann calls on this motif found in both the Eastern and Western trinitarian traditions. The social doctrine of the Trinity maintains the distinctiveness of the persons as well as the unity of their community of love. God is neither a simple substance nor an indivisible self. The abiding contribution of the Western trinitarian tradition is the translation of the Greek *hypostasis* into the Latin *persona* (person), thereby meaning a distinct person with unique characteristics and a nonexchangeable existence.[11] The Eastern fathers contributed the notion of the unity of the community of distinct persons in their concept of *perichoresis* (mutual coinherence). God is a community of persons united in giving themselves each to the other and to the world. The triune God is the inexhaustible life that the three persons share in common, in which they are present with one another, for one another, and in one another. Everything is shared except their personal attributes and peculiar commissions.

We turn now to a juxtaposition of the problems of property and the social doctrine of the Trinity. The social doctrine of the Trinity is particularly aware of the constant tendency to project onto God our dominative uses of property and then to use the resulting view of God as justification for property. Traditional metaphysical attributes of God when applied to the human being describe what is required by the modern conception of exclusive private property, namely, the ability and right to possess, use, manage, gain revenue from, devise, hold a perpetuity to, consume, waste, alienate, and destroy property. This notion of exclusive alienable property and the ideologies connected with it are grounded, at least in part, in the concepts of God's freedom as the power to dispose property, God's exclusive property in all things, and God's self-possession.

The Lordship and Freedom of God and Concepts of Property

The mystery of property is its connection to power, and the mystery of property's connection to God is its need to be justified, for all modes of property can potentially lead to the dehumanization of life.[12] Property, once justified by the conscious or unconscious approbation of God, becomes axiomatic for human relationships. The first function of the doctrine of the social Trinity is the criticism of the concepts of God employed in the justification of dehumanizing doctrines of property.

The great promise of property has always been that it would give the human being freedom.[13] Having property means that one is less likely to be dependent on others for livelihood, reduced to servitude, made a client, or left defenseless against fate. Thus, in the history of civil society, those who have property are also said to possess liberty, independence, and responsibility. If the promise of property is liberty and security, then the threat of property is domination. Property and dominion seem married. Those who gain their own freedom and guarantee their own future through property are often prone to deny property to others. Property is thus also the threat of mastery.

There is consequently a qualitative difference in kinds of property. Property that is access to life is vastly different from property that gives one the power to exclude others from access to life. Property that makes one independent is qualitatively different from property that makes others dependent. The former is a means of realizing one's vocation as a human being; the latter is potentially a means of destroying the humanity of others and one's own humanity. The profound ambiguity of property is that it can mean both power for life as inclusion in livelihood or power for death as exclusion from livelihood. Property promises freedom, but it also threatens to destroy human dignity.

The liberal theory of property changed the right of persons not to be excluded.[14] As a result, the meaning of property has been drastically narrowed in the modern world.[15] The most momentous change was the loss of the traditional inclusive property right. The kind of property necessary to the logic of the market is the right of an individual or corporation (natural or artificial individual) to exclude others from some use or enjoyment of something. Only exclusive rights can be marketed. The right not to be excluded from use or enjoyment of something cannot, by its very nature, be marketed. This second right virtually dropped out of sight.

In light of the dehumanization resulting from property defined only as private and exclusive, the social Trinity presents an alternative understanding of God's freedom and of our freedom. For much of the theological tradition, God's freedom has been viewed as God's unlimited power to dispose property. Absolute divine lordship has been construed as absolute freedom. That God is free to do whatever God likes, including disposing God's property according to God's whim, is taken to be the essence of God's lordship and sovereignty. When God's freedom is conceived as mastery, so also is human freedom.

The biblical narratives, however, do not speak of God's freedom as the power of exclusive and alienable ownership. Also, God's freedom is not *free choice*. God's freedom is God's love. The notion of God's freedom as *free choice* based on the ability to dispose property denies God's nature as love. According to Moltmann, God

> does not have the choice between mutually exclusive possibilities . . . between being love and *not* being love. If he is love, then in loving the world he is by no means "his own prisoner"; on the contrary, in loving the world he is entirely free because he is entirely himself. If God is the highest good, then God's liberty cannot consist of having to choose between good and evil. On the contrary, it lies in doing the good which he himself is, which means communicating himself.[16]

God cannot just will and do anything imaginable. God limits Godself through faithfulness to God's promise. God's freedom consists of God's communicating immanently and economically the love that God essentially is. The unity of the Trinity as the love expressed among the persons of the community negates the notion of God's freedom and unity construed as property ownership and disposal.

God has a claim on the creation and all creatures as creator and redeemer, not as maker (labor theory of property) or owner (first occupancy). At the heart of God's act of liberating/creating is God's suffering and self-giving. God's work of suffering is the source of God's claim in, that is, God's property in, creation. God brings the world into being through God's costly struggle against the power of the *nihil* (nothingness). God has suffered for the creation and will not allow it to fall into vanity or be alienated. The creation is properly God's because God's power of righteousness makes its life fundamentally a gift of God's grace. Since no one else has the power to suffer and prevail against the power of nothingness; no one else has the right to everything in creation which is yet subject to death and which must yet be redeemed from the threat of nothingness.

THE SELF AS PRIVATE PROPERTY AND GIVING

Many proponents of the market system would say that *liberty* is its most essential component. There must be in place custom and law that secure the ability of human beings to use and control their bodies and energies and to move and enter into transactions as they will.[17] The market view of the human being requires the assumption that I have a property in myself. I own and possess myself.[18] Economic freedom comes to mean having no claims laid upon oneself by others. To conceive of myself as my ultimate property, which I must protect at all costs, is to make me unable to give myself away to the other and to recognize the other's right not to be excluded from what he or she needs to live abundantly. Is this, however, really freedom; or is it a kind of subjugation to a system that may offer freedom from restraints but not the freedom for the engagement with others for life that is ultimately the only real freedom? A humane economy requires that human beings not be determined by a narrow view of freedom as the ability to choose among commodity and service options. Human beings become genuinely free through their calling by God for a life with and for others.

The description of God as a simple, undivided, atomistic essence lends itself to the description of the human being as a private individual in our economic life today. The doctrine of God in Western teaching has often conceived God modalistically as a self-possessor, a self-proprietor. Behind the three divine persons is the absolute being, a simple, indivisible, self-sufficient individual. God's absolute existence is in and for God's self. With Augustine the West came to think of the Trinity on the model of the radically individual human being who would claim I constitute myself, I am proper to myself, and I am property of myself. On this model God exists for God's self, God is proper to God's self, and that means God's self is the property of God.

The doctrine of the social Trinity, however, claims that God's owning is not grounded in self-possession but rather in self-giving.[19] It is the character of God to give Godself to us and to give us all things with Godself (Rom. 8:32). God owns by giving. God "has" God's self precisely in giving God's self. If God is not a self-possessor who dominates by excluding others from access to what is necessary for life, then it is also true that God's mode of possessing cannot be the model or justification for understanding all property as absolute exclusive property. It is God's self-giving which is the font of human livelihood in community. The commonality of human claim to God's goodness in creation is based on God's self-giving for all.

Christian anthropology stresses a universally recognized *inclusive* property right in what it takes to be human. What belongs to each and is due each cannot be decided simply by modern theories of exclusive property irrespective of God's creation and redemption of each human being. All human beings have a property in or claim on what is appropriate to life against death and what he or she needs to fulfill his or her humanity (*imago Dei*, God's likeness or God's image) by serving God and neighbor. Human hospitality (giving the other the goods and space for life) is the other side of God's goodness extended to all of God's creation. God excludes no one from life; neither may we.

PROPERTY AS GIFT AND COMMODITY

Karl Polanyi argued that in order for the modern market to come into being, land, labor, and money had to become exhaustively commodities.[20] As a result, the most obvious characteristic of a market society, now exacerbated by instantaneous global communication, is that everything tends to become a commodity, that is, something that can be valued or priced for buying and selling. If everything is a commodity for sale, then the market must solve all human problems. The criticism of this delusion is the first step toward economy with a human face.

In the midst of the unabated commodification of human life, Christians and Jews who are not suffering from amnesia should know that justice, healing, and learning, for example, should not be commodities. Obviously, however, the benefits of our judicial systems, our health care systems, and our educational institutions tend to be closed to those who have nothing to exchange. The practices of these systems are regularly commodified. The media are full of concocted arguments that things human beings used to think could in no sense be commodities should now be properly commodified: blood, organs, fetuses, personal genomic information, children, and air.

What should not be a commodity? What is necessary for life should not be a commodity or exhaustively a commodity. Only the shared life of a community can decide what is a commodity and what is not.[21] At present in the United States, persons have a property in health care delivery only as purchased through insurance or provided by the state. The commodification of health care delivery leaves about forty-three million persons without a property in health care. Robin Cook has argued that our conception of a property in health care delivery will have to change drastically not only because of the social value of equality of access but also because, with advances in genomics, we can increasingly predict presently untreatable diseases that mean progressive disability and death.[22] Because of ever-expanding microarray technology, for-profit private insurance companies have strong incentives to use this "cruel extended death sentence" to protect their bottom lines by denying service or even coverage.

> It is precisely this danger, however, that may lead to a great breakthrough: the inevitable movement to universal health care. In this dawning era of genomic medicine, the result may be that the concept of private health insurance, which is based on actuarially pooling risk within specified, fragmented groups, will become obsolete since risk cannot be pooled if it can be determined for individual policyholders. Genetically determined predilection for disease will become the modern equivalent of the "pre-existing condition" that private insurers have stringently avoided.[23]

If the equal access of all persons to what they need for life and what they need to contribute to the lives of others is the norm pictured in the social Trinity, then property has to be understood also in terms of reciprocity, redistribution, and gifting.[24]

The market system depends on the logic of exchange, *quid pro quo* (this for that). No one can doubt the great benefit of exchange relationships in the distributing of goods and services. On the other hand, the history of economies that are ruled exclusively by the logic of exchange shows that the accompanying logic of debt becomes destructive of the social fabric.

As over against the logics of exchange and debt, the social Trinity points to the Triune Community's freeing of human giving from the reality of debt. This freeing of human giving is apparent first in the way God gives in creating. God gives without the guarantee of return.[25] This generosity is so because God gives everything that we are, and thus there is nothing in us that could establish an obligation toward God. Paul reflects this same perspective: "What do you have that you did not receive? And if you received it, why do you boast as if it were not a gift?" (1 Cor. 4:7; cf. Rom. 8:32). Furthermore, God gives us Christ and in him union with the Triune Community simply because of our need, not because we are deserving. God's *pleroma* (fullness, totality) lacks nothing we could pay back. We have nothing more to return than what God has already given us.

In the cross God cancels the possibility of debt itself and therefore debt economy as the source of obligation and security.[26] If God accounts us as having no debt, the possibility of our being restored to God's economy of graceful giving is opened up. In this sense God's redeeming work transforms the economy of debt into the economy of grace. The appropriate prayer to be prayed in the economy of grace is, "Forgive us our debts as we forgive our debtors." To be the *homo economicus* (economic man) in God's economy of grace means that we are shaped by God's giving rather than by maximizing utility.

God's gift of Christ is given to sinners without preconditions of any kind. Sinners deserve this gift because they need it. God's gifts to us are not loans, nor does God stop giving when we squander or misuse God's gifts. Even when we fail to give, God is willing to give more. Our failure to give, to be sure, removes the blessing of giving that God intends for us; but it does not cease God's giving. Everything about our lives should be a reflection of this gift.

If God gives to the creation in a way that undermines debt economy, we are left with the question *how* we should give. God's excessive giving creates space and time for human reciprocity. Our obedience in giving is not a matter of clearing our debt to God, and yet God does give to us with the expectation that God's giving will be reflected in our giving.

What, then, is the horizon or framework in which our giving of God's gift can express God's grace rather than the obligation of debt? In what sense does our gifting properly reflect trinitarian giving? This giving is best seen in the life-serving shape of human life in the eucharistic existence gifted at the spreading of the Lord's table. Our obligation is to give as God gives, that is, to meet the needs of the creatures for whom Jesus Christ has died. Whereas commodity exchanges are anonymous, the emphasis in giving as God gives is on the persons brought into relationship, not on the objects that are exchanged. Gift giving creates communal relationships of interdependence. A commodity transaction ends the relationship as soon as goods are exchanged so that one is free immediately to enter into another transaction. This exchange may serve equilibrium but not reconciliation and mutual life with the different other. Commodity transactions cannot proffer the most important right to life because of God's claim on every human being, that is, the right to be included, the right to belong to a primary community in which the conditions of life are mediated.

For the household of God, the tendency of property to create domination is to be overcome in *oikos* (household) relationships of mutual self-giving in which possessions are used for the realization of God's will in the community. The self-giving life of the trinitarian community of God is a criticism of the self as private property. Human possession of all kinds is basically a means to nurture *koinoia* (fellowship); hence, under whatever arrangements of ownership, the primary communal purpose of human goods ought to be safeguarded. Property is not only a right against community but also a right to the life-giving powers of community. Ownership is a means of fulfilling our calling to be God's stewards through community with God, other human beings, and nature. Property is a function of the community, a performance of a social function.

CHAPTER 3

THE SPIRIT OF LIFE AND
THE REVERENCE FOR LIFE

William Schweiker

> *Whether humanity* ought *to* live, *or ought to become extinct, is a question which cannot be answered through the dictates of rational expediency, but only out of a love for life.*
> —Jürgen Moltmann, *The Spirit of Life: A Universal Affirmation*

Jürgen Moltmann has argued that there is a necessary connection between the experience of the God of life and reverence for life. In one book he writes that because "life comes from 'the source of life'—the creative divine Spirit—and is alive in the Spirit, it must be sanctified. Life is sanctified when we encounter everything living with reverence before God."[1] While Moltmann has not produced an ethics, the idea of the reverence for life enables a theologian interested in ethics, a theologian like myself, to engage Moltmann's work at its most humanly salient point.[2] What is at stake in this engagement is nothing less than the perspective of Christian faith on reality and also the most basic good that can and ought to orient human life and action.

I agree with Moltmann that a new sensibility for the worth and fragility of life is profoundly needed in an age of global suffering and ecological endangerment. The discourse of reverence for life resonates deeply within present moral and religious longings. The question is whether or not an ethics of the reverence for life articulates the proper expression of Christian moral thinking in our time. On that question, I have profound reservations. What follows, then, are reflections on the *necessity* of the connection between the Spirit of life and an ethics of the reverence for life. These reflections are offered in gratitude for the many things I have learned from Jürgen Moltmann about the kinds of virtue, scope of generosity, and creativity that can and should characterize theological reflection. It is a genuine honor for me to be able to contribute to this volume.

CHRISTIAN FAITH AND THE REVERENCE FOR LIFE?

On first glance it might appear that a conviction about the living God would naturally lend itself to an ethics of the reverence for life. The divine life, the *perichoresis* in the being God, is the power and energy of life and also the vibrancy of new life. When God's coming provides a way to view all reality, then a reverence for life seems necessarily to follow. The sanctification of life on Moltmann's account entails trust in God, respect for others and self, and also reverence for all life. Little wonder, then, that he writes, if "life itself is sanctified because it is holy, the conclusion that has to be drawn is an ethics of *reverence for life*."[3]

Despite Moltmann's interest in a theology of life, it is not immediately obvious why Christian theologians concerned about ethics ought to bother themselves with reflection on reverence for life. The ethics of reverence for life is most often associated with Albert Schweitzer's ethical mysticism. "Only by serving every kind of life," he wrote, "do I enter service of that Creative Will whence all life emanates . . . . . This is the mystical significance of ethics."[4] Most contemporary moral reflection, Christian or otherwise, rejects any connection to mysticism and, most basically, to the metaphysics of will that Schweitzer's thought presents. Our age, ethically speaking, is anti-metaphysical, anti-mystical, and increasingly anti-universalist, that is, particularistic. Furthermore, thinkers interested in the domain of the mystical in life return the compliment. Rarely do they make any connection to ethics. They usually renounce the aspiration to moral rationality as effacing the complex texture of the spiritual life. Finally, in a world increasingly under the dominance of global economic forces, the spiritual and moral longings of peoples are often relegated to private thoughts and practices or find uneasy expression in the inherited religions. For all of these reasons, it is unclear why anyone should reflect on an ethics of reverence for life that too easily floats between vague spirituality and the ardent rationalism of global systems.

Matters are more complex, however. In various ways the idea of reverence for life does resonate deeply in the moral and religious sensibilities of peoples around the world. These sensibilities arise in part as a protest to endangerments to life: ecological destruction, global poverty and oppression, the denial of the needs of future generations, the destruction of local cultures and traditional religious forms by means of worldwide political and economic systems, and, most pointedly, a loss of awareness of the inviolability and mystery of life. What is more, the reverence for life is often bound to spiritual awakenings among people within new religions and spiritualities as well as to the fresh vitality seen among forms of the classical, global religions. For example, the Buddhist priest and peace advocate Thich Nhat Hanh has insisted that reverence for life is the first precept of a viable moral and religious outlook for our age.[5] Even new spiritualities, such as forms of ecofeminism and holistic theologies of creation, use the language of reverence of life to articulate their moral visions.[6] Conservatives and fundamentalists in all of the religions, especially among Christians, have likewise embraced *the right to life* and the *sanctity of life* that evoke reverence.

The widespread resonance and rejection of the idea of the reverence for life warrants some reflection on it as a theme in contemporary Christian theology. Furthermore, at the heart of Christian conviction is the living God who graciously bestows life, even new and eternal life, on human beings and all reality. The task of Christian existence is to dwell within the power and presence of God. Thus, there are many good reasons to engage critically the idea of reverence for life within Christian theological and ethical reflection. How does Moltmann do so? In order to answer that question and to isolate distinctive features of Moltmann's thought, I must briefly explore Albert Schweitzer's original formulation of an ethics of the reverence for life.

ABSOLUTE REVERENCE FOR LIFE

Albert Schweitzer argued that an ethics for the reverence of life is *absolute* since it articulates a moral demand and possibility that can never be fully realized in human history. The struggle to fulfill this responsibility deepens human life and mitigates the conflicts of existence. The ethics of the reverence for life also articulates a fundamental conception of reality. In fact, Schweitzer held that the "loss of real civilization is due to our lack of a theory of the universe."[7] An adequate theory, he further held, must be ethical and be affirmative of the world and of life. The idea of an ethics of reverence for life is meant to meet this twofold demand. How so?

In continuity with eighteenth-century rationalism and especially with the reflexive philosophy of Descartes, Schweitzer seeks to grasp immediate self-consciousness in order to ground his ethics. When one does so, he argued, one comes to realize that the core of consciousness is not the *cogito*, the "I think." "'What is the immediate fact of my consciousness?'. . . 'To what do I always return?' we find the simple fact of consciousness is this, *I will to live.*"[8] If one thinks this awareness through to its conclusion, it is obvious that the will-to-live is a primary feature of the universe, a reality that I affirm and reverence in myself and must acknowledge in all things. Yet this insight, this affirmation of life as a spiritual act, is hardly piously optimistic.

> The world is a ghastly drama of will-to-live divided against itself. One existence makes its way at the cost of another; one destroys the other. One will-to-live merely exerts its will against the other, and has no knowledge of it. But in me the will-to-live has come to know about other wills-to-live. There is in it a yearning to arrive at unity with itself, to become universal.[9]

The affirmation of the will-to-live is the first spiritual act of experience, as Schweitzer calls it. However, it is not obvious that an affirmation of my life entails the demand to reverence all others' lives. It would be possible to reverence the will-to-live in oneself and no others.

Schweitzer argued that on purely rational grounds the attitude one can and ought to take to other life must be consistent with self-appraisal. "If I am a thinking being," he writes, "I must regard other life than my own with equal reverence."[10] Further, he endorsed Kant's principle of universalizability as the "form" of the ethical. An ethics of the reverence for life means that every type of life is given equal reverence. This equality led Schweitzer to acknowledge the moral standing of non-human life. Evil is simply what annihilates or hinders or hampers life; good is just the helping or saving or enabling of life to its highest development. So, reverence for life arises from a rational reflection upon and universal extension of the primitive datum of consciousness, the affirmation of the will-to-live. It specifies good and evil in terms of what promotes or destroys life. Furthermore, the ethics not only has universal and rational qualities, it also fosters activism. It seeks to perfect the self and also enable all life to develop. "A man is truly ethical," Schweitzer summarized, "when he obeys the compulsion to help all life which he is able to assist, and shrinks from injuring anything that lives."[11]

Schweitzer was, of course, keenly aware that life competes with life. He acknowledged a "division in the will-to-live" that is the ghastly drama of existence. As he notes, it is "a painful enigma for me that I must live with reverence for life in a world which is dominated by creative will which is also destructive will, and destructive will which is also creative."[12] The fullest meaning of an ethical act, any aid given to another living being, is that the will-to-live becomes one with another will-to-live and, thereby, fleetingly the division of the will-to-live is put to an end. The destiny of ethical existence is to "choose for my activity the removal of this division in the will-to-live against itself, so far as the influence of my existence can reach." Schweitzer concludes, "[K]nowing now the one thing needful, I leave on one side the enigma of the universe and of my existence in it."[13]

Schweitzer's ethics embraces as metaphysical fact that the will-to-life is divided against itself. Creative will is destructive will. An absolute ethics of reverence for life does not seek to compromise with this situation, but, rather, to provide an ethical triumph over the truth of reality. In the face of the division in the will-to-life, the ethical person in acts of goodness brings to a momentary end the ghastly drama of reality. When one so acts, Schweitzer insists, one experiences a union, a mystical participation, in the infinite Will in which all are one. That oneness is the mystical significance of ethics and the moral justification of the human adventure. Not surprisingly, the ethics moves then between theism and pantheism. Ethical theism, as Schweitzer called it, "presupposes a God who is an ethical Personality, and who is, therefore, so to speak, outside the world . . . (and) it must hold fast the belief that God is the sum total of the forces working in the world—that all that is, is in God."[14]

Schweitzer's ethical theism, metaphysics of Will, and mysticism seem to be profoundly at odds with Moltmann's arguments about "the coming God." Why then would Moltmann use the discourse of reverence of life? I turn next to what can be called Moltmann's eschatological reverence for life.

ESCHATOLOGICAL REVERENCE FOR LIFE

Jürgen Moltmann's most recent books have been part of his "Systematic Contributions to Theology," a project in continuity with *The Crucified God* and *The Theology of Hope*. The point of continuity is an eschatological perspective. It stands in radical contrast to any apocalyptic outlook focused on a final resolution of ambiguity, suffering, and injustice. "But *Christian* eschatology," Moltmann writes, "has nothing to do with apocalyptic 'final solutions' of this kind, for its subject is not 'the end' at all. On the contrary, what it is about is the new creation of all things."[15] The end will be the beginning: true creation is to come and thus is ahead of us. Moltmann is clear that an eschatological stance and its expression in a theology of hope is the fundamental "form" of theology.

Importantly, while hope and eschatology provide the form of theology, in recent works Moltmann has been concerned with the *content* of theology. His theology comes to focus on life, new life, and new creation as the necessary content of thinking eschatology otherwise than in apocalyptic terms. If, as he says, theology is "*imagination for the kingdom of God* in the world, and for the world in God's kingdom," then it is centrally concerned with how God comes to dwell in creation.[16] This theology is, so it appears, the backing for Moltmann's concern for new life.

Consistent with his eschatological focus, Moltmann rejects any account of experience as self-constituting, a claim already seen as basic to Schweitzer's ethics. One must abandon, as Moltmann says in *The Spirit of Life*, "the narrow reference to the modern concept of 'self-consciousness', so that we can discover transcendence in every experience, not merely in experience of self." This discovery means, further, that the "*experience of God* is not limited to the human subject's experience of self. It is also a constitutive element in the experience of the 'Thou,' in the experience of sociality, and in the experience of nature."[17] For Moltmann, the most basic datum of experience is not the will-to-live that one comes to grasp as divided against itself, but, rather, the reality of the living God. More pointedly, the eschatological moment, not self-consciousness, awakens one to the reality of God in all things and of all things in God. Moltmann speaks of the Spirit to articulate this divine reality. He conceives of the Spirit as "the divine field of force which permeates us through and through."[18] The Spirit is an environment and also the inward vitality of life. The Spirit's being is the source of life and its worth.

Now, the logic of the ethical argument entailed in these claims about the Spirit of Life seems to include these points: (1) the divine source of life is the creative Spirit; (2) because of life's source in the Spirit, it must be sanctified; and (3) life is sanctified when *everything* is encountered with reverence before God. Importantly, the correlate argument is (1) that the meaning of reverence is universalized so that one reverences *all* life not because of the rational demands of universalizability but because its source is God, and (2) the final grounding of the ethic is the triune life of God rather than the actual dynamics and conflicts of finite life and its ghastly drama. Reverence for life is really about the divine life in all things. The future of history, Moltmann consistently argues, is the coming God, the new creation, God's Sabbath and indwelling in reality. The reverence for life must center on this reality shorn of apocalyptic dread, moral perfectionism, or the attempt through action, as Schweitzer taught, to surmount the division within the will-to-live.

Moltmann is profoundly mindful that death, destruction, and suffering characterize current existence. The distress that drives created being to cry out to God is, he notes, a double distress. "It is distress over the inexorable, progressive destruction of nature by human beings, and it is distress over the destructibility inherent in nature itself: the destructibility that makes this human aggression against nature possible."[19] The tyranny of time and death is the condition for human aggression and injustice to human and nonhuman life, and it is a feature of "nature" as the immanent side of creation longing for redemption. Under the power of time and death, life wars against life in a deadly cycle of violence and oppression. Moltmann thus admits that under present conditions the theological imagination is somewhat limited. It tends to use negative images to speak of the reign of God: when mourning or crying or pain will no longer endure; when death shall be no more (Rev. 21:4). Positive images are possible, too: the kingdom of God, the resurrection of Christ, eternal life, and the reign of righteousness and justice.

However, no one presently has a full experience of the kingdom. This partial experience is why theology is an imaginative act. In anticipation of God's reign, one has to be awakened to the eschatological reality of God's presence in which God suffers with creation seeking to turn creatures from death to life. "Out of hope for eternal life, love for this vulnerable and mortal life is born afresh . . . [W]e Christians are what Christoph Blumhardt called 'protest-people against death.'"[20] The content of ethics, seemingly, is a hope that warrants protest against death and seeks to sanctify all life before God. What is distinctive about the Christian vision is not specific moral rules, norms, values, or agendas, but, rather, reverence for life born from an eschatological awakening to new creation. It is to live in newness of life in the coming of God. What justifies the continuation of the human project is God's coming that empowers reverence for life.

Moltmann's theology of life can be seen as a negation of Schweitzer's ethics but also an eschatological transformation of a widespread sensibility captured in the discourse of reverence for life. If that negation is indeed the case, then the orienting question of this essay returns. Does an "ethics" of the reverence for life, even recast in eschatological terms, articulate the proper expression of Christian moral thinking in our time? I want to conclude these reflections with that question in mind. My point is not to deny the sensibility of reverence for life as important for this age.

It is, much more, to think carefully through the kind of *ethics* we need to embody that sensibility in actual life.

RESPONSIBILITY FOR THE INTEGRITY OF LIFE

Moltmann's theology of life advances thinking about a properly Christian perspective on reality and also about the most basic good that can and ought to orient action. It is, thereby, genuinely important to contemporary theology and is additionally an enduring contribution to the worldwide church. Problems nonetheless remain. It is not at all clear on theological or philosophical grounds that *life* articulates a necessary good that can and ought to be reverenced in all situations. *Life* is not a second god. It is a great good but not the supreme good. To think otherwise is to fail to acknowledge rightly the worth of finite *life* precisely in its finitude as well as the difference between God and reality. Christians love life. Yet even when seen within the life of God, finite *life* is and will remain radically finite. Its goodness, we must say on theological grounds, is inseparable from its finitude. Anything other than that judgment is a form of nihilism and the denial of the creation, which, open to the divine presence, is nevertheless not divine.

Moltmann seems to agree on this point. On close reading, he distinguishes between *sanctifying* life and *reverence* for life. To sanctify life, it seems, requires a good or end that one seeks to acknowledge and realize within finite existence. Moltmann writes:

> Harmony with God is called sanctification. Harmony with ourselves as God's image and his children is called happiness. In this sense sanctification leads to true self-realization. . . . Trust in God, respect for our own lives and the lives of others, as well as reverence for everything living, in which God is present: these are the things which characterize and determine the sanctification of life.[21]

Notice that *reverence* is an attitude, a sensibility, about forms of life that is conceptually distinct from the good to be realized, namely, *harmony* with God, self, and others. It is also distinct from other sensibilities, trust, and respect. On my reading, there is then in Moltmann's texts the need to distinguish between *reverence* as a sensibility related to trust and respect and the end or good that can and ought to guide all human actions and relations (harmony/sanctification).

Reverence, we can summarily say, is the active willingness to acknowledge the moral standing and worth of all realms of life just as *respect* does with self and others and *trust* characterizes a right relation to the living God. It is then a grave mistake to collapse the sensibility of *reverence* and the content of the good, that is, harmony or sanctification. The confusion of a sensibility that motivates action and the good that is the norm and object of the sensibility too often bests an ethics like Schweitzer's. What is more, one must insist that human beings bear the responsibility for the use of power at their disposal even when they lack the moral sensibilities one would hope to motivate life. Sometimes duty itself and not more refined motivations like reverence or respect or trust (not to mention love) must have its say!

What then can we do? While the concept of reverence designates an attitude or sensibility about what bears worth, the good that ought to guide and orient conduct is best conceived along lines intimated by Moltmann's argument about *sanctification* and *harmony*. Yet here too more precision is needed. The idea of *harmony* is hardly obvious, since, for example, it is unclear what is to be harmonized in the self or what would count as a harmonious community. In order to avoid this confusion, I contend that the *integrity of life* best articulates what can and ought to be respected and enhanced in actions and relations.[22] To be sure, *integrity* can and must evoke reverence as well as a host of others sensibilities and motivations. Yet we make a decided gain in thinking by developing an ethics of responsibility for the integrity of life, thereby avoiding the confusion of sensibility and a conception of the good in an ethics of the reverence for life (Schweitzer) as well as the vagueness of ideas about *harmony* (Moltmann). I can, therefore, finish these reflections with a few remarks about the *integrity of life* and what it means for a theological ethics committed, like Moltmann's, to a construal of all things in God and God in all things.

By the *integrity of life* I mean two related but distinct things. First, integrity designates the project of any living being, namely, to integrate or draw together a range of goods sufficient to fulfill basic needs and express capacities necessary for that form of life to continue to exist, to resist nonbeing.[23] Obviously, the range or kinds of goods differ depending on the form of life considered. A human being, for instance, has needs and capacities for reflection and meaning missing at organic levels of life even as a human being, no less than a cell or animal, must metabolize energy through interaction with his or her environment. In each case, some integration of a being is enacted. The analogical use of the concept of life across its diverse forms is thereby rooted in the dynamic of integration that is simply a concept for the vitality or power of living. The main threat to any kind of life, accordingly, is disintegration, the weakening of the life process to the point of nonbeing or death. Even the concept of death is analogically predicated of beings owing to the diverse ways they integrate their being. This is why, as Christians have long known, human beings can die in many different ways: physical death, social death through the disintegration of community, existential death in the loss of meaning in life, and even spiritual death or the denial of the spiritual integrity of existence. So too, one can be physically alive and spiritually dead; existentially alive and yet physically dying.

Theologically construed, the power of integration is, of course, the presence of the divine spirit, the vitality of life experienced and manifest in the capacity of a being to draw together its being into living expression. This divine power is experienced at diverse levels of life, from the physical to the existential and spiritual in relation to other forms of life. This is why it makes sense to speak of God in things and things in God or God's spirit as vitality and also environment. The mark of finite life is that this capacity for integration at all levels is never complete and thus in time is either destroyed or dissipates to the point of disintegration and thus death. Further, any form of life advances or thwarts the integration of life in itself and others; there is real conflict as well as real concord in reality. What we mean by *good* and *evil* on this meaning of integrity are relations and actions that advance or thwart the integration of existence among beings.[24]

My first point is that by insisting on the *integrity* of life one has a complex understanding of what, in fact, aids or thwarts any living being and, thereby, gains precision in reflecting how we can and ought to relate to others and ourselves. This provides a finer grained conception of *goodness* than found in the vague idea of *life* that an ethics of the reverence for life hopes to serve. The account offered here also helps us to understand the threats to life of greatest moral and religious significance, for instance, the conflict between forms of life and forms of death that beset us mortal creatures.

Rather than continue to explore the range of needs that must be met, the capacities exercised, and the goods attained for life to be integrated, we can turn to the second meaning of *integrity* important for reflection on human responsibility. Integrity in this second, but related sense, denotes a unique form of goodness that arises within the life of someone dedicated in action to respect and enhance the integration of life in others as well as oneself. This meaning of integrity specifies the *moral good*, as a form of goodness that is only attainable, no matter how momentary or fragmentary, through responsible action. In other words, a life of moral integrity is one that is integrated not simply in terms of the range of goods that meet (basic, social, reflexive) needs and capacities, but, more radically, through a committed project of respecting and enhancing those goods in, with, and for others. A person of *integrity* is someone whose strength of conviction is manifest in a specific intentionality and orientation of actions and relations. The *integrity* of life in this sense denotes the moral vocation of human beings. It is a unique good of the spiritual core and dynamic of human life.

The idea of *moral integrity* arises not with the brute awareness of the power to integrate life or even with needs and capacities. It is, rather, an attribute of the exercise of capacities for action in, with, and for others wherein the power to act is deployed to respect and enhance, not demean or destroy, the integrity of others' lives. The truly moral person is one who acts to respect and enhance the integrity of life not for the sake of integrating her or his own life, but, rather, because that is the hallmark of the responsible life. Put in more classical terms, and ones that Moltmann uses, in the genuinely moral act holiness and happiness meet. The amoral person or community abides by the demands of responsibility in order to meet needs and secure wants. The amoral seek happiness and see the demands of holiness, of moral integrity, as a *means* to that happiness. This type of seeking is the definition of the easy conscience that makes the spiritual life instrumental to other goods. But what would it profit a man if he gained the whole world and lost his soul (see, Mark 8:36)?[25]

Accordingly, the real, ethically construed struggle of human existence is not the fact that we are subject to time or death or that we live within a ghastly drama of life divided against life. Difficulties and conflicts and sorrow abound, of course. Still, the real struggle of existence is to answer the call of conscience to live with moral integrity, to use one's power to respect and enhance the complex array of goods integral to life, to have nothing but the hope that happiness will, in fact, be attained in a life so committed. The resolution of this challenge has sometimes been called the moral paradox, namely, the insight that "egoism is self-defeating, while self-sacrifice actually leads to a higher form of self-realization."[26] As Christ put it, "Those who find their life will lose it, and those who lose their life for my sake will find it" (Matt. 10:39). The truly moral person or community is one who attenuates immediate and wholesale attention to the needs and capacities required to integrate life in order to have their existence defined by the demands of responsibility. In doing so, a new life is found; a higher kind of being and what is best called *moral integrity* are found. Happiness and holiness are one. Obviously, this *moral integrity* does not mean self-neglect or abasement. *Moral integrity* is not another name for servitude, but is rather a proper self-relation mediated by the realm of responsible actions and relations. Accordingly, a range of proximate judgments consistent with the demands of justice guide actions amid the conflicts between forms of life—including love of self—with respect to basic, social, and reflexive goods. The good of *moral integrity* entails the commitment to respect and enhance the integrity of life in, with, and for others as well as self. It designates the kinds of harmony Moltmann notes. To be more precise, *moral integrity* articulates the meaning for ethics of what John Wesley meant by perfection in love.[27]

Why then *ought* humanity to continue to exist? Is it to bring to a momentary end the ghastly drama of life against life? Is our moral vocation to live within the eschatological presence of God as people of protest against death? An ethics of responsibility for the integrity of life drawn from the resources of Christian faith answers that what morally justifies the fateful and costly human adventure can be found only in the fact that through the renewal of our hearts we can and may and must deploy the power at our disposal in the service of life and thereby enact amid the turmoil of existence the triumph of spirit over force. It is, to put it otherwise, to live out the primal Christian plea to have God's will be done on earth even as it is in heaven. The world around us is neither a ghastly drama nor is awaiting its true creation, but is fully marked by sorrow and pain and also joy and is much more the *agora*, the arena or stadium, of responsibility in which human beings can and may and must cooperate with divine purposes for life.

CONCLUSION

In these reflections I have attempted to think along with Moltmann's theology of life. I have tried to clarify why on Christian grounds we can and must develop an ethics of responsibility for the integrity of life. Surely what is most crucial is not the precision of concepts or the imaginative depths of a theology. What is most important is the tenure and orientation of our lives in a world riddled with hatred, violence, and sorrow. All who know Jürgen Moltmann and who have engaged his thought can be thankful that his life and creative energies have been dedicated to lifting up the lowly and announcing the acceptable day of the Lord. In those acts are to be found, I submit, testimony to the Spirit of Life.

CHAPTER 4

"Speak, 'Friend,' and Enter"
Friendship and Theological Method

Nancy Elizabeth Bedford

W hen I was an adolescent, my best friend was almost mute, which is what made our closeness possible." With these ironic words, Rosario Castellanos begins her short story "Las amistades efímeras." Both the reference to "fleeting friendships" in the title and the introductory statement imply that this will be no lasting friendship. Indeed, the relationship begins to dissolve almost immediately; yet it is through her conversations with her friend Gertrudis, flawed as they may be, that the narrator is able to begin to discover her calling: "I didn't have the least idea of what I was nor of what I was to be, and I felt the urgency of organizing and expressing myself through words, more than through actions."[1] By listening to those words and later by finding a voice and words of her own, the friend creates a space in which the narrator is able to discover her own vocation as a writer. At the end of the story, the two friends have grown so far apart that communication breaks down. Faced with the end of the friendship, the narrator, who speaks in the first person but remains nameless, opens up a notebook to write but cannot: "I wanted to write but was not able to do so. What for? It is so difficult! Perhaps—I repeated to myself, with my head between my hands—it would be simpler just to live."[2]

Even an ephemeral friendship, it would seem, can contribute fundamentally to the process that leads to words being crafted together meaningfully, whereas the absence of a friend and dialogue with her leads to a blank page. At least in this short story, then, the nexus between simply living and making sense of living in a way that can be written down and shared is provided by *conversation among friends*. Castellanos's story probably strikes a chord with me because just as her narrator's craft flourishes in a context of friendship, so does my own theological vocation, for which writing is, of course, not unimportant. I cannot imagine writing theology without the stimulus of conversation with friends: conversation with friends or acquaintances with whom relationships are "fleeting," certainly, but mostly with those friends in the sense of people with whom we share our lives across time, persons not necessarily bound to us by kinship or by marriage, yet without whom we simply could not imagine making sense of life. I am not referring primarily, then, to the practice of sending one's theological texts, once largely written, to certain friends and colleagues for their critique and revision, a process often documented in the acknowledgments section at the beginning of a book. Rather, I am thinking of the largely dialogical process by which we come to our best insights in the first place, a process that is permeated by grace: friends and the insights that they provoke by their comments, looks, presence, and even exasperated huffs are some of the greatest gifts we experience in God's economy of grace. Jürgen Moltmann's recognition of this process, I think, is one reason why he is so fond of quoting 1 Corinthians 4:7 when he speaks of the influence of his teachers and friends on his own theology: "What do you have that you did not receive?" In what follows, as a tribute to my teacher and friend, I propose to probe the matter of conversation in friendship as an integral part of a theological method born out of faith in the triune God.

FRIENDSHIP AS A TRINITARIAN LOCUS

Theological reflection on friendship often draws on classical sources such as Aristotle's *Nicomachean Ethics* or on Cicero's *Laelius sive de amicitia;* and this selection is understandable, not only because those works have beauty and value in themselves, but also because classical Greek and Roman understandings about the character of friendship were part of the ethos of the cultural world in which the New Testament was written. This cultural milieu is one reason why the New Testament can be read profitably through the lens of friendship,[3] and is also why, as Luke Timothy Johnson rightly points out, it would be insufficient to look up *philein* (to be friends with) or *philia* (friendship) and their cognates in the New Testament and, upon seeing that their frequency is low, conclude that friendship is secondary to New Testament understandings. Admittedly, some Christians actually did refer to each other as *philoi* (friends) as John 15:14; Acts 27:3; Titus 3:14; and 3 John 15 indicate. Beyond the precise lexicon used, the classical ideals of friendship have important similarities to the ways that the early church used language to convey reciprocity, being of one spirit, having the same mind, being of one accord, enjoying fellowship, or having all things in common.[4]

One of the characteristics of such *philia*, both in classical and in New Testament understandings, is its material component: friendship is a *material practice* that is reflected in the way we live; in other words, it requires a commitment that has concrete and practical consequences. This element is too easily forgotten in theological reflection if we consider friendship in the abstract or if we paint a concrete but individualized picture of Jesus the Friend. Consider the hymn "What a Friend We Have in Jesus," or as we sang it in the Argentine churches in which I grew up, "*¡Oh, qué Amigo nos es Cristo!*"[5]—a tune that comes to my mind immediately upon thinking of friendship in the context of the Christian faith, perhaps because I was raised in a context where such hymns were often played and sung. What strikes me about this hymn is not so much its depiction of Jesus as our Friend, but rather what it asks in the third verse: "Do thy friends despise, forsake thee? Take it to the Lord in prayer" (or in the Spanish version: "*¿Te desprecian tus amigos? Cuéntaselo en oración*"). The verse implies that earthly friends are unreliable; only Jesus is the true Friend. A binary is thus proposed: the true and somewhat exclusive friendship of Jesus as opposed to the fleeting and unreliable friendship of mere human beings, who are prone to despise us when we are "weak and heavy laden." In such a depiction, the communal dimension of our friendship with Jesus all but disappears.[6] Lest this tendency toward the privatization of Jesus' friendship, to the detriment of our community of earthly friends, be attributed solely to Anglo-American individualism, we should remember the well-known sonnet by Spanish poet Lope de Vega (1562–1635), which also frames friendship with Jesus as an individual and exclusive exercise, beginning with the question "Why do you seek my friendship?"

> *¿Qué tengo yo que mi amistad procuras?*
> *¿Qué interés se te sigue, Jesús mío*
> *Que a mi puerta, cubierto de rocío,*
> *Pasas las noches del invierno escuras?*[7]

Notably, neither Lope de Vega nor Joseph Scriven allude to the context from which the christological title Friend primarily springs, namely, the Johannine Jesus: Lope de Vega's metaphor presumably comes from Revelation 3:20, while Scriven hovers in the vicinity of Matthew 11:28.[8]

Throughout the Gospel of John, the vocabulary of friendship (*philos, phileo*) appears: John the Baptist is the "friend" of the bridegroom (John 3:29); and Lazarus, Mary, and Martha of Bethany are depicted as friends of Jesus (John 11). In John 15:13-15, the language becomes even more pointed: the Johannine Jesus uses the image of someone giving his life for his friends as the greatest possible manifestation of love, and then goes on to say: "You are my friends, if you are doing what I am commanding you. I will not call you servants. . . . I have called you friends." His words are not spoken as an invitation to individual and privatized friendship, but rather in the context of a community of friends who interact among each other as well as directly with him. As Howard-Brock points out, when Jesus speaks of giving one's life for one's friends, it is not a matter of abstract self-sacrifice, but rather "an expression of commitment that flows directly from the relationship among friends."[9] In the Johannine context, those friends are not a select group of persons close to Jesus, but rather all those in the community of faith.[10]

As Sharon Ringe puts it, then, Jesus is the Lover/Friend whose love effects life in the beloved by granting them an intimacy with God that can be called friendship with God.[11] Jesus as the Friend, then, should be imagined as firmly committed to his *friends*—in the plural—as his friends are also committed to him, as manifested in their resolve to walk in the way he has shown them. Precisely in the point of the relationship to his friends, the language becomes explicitly trinitarian: "I have called you friends, because all the things that I have heard from my Father, I have made known to you" (John 15:15). In one of his essays, Moltmann picks up on this dynamic of trinitarian friendship in the Gospel of John and makes the further point that it is traversed by a pneumatic dimension:

> In the Spirit a freedom is experienced that goes even beyond the filial relationship: *friendship with God*. God's "friends," both male and female, no longer live "under" God, but rather with God and in God. They participate in God's pain and in God's joy. They have become "one" with God (John 17:21).[12]

Moltmann thus understands friendship with God as a relationship that surpasses not only that of "servants," as in John 15, but even that of the "children" of God, as in Romans 8. This argument is trinitarian and requires a *Chalcedonian* Christology in the sense that the Son is seen both fully human and fully divine: only then can our designation by Jesus as "friends" be correlated meaningfully with a friendship with God experienced in the Spirit.

If, as implied in John's Gospel, and parsed out explicitly by Moltmann, our promised relationship with the trinitarian God can and should be described in terms of *friendship*, what does it mean for theology? I would posit that *theology*, inasmuch as it is God-talk among friends of God, is inseparable from such friendship. Theology can be seen as an exercise in gratitude for God's friendship, carried out in friendship with others. As such, it can become one of the dimensions in which friendship is played out: one of its *material practices*.

CONVERSATION AMONG FRIENDS AND THEOLOGICAL METHOD

How might this insight about our trinitarian friendship with God and with each other be distilled into theological method? I would like to focus on one way that it manifests itself: in conversation.[13] Various sorts of highly stylized dialogues have, of course, been used in philosophy and theology for a long time, for we need only think of the Socratic method as represented in Plato's *Republic* or of Justin Martyr's *Dialogue with Trypho*. What I wish to explore here is something quite different: the place of conversations among friends in the *doing* of theology, particularly as a spur to theological thoughts and insights.

One poignant example of this conversation is that of Augustine with Alypius and Ponticianus in *Confessions* 8, in the passages immediately prior to the description of his conversion. Augustine vividly describes both his conversation with Ponticianus and its effects: "On a certain day, then, when Nebridius was away—for some reason I cannot remember—there came to visit Alypius and me at our house one Ponticianus, a fellow countryman of ours from Africa, who held high office in the emperor's court. What he wanted with us I do not know; but we sat down to talk together."[14] During the conversation, Ponticianus notices a codex by the apostle Paul on a game table and is delighted to find that rather than a book on rhetoric as he had feared, it is a portion of Scripture, for as it turns out, he is himself a baptized Christian. Ponticianus then leads the conversation to Anthony the Egyptian monk, of whom Augustine had never yet heard, and tells Alypius and Augustine about visiting the cottage where the *Life of Anthony* had been written, an experience that led two colleagues of Ponticianus, *agentes in rebus*—a phrase that Outler renders "secret service agents"—to find their way to the Christian faith. This story within Augustine's story itself centers on a conversation between friends: Ponticianus narrates that one of the "secret service agents" reveals to his companion that rather than seeking to become one of the "friends of the Emperor" (*amici imperatoris*), he is now resolved to be a "friend of God" (*amicus Dei*). The colleague and friend replies that in the face of that decision, "he would continue bound in his friendship"; indeed, he immediately likewise resolves to become a servant and friend of God. These two in turn tell Ponticianus and a fourth colleague, who have been walking around the garden, of their resolve to abandon imperial service in order to pursue the service of God. Ponticianus does not follow their example, but he seemingly admires their decision. This story in turn mightily affects Augustine, who while he listens to Ponticianus's narrative, compares himself negatively to these two exemplary men who have "set their affections on heavenly things." Augustine writes: "Thus was I inwardly confused, and mightily confounded with a horrible shame, while Ponticianus went ahead speaking such things. And when he had finished his story and the business he came for, he went his way. And then what did I not say to myself, within myself?" (8.7.16).

Much has been written about Augustine's conversion and about the literary construction of the eighth book of the *Confessions*; as is quite transparent, the story of the conversion of the "secret agents" mirrors closely Augustine's own conversion narrative and is the second in a chain of conversion stories that begins with an account by Simplicianus of the conversion of Marius Victorinus (8.2.3) and ends with the dramatic narrative of Augustine's own conversion—and that of Alypius. What I want to center on here, however, is not on the presumed effect of the reported conversations on Augustine's conversion, but rather on the conversations in the light of the *Confessions* as *theology*. The *Confessions* is, of course, not some sort of pre-theological text of Augustine's, but is rather a text that was written *as theology*, albeit in a more narrative form than most of his other works. The description of conversations and interaction with his friends are central to the literary structure of the work; the autobiographical structure allows Augustine to bring to light how he has reached certain fundamental conclusions about the nature of God: certainly through the leading of the Spirit of God and the reading of Scripture, but also in and through *conversation,* both with God (whom he constantly addresses in the vocative in the prayers interspersed throughout the work) and with friends and acquaintances. The story about the *agentes,* which constitutes the middle link in the literary chain mentioned above, has in turn at its heart the decision of the two men to become *friends of God.* Augustine's narrative theology thus links here the notion of *friendship with God* with the importance of conversation among friends in the process of articulating the meaning of that divine friendship or *amicitia Dei.*

In a sense the historical shift that led to the practice of reading in silence rather than aloud leaves us more than ever in need of the company of others with whom we can try to "find our voices." As de Certeau reminds us, in earlier times readers made "the body of the other" with their own voices, whereas today for the most part, a text no longer manifests itself through a reader's voice. The body withdraws itself from the text and comes into contact with it only through the mobility of the eye, which skips over the page as quickly as it can, rather as the airplane detaches itself from the soil to cover distance more rapidly.[15] Besides the subconscious gestures, tics, rustlings, and rumblings that de Certeau mentions as residual signs of our bodies' engagement with texts, we do still read aloud in the context of friendship and community: reading a story to our children, reading Scripture in church, reading a line that has caught our fancy to a friend, even mumbling in response to newspaper headlines. By doing so, we re-embody these texts and resist their privatization. Meaningful conversation with friends likewise allows an embodiment of our ideas, as we gesticulate and articulate, giving voice to what otherwise would remain silent. Even sitting in silence together does not allow for a disembodied silence: we breathe, exchange glances, feel each other's company, and come away from the encounter subtly changed.

Admittedly, the recognition of conversation as a key piece in the articulation of one's discipline is not exclusive to theology. Take, for instance, the case of Latin Americanist Walter Mignolo, who reflects lucidly on this topic in the preface to his book *Local Histories/Global Designs,* a work that he goes so far to define as a journey of his conversations.[16] "The main research for this book consisted in conversations," he states, by which he means casual conversations of all kinds, not interviews. He goes on to explain:

> By conversations I do not mean statements that can be recorded, transcribed, and used as documents. Most of the time the most influential conversations were people's comments, in passing, about an event, a book, an idea, a person. These are documents that cannot be transcribed, knowledge that comes and goes, but remains with you and introduces changes in a given argument.

This matter is delicate, of course, because it hints at the possibility of "milking" the ideas of others without giving them credit. The awareness of that danger makes one appreciate anew Augustine's careful descriptions of his conversations, even if they serve primarily as a literary artifice. The quandary of low-intensity plagiarism is particularly true for academics such as anthropologists and theologians who often have their finger on the pulse of aspects of popular culture and make use of ideas they encounter in conversation with people who will likely never read scholarly books or journals.[17] Mignolo's careful depiction of conversation *as method* is in itself a salutary exercise in honesty, as when he writes that his "acknowledgment goes mainly to the people who guided my thinking with their wisdom, though I cannot quote what they said, and perhaps they do not even remember it." Beyond the trickiness of faithful attribution, it also points to one of the richest aspects of fruitful conversation: its ability to modify the course of one's insights, thoughts, or convictions in unexpected ways. This latter ability is reminiscent of the work of the Spirit: often unexpected, deceptively simple, the batting of the butterfly's wing that grows into a buffeting wind and changes the course of our lives. What theology *can* do that other disciplines most often do not, either because they cannot or they will not, is consciously reflect on how the Spirit's agency is manifested in the course of such conversations.

Virginia Azcuy articulates this pneumatic agency and its consequences for an ecclesial and social ethos in a narrative fashion, by situating in (auto) biography some of the theological conversations that have helped give shape to her own theological method.[18] She does so vividly by making use of conceptual tools developed by Alfonso López Quintás: *entreveros* and *entreveramientos.*[19] These Spanish nouns, derived from the verb *entreverar* (to mix or intermingle), can imply on the one hand a material encounter that is often disorderly somewhat in the sense of an entanglement or a melee (as in ancient cavalry battles), and on the other hand, in a more positive sense, participation and involvement in the life of another. In this second sense Azcuy uses the two nouns to describe the personal and dialogical ethos of much of Latin American and Latino/Latina theology, which emerges in great part through a biographical interweaving of conversation and interchange. She admits that the conflict and complications that are part of the semantic universe of *entreverar* are often also part of the theological process, for human lives are complicated and so are their interrelationships. Indeed, one element that I find compelling in her use of the semantic field of *entreverar* is that the richness and ambiguity of the word reflects an openness to factor in the *messiness* involved in living out theology in the quotidian, in the materiality involved in the intersection of the global and the local that is reflected in each of our lives. Azcuy argues that precisely our awareness of both the possibilities and the limits of human relationships can lead us to move more decidedly to work on the mutuality of our encounters.

The idea of mutuality, particularly as it is expressed in the relationship between friendship and self-disclosure, is a trope of the classical tradition that reappears in many early Christian authors. Ambrose, for instance, who crafts his work *De officiis ministrorum* with obvious admiration for Cicero (who had earlier written the treatise *De officiis*), speaks of such mutuality in self-disclosure: friends should reveal to each other what is "on their chests" or "in their bosoms" ("*ostendamus illis nos pectus nostrum, et illi nobis aperiat suum*"). Such mutuality is, however, premised on a Trinitarian dynamic. Ambrose quotes John 15:14 and then adds, "A friend, then, hides nothing, if he is true; he pours forth his mind, just as the Lord Jesus poured forth the mysteries of the Father."[20]

I find this passage from Ambrose suggestive, inasmuch as I wonder what would happen in conversation if as theologians we practiced moving toward mutuality and self-disclosure in this Ambrosian sense, but with a *caveat*: with the explicit awareness of power dynamics that Azcuy's model of *entreveramientos* requires, lest self-disclosure serve only for the more powerful of the interlocutors to erase the other. A movement toward mutuality in this sense would manifest itself in an explicit commitment to "take to heart" the perspective of the person to whom we want to be a friend:[21] to allow her to pour forth her mind, while remembering that from the perspective of a society's hegemonic "common sense," any minority's voice tends to be held as personal, subjective, anecdotal, and unreliable, whereas that of the majority tends to be seen as impersonal and thus truthful and objective.[22] This principle means that if in any given interaction with someone "to whom we want to be a friend" (even if friendship has not yet fully emerged), if we find ourselves to be the person with more power or status in that situation, we should remember continually that our interlocutor, by virtue of his or her social location, is in the position of being heard less than we would likely be. On the other hand, if we should find ourselves to be on the side of those who have less power in a given situation, we should proceed with a good measure of caution and a sense of self-preservation, while preserving the willingness to "bless those who persecute us" in imaginative ways.[23] It is impossible to prescribe beforehand exactly how these interactions will or should take place, since the interplay of *difference* is always contextual and particular, even while it is embedded in larger structures.[24]

Such an exercise would constitute a departure from Ambrose's framework inasmuch as he, following classical writers, presupposed that friendship would take place between persons (presumably male) of a similar social standing who spoke the same language in the same rhetorically sophisticated way. On the other hand, it must be also admitted that upon introducing a Trinitarian rationale for self-disclosure in mutuality, Ambrose also opens the door analogically to the possibility of relations of mutuality and friendship between persons whose social standing is quite different, by virtue of being loved equally by the God whose love was manifested in the Incarnation.

Let us for a moment imagine this kind of movement toward mutuality, not using the lens of race, class, or gender explicitly, but rather—and perhaps jarringly—that of access to communication technologies, particularly the Internet. Néstor García Canclini analyzes the disparities between those who have both access to the Internet and the ability to use it and those for whom access to electronic media is primarily the consumption of noncable television. Although this polarity exists in all countries, it is all the greater in those where economic growth is slow, work is precarious, and foreign debt is high. For example, in Mexico, although 77 percent of homes that include young people have televisions, only 6 percent of those homes have an Internet connection. At the same time, all of those young persons, as is the case with all Latin Americans, share the common experience of owing 1,550 dollars as their portion of the foreign debt, from the moment of their birth. All are debtors, although not all are equally affected by the foreign debt; all of them have been globalized, but not all in the same way.[25] What might the move toward conversation and mutuality mean for two young persons who respectively do and do not have access to the information deemed necessary to adapt and perhaps—in some cases—even to thrive for a time in the context of globalized capitalism? In what way might that conversation prove theologically fruitful? It would not, for one, be possible to hold such a conversation in a virtual chat room; friendly conversation would require the materiality of a face-to-face encounter as well as "real time." It would, in short, have to stand in the way of the liquidation of time and space that constitutes one of the most disquieting and dehumanizing markers of the postmodern condition.[26] Even that simple observation has profound significance theologically: *real presence* is required.

García Canclini, speaking as an anthropologist, observes that the most fecund space for an academic with access to information and the material possibility of producing knowledge, is neither a refuge in the biases of First World elitism nor an understanding of the subaltern as an ontologically privileged and untainted fount of knowledge, but rather the *intersections* in which "subjects are able to speak and act, transform themselves and be transformed."[27] The placement at the crossroads, at the intersections, and in the third spaces would seem to be one of the factors which allows for fruitful conversation although placing oneself there, in what Bhabha terms the "interstitial time and space," often also means "living in the incomprehensible."[28]

It seems to me that as theologians we often hope to weave in and out of our interaction with others by the perichoretic rhythms of God. Too often we succeed only in making a tangle of things, even when our intentions are good; yet, by God's grace, in that very messiness can be found unexpected theological richness that is worth disentangling. Such messiness may well be distasteful to the classical tradition, which desires above all harmony and symmetry. Aristotle writes that the kind of friendship that is "perfect both in respect of duration and in all other respects" is the friendship in which "each gets from each in all respects the same as, or something like what he gives; which is what ought to happen between friends."[29] This portion of the Nicomachean ethics is quoted more than once with distaste by Moltmann precisely because it seems to him to imply an exclusive friendship between persons of identical social status, rather than the open friendship practiced by Jesus in the Gospels. The "friend of tax collectors and sinners" (Luke 7:34) and the community that emerged in his Spirit (Rom. 15:7) presuppose a divine and cosmic friendship by which God invites all of creation to an open friendship not based on defensiveness or dividedness.[30] Methodologically, the result of Moltmann's conversations with many different friends are expressed paradigmatically in the section on "Mirror Images of Liberating Theology" of his *Experiences in Theology*, where he tells of his dialogue with black theology as a white person, with liberation theology as a German, with feminist theology as a male, or with Minjung theology as a person of privilege in the First World. [31] Such conversations have shaped his theology in unexpected ways and helped it to continue to unfold creatively.

SPEAK, "FRIEND," AND ENTER

An important turning point in J. R. R. Tolkien's *The Fellowship of the Ring* (the first volume of his trilogy The Lord of the Rings) is the moment when the group of friends who have been commissioned with the task of accompanying Frodo the ringbearer on his way toward Mount Doom come up against the sealed entrance to the mines of Moria, through which they have no choice but to go. Across an arch over the top of the doors can be seen, written in an ancient tongue, the words "Speak, friend, and enter." Gandalf the wizard, whose task it is to find the password that will open the doors, tries for hours to speak the combination of words able to unlock them, in a variety of languages, finally banging his staff against the doors in frustration, but to no avail. It is a passing question by one of the hobbits, Merry, that holds the key to opening the doors: "What does it mean by *speak, friend, and enter?*" Through mulling over that fragment of dialogue with Merry, Gandalf finally is able to guess the riddle and open the door, simply by saying the Elvish word for "friend." [32] In this instance, conversation with a friend literally provides the key for unlocking a door. Unlike the conversations that Augustine describes in his *Confessions,* however, this interchange occurs not among persons of roughly equal status in society, but rather crosses boundaries of age, social standing, and "kind." Likewise, when conversations among friends are able to cross such boundaries, they are often the most valuable nudges in the development of theological insight.

Theology cannot enter into all the places it needs to go unless theologians are able to grasp the importance of conversations with friends, precisely because such conversations are a material practice that can help us avoid the trap of living, thinking, and writing in a solipsistic manner. But if the circle of friends with whom we converse is limited to those very similar to us, following the classical model of friendship, that excludes the potential for conflict and misunderstanding, for messiness, then we also will have missed the opportunity of finding new spaces for transformation. For Rosario Castellanos's character, the reason for the demise of her friendship with Gertrudis was neither her friend's initial reticence to talking nor the considerable differences between them, but rather the sense that her friend, though amiable, was finally indifferent to her. Toward the end of the relationship, she observes: "Our conversation was agreeable, balanced. We were happy, as if we did not know that we belonged to different species."[33] The friendship failed to prosper not because they did not belong to the "same species" but rather because one of them chose to be oblivious to that difference. It seems to me that what is particularly promising for theology is not primarily the prospect of the amiable dialogue of birds of a feather, though at times such may be needed, but also the challenge of tense, messy conversations along the way with those who are or may become our friends. As in the case of the disciples on the road to Emmaus, who were "talking and arguing among themselves" (Luke 24:15), in the midst of heated conversation we may unexpectedly find Jesus walking along with us—and our theology will be the better for it.

Chapter 5

Wisdom, Theological Anthropology, and Modern Secular Interpretation of Humanity

David H. Kelsey

Because both Christian theological anthropologies and several human and life sciences address the same descriptive question—*What* is a human being?—it is desirable that theological anthropologies be conceptually hospitable to anthropological claims warranted well by those sciences. If theology values consistency and coherence of knowledge, regardless of its sources, and if it wants its own claims to be taken seriously in public forums, its anthropology has everything to lose by systematically ignoring and excluding scientifically warranted anthropological claims. That consideration raises a secondary question from the side of Christian theology: How should we relate theological claims about what human beings are to secular anthropological claims warranted by the life and human sciences? Building on Professor Jürgen Moltmann's[1] recent recommendation, I shall argue that canonical Wisdom literature provides a creation story whose implied answers to the questions of what is a human being are more hospitable to scientifically warranted secular anthropological claims than are the anthropological implications of the Genesis creation stories that have traditionally provided norms for Christian anthropology.

Genesis and Theological Anthropology

In theological anthropology, the question, what is a human being? has traditionally been treated as a subtopic in a doctrine of creation warranted by the creation stories in Genesis 1:1—2:24. More exactly, the question has received a warrant through an interpretation of Genesis that assumes chapters 1–3 are the best hermeneutical lens through which to interpret not only Genesis, but the entire Pentateuchal narrative of the Israelites' deliverance from Egypt and the creation of Israel. This interpretation involves construing the anthropological aspects of the creation stories in Genesis as narratives of origins: the origin of humankind as fully actualized, physically perfect, undying creatures in proper relation to God; the origin of the imperfections of hard labor, suffering, and death that befall human creatures in consequence of that disobedience; and hence the origin of the need for the event of deliverance to which, for Christians, not only the Pentateuch, but the entire canon witnesses. This anthropological story about creation and the fall is told in a way that is ordered to and governed by the telling of another theologically more central story of divine deliverance. I particularly want to stress that as an anthropological account of what human beings are that is focused on questions of origins but *ordered to* a soteriological account of divine deliverance, anthropology about the creation and the fall has had great difficulty being hospitable to apparently competing genetic and etiological claims from extrabiblical sources such as the sciences about what human beings are.

Against this background, in his commentary on Genesis and in related texts, Claus Westermann[2] argues that when Genesis 1:1—3:24 is properly interpreted in context, it can no longer be taken in the traditional way to warrant existentialist and individualistic anthropologies about creation and the fall that focus on one's own existential relation to God and on the consequence of wrong relation to God.[3] This claim does not imply that Westermann has any agenda regarding the question of Christian anthropology's conceptual hospitality to anthropological claims warranted by the sciences. Nor does he suggest that a theological address to the anthropological question, what is a human being? ought not to be a subsection of a doctrine of creation. He does insist, however, that Genesis 1–3, properly understood, does not warrant a traditional kind of theological anthropology.

Westermann's analysis of Genesis 1–11 has even larger implications for anthropology. I shall argue in the next two sections that his analysis provides both reasons *against* relying on Genesis 1–3 to establish a norm for *any* theological anthropology, and reasons *for* privileging creation stories from canonical Wisdom literature, rather than Genesis 1–3, to provide a norm for answers from Christian anthropology to the question, what is a human being? I shall then argue in a final section that a theological anthropology guided and provided norms by the creation story of canonical Wisdom literature is conceptually very hospitable to modern secular interpretations of humanity.

The heart of Westermann's case against Genesis 1–3 as authorizing traditional existentialist anthropologies that focus on the creation and the fall lies in his analysis of the literary structure of the Pentateuch, the role of Genesis within it, and the role of Genesis 1–11 within Genesis. In short, as Westermann reads the Pentateuch, its "central part . . . tells the story of the rescue [or 'deliverance']"[4] at the Reed Sea (Exod. 1:18). Editors shaped Genesis into its received canonical form to provide two types of introduction to this story of deliverance: chapters 12–50 and chapters 1–11. Each differently sets the story of Israel's deliverance in a larger context in order to give it universal significance. Chapters 12–50 "present the history of Israel before it became a people," showing that Israel emerges out of a universal process across time that leads inexorably from generation to generation; but chapters 1–11 place the events of deliverance in "a much wider horizon, extending them to world events in the broadest sense of the word."[5]

Our focus falls on chapters 1–11. According to Westermann, these chapters function to characterize *primal time*, that is, the background of the event of the deliverance and formation of Israel narrated in the rest of the Pentateuch, viz., the continuity of the generations through a process of "growth, expansion, prosperity, and fertility."[6] These processes are the "necessary preconditions" of historical events such as the event of deliverance. They characterize the universal context of human life as marked by a "forward-thrusting, ever-pregnant power of becoming."[7] Genesis 1–11 "trace[s] back to its source [this] power which carries on [human] existence from generation to generation."[8]

Westermann holds that these chapters constitute a freestanding literary unit that must be interpreted on its own terms.[9] According to Westermann's analysis, the unit consists of two different types of writing: genealogies, which Westermann calls "numerative" writings, and narratives of different sorts. The genealogies function to stress "the continuity of successive generations"[10] that characterizes *primal time*. The upshot of his analysis is that the genealogies form "the framework of everything that is narrated in Gen 1–11."[11] They are the hermeneutical lenses through which the narratives are to be interpreted.[12] In Westermann's analysis, the editors of the received canonical form of Genesis appropriated stories of creation from Israel's neighbors and their predecessors, whose accounts served to give a cosmogony. As edited in Genesis 1–3, the creation stories serve, not to *explain* the origin of the cosmos, but to *stress* that God's creative blessing, the "power which carries on [human] existence from generation to generation," is the universal and necessary precondition of God's deliverance of Israel at the Reed Sea and is to be traced back to its source: God's blessing on creation. So too, stories of crime and punishment (e.g., Adam and Eve in chapter 3; Cain and Abel in chapter 4; the flood in chapters 6 and 7; and Noah's sons in 9:18-28) all have the same function. They were appropriated from other cultures and edited to stress that *primal time* includes God's creative blessing, but also that "[s]in, guilt, and revolt," which "are not the results of a long encounter with God [beginning with the event of deliverance at the Reed Sea] as are the sins of Israel." Rather, "they belong to human existence as such and are common to all people in all places."[13]

This analysis reverses the traditional assumption in doctrines of creation and anthropology that the creation narratives in Genesis 1 and 2 and the story of Adam and Eve's disobedience in chapter 3 are the hermeneutical lenses through which the rest of Genesis is to be read. The story about the disobedience of Adam and Eve no more serves to *explain* the origin of sin and suffering from which humankind needs to be *delivered* than the creation narratives serve to *explain* the existence of a good world in which a wrong existential relation to God and a radical *fall* of a good creation are possible. Instead, the creation narratives serve to describe the precondition of the event of deliverance as the power that carries on human existence from generation to generation; and the stories of crime and punishment describe that precondition as marked also by universal human estrangement from God. Clearly, when the creation stories in Genesis 1–3 are interpreted through the hermeneutical lenses of the Genesis genealogies, they cannot warrant existentialist anthropologies about creation and the fall.

The Narrative Logics of Scriptural Stories of Creative Blessing, Echatological Blessing, and Deliverance

Westermann's analysis implies three further points more radical than his conclusion, points that cumulatively suggest that the stories in Genesis 1–3 ought not to be the scriptural norm for *any* theological anthropology. He makes two of the points explicitly; I shall argue that the third, which goes far beyond anything Westermann explicitly proposed, is implied in the first two.

First, Westermann draws a conceptual distinction between two ways in which the Pentateuch says God relates to humankind: in events of deliverance (the central story of the Pentateuch) and in blessing. The two ways "cannot be reduced to a single concept because, for one reason, they are experienced differently. Deliverance is experienced in events that represent God's intervention. Blessing is a continuing activity of God that is either present or not present. It cannot be experienced in an event any more than can growth or motivation or decline of strength."[14] A story of deliverance is a story about an episode. A story of blessing is a story of a continuing condition.

The second is a distinction between two sorts of blessing implicit in Genesis 2 and explicit elsewhere in the Christian canon. Westermann distinguishes between God's creative blessing on creation (whose paradigmatic expression is in Genesis 1–3) and God's eschatological blessing on creation (whose paradigmatic expression is in Isaiah 65 and Revelation 21–22).[15] Both, when they prevail, are about constant conditions or states, not about episodic events in history.[16] Westermann holds that a story about God's relating to humankind in eschatological blessing is implicit in Genesis 2:2, 3. In his view, when the Priestly editors of the received canonical text of Genesis 1:1—2:4 appropriated internationally shared stories of creation, conflating eight works of creation into six days of creation followed by God's day of rest, the seventh day "pointed to the continuation of this process [of stages of creation] as it moves toward a goal which transcends the works of Creation."[17] The course of human history "runs to its goal just like the days of the week," and that goal is "the eternal rest which has been suggested in the rest of the seventh day."[18] Thus the story of creative blessing is ordered not only to a story of deliverance, but also to a story of eschatological blessing.

Westermann is vague about whether God's creative blessing and God's eschatological blessing are variations on one selfsame way God relates to humankind or are fundamentally different. I suggest, however, that the principle by which Westermann distinguished deliverance from blessing requires an equally basic distinction between creative blessing and eschatological blessing. They are experienced differently. Creative blessing is experienced as a continuous condition of God's actively relating here and now to provide the "power which carries on [human] existence from generation to generation"; but by definition eschatological blessing cannot be experienced here and now as a continuous condition because it is precisely what does not yet obtain, at least not fully. As Moltmann has shown in his pathbreaking *Theology of Hope*,[19] eschatological blessing can only be *experienced* in hope that responds to at least hints of a promise of eschatological blessing. Human beings may *experience* the *promise* as a continuous condition, but they do not yet experience the blessing itself as a continuously realized condition. I conclude that although Westermann only distinguished explicitly between the two ways in which canonical scripture narrates God's relating to humankind, that is, to deliver and to bless, he implicitly points to distinctions among not two, but three, ways in which God relates to humankind: to deliver, to bless creatively, and to bless eschatologically.

Building on Westermann's distinctions, I want to urge a formal point about the way in which canonical scripture provides norms for Christian theological anthropology—a point with which, for all I know, Westermann might have had little sympathy. This point is important because it shows why no theological anthropological address to the question, What is a human being? ought to be provided norms by Genesis 1–3. The point is that as deliverance, creative blessing, and eschatological blessing can be distinguished because each is differently experienced, so too in the Christian canon, stories of each way God relates to humankind must be distinguished because, formally speaking, they each have a different narrative logic.

The notion of *narrative logic* requires more explanation. Consider how the movement of each type of story is plotted. Canonical stories of God's drawing humankind to an eschatological consummation are told as stories of how God goes about fulfilling a promise to bless humankind with an eschatological blessing that goes beyond anything that human creaturely life is otherwise capable of doing, but in such a way that human beings do not cease to be specifically human and finite creatures. In their New Testament versions, the movement of such stories is plotted as the breaking in of God's intended future for the world in the resurrection of the crucified Jesus of Nazareth so that God's future is now actually in humankind's shared world in a way that neither violates nor annihilates their creaturely human finitude. Not yet fully actualized, God's future drives on toward full actualization. The plot of this type of story of God's relating to humankind is moved neither by a problem God needs to solve nor by a brokenness God needs to heal. On the other hand, the plot of Christian canonical stories of God's relating to reconcile estranged humankind *is* moved by a brokenness only God can heal and a problem only God can solve.

Humankind's estrangement from God entails a deadly distortion of *what* humankind is by God's creative relating, a distortion humankind is itself unable to correct. Like the plot of New Testament stories of God's relating to draw humankind to eschatological consummation, the plot of this set of stories is also moved by the narrative logic of the concrete way God goes about righting this distortion and reconciling humankind's estrangement, viz., through a story of the crucifixion and the resurrection of Jesus of Nazareth as the story of Godself not only being one among Jesus's human sisters and brothers in their creaturely finitude, but also being in solidarity with them in the deadly consequences of their estrangement from God and from one another. That is to say, it is inherent in the narrative logic of this set of stories that God relates to reconcile humankind on terms that are set, not only by the givens of finite human creatureliness, but *also* by the "adventitious" (Calvin) given of death-dealing human estrangement.

The formal differences between these two sets of stories ties them together in an asymmetrically reciprocal relation. They are reciprocally related because the story each tells of a different way in which God relates to humankind (to bless eschatologically; to deliver from estrangement and its consequences) simply *is* the story of Jesus of Nazareth. Neither can be told except in relation to telling the other; however, because of their different narrative logics, this relation between them is asymmetrical. A canonical story of eschatological blessing presupposes that those who are blessed are not estranged from God. In principle, it could be told coherently even if, contrary to fact, humankind were not estranged and there were no need for a story of deliverance. On the other hand, if humankind is estranged from God, God's faithfulness to the promise of eschatological blessing entails God's event of deliverance, for there can be no fulfillment of the promise of eschatological blessing for those who are not delivered from the consequences of estrangement from God. Thus a canonical story of deliverance presupposes not only human estrangement from God but also a story of eschatological blessing, and cannot be told coherently apart from such a story.

In contrast to both of these sets of canonical stories, however, canonical stories of God's relating to humankind in creative blessing are moved neither by the narrative logic of making and keeping promises enacted within conditions set by creaturely finitude, nor by the narrative logic of restoring broken relationships and righting distorted human beings enacted within conditions set by both creaturely finitude and human estrangement. There is no reality independent of and antecedent to God's relating creatively that could set the terms on which God relates creatively. Instead, when told for their own sake, canonical stories of God's relating in creative blessing are moved by the narrative logic of spontaneous play or an expressive gesture. God relates creatively solely for the sake of doing so, not to accomplish some further end such as making good on a promise or healing a brokenness. These stories render God's relating creatively purely in the delight of doing so for its own sake. God loves doing it, declaring it good to do it.

The distinctive narrative logic of stories of God's relating in creative blessing means that they are asymmetrically related to the other two sets of stories. Stories of God's relating in eschatological blessing and stories of God's delivering estranged humankind from estrangement and its consequences both presuppose stories of God's relating creatively to reality other than God, including humankind; otherwise there is nothing "there" to be either blessed eschatologically or delivered. On the other hand, nothing in the narrative logic of stories of God's relating creatively entails that God also relates in the other two ways. That is precisely what warrants calling the other two *grace*. They are not exacted ontologically, morally, or logically by God's also having related to humankind creatively.

The differences in the narrative logics of each of these three sets of canonical stories shows that they cannot be conflated as though they were mere variations of or different moments in basically the *same* story. They are not the same; they have different narrative logics. Westermann implicitly makes this point. Although he agrees with Gerhard von Rad[20] that confession of faith in God's act of deliverance at the Reed Sea is the *middle* of the Pentateuch's salvation history, he rejects von Rad's characterization of the Genesis creation stories as the first event in salvation history. Creation is not an event of deliverance of anything from anything. The creation stories in Genesis have the narrative logic of stories of God's creative blessing, not the narrative logic of stories of God's act of deliverance. Scriptural creation stories cannot be conflated with scriptural deliverance stories as though they were their first chapters.

The point can be generalized. These three sets of canonical scriptural stories cannot be strung together in any one order of sequence as though they were the beginning, middle, and end of one grand story that has a coherent narrative logic. Nor can they be told separately in isolation from one another. Rather, each must be told in relation to a telling of the other two in a way that braids them together without conflating them with one another.

Conflation of these stories is not to be confused with the practice of telling one set of the stories in a way that uses tropes and images from either of the other two sets of stories. That rhetorical practice is unexceptionable and has plenty of instances in Christian canonical scripture. For example, in Romans 5, the apostle Paul appropriates tropes from the Genesis story of Adam in the service of telling a story of divine deliverance in Christ. However powerful and effective that may be in telling the story of deliverance that Paul wants to tell, Westermann points out that, subordinated to the narrative logic of a story of deliverance, the story of Adam is no longer told according to the narrative logic of the story of creative blessing in Genesis 1–3. Consequently, soteriology aside, Westermann questions the value to theological anthropology of the apostle Paul's pairing of Adam and Christ in Romans 5. Since the story of Adam in Genesis is part of the story of creative blessing in Genesis 1–11, it corresponds most closely not "to Christ" and a story of deliverance but to a story of eschatological blessing, "to the events of the end, and specifically to what is said about mankind as transformed at the events of the end, as for example, in Isaiah 65 and Revelation 21–22."[21] Moreover, as long as Adam is correlated with Christ, deliverance through Christ is limited to deliverance from sin and death as in Romans 6. But when Adam is correlated with Revelation, then what Christ delivers humankind from extends also to "the suffering which results from . . . being a creature" as in Revelation 21:4.[22] Westermann's analysis of the role of Genesis 1–3 within the larger context of the Pentateuch as a whole shows that it is a paradigmatic case of this very rhetorical practice. Tropes from a story of creative blessing are used to tell a quite different story of divine deliverance, for the narrative logic of the creation story is *bent* under the conceptual gravitational force of the narrative logic of the second type of story.

If a theological anthropological address to the question, what is a human being, is a subtopic of a doctrine of creation, it should be provided norms by canonical creation stories moved by their proper narrative logic of creative blessing, not by the narrative logic of either of the other two sets of canonical stories of God, i.e., by relating to humankind in eschatological blessing or to deliver them from the consequences of estrangement. Westermann has shown that Genesis 1–3 does not tell creation stories "for their own sake," but in the service of another set of stories about God's relating to humankind to deliver them. The creation stories are governed by the latter's narrative logic and do not warrant traditional anthropologies concerned with creation and the fall, and should provide norms for no theological address whatsoever to the anthropological question, what is a human being? Rather, theological answers to the question, what is a human being? should be provided norms by the narrative logic of canonical stories of God's creative blessing that are told for their own sake and not told in the service of stories either of eschatological blessing or of deliverance. When we turn to the narrative logic of canonical stories of creative blessing to provide norms for theological anthropological remarks about *what* human beings are as creatures, we need to look elsewhere than to Genesis 1–3.

GENESIS, WISDOM, AND GOD RELATING CREATIVELY

An alternative is the creation story told in canonical Wisdom literature, which, as Walther Zimmerli pointed out long ago,[23] "thinks resolutely within the framework of a theology of creation." I shall argue that an address to the anthropological question, "What is a human being?" which has been provided norms by the narrative logic of Wisdom's creation story, can be more hospitable to scientifically well warranted anthropological claims than when it has been provided norms by the Genesis creation stories. Canonical Wisdom literature texts tell a story of God's creative blessing whose narrative logic is not *bent* by its appropriation in the telling of some other story. Its narrative logic is a strong candidate for providing norms for theological anthropology. By canonical Wisdom literature, I mean those texts acknowledged by both Roman Catholic and Protestant Christians: chiefly Proverbs, Ecclesiastes, Job, and Song of Songs. They all think within the framework of a creation theology, but they think variously. I take Proverbs to express the mainstream conventions of the Wisdom tradition, while Ecclesiastes and Job press hard in different directions against those conventions. As Brevard Childs observes, the variations within canonical Wisdom literature all "move to *expand* different aspects of wisdom through theological reflection within basically a creation theology."[24]

Wisdom's creation theology is explicitly affirmed in only a few places in Proverbs and Job; mostly it is implicit, functioning as a background to what is explicitly affirmed. Even more rarely is a story told of God's relating creatively to reality other than God. The notable exceptions are Proverbs 3:19; 3:20; and 8:21-32, where so little happens that the texts barely manage to be narratival. *Nonetheless*, a creation theology is here and a creation story is told for its own sake. It is not employed in the service of telling stories of eschatological blessing or deliverance. Canonical wisdom makes no reference to God's acts of deliverance and hardly any reference to either Law or cultic worship.[25] The editors of Proverbs in its canonical form appear to have framed the text by two editorial insertions, one at the end (30:5-6) and the other at the beginning (1:1), in a way that identifies the book as an independent voice in the canon of the Hebrew Bible, neither a subset of the Law nor of the Prophets. Proverbs 30:5-6 combines variants of 2 Samuel 22:31 and Deuteronomy 4:2 to put the attentive reader on notice that this collection of wise sayings has the same status as God's promises (as made to David in 2 Samuel 22:31) and God's Law (as enunciated by Moses in Deuteronomy 4:2). Childs argues that these collections of sayings were canonically edited to establish that they are as religiously authoritative as canonical historical and prophetic scriptures.[26] The superscription for the entire book (1:1) ascribes to Solomon all the collections of wise sayings that make up the book, even though some of them later in the text are also ascribed to others. This ascription suggests that the question of authorship was not the question of who originally wrote the book but rather a question about the grounds of its religious authority: Why privilege this text of Wisdom as normative for our common life of faith? Just as the traditional attribution of the Pentateuch to Moses grounds its authority in the covenanting history of YHWH with Israel, and the attribution of the Psalms to David grounds their authority in the history of Israel's (ambiguously) divinely established monarchy and cultic worship of YHWH at Zion, so Proverbs is attributed to one who in 1 Kings is explicitly linked to Eastern and Egyptian wisdom. The creation story told by canonical Wisdom literature is told for its own sake, that is, on the authority of Wisdom's own independent voice in the canon, not on the authority of other voices in the canon, whether stories of deliverance or stories of eschatological blessing, in whose service the rhetoric and imagery of creation stories might be used.

The narrative logic of Wisdom's creation story as told in Proverbs 3:19; 3:20; and 8:21-32 is moved, not by the logic of the promise of eschatological blessing nor by the logic of deliverance from estrangement and its consequent broken-ness, but by the narrative logic of spontaneous play or of an expressive gesture. In Proverbs 3:20, creation happens abruptly. It erupts. In Proverbs 3:19 we learn that God founded the earth "by wisdom." Then in Proverbs 8:21-32 wisdom is personified as Woman Wisdom: "The Lord created me at the beginning of his work, the first of his acts long ago" (8:22). Personified in a literary trope, she does not stand in for God (much less for one of the persons of the Trinity), but rather for how God relates to creation. The way God relates to Woman Wisdom and the way Wisdom relates to the rest of creation are both paradigmatic of the way God relates creatively to reality other than God.

God's relation to Woman Wisdom is intimate, modeling God's creative relation to humankind. Wisdom is beside God when God creates: "I was daily his delight / rejoicing before him always / rejoicing in his inhabited world / and delighting in the human race" (8:30-31). This mini-story about creation has the narrative logic of spontaneous play. God's creative relating breaks out spontaneously, delights in what it does, and is attentive to and committed to continuing what it is doing. God's creative relating is a kind of loving. Enacted wholly on its own terms, it is also radically free. With some complacency about its self-evidence, Proverbs famously stresses that God's creative blessing imbues creation with an inherent moral order so that wise behavior brings flourishing life and foolish behavior brings death. However, without explicitly challenging the belief that God creates such order, Ecclesiastes stresses how difficult it is to discern where and how God's just order is effective; and Job laments that God is too elusive to allow a showdown about the justice of Job's suffering. God is creative at God's free initiative. If God's creative relating is so radically free of all prior conditions, then what human beings are as God's creatures is not simply their empirically discoverable *nature*, but their *creatureliness*, i.e., their dependence on being related to creatively by God for sheer existence. If God's creative relating is loving as well as free, then what has the property of being related to creatively by God may fairly be called a gift. What human beings are as God's creatures is not simply their empirically discoverable *nature*, but their character as an ontologically contingent gift.

The major metaphor in Proverbs for Wisdom Woman's relation to creatures, and especially to humankind, modeling God's creative relation to humankind, is tree of life. The function of the wise sayings that constitute the literary content of Proverbs provides the book's two dominant images for just how Woman Wisdom is a tree of life, viz., by calling human beings to be wise in their actions and by engaging human beings in a practice of teaching and learning short Zen-like sayings, a practice through which wisdom is elicited. In Proverbs, Wisdom's opposite is folly and regularly leads to death. As Proverbs' characterization of death shows, the life nurtured by wisdom embraces much more than biological life. Death is consistently imaged, not merely as death of the body, but as shallow, broken life, both individual and social, that is but a living death. In Wisdom's creation theology, creaturely life embraces biological, emotional, intellectual, moral, social, and cultural vitality alike. The tree of life, which symbolizes a nurturing of life through a call to be wise and a pedagogy to elicit wisdom, characterizes God's creative relating as ongoing relating, resonating with Westermann's characterization of creative blessing as an ongoing condition rather than an episodic event. However, Wisdom literature's story of that divine relating is not oriented either to the promise of an additional eschatological blessing or to a characterization of the necessary universal preconditions of an event of deliverance. God creatively relates to reality other than God for its own sake.

In canonical Wisdom, *what* God's wise, attentive, and self-committed delight creates is a society of diverse physical beings, including human beings, that constitutes human beings' ordinary, everyday, lived world, the quotidian. Proverbs simply assumes a largely *petit bourgeois* quotidian, mostly located in villages and towns, whose patriarchal culture is ancient Middle Eastern and whose economy is agricultural. However, none of these features is definitive of what is the *creaturely* quotidian. What defines this society of physical beings as *creaturely* is its finitude, i.e., its limitedness. It is finite in at least three respects. First, creatures' resources of physically based energy and of capacities to regulate that energy, are intrinsically limited and are eventually exhausted. All creatures' time spans are limited. In particular, the creation theology of canonical Wisdom literature assumes a remarkably physical picture of human life. It is physically based and inherently mortal. Second, the quotidian lived world is finite in that it is a society of interacting physical beings, including human beings, that depend on one another for their well-being, but whose interdependence also leaves them vulnerable to conflict, collision, and damage. Its creatureliness means that the quotidian is inherently accident-prone. Third, as noted, the quotidian is finite in that the entire network of the society of interdependent creatures is radically dependent for its existence on God's relating to it creatively.

In Wisdom's creation story, human beings are, by God's creative relating, at home in this quotidian. In contrast to the Genesis creation stories, *what* God creates are not normatively *perfect* human beings who, though having physical bodies, are free of struggle, damage, pain, and death, though, if they prove faithless to God, they may be cursed with labor, pain, and death. That *perfection* of the human beings that God is said to create in Genesis is a function of a creation story being told in the service of a quite different story of divine deliverance. It serves to universalize the background need for deliverance. Canonical Wisdom literature, by contrast, assumes that God creates beings whose physical bodiliness is *inherently* mortal, obliged to labor for its life, and vulnerable to all manner of violation and pain. In Proverbs, human beings do not get their status as human by rising above or standing out of the quotidian. Rather, what marks them off from other creatures in the quotidian is their capacity, precisely as enmeshed in the quotidian, to hear in and through details of the quotidian God's call to be wise in their actions for the well-being of the quotidian. That call is what the trope of Woman Wisdom expresses.

Wisdom's creation story moves according to the narrative logic of an expressive gesture or spontaneous play, done by God for the sheer delight of doing it. What God creates by relating creatively and specifically to human beings are physical creatures capable of responding to God's call to be wise in their exercise of their finite energies for the well-being of the creaturely quotidian for its own sake—not for the sake of some further eschatological telos or for the sake of an act of deliverance from the quotidian conditions of finitude. Of course, that does not rule out the possibility that God also relates to what God creates to draw it to an eschatological consummation, or that God also relates to what God creates, when it is estranged from God, to reconcile it and deliver it from the deadly consequences of its estrangement. But those modes of God's relating must be told in stories with narrative logic different from those of stories of God's relating creatively.

MODERN SECULAR INTERPRETATION OF HUMANITY

The narrative logic of canonical Wisdom literature's creation story has anthropological implications that are conceptually hospitable to a widely shared modern secular interpretation of humanity. Perhaps it is worth noting in passing that canonical Wisdom literature's practice of appropriating from Egyptian and Babylonian sources wisdom about how the natural and social worlds work, like the practice of the editors of Genesis on appropriating and *bending*[27] creation stories and genealogies from Canaanite and Babylonian sources, provide a kind of scriptural precedent for contemporary theological anthropologies' appropriation of interpretations of humanity widely shared in contemporary culture.

The theologian Wesley Wildman has helpfully summarized one interpretation of humanity widely shared in modern culture in an article[28] that he abbreviated MSIH ("Modern Secular Interpretation of Humanity"). He charts the points at which MSIH presses hardest against views of human nature in all major religious traditions. I will confine myself to places where it might press against traditional Christian anthropology.

Wildman identifies five major themes in this interpretation of humanity. Before we briefly identify each of them and comment on them theologically, it is important to put them in perspective by noting four important general features of MSIH.

First, MSIH is neither a rigorous, comprehensive, and systematic philosophy of humanity nor a systematic comprehensive theoretical synthesis of the results of scientific inquiry concerning a global scientific theory of everything human. Much less is it in its own right a scientific research program. Rather, it is expressed relatively informally in a set of claims about humankind that are based in some way on the data and the theories of several sciences. Evolutionary biology, genetics, neurology, endocrinology, paleo-anthropology, cultural anthropology, and sociology have provided especially important warrants.

Second, MSIH makes the important assumption that there is a rough hierarchy among the sciences on which it is based, with "each level corresponding to a special science, and the space between each two levels corresponding to the relationships obtaining between the higher level and the lower level science."[29] It is assumed that there is no explanatory gap at any level of this hierarchy. The hierarchy among the sciences gives MSIH its *unity*. At the same time, MSIH is sufficiently independent logically of the current state of each science that it neither has to deny ongoing disputes within each science nor leave its claims about *the human* vulnerable to the latest scientific discovery or theoretical development in each discipline.

Third, MSIH is minimalist in its claims about human beings. It recognizes the distinction in each science between a center of agreement and a periphery of ongoing debate. "It is defined primarily by the unanimous core and secondarily by contested issues in the sciences, together with a series of cautious postures toward those debates."[30] MSIH is also minimalist in that it does not claim that it includes every worthwhile insight into human life. It may expand to include new insights if it can coordinate them with the ones based on the sciences.

Fourth, MSIH is ontologically modest. It remains neutral to nonphysical, transcendental realities. MSIH feels no need of hypotheses beyond those constructed from the raw materials of physicalism. Likewise, MSIH sees no justification for rejecting such hypotheses outright. In particular, it is neutral with regard to religious realities.

According to Wildman, the content of MSIH consists of five themes. Our questions about each are whether the narrative logic of Wisdom's creation story, taken as a norm for theological anthropology, would allow these themes to be appropriated by theological anthropology today; and in what ways, if any, it would require them to be *bent* in the process. Let us consider the first two themes. First, on the basis of the neurosciences, MSIH holds that "human brains are necessary for human minds"[31] and inclines to the view that there is a "gapless continuity from the lowest, least complex organization of matter to the highest, most complex level"[32] that exhibits consciousness. Second, on the basis of evolutionary biology, it views human beings as "the complex, provisional products of an ongoing process . . . driven by chance variations in the genetic makeup of organisms, competition for resources . . . , and the natural selection of genetic variants that best succeed in reproducing."[33] Two features of the narrative logic of canonical Wisdom's creation story make its anthropological implications conceptually hospitable to these themes. First, it assumes a remarkably *physicalist* picture of what human beings are by God's creative blessing. Second, its logic is not that of a story that explains how humankind came to be. It does not equate a doctrine of creation with cosmogonic or etiological explanations of either the cosmos or humankind. *If* "human brains are necessary for human minds" is conceptually coherent, *and if* appropriate types of research warrant the notion, *and if* it is well established that human living bodies have evolved as part of a larger process that is driven in the ways specified above, *then* the narrative logic of Wisdom's creation story issues something like a conceptual *nihil obstat*.

Some caveats are in order. Those conditions are open to questioning, in principle subject to continual testing. The anthropological implications of Wisdom's creation story have no conceptual stake one way or the other in whether these particular claims about how human beings came to be, how they came to be conscious, and how they came to have minds. On the other hand, if these explanations are correct, they are consonant with a theological anthropology provided norms by the narrative logic of Wisdom's creation story. The anthropology has nothing to gain by refusing to appropriate them. Furthermore, one centrally important claim in this theological anthropology cannot be abandoned in appropriating these explanations, viz., that the entire network of interrelated and interactive physical beings develops in the ways MSIH says it does, such that each of those beings individually, as long as it does exist, has the property "related-to-creatively-by-God" and depends on that relation for its existence. I return to this point below.

Wildman notes additional themes that must be mentioned. Third, on the basis of the social sciences, MSIH views human beings as "adaptable, anxious, and curious; led by powerful psychological drives and needs for communal identity; liable to violence, mental disease, and fantasy; and embodying ultimate and preliminary commitments to linguistic habits, symbolic systems, and social organizations."[34] Fourth, on the basis of sociobiology and evolutionary psychology, MSIH holds that human beings' drive to make social and cultural worlds can be at least partly explained by "a struggle to ensure genetic self-perpetuation."[35]

In addition to the two noted above, a third feature of the narrative logic of canonical Wisdom's creation story makes its anthropological implications conceptually hospitable to these two themes. The creation story it drives assumes that human beings are, by God's creative blessing, social and cultural as well as biological creatures. It blurs our culture's received distinction between civilization as an *artificial* human construct imposed upon God's *natural* creation. Instead, it takes the social and cultural dimensions of human life to be as integral to its creatureliness as is its biological life. Combined with its *physicalist* assumptions about what human creatures are, the narrative logic of Wisdom's creation story issues a *nihil obstat* here as well. Of course, the caveats noted above in connection with the first two MSIH claims apply here as well.

Wildman's fifth theme remains. On the basis of theories of ethics and religion, this theme views human beings' religious practices and beliefs functionally. Religious beliefs may be projections, perhaps illusions; but the projection functions positively to satisfy "psychological needs for orientation to the world and for social stability—arising in part from evolutionary drives."[36] In the nearly total absence of references to revelation, divine deliverance, and religious cult or to the observance of divine law, the nearest recognition that canonical Wisdom literature makes about the *religious* is its stress on Woman Wisdom's call to human beings to be wise for the well-being of the quotidian. Ecclesiastes' and Job's stress on the difficulty of identifying just what counts as being wise and Proverbs' occasional acknowledgment of the same point, combined with Proverbs' repeated stress on the variety, subtlety, and destructive power of humankind's capacity for deception and false speaking in social and cultural life, however, make Wisdom's anthropological implications hospitable to this theme also. The caveats noted above apply here too. In addition, it needs to be kept clear that adoption of this theme in a theological anthropology would not necessarily commit one, on pain of inconsistency, to a skeptical position on questions of religious knowledge. It might, however, incline a theological anthropology to a skepticism of human religious phenomena as fierce as Karl Barth's.

Does MSIH itself have a certain normative force that theological anthropology, shaped by the norms of the narrative logic of canonical Wisdom's creation story, would need to resist by conceptually *bending* what it appropriates from MSIH? On the surface, MSIH has a certain formal and material normativity.

Its formal normativity is not that of any of the sciences on whose authority well established data and theories are accepted as true. It is not the data and theories of any or all of the relevant sciences, but rather the relatively informal, unified, minimalist, ontologically modest set of themes in MSIH's claims that have the formal normative status of anthropological truth that Wildman urges theological anthropology to engage.

His proposal warns us against engaging in thinking rigidly about the conversation between theology and science, as though theology and science each named an intellectual monolith. It may be most helpful to ask, not about theological implications of science, but about the implications of the data and theories of separate sciences one by one. Conversely, it may be most helpful to ask, not how the data and theories of various sciences bear on theology, but rather how they bear on individual theological *loci*. It may be, as James Gustafson urges,[37] that a discussion of the doctrine of God's providential governance of human affairs in relation to some particular human event, say the collapse of a building or the onset of a genetically based disease, ought to take direct account of the data and theories of particular sciences that deal with those types of events. It may also be, as Jürgen Moltmann has suggested,[38] that a discussion of the doctrine of the creation of the world *ex nihilo* ought to take account of the data and theories of scientific cosmology only indirectly, as they are mediated by systematic philosophical reflection on their epistemological and metaphysical assumptions and implications. When it comes to anthropology, however, there is merit to Wildman's suggestion that discussion of the anthropological question of what is a human being ought not to engage particular scientific data and theories directly, nor ought it to engage them indirectly as mediated by a systematic metaphysics. Rather, it ought to engage relevant scientific data and theories indirectly as mediated by this relatively informal modern secular interpretation of humanity.

The chief reason that formal anthropological normativity can be attributed to the secular interpretation of humanity, not the scientific data and theories from which it arises, nor any widely shared systematic philosophical system, is that it constitutes the set of beliefs about human nature that are most widely shared by scientists and nonscientists alike in our common culture. Just how MSIH is based on the data and theories of these sciences is not rigorously clear, but there is consensus that the beliefs that constitute MSIH are warranted by those theories and data and are by and large correct. If it seeks a public forum for its claims, Christian theological anthropology has nothing to gain by denying or ignoring MSIH, for in our culture it does have a certain formal normativity.

Wildman also claims a material normativity for MSIH. In particular, he suggests two themes in traditional Christian anthropologies that would apparently have special difficulty satisfying MSIH when taken as a criterion of adequacy. He notes that "theological anthropologies that assume a nonphysical basis for personhood"[39] such as a nonphysical soul, will have a hard time with the MSIH view grounded in neurology that human brains are necessary for human minds. I have addressed this concern above in the discussion of the first two themes in MSIH. Wildman also notes that "the joint message of [scientific] cosmology and biology"[40] is that a theological anthropology that privileges the human species as the central character in a [single] cosmo-historico-theological narrative, such as some Christian anthropologies do, will have a hard time with MSIH. That seems true of traditional anthropologies with themes of creation, fall, and redemption whose norms have been provided by a reading of Genesis 1–3 that takes it as the hermeneutical lens through which the rest of Genesis and the Christian canon is interpreted—the reading, and hence the anthropology, that Westermann's analysis of Genesis disallows. Such anthropologies would especially need to *bend* the second MSIH theme above quite a lot. However, the anthropological implications of the creation theology through which Wisdom thinks so resolutely entails no single cosmo-historico-theological narrative whose narrative logic would be theological anthropology's sole norm.

There is yet another sort of normativity sometimes ascribed to MSIH that would be resisted in a theological anthropology provided norms by the narrative logic of Wisdom's creation story. It requires a not uncommon construal of MSIH that violates two of the general characteristics of MSIH: minimalism and ontological modesty. This violation does not necessarily consist in supposing that MSIH requires an ontologically immodest denial of nonphysical, transcendental realities, especially religious realities, although it may lead to that supposition. It consists rather in construing MSIH's anthropological claims *as* a set of ontological claims (most likely of a *physicalist* type) that give a maximally exhaustive account of what it is basically to *be* a human being. Wherever the claims constituting MSIH are construed in this way, theological anthropology shaped by the norms of the narrative logic of canonical Wisdom's creation story will need to *bend* them, construing them in more minimal and ontologically modest ways. For such a theological anthropology, we might say, the *primitive concept*[41] in an account of what it is God creates in creating human beings is *creature*. For such a theological anthropology, *related-to-creatively-by-God* constitutes the reality of human creatures, to which all their other properties are ascribed. Any number of other well-warranted claims about what human creatures are may be ascribed to human creatures by a theological anthropology, including the claims that constitute MSIH. Theological anthropology is not an integral part of any one systematic ontology or metaphysics, but it does make ontological and metaphysical claims about human beings. MSIH is neither a systematic metaphysical claim nor an ontology; and whenever it is construed as though it were part of such systems, the normative force of the narrative logic of Wisdom's creation story requires its *bending* when theological anthropology appropriates it so that it is deprived of its status as a systematic ontological or metaphysical claim.

Chapter 6

Jürgen Moltmann's Engagement with the Natural Sciences

John Polkinghorne

When I was preparing to leave theoretical physics and begin the study of theology in preparation for ordination to the Anglican priesthood, someone recommended that I read *The Crucified God: The Cross as the Foundation and Criticism of Christian Theology*. I did so and was bowled over by the experience. It opened up for me a new insight into the power that theological thinking possesses when a profoundly creative theologian undertakes it. Subsequently, I have reread the book several times and become a regular student of Jürgen Moltmann's other writings too. Of all contemporary theologians, he is the one whom I have found most helpful and illuminating; and it is a privilege to have this opportunity of expressing my debt of intellectual and spiritual gratitude to him.

People working at the interface between science and theology are always on the lookout for those who might join them in the traffic between disciplines. Most of my face-to-face meetings with Jürgen Moltmann have been in this interdisciplinary context, most notably in the course of three years working together as members of a research project on contemporary approaches to eschatological issues, sponsored by the Center of Theological Inquiry at Princeton.

There could scarcely have been a more appropriate intellectual meeting ground than that afforded by this eschatological enquiry. As one of the theologians of hope, Moltmann's thinking has a strong orientation toward the future and exhibits a powerful concern to engage with eschatological issues. While much classical theological understanding of the world was based on the notion that its state represented the degenerate effects of the aftermath of the fall, Moltmann argues for a reversed perspective, "turning things upside down and arriving at an eschatological understanding of creation" so that " eschatology is no longer seen only in the light of creation; creation is also understood in the light of eschatology."[1]

Certainly, science offers no support for the idea that the contemporary state of affairs has resulted from a decline from a past paradisal situation. This realization enforces on theology a revaluation of how to understand the fall.[2] It is also the case that the prognostications of the physical cosmologists, peering into the future and envisaging the eventual collapse or decay of the present universe, pose an equally serious challenge to theology, in this case concerning how this future cosmic futility is to be reconciled with the concept of the universe as God's creation. In common with many of those engaged in considering this latter issue,[3] Moltmann responds to the problem posed by science's prediction of the eventual death of the universe, by a vision of God's creative act as one that unfolds in a second phase: the present old creation followed by its transformation into the new creation. He writes that "these are two qualitatively differentiated eons" and adds that "this world-time is the time of a world that is transitory—the future world-time is the time of an abiding and hence eternal world."[4]

Moltmann assigns great significance to the role of the future, in contrast to the roles of past and present. He points out that Revelation 1:4 speaks of God in terms of "him who is and who was and who is to come" (rather than "who will be") and that "the linear concept of time is broken through that third term."[5] For Moltmann, the future is not simply *futurum*, just further steps in an already unfolding process, but *adventus*, a coming event "on the way towards the present,"[6] thereby exercising a contemporary influence. This latter idea means that there is a realized element in Moltmann's eschatological thinking, since *adventus*, used in this manner, seems to function as a theological concept expressive of the effects of that current activity of God that is already seeking to draw creation toward the fulfillment of divine teleological intention.

Yet any attempt to relate this concept of the influence of the future on the present to a scientific understanding of temporality poses problems for the physicist. Scientists work with so-called retarded solutions of their fundamental equations, which privilege the influence of the past over effects of the future. There are also advanced solutions, for which the roles of past and future are interchanged; but they do not appear to be relevant to physical process as it is actually observed.

Much of the discussion in Moltmann's collection of essays, *Science and Wisdom*, is centered on wrestling with how one should conceive of the nature of temporality, an issue that he had also addressed in *God in Creation*. A number of key concepts control the discussion. One of these is the importance and significance of open systems, for which the future is not merely a rearrangement of what was already there in the past, but includes the emergence of genuine novelty. Here Moltmann's approach exhibits a good deal of consonance with ideas circulating in the science and theology communities.

Twentieth-century physics displaced the Laplacian notion of a world of tight and predictable mechanisms. Its discovery of the presence of widespread intrinsic unpredictabilities in nature, first at the level of quantum theory's account of subatomic processes and then at the macroscopic level of chaotic systems, so exquisitely sensitive to the fine detail of their circumstances that their future behavior could not reliably be foreseen, implied that physical reality must be something more subtle and more interesting than a collection of tame and controllable pieces of clockwork. Exactly what this implies has been a matter of much discussion. After all, unpredictability is an epistemological property (one cannot know what behavior will be in the future), with no necessary entailment of specific ontological consequences. Consequently a good deal of argument has transpired about what would be the best interpretation to espouse. Is intrinsic unpredictability simply a sign of an unfortunately invincible scientific ignorance (a kind of apophatic physics), or is it an indication that there is some form of actual openness in relation to the future? Responding to these questions is a matter for metaphysical decisions rather than scientific determination so that a variety of strategies are actually possible. In the case of quantum theory, for example, one can follow the conventional indeterministic understanding of Niels Bohr and his successors; or one may embrace the deterministic views of David Bohm.[7] Experiments do not offer a way of settling the issue, since the two interpretations lead to identical empirical consequences. The choice is, therefore, metaphysical; whatever stance is chosen will have to be defended on metaphysical grounds.

Those of a realist cast of mind will consider epistemology a reliable guide to ontology and will make the philosophical decision to seek as close an alignment as possible between what is knowable and what is the case. This stance is a natural one for scientists to adopt since their work would lose much of its point if it were not actually telling us what the physical world is like. It should also be congenial to theologians, for it implies that the Creator's Book of Nature does not mislead us by the way in which it is written. If this is the case, unpredictability will be considered as a signal of causal openness, i.e., that the grain of nature is not drawn so tight that there is no room for the operation of causal principles over and above the effects of the exchange of energy between constituents, which is the canonical account of conventional physics. Those who take this open line, including the present writer, are led to take seriously the concept of top-down causality, in which the influence of the whole shapes the patterns of behavior of the parts.[8] Such a metaphysical hypothesis offers a glimmer of insight into how agency might be exercised, whether it is human intentional activity or the workings of divine providence.

Causal openness abolishes mechanical determinism and leaves room for a genuine role for contingency. Moltmann sees the past as a closed realm of realized actuality but the future as an open realm of possibility, in a way that gives the latter its particular significance: "Possibility and actuality are qualitatively different modes of being and the way we deal with them is qualitatively different too. Remembered past is something different from expected future. . . . So among the modes of time future must have priority."[9] This priority has theological consequences for Moltmann: "If we switch over from the metaphysics of reality to a metaphysics of possibility, we

GOD'S LIFE IN TRINITY

can view the divine Being as the supreme possibility, as the source of possibilities, and as the transcendental making possible of the possible."[10] One is reminded of Arthur Peacocke's favorite metaphor of creation as the unfolding of a grand improvisation rather than as the performance of a fixed score.[11] Considering this musical image also suggests some modification of what one might call Moltmann's "preference for the future." An improvised fugue has to find its way from stated theme to final resolution, but the way it does so continuously incorporates past developments into present music. Analogously, in an evolving universe, past history is not simply what has been; it is also constitutive of what now is. James Hutton's geological insights and Charles Darwin's biological insights made it plain that the present can only properly be understood in the light of the continuing influence of past events. Eventually, big bang cosmology led physicists to the same conclusion. Moreover, if the future is open and the universe is a world of true becoming, then it would seem that the future of creation does not yet exist, and so theological thought about its postulated influence on the present becomes problematic.

Jürgen Moltmann might find it helpful to take into account more explicitly this way that science influences thinking about the temporal processes of the present universe. There is a general insight that the emergence of novelty takes place in regimes "at the edge of chaos," where circumstances are neither so rigid that nothing really new can form nor so haphazard that nothing new can persist. Further insight into the character of open systems could be gained by considering the infant science of complexity theory. The study of computer simulations is just beginning to afford the opportunity for detailed consideration of the nature of systems of moderate complexity. Remarkable and unexpected results have already emerged, for these systems prove capable of spontaneously generating an astonishing degree of patterned behavior. An example drawn from the work of Stuart Kauffman illustrates the point.[12] He considers the logical model of a Boolean net of connectivity two, but it will be more convenient for us to think about the matter in equivalent hardware terms. Consider a large array of electric lightbulbs, each of which is in one of two states, *on* or *off*. The system develops in successive steps; and there are simple rules that determine the state of each bulb at the next step, formulated in terms of the present states of two other bulbs in the array with which it is correlated. The system is started off in some random configuration of illumination and then is allowed to develop according to these rules. One might have expected that nothing very interesting would happen and that the array would just twinkle away haphazardly for as long as it was permitted to do so. In fact, this is far from being the case, for the system soon settles down to a highly ordered behavior, cycling through a very limited number of patterns of illumination. This behavior represents the spontaneous generation of an amazing degree of order. For example, if ten thousand bulbs are in the array, then there would be about 103,000 different states of illumination in which, in principle, it might be found. Yet it turns out that the array will soon simply cycle through only about a hundred such states. This behavior is a holistic feature of the total system that is quite unforeseeable in terms of the individual correlations of its constituent elements.

At present, no known general theory explains this degree of self-organization, but clearly there must be a deep foundation for these striking effects. Big discoveries seem to be waiting to be made. I believe that by the end of the twenty-first century, the concept of information (the specification of dynamical pattern) will become a fundamentally important category in science, taking its place alongside energy as a foundational idea for understanding the physical world. Nevertheless, when Moltmann says, "Our premise is the principle that the more complex system explains the simple one, because it is capable of integrating it,"[13] I think that this premise is only half the story. The science of the future may be expected to strike a complementary balance between top-down holistic thinking, framed in terms of information, and bottom-up constituent thinking, framed in terms of energy exchange. Influences flow in both directions. I feel more in tune with Moltmann when he says, "Creation contains neither spiritless-matter nor non-material spirit; there is only informed matter."[14] One can just begin to conceive how agency, whether human intentions or divine providence, might be exercised through the input and flow of information bringing about purposefully intended patterns of behavior.

We have seen that a key feature for Moltmann's thinking is the nature of time itself, particularly in relation to eschatological expectation. For a scientist-theologian, the positive presence of the past gives a value to evolutionary process that can be expressed theologically through the concept of *creatio continua* (continuous creation). Yet in such an evolving creation that is "making itself" (in Charles Kingsley's pregnant phrase), the fruitfulness of temporality has the inescapable shadow side of individual transience, for one generation must give way to the next. However, there is no reason to suppose that in the world of the new creation, there cannot be a new kind of *time*, whose processes will have a different character, one no longer condemned to the thermodynamic drift to disorder that is characteristic of this present world. I believe that this new *time* will be linear like the time of this world, and its unfolding development will enable the redeemed to enter into the unending exploration of the riches of the divine nature. Indeed, if finite beings were to engage with the infinite reality of God, something like this everlasting process of unrolling revelation would seem to be a necessity.[15]

Moltmann rightly rejects the notion of a timeless destiny for human beings. For him, "Instead of timeless eternity, we would therefore do better to talk about *eternal time* (*aeon, aevum*)."[16] Yet sometimes his thinking seems to suspect that linearly unfolding time will always involve transience and the irreversible loss of the past. This suspicion leads him to invent his novel temporal concept of eonic time, relating to the temporality of the world to come: "The time of the invisible multiverse [the new creation] is *aeon, aevum*, the reversible temporal structure of cyclical time, for the circle of time counts as the image and reflection of eternity."[17] I have some difficulty here. Of course, science derived from this world cannot be used to forbid the conception of a kind of cyclical time in the world to come,[18] but the idea seems at odds with the preservation of true humanity in the life of the redeemed. Just as the Christian hope of the resurrection life corresponds to the insight that it is intrinsic to humanity to be embodied in some way (though, of course, not necessarily in the flesh and blood of this world as Paul recognized in 1 Cor. 15:50), so it seems to me that it must be equally intrinsic to true humanity to be able to experience progressively unfolding process, albeit in the *time* of the new creation.[19] (It seems a coherent expectation that the *matter* of the new creation will be endowed with such strong self-organizing properties that it will not be subject to the thermodynamic laws that induce decay in the matter of this world and give its time the character of transience.) Whatever Moltmann's ideas of reversibility and cyclicity might be held to express, they do not seem consistent with that continuity-in-discontinuity that appears such an essential aspect of credible eschatological hope.[20] At the very least, the image of the circle, with its overtones of endlessly repeated return, needs to be replaced by that of the spiral, moving ever closer to the heart of encounter with the life and energies of God.

At other times, however, Moltmann appears open to a different kind of temporal expectation, as when he says:

> It is also even permissible to assume that in the kingdom of glory there will be time and history, future and possibility, and these to an unimpeded degree, and in a way that is no longer ambivalent. Instead of timeless eternity it would be better to talk about "eternal time"; and instead of "the end of history" we should talk about the end of pre-history and the beginning of the "eternal history" of God, human beings and nature. This of course means thinking of change without transience, time without the past, and life without death. But this is difficult in the history of life and death, becoming and passing away, because all our concepts are molded by these experiences of transitoriness. Yet finitude is not necessarily bound up with mortality.[21]

In fact, it is precisely this separation between finitude and mortality that may be expected to distinguish the new creation from the old creation, for indeed "flesh and blood cannot inherit the kingdom of God, nor does the perishable inherit the imperishable" (1 Cor. 15:50).

Important thematically in much recent reflection on the doctrine of creation and central in Jürgen Moltmann's thinking has been the recognition that divine creation involves a kenotic act of self-limitation on the part of the Creator in allowing the created other truly to be itself and to make itself. The God of love could never be simply the manipulator of a cosmic puppet theater.[22] This insight offers significant help in the endless theological task of wrestling with the mystery of suffering, for it implies that not everything that happens—whether it is the act of a murderer or the occurrence of an earthquake—is a direct expression of the Creator's will. Moltmann has been one of the most powerful and persuasive expositors of this understanding of a divine who makes ways to accommodate the freedom granted to creation. In *God in Creation* he writes, "It is only a withdrawal by God into himself that can free the space into which God can act creatively. The *nihil* for his *creatio ex nihilo* only comes into being because—and as far as—the omnipotent and omnipresent God withdraws his presence and restricts his power."[23] (This is the prelude to Moltmann's celebrated invocation of Isaac Luria's kabbalistic concept of *zimzum*.) Later he says, "But if creation *ad extra* takes place in the space freed by God himself, then in this case the reality outside God still remains in the God who has yielded up that *outwards* in himself."[24] In this manner, Moltmann nuances his subtly qualified form of panentheistic thinking.[25] He emphasizes the resulting implication of a divine acceptance of vulnerability, speaking of "the God who in patience bears and endures the history of nature and human beings, allows them time and gives them time, and in so doing makes possible ever-new possibilities, which are either realized or not realized, which can be used for further development but also for annihilation."[26]

Kenotic insight also endorses the approach of a kind of theistic naturalism in which God acts through nature and in concert with nature, but does not arbitrarily interfere with those processes whose unfolding consequences are also a permitted part of the history of creation and whose regular forms are expressions of its Creator's will. If Moltmann had done no more for science and theology than to express these kenotic insights, by that alone he would have left the subject greatly in his debt.

Scientist-theologians often criticize their systematic colleagues for taking a too narrow, anthropocentric view of God's creation so that *the world* is just planet Earth, and *history* spans the few thousand years of recorded human culture rather than the fourteen billion years of cosmic evolution. Moltmann sets his face against such terrestrial parochiality. He tells us that "the salutatory *Christological concentration* of Protestant theology must be matched today by an extension of theology's horizon to cosmic breadth, so that it takes in the whole of God's creation."[27] Later he says that "no theological doctrine of creation must be allowed to reduce the understanding of belief in creation to the existential self-understanding of the person. It must mean the whole knowable world. If God is not the Creator of the world, he cannot be my Creator either."[28] In pursuing this cosmic theme, great emphasis is laid on the role of the Spirit. He asserts, "By the title, 'God in Creation' I mean God the Holy Spirit. God is 'the lover of life' and his Spirit is *in* all created beings."[29] The suggestion made above that we can understand God's providential interaction with the history of creation through the input of information into its developing process seems particularly consonant with Moltmann's pneumatological approach, especially when he writes: "The Spirit is the principle of creativity on all levels of matter and life. He creates new possibilities, and in these anticipates the new designs and 'blueprints' for material and living organisms. In this sense, the Spirit is the principle of evolution."[30]

Nothing reliably known to science forbids a belief that the hidden work of the Spirit, acting within the cloudy unpredictabilities of the world, has been part of the unfolding fruitfulness of evolutionary contingency. The theological picture being proposed is one of continuing divine interaction operating within the open grain of nature, not one of occasional divine interruptions of nature. If the Creator works through an evolutionary process whose character is the fruitful interplay of contingency and lawful regularity, then one must surely expect God to be active within the processes of history and not solely confined to the role of the sustainer of cosmic order. The Creator must be present in chance as well as in the necessity of the world.

This divine immanent presence to the created universe of space and time is represented in Moltmann's thinking by the symbols of the indwelling of the divine Shekinah and the role of the Sabbath rest. He also wants "to take up again the ancient theological doctrine of the *vestigia Dei* (traces of God). Anyone who understands nature as God's creation, sees in nature not merely God's *works*, but also *traces of God*, ciphers and hidden tokens of his presence. God's signature is on the whole of nature."[31] This endorsement of a role for a modest natural theology is congenial to those who approach these issues from a background in science.

Perhaps the aspect of what modern science has to say that is most obviously consonant with the trinitarian thrust of Moltmann's thinking is its strong emphasis on the presence of relationality in the physical world. The Newtonian scheme had pictured individual atoms moving in the container of space and in the course of the uniform flow of an absolute time, but this scheme has now been replaced by an altogether more integrated account. Einstein's theory of general relativity ties together space, time, and matter in a single unified package. Matter curves space-time, and the latter's curvature in turn affects the paths of matter. An even more profound relational discovery is the nonlocality (togetherness in separation) present in the quantum world. Once two quantum entities have interacted with each other, they remain mutually entangled however far they may subsequently separate so that effectively they constitute a single system.[32] It seems that even the subatomic world cannot be treated atomistically! Nature fights back against a crude reductionism. Insights of this kind are certainly consistent with their being understood as vestiges in creation of the triune God, whose nature is constituted by the perichoretic exchange of love between the divine persons.

A different vestige of creation may be located in the experience of scientists themselves. The universe that is disclosed to scientific investigation is rationally beautiful; and *wonder* is an indispensable word in the scientist's vocabulary, even if it seldom finds its way into the formal papers that they write for the learned journals. Wonder testifies to the intellectual delight that rewards all the weary labor and routine that are inevitable parts of scientific research. In *God in Creation*, Moltmann speaks of "forms of meditative knowledge," quoting Augustine's remark that "We know to the extent that we love."[33] There seems to me to be a connection here with scientific wonder. Whether scientists know it or not, whether they acknowledge it or not, this experience of theirs is an implicit religious experience of a meditative kind, a tacit act of worship of the Creator. Moltmann is right to say that "Perception of the world as creation confers felicity on existence."[34]

Jürgen Moltmann has always been concerned with orthopraxis as much as with orthodoxy. His writing exhibits a strong element of concern for the political will to act for the common good. In his thinking about creation, this tendency is manifested by a deep ecological concern:

> Faced as we are with the progressive industrial exploitation of nature and its irreparable destruction, what does it mean to say that we believe in God the Creator, and in this world as his creation? What we call the environmental crisis is not merely a crisis in the natural environment of human beings. It is nothing less than a crisis in human beings themselves.[35]

If human freedom is not to be exercised destructively, human beings must learn how to make right choices in using the technical power that scientific knowledge affords them. Moltmann calls for efforts to ensure that "a new attempt to see science and theology in the context common to them both is made on the level of wisdom."[36] The appeal to wisdom combines both the quest for knowledge and the search for right ethical judgment. The wisdom writers of the Hebrew Bible have been a favorite scriptural resource for writers on science and theology.[37]

Moltmann has consistently opposed any isolation of theology by retreat into a fideistic ghetto. "Theology must abandon its confinement to church, belief, and the inwardness of heart," he says, "so that with all others, it may search for the truth of the whole, and the salvation of a torn and disrupted world."[38] The dialogue between science and theology is a part of that wide truth-seeking engagement. Nevertheless, Moltmann feels that "up to now the attempt to bring pure science and scientific, or scholarly, theology into dialogue has borne only limited fruits."[39] I am somewhat more sanguine about what has already been achieved, but there is more work to be done. Future gains depend upon taking seriously not only the methodologies and general tone of the two disciplines, but also the need to pay a greater degree of detailed attention to their content. For example, making progress in the consideration of the nature of time, and understanding the character of open systems will require a willingness to pay careful attention to the specific insights afforded by recent scientific advances as a means of advancing from rhetoric to argument. We have seen that Moltmann's work can certainly expect to gain positive benefit from such an engagement.

The intense specialization of the contemporary academic world undoubtedly makes interdisciplinary encounters matters of some difficulty. Although Molt-mann is regrettably and largely correct in saying that "the book of nature has long since ceased to be studied by theologians of Holy Scripture,"[40] we cannot rest content with that state of affairs. Moltmann considers that philosophy might prove a mediating discipline to bring science and theology together more effectively. Another possibility, which to some of us seems a somewhat neglected one, would be to pay a bit more attention to the writings of the scientist-theologians who seek to have a foot in both camps.[41] No doubt we have our limitations, but I think that we can also play a modest role in helping to facilitate that ongoing engagement of theology with the natural sciences that is surely necessary for the former's development and for its contemporary credibility. Be that as it may, we scientist-theologians are deeply grateful to have Jürgen Moltmann as so stimulating a conversation partner in the dialogue between those two great truth-seeking disciplines, science and theology.

Part TWO

TRINITY
AND RELIGIOUS TRADITIONS

CHAPTER 7

CHURCH UNITY IN FREEDOM

Dirk J. Smit

"INTEGRAL TO THE CONFESSION OF THE TRIUNE GOD"? MOLTMANN ON THE CHURCH

The statements about the church in the Apostles' Creed and the Nicene-Constantinopolitan Creed respectively, according to Jürgen Moltmann's *The Church in the Power of the Spirit: A Contribution to Messianic Ecclesiology*, "form a component part of the creed."[1] This claim means that they are "integrated components of the confession of the triune God, and cannot be detached from this context." The so-called true church is the church that participates in and is determined by the truth of the triune God:

> They belong to the article about faith in the Holy Spirit, and are only justified and comprehensible in the framework of the creative workings of that Spirit. . . . They (only) make sense if we see the church in the context of the divine history in which the acknowledgment of the triune God puts it. . . . They are characteristics which this object receives through a history external to itself. The church receives the attributes named from the activity of Christ in the workings of the Spirit for the coming kingdom. But as these extend and link together, the attributes become the inalienable signs of the true church, which is to say the church in the truth of God.[2]

These comments should not be surprising. After all, his book on the church was the third and final volume in his three programmatic studies between 1964 and 1975, which made him well-known almost worldwide and certainly also in South African church and theological circles. *The Church in the Power of the Spirit*

(1975/1977) followed the *Theology of Hope: On the Ground and the Implications of a Christian Eschatology* (1964/1967) and *The Crucified God: The Cross of Christ as the Foundation and Criticism of Christian Theology* (1972/1974) and concluded these two groundbreaking works. The trinitarian assumptions of these programmatic works were already discernible and often discussed, and they challenged, informed, and inspired many audiences and contexts in the ecumenical church.

Even more, the trinitarian logic of *The Church in the Power of the Spirit* itself was unmistakable and crucial to the argument and thrust of the whole book and of his emerging ecclesiology. The church of Jesus Christ today—missionary, ecumenical, and political, according to Moltmann's descriptions of its key dimensions[3]—should be seen in the context of history; and for him that context means "the trinitarian history of God." Since the church receives its existence and meaning, its identity, and its calling through its participation in the history of the triune Godself, it is impossible to talk about the church or to understand the deepest nature and purpose of the church apart from this historical context. "The church of Jesus Christ" is "the church of the kingdom of God," which is "the church in the presence of the Holy Spirit" and therefore also "the church in the power of the Holy Spirit"—the sequence in which Moltmann retells the story of the church in trinitarian terms.[4]

It is therefore not surprising that he concludes this story with a final chapter on *the marks of the church* in which he then claims that the statements about the church should also be seen as integrated components of the confession of the triune God, not as descriptions of the church as an object in itself. Because we confess that God is like this, the church receives a role not in the story, but in the history of this triune God, namely, this very specific role that is expressed in the four so-called *marks of the church*. For Moltmann, the precise claim of these *marks* or elements within the history of the triune God will, in fact, only become clearer if each of the four is qualified and explained further by adding another element, integral to the specific mark. For this reason he speaks of "unity in freedom," "catholicity and partisanship," "holiness in poverty," and "the apostolate in suffering."[5] For him, these qualifications help us see the thrust of these respective claims within the history of the triune God somewhat better than when the *marks* are taken on their own and accordingly often separated from this history.[6]

Of course, one should not overestimate the importance of the church, or rather, the importance of ecclesiology and of theological reflection on the church in Moltmann's own project. He was seemingly less interested in the church, or rather in ecclesiology in a technical and traditional way, than many may perhaps presume. Many reasons may account for this fact; but as some have speculated, perhaps his early work on the church simply did not receive the same interested and enthusiastic reception as his works on other topics. The first two programmatic works, for example, received discussion volumes, respectively in the form of *Diskussion über die "Theologie der Hoffnung" von Jürgen Moltmann* (1967) and *Diskussion über Jürgen Moltmanns Buch "Der gekreuzigte Gott"* (1979), both demonstrating widespread interest and further contributing to that interest.[7] No such published work followed *The Church in the Power of the Spirit*, which simply did not generate the same enthusiasm, at least in many circles.[8]

It is therefore not surprising that he did not include another volume on the church in his six very important "Contributions to Systematic Theology" published between 1980 and 1999, in many ways representing his lifework. In fact, when one could expect a discussion on the church in *The Way of Jesus Christ: Christology in Messianic Dimensions* (1989/1989), he only refers readers to the relevant chapters in *The Church in the Power of the Spirit* so that an informed commentator like Geiko Müller-Fahrenholz speaks of "a missing part."[9] In a way, the same is true of the volumes on *The Spirit of Life: A Universal Affirmation* (1991/1992), and perhaps even—albeit to a lesser extent—of *The Coming of God: Christian Eschatology* (1995/1996) and *Experiences in Theology* (1999/2000), and looking back, also of the early *The Trinity and the Kingdom of God: The Doctrine of God* (1980/1981). Where one would—or at least could—expect detailed discussions of the church, they seem to be absent.

Through the years, readers also waited and searched in relative vain for in-depth reflection on the church in his many other essays and papers, journal articles, sermons and meditations, volumes of collected contributions, shorter monographs, edited works, and dialogues with other authors.[10] He was such a prolific author, yet he never again focused on ecclesiological issues. In passing he sometimes talked about the church, but mostly in relation to other themes—like the task of the ecumenical church, the mission of the church, the political nature of the church, the church's responsibility regarding human rights, spirituality and prayer, the changing nature of theological education, and similar topical themes. It was as if the classical topics and questions of ecclesiology were somehow not directly in sight.

Part of this absence may perhaps be explained by the fact that he did not use *church* in a very technical sense, but rather vaguely and, therefore, could use several other terms as synonyms, including *congregation* (probably his favorite synonym), *community, life in community, a new community of men and women, human life in relationships, Christian fellowship, Christianity, discipleship,* even *the Christian life.* For him, the revolutionary view of God unfolding in the history of the triune God calls for a form of human community that is also revolutionary, new, and constantly renewed; and for this new form of community, solidarity, fellowship, and life-in-community, the traditional expression *church* is not the best term to use since what is normally and traditionally understood under *church* may precisely be part of the structures of patriarchal monotheism that must be overcome. The expression *congregation* that he finds in his Reformed legacy and particularly through the lenses of his teacher Otto Weber is much more suitable to describe this form of community to which Christians are called.[11]

In addition, however, the forms of community called forth by the history of the triune God are often found outside the walls of the traditional church and congregation so that the term *church* is even less suitable to use. Of course, each of these synonymous expressions generates its own set of questions and issues and causes a retreat of other questions and issues into the background, which probably provides the best explanation why many theological questions and issues traditionally related to *the church* do not feature prominently in Moltmann's theology.

Still, from a South African perspective, his views on the *church* were already challenging, informative, and helpful in the three programmatic studies, specifically in *The Church in the Power of the Spirit*; but his views scattered through his later writings were as well.[12] In the struggle against apartheid and the theology justifying apartheid, his theology played an instructive and helpful role.[13] In the struggle for the unity of the church—which was crucial, albeit in different ways, in about every Christian tradition and community in South Africa at the time, certainly including most Protestant denominations[14]—his ideas were directly relevant.

Perhaps this relevance was true in a very special way for the Reformed tradition and community since it is possible to argue that apartheid was originally born in the heart of Reformed worship and the Reformed church and because the struggle concerning the unity of the church—against the divisions caused and sustained by race, nation, *volk*, culture, language, and blood—was especially acute and critical in these churches, in fact, even today.[15] Many Reformed Christians, theologians, and church leaders in South Africa could, therefore, immediately relate with the seemingly typical Reformed way that Moltmann described the situation in the Christian church, the challenges facing the congregation, the temptations leading the community astray, the real issues at stake, and the calling truly involved in the search for unity.

His point of departure in the local congregation and in the church as community; his trinitarian understanding of the church; his ecumenical vision of the church; his emphasis on the calling of the church and on its mission, but also on its continuous renewal and sanctification, including personal, economic, and political sanctification; his stress on solidarity with the suffering and the excluded; his ongoing interest in discipleship, the Christian life, ethics, and passionate commitment; and his conviction that the truth of the church calls for visible embodiment— these well-known emphases in his theology and ecclesiology, all so characteristic of the Reformed tradition, immediately appealed to many Reformed Christians and theologians involved in the church struggle in South Africa. We recognized the voice.

Reading the short paragraphs in 1975 on the marks of the church in *The Church in the Power of the Spirit* (translated 1977) was similar to doing a close reading of the situation within the churches in South Africa, particularly the Reformed churches, and to listening to a running commentary on the situation at the time in our congregations and denominations. Looking back, it becomes possible to recall and to reconstruct many of those questions, issues, and challenges by doing a close reading today of these paragraphs in Moltmann's ecclesiology of three decades ago and by doing running commentary on what he wrote at the time and what we heard him say to us in our particular sociohistorical context and experiences. To many of us, his words were indeed like the voice of a contemporary and a friend.[16]

Unity in Freedom? Moltmann on the Mark of Unity

It may have been better to perform a close reading of his discussion of all four *marks of the church* since they were all directly relevant to the South African context and experience, but it is fair to claim that his discussion of the *mark* of unity showed itself to be of special relevance at the time. According to Moltmann, the church's unity is a *unity in freedom*; and he develops this idea in three ways. He discusses *unity in freedom* in the gathered congregation, *unity in freedom* between the congregations, and *unity in freedom* as witness to the world.

Unity in Freedom in the Gathered Congregation

> The unity of the church is experienced first of all in the gathered congregation. The congregation is gathered through proclamation and calling. It gathers for the one baptism (Eph. 4.5; I Cor. 12.13) and for the common Lord's supper (I Cor. 12.13; 10.17). It lives in the spirit of mutual acceptance (Rom. 15.7) and maintains the unity of the Spirit through "the bond of peace" (Eph. 4.3). In the church people of different social, religious and cultural origins become friends who "forbear one another in love" (Eph. 4.3), do not judge one another, but stand up for each other, especially for the weak among them. The unity of the gathered congregation is visible and experienced in the fellowship of people who are in themselves different. It is in no way a fortuitous result of the proclamation and the administration of the sacraments, but is, in association with these, itself the sign of hope. The fact that Jews and Gentiles, Greeks and barbarians, masters and slaves, men and women surrender their privileges, or are freed from oppression as the case may be, is—like the gathering of the new people of God itself—the sacrament of the kingdom and the beginning of the messianic era.[17]

These first sentences already draw together many of the characteristic themes of Moltmann's theology and ecclesiology; they also draw together many themes that were at stake in the struggle with a theology and ecclesiology of apartheid.

The unity of the church is "experienced first of all in the gathered congregation." This setting probably betrays Moltmann's Reformed background, his own preferences, and his context. At the same time, this setting was precisely the crisis in South African churches, especially Reformed churches. It was in the local congregations, in its worship, its celebration of the Lord's Supper, and its local activities as congregations that the class and race divisions originally entered in the churches, and where apartheid was practiced and ideologically maintained. Ironically, for us, the disunity of the church was experienced first of all in the gathered congregation. Also for that reason, the struggle was for a church in which a real, living unity would indeed become an experienced reality, not merely on the regional or national level of synods and structures, but also on the so-called grassroots-level, that is, in local structures and worshipping congregations.

Second, his references to the sacraments of one baptism and the common Lord's Supper and his biblical allusions, for example, to the calling to accept one another, to live together with those who are different, to become friends who practice peace and love in the Spirit, and, in particular, to stand up for the weak, were precisely the kind of biblical allusions that were also inspiring and powerful in the preaching and teaching, the piety and spirituality, the theology and public debates of the struggle years.[18]

Third, his conviction that the gathered congregation should be "visible and experienced" in the fellowship of "people who are in themselves different" was precisely expressing the theological vision of different generations of South African Reformed theologians and church leaders like Beyers Naudé, Ben Marais, Willie Jonker, Jaap Durand, Adrio König, Allan Boesak, Chris Loff, Daan Cloete, Russel Botman, and many others. Deeply emotional debates about the so-called visible or invisible unity of the church were at the heart of the struggle for several decades, and the conviction that the unity should be visible and experienced was central to the Reformed claims—already from Calvin, but again powerfully expressed in the *Theological Declaration of Barmen*—which were so influential in opposing apartheid. Indeed, the differences and otherness that resulted from "different social, religious and cultural origins" should not divide believers into separate, apartheid churches—"that was the acid test," in the words of Jaap Durand and the World Alliance of Reformed Churches.[19]

Finally, Moltmann suggested that this congregational unity would become a sign of hope. His words that the congregation would become a sacrament of the kingdom and would announce the beginning of the messianic era whenever people from diverse backgrounds would surrender their privileges and be freed themselves, echoed the words of South African theologians like David Bosch, Flip Theron, and many others about the church practicing real and living unity as an alternative community and as a cosmic-eschatological sign.[20]

For Moltmann, however, this emphasis on the unity visible and experienced in the gathered congregation immediately called for the qualification that it should be a unity "in freedom."

> The unity of the congregation is a unity in freedom. It must not be confused with unanimity, let alone uniformity in perception, feeling or morals. No one must be regimented, or forced into conformity with conditions prevailing in the church. Everyone must be accepted with his or her gifts and tasks, his or her weaknesses and handicaps. This unity is an evangelical unity, not a legal one. The charismatic congregation gives everyone the room they need to be free in their dealings with

other people and to be at their disposal when they need them. Because it is Christ who gathers it and the Spirit of the new creation who gives it life, nothing that serves the kingdom of God and the freedom of human persons must be suppressed in it. It is a unity in diversity and freedom.[21]

Again, these convictions were also central in the church's struggle against apartheid theology. One form of oppression should not replace another form. Believers should be free and feel free. The living, real, and visible unity should be the result of freedom. Unity in the church should not result from the law and legalism, from pressure and oppression. Church unity is not to be confused with unanimity or uniformity. Instead, through the gathering Christ and the life-giving Spirit, the diverse gifts and tasks, even the weaknesses and the handicaps that some may suffer, all become opportunities for mutual enrichment and service in the one church.[22] The crucial thrust of the rejection of the theology of apartheid meant never to deny the wonderful richness of creation, humanity, culture, language, and background at all, but rather to accept, appreciate, and celebrate all these wonderful riches from God as life-giving and life-enabling opportunities of grace—all within the one church.

Moltmann, however, also immediately recognizes the temptation that may be hidden in this diversity, and warns against a celebration of diversity that may, in fact, hinder or deny the bond of real unity.

But the congregation's unity is also freedom and diversity in unity. Where old enmities flare-up again in it, where people insist on getting their own way and want to make their perceptions or experiences a law for other people, not only is the fellowship between people threatened, but so (in a deeper sense) is the fellowship with God himself. Through claims to domination and divisions of this kind Christ himself is divided (I Cor. 1.13). Anyone who uses freedom in order to destroy freedom is not acting in accordance with that freedom. Freedom can be destroyed through the mania for uniformity, just as it can be killed by ruthless pluralism. In both these dangers, the important thing for the committed congregation is to return to the foundation of its unity in diversity, and to experience the open fellowship of Christ in his supper. For the committed congregation is *his* people and it is only in *his* Spirit that unity and diversity can be so intertwined that they do not destroy one another.[23]

His words almost sound like a warning against apartheid and its influence in the church. Where old enmities flare up, where people insist on getting their own way, where people make their own perceptions or experiences a law for others— there the fellowship with others but also the fellowship with God is threatened. Claims of domination and division threaten to divide Christ himself. Indeed, freedom can be used to destroy the freedom of others. "Ruthless pluralism" can also destroy the freedom to belong, to love, and to serve that the gospel brings, just as "the mania of uniformity" can destroy that freedom—and apartheid was such a form of "ruthless pluralism."

What, then, is the way forward? According to Moltmann, the committed congregation needs to return to the foundation of its unity in diversity and renew its experience of the open fellowship of Christ in his supper, for only through Christ's Spirit will unity and diversity not destroy one another—but that kind of return was precisely the difficulty, the seemingly impossible move at the time in our churches: to experience the open fellowship in Christ in his supper and in the common worship of the triune God. How could believers experience the open fellowship in Christ in the Lord's Supper if the celebration of the Supper was *not* open, but precisely the moment and place where historically the divisions originated?[24]

Unity in Freedom between the Congregations

Moltmann is, however, aware that the unity of the church extends further than the gathered congregation. In a second comment he, therefore, also reflects on the *unity in freedom* between congregations. In his later work, his ecclesiology seems to leave many concrete, practical questions about this aspect unanswered. It was as if these more denominational, institutional, and ecumenical issues moved to the background in his thought and work. At this time, however, he (seemingly) still continued to explore the importance of what is called *kerkverband* in many Reformed circles, the *verband* or bond, the relationship between the local, gathered congregations.

> Every congregation gathered together in one place is one in Christ with every other congregation gathered together in other places and at other times. A community which does not see the suffering and testimony of other communities as its own suffering and its own testimony is dividing the one Christ who suffers and acts in all places and at all times. Communities which are divided in space and time recognize one another through their identity in Christ and the common Spirit. They will therefore experience this common identity of theirs and make it visible through fellowship and friendship with one another. They will recognize one another as members of the one church of Christ. "If one member suffers, all suffer together; if one member is honoured, all rejoice together" (I Cor. 12.26). This demands a solidarity beyond the limits of one's own community and must be proved in times of persecution. Every repression of a single Christian or a single community in the world affects all Christians and the whole church. It is only through this living solidarity and full identification with its persecuted members that the church will be able to resist the oppressor's tactics of "divide and rule."[25]

Although Moltmann does not use the expression, this relationship seems to refer to what the famous New Delhi Statement of the World Council of Churches

(1961) described as "(unity) with the whole Christian fellowship in all places and ages," therefore including the universal, catholic, global dimensions of the church. The differences between his description and the description of New Delhi are, however, remarkable. For the World Council, this unity consists in "such wise that ministry and members are accepted by all, and that all can act and speak together as occasion requires for the tasks to which God calls his people." For Moltmann, this unity consists in suffering and solidarity. In a quite remarkable way, he uses these expressions again and again to show what ultimately binds congregations together—seeing the suffering and testimony of other communities as their own suffering; seeing the one Christ who is suffering and acting in all places and at all times; recognizing common identity and making it visible through fellowship and friendship; suffering together with other members; practicing solidarity beyond one's own community; proving solidarity in times of persecution; living solidarity and full identification with the persecuted members; and resisting the oppressors' tactics to divide and rule. In short, the living unity between congregations seems to consist almost fully, according to him, in freely suffering with others, in experiencing solidarity in persecution, and in resisting oppression.

For Reformed Churches in South Africa, several issues of major importance, causing serious theological controversies, were involved in what Moltmann dealt with in this short paragraph.

First, the questions whether the unity between congregations is indeed important, whether visible, real, and lived unity between congregations belongs to the nature and integrity of the church, or whether unity is something of less importance, something arbitrary, something that could sometimes be wholesome and beneficial but sometimes also unnecessary, unwelcome, and counterproductive, were major questions in the church struggle. To justify the existence of separate churches on ethnic, racial, and cultural grounds, the theology of apartheid argued that unity between congregations belongs not to the being, but to the well-being of the church—a claim that meant that, if unity across ethnic, racial, and cultural barriers would lead to tension and conflict in the church, the right way would be for the church *not* to search for expressions and forms of visible and living unity, but rather to keep the believers and congregations apart, along the lines of their natural and cultural divisions and enmities. Believers struggling against this theology of and in the church were convinced that unity between congregations is indeed—in Moltmann's spirit—of extreme importance for the church of the triune God and an integral part of its very being and identity.

Second, again agreeing with Moltmann, Reformed Christians in South Africa were deeply convinced that seeing the suffering of others, accepting their suffering, suffering with them, being in solidarity with the persecuted and those in need, and resisting the divisive and repressive tactics of the oppressors were all indeed integral to the calling of the church to be one. They were also claiming that the necessary, living unity between congregations would include "solidarity, fellowship, and friendship," although they mostly used different terminology, like *unity*, *reconciliation*, and *justice*. For them the deepest claim in the calling of the church to practice *unity in freedom* between congregations was also given in the fact that merely institutional, structural, and organizational unity would not be enough to witness to the reality that they belong to one another as congregations of the church of the triune God.

Third, however, the very use of the term *friendship* may be too weak to do justice to the importance of this aspect from a South African perspective, precisely since Moltmann was using *friendship* very deliberately as an alternative to *brothers and sisters* in order to emphasize the role of free choice in this regard. For South Africans, the emphasis was precisely on the fact that as Christians they *cannot* choose their brothers and sisters, but receive them as gifts from the triune God—a conviction that Archbishop Tutu very often expressed in public and one at the heart of the rejection of the theology and ecclesiology of apartheid. It should perhaps not be surprising that notions of friendship and free choice of association in congregations and churches have become popular in South African church circles since the demise of apartheid. These developments may not be as innocent as they seem, and they certainly do *not* represent the understanding of unity that was alive in the churches that struggled against apartheid.[26]

Fourth, these South African Reformed Christians were pleading for more than what Moltmann was seemingly interested in or willing to argue. For them, the institutional, structural, and organizational unity between congregations was also extremely important, not merely a rather vague and invisible practice of solidarity. Much of the theological debate and ecclesial struggles in South African circles has precisely been—and, in fact, still remains until today—about the need to (re)unite as churches (congregations, denominations) in order to truly be able to practice the living unity, the solidarity, the reconciliation, and the justice called for. In that sense, the Reformed Churches did not see an alternative between the World Council's call for visible unity and Moltmann's call for solidarity and friendship. They would want to affirm both and strive to practice both.

It is unclear whether Moltmann's lack of interest in the structural forms of unity between congregations (and denominations) was caused by his own particular context, in terms of which he could simply take the existence of the Protestant churches for granted, or whether it was based on more material theological concerns, for example, a conscious and growing commitment to a radical reformation ecclesiology. The very next sentences in his discussion of the unity in freedom between congregations, in fact, make this ambiguity, if not lack of clarity, even stronger.

> That is why it is not enough for the fellowship between the individual communities to exist merely in an organization over a large area. The hierarchical build-up of large-scale church units and of administrations over a large area becomes abstract

if it loses its contact with the "grass roots." It is true that many of the community's tasks can be carried out regionally or territorially by the church authorities: questions of finance, schools, dealings with government departments. But this does not affect the *specific* tasks of the local community—proclamation, mission, charitable work, fellowship, and so forth. Individual communities cannot delegate their specific duties to supra-regional units, and so shed their own responsibility for them. If they did so they would become poverty-stricken and reduce their work at the "grass-roots." Even fellowship at the local level is one of the community's own specific duties. It must be performed by the community itself and cannot be delegated.[27]

What does he really mean? What is his rhetorical point? Against what kind of practices is his argument precisely directed? These questions are not easy to answer, especially from a South African context. It may be that he is simply taking the organizational unity between congregations as necessary and already in place but as not fully sufficient. Several expressions, such as "not enough," "becomes abstract if it loses its contact," "it is true . . . but," all point in this direction. In that case, he would simply be pleading for local congregations and communities not to delegate their intrinsic responsibilities and callings to be the church to any overarching organizational structure, but to practice their own calling locally as a congregation.

In that sense, his plea would simply reflect a very central Reformed conviction about the local congregation as fully church. It would also reflect the crucial aspect of the unity of the church emphasized in the New Delhi Statement that later became known in the now famous expression that ecumenism (or the unity of the church) "must be local in order to be real." New Delhi explained more fully that "the unity which is both God's will and his gift to his Church is being made visible as *all in each place* who are baptized into Jesus Christ and confess him as Lord and Savior are brought by the Holy Spirit into one fully committed fellowship, holding the one apostolic faith, preaching the one Gospel, breaking the one bread, joining in common prayer, and having a corporate life reaching out in witness and service to all."

In that sense, he would certainly also be formulating a conviction that Reformed South Africans also held deeply as they were struggling against an apartheid ecclesiology. Ecumenism (or the unity of the church) was meaningless and, in fact, practically denied when representatives from different churches and denominations met one another for a few days somewhere distant in the world; but back home, while living in the same community, they never met one another, never shared any aspect of one another's life, and never experienced any *koinonia* or community. Indeed, the living unity of the church should be "grass-roots" according to Moltmann; but so also according to many South African church documents from the time. It should be local in order to be real.

Was that indeed all that Moltmann meant, or was he more fundamentally critical of church structures themselves? Was he anticipating a totally new form of being the church—only community, only congregation, only solidarity, only freedom—without the traditional structures of the church? Was he perhaps more deeply skeptical of church in the traditional sense? Was this skepticism the reason why so many of the classical questions of ecclesiology never seemed to interest him? Was he seeing or construing a real alternative where most South African Reformed Christians at the time would not be going? His subsequent paragraphs in which he specifically focuses on the nature of the unity between the congregations and the necessity of larger forms or structures of the church still do not resolve these questions.

> The community can assign particular charges connected with their mutual fellowship. The apostles performed this function in the early Christian churches. Later it was given to bishops. In state churches it was possible to leave this task to the state authorities. On the other hand regional and territorial synods grew up which represented and expressed practically the common fellowship between the different congregations. But the episcopal organization is in danger of absorbing the actual congregation into abstract units under the name, in Germany, of *Landeskirchen* (churches belonging to a particular federal *Land,* or state); and on the other hand the synodal organization is in danger of seeing itself solely as the representative of the congregations, over against a central church government. In both cases organizations above the local level lose the character of the "committed congregation". The governing bodies and the synods then see themselves as institutions for the support of the congregations, or even as "the church" compared with "the congregations". The all-important thing is therefore to present and organize the fellowship between local churches not from above but from below. Church governments and synods cannot set themselves up "above" the congregations; they themselves can only be again the congregation gathered round word and sacrament.[28]

Here, his German church background becomes very clear, and so also his very critical, skeptical theological evaluation of tendencies which he observes endangering and reducing the life of local congregations. This criticism, of course, makes very good sense in the light of several of his other writings on the church, in which he openly declares his own commitment to what he calls *congregationalism*. He certainly sees the future of the church in the life of local congregations (and local congregations in real solidarity with one another), not in any more organized, structural form of the church. Today, many believers and theologians in many other contexts would probably show strong sympathy with his sentiments. But how far is he really willing to go? Does he see any real alternative for the future? What does his vision mean in actual practice? He continues to spell that out, but still not very clearly.

> The unity of the congregations depends on what the congregations do. The fellowship of the fellowships should be lived as fellowship. The open friendship of

Jesus, which is experienced and lived in the gathered congregation, and "the unity of the Spirit in the bond of peace," cannot be surpassed. It is only when the unity of the congregations with one another is itself realized as a congregation that unity in freedom and freedom in unity can be experienced. For all inter-congregational fellowships and organizations, therefore, the fellowship in word and sacrament is fundamental, and the things that have to be administered and the affairs that have to be ordered must be settled in the fellowship of the Spirit.[29]

What could it practically mean, for example, in the context of the South African church struggle for unity in the divided church that "the fellowship of the fellowships should be lived as fellowship," that "the unity of the congregations with one another" should itself be "realized as a congregation," that also for "all inter-congregational fellowships . . . the fellowship in word and sacrament is fundamental"? How could the other forms of the church—ecumenical, denominational, structural, conciliar—really be conceived as *congregation*, as *fellowship*?

In short, the fact that Moltmann also affirmed the importance of *unity in freedom* between congregations certainly agreed with very strong convictions among antiapartheid Reformed Christians. The fact that he affirmed the importance of unity between congregations in the form of sharing in suffering, solidarity, and resistance against oppression also agreed with deeply held convictions in the South African context. His lack of interest in the visible forms and structures of being the church, however, was unhelpful in addressing the deeply structural and systemic challenges that ethnic, racial, and class divisions offered to the life of the church—and his lack of interest could, in fact, be construed in ways that would draw the attention away from these crucial institutional and structural issues and questions that real churches were and still are facing in South Africa.

Unity in Freedom as Witness to the World

Moltmann was, however, also aware that the unity of the church was important because of the mission of the church, and that unity hangs together with witness, with the credibility of the gospel that constitutes the church, and with the prayer of Jesus that his disciples should be one so that the world might believe (John 17:21), *the* central concern behind all ecumenical visions and initiatives. In a third section of his discussion, he therefore dealt at some length with the *unity in freedom* as witness to the world and, once again, in a chain of thought and convictions that corresponded very closely with that which Christians in South Africa were concerned.

Unity in freedom is not merely a mark of Christ's church; it is also a confessional mark, a sign of the church's creed in a divided and estranged world, "that the world may believe" (John 17.21). The word and the sacraments have a power that gives fellowship and freedom in the church and—through the church—in the whole world of men and women as well.[30]

Indeed, the unity in freedom is also a confessional mark, a sign in a divided and estranged world, a visible reality so that the world may believe. It is important for his own theological understanding that he refers in this regard not only to the word, but also to the sacrament. Not only the word, but also the sacrament has "a power" that gives both "fellowship and freedom" both "in" the church, but also "through" the church in the whole world of men and women. Together, word and sacrament, therefore, produce forms and experiences of fellowship and of freedom, not only in the traditional forms of the church in and between gathered congregations, but, indeed, somehow also in the whole world where forms of division and estrangement like those between men and women—but implicitly all other systemic and structural powers of division, like race, ethnicity, and culture—are overcome as a sign. In fact, it is important for him to stress the unity outside of the church since that is the real unity, the real unity of Christ.

> As a unifying force, the church is the messianic people of Christ, for unity is not merely an attribute of the church; it is the church's task in the world as well. If the assembled church is the confessing church, then it will represent the unity in Christ and the Spirit that makes all things new in the midst of the conflicts of its social and political situation. That is why the unifying power of the sacraments cannot be separated from the tasks and forces of social and political justice. The unity of Christ, which must not be divided, is not only unity with his disciples and the fellowship of believers but, based on that, is also his unity and fellowship with the oppressed, humiliated and forsaken.[31]

Thus, unity is not only a characteristic of the church, but as confessing church, it is called to become a unifying force in the world itself, bringing unity in the midst of social and political conflicts. Why? The unity that the church is called to serve is "the unity in Christ and the Spirit" or "the unity of Christ"—a unity that involves much more than merely the unity within the church itself, the unity in and between congregations. Here careful readers would not misunderstand his intentions, which were integrally embedded in the whole of his theological project over many years. The unity to which the church should contribute in the world should not be understood in any innocent or neutral sense as always on the side of harmony, agreement, and objectivity and as never getting involved, never making options, and never taking sides. No, the unity of which the church should be a sign and an instrument is the unity of Christ, which for him means unity with the oppressed, the humiliated, and the forsaken, like Jesus Christ. He is obviously concerned to spell that out very clearly.

> The church would not witness to the whole Christ if it were not a fellowship of believers with the poor, a fellowship of the hopeful with the sick, and a fellowship of the loving with the oppressed. Its unity would no longer be a "predicate of the

time of salvation" if it were not to achieve liberation for the downtrodden, justice for those without rights, and peace in social conflicts. It is not "one" for itself; it is one for the peace of divided humankind in the coming kingdom of God. In this respect "unity in freedom" and "freedom in unity" become particularly important.[32]

Fellowshipping with the poor, bringing hope to the sick, bringing love to the oppressed, achieving liberation for the downtrodden, working for justice for those without rights, contributing to peace in social conflict and division—these actions are what the church's witness to unity calls for if this unity is indeed qualified by "the unity of Christ and the Spirit."

Why do *unity-in-freedom* and *freedom-in-unity* become so particularly important in this respect, according to Moltmann? They have importance because the church itself should first of all be liberated from these same realities within its own life and being, including division, injustice, conflict, and hopelessness. In order to become a sign and an instrument of the messianic truth and power, the church itself should become free and liberated and should experience and practice *this* form of unity in freedom. This practice will not be easy at all.

> The church itself acquires its practical unity as it experiences and lives in liberation from claims to domination in the society in which it exists. It is only a church liberated in this sense that portrays that unity. But this also means, as experience shows, that a church that suffers because of its resistance to claims of this kind becomes assured of its unity in Christ in a particular degree. The church will seize every opportunity to work for unity through liberation, and for peace through justice, in social and political conflicts. It does this when it works for the liberation of people whose rights have been taken from them and who have to suffer injustice helplessly. It does this when it offers open friendship to the people who have to suffer enmity and contempt. It testifies to the fellowship of the crucified Christ when it offers this fellowship and helps the people who are poor, oppressed and rejected to find fellowship themselves.[33]

In the South African church struggle, these convictions were crucial. The church should, indeed, practice what it preaches. The church should embody its own confession. The church should live its own truth. The structure and the order, the life and the practices of the church should not contradict and even deny its own confession and proclamation, its own witness and claims of truth.

Again, these convictions, in fact, belong very fundamentally to the Reformed faith and tradition. Behind these positions in South African circles were many voices from the Reformed tradition since Calvin himself, but also voices from the German Church Struggle, including those from Barth and some of his followers, Bonhoeffer and some within his legacy, such as Wolfgang Huber, and the tradition of the *Theological Declaration of Barmen*. These voices both informed and inspired many of the believers, church leaders, and theologians involved in the South African churches, among them, for example, the well-known Beyers Naudé.

So, the church itself should experience *this* form of unity and, therefore, *this* form of liberation from simply being a mirror image, a reproduction of the realities in the society of the day. Such a process will, however, not be an easy one for the church because resistance will seek to thwart these kinds of claims and convictions as the South African believers most certainly experienced. Moltmann points out, again very helpfully, that such resistance will not and does not merely come from without, from those powers and realities in society that are being confronted with the church's witness about this messianic form of unity in freedom; but the resistance comes also and sometimes primarily and very strongly from within. These claims for following the unity of Christ and the Spirit lead to new forms of conflict *within* the church, which raises questions concerning the unity of the church in a dramatic, even radical new way, as Moltmann realizes and underlines.

> But when the church believes, hopes and practices unity in, with and beneath the real conflicts of society, it is also taking new conflicts on itself. The church's inward orientation towards its own unity would remain abstract and remote from its messianic mission if this political trend of its unity were not discerned and accepted.[34]

In other words, these conflicts that are now caused within the church itself raise the question for Moltmann whether the choice should be for (continuing) unity within the church with those who, in fact, oppose the unity in Christ with the suffering of the world or rather for a (new) unity outside of the church with the suffering and hopeless instead of a continuing unity in the (so-called) church? Once again, it would seem—at least from the perspective of the majority of South African Reformed Churches and believers at the time—as if Moltmann is here again almost on the borderline of what may very easily become an unfortunate and unnecessary, if not false and misleading, alternative. It may almost seem as if he is again propagating the same choice for a new form of ecumenism, even a new form of church, leaving the traditional forms of the church behind for a new form of somewhat vague and invisible church and ecumenism, perhaps a movement rather than "the fellowship in word and sacrament."

> The ecumenical movement of the separated churches has made great progress in the field of dogma, and has been able to overcome traditional conflicts about baptism, the Lord's supper and the ministry. But for a number of years a growing sense of the social and political tasks of messianic action has introduced new conflicts into these endeavours on the part of the church for unity and fellowship. It is no longer merely true that "doctrine divides but service unites"; now it is

often the case that "doctrine unites but politics divide". Here the question of which kind of unity has priority is especially delicate. Is it the fellowship in word and sacrament that unites a person with his political enemies, or is it fellowship with the poor and all those who are standing up for them that divides the one from the other?[35]

His questions are, indeed, penetrating and challenging, if, indeed, taken as real questions, not merely as rhetorical positions. For us in South Africa, these kinds of questions and challenges were simply too real and practical than to be merely rhetorical. Was there also a fellowship in word and sacrament that could unite believers with their political enemies, or was there only a fellowship with the poor and their advocates dividing them from other believers? These were real, concrete, everyday questions—the question of the real unity of the church in a new and very practical, but also dramatic way. But was this alternative a real one or a false one?

> When does a political situation become so acute that it becomes a matter of creed? Does Christian fellowship exist between the hangman and his victims? Can there be Christian fellowship with both the hangman and his victims at the same time? How far can the church settle conflicts of this kind within itself, and when does Christian fellowship run aground on them? Can we witness to our unity even through confrontation and conflict about the truth? Can the church confine itself to word and sacrament, and keep out of the quarrel altogether as an institution, while individual Christians take different and opposing sides in the various conflicts? Can political enemies "remain one under the gospel"? How long can they do this? And what does it mean for their conflict itself? Does this not make "the gospel" an abstract and ineffective power? These are some of the practical questions facing the church and many individual Christians today.[36]

In South Africa, the political situation, indeed, became so acute that it became a matter of creed, or rather of confession. A *status confessionis* was declared following the Lutheran World Federation and the World Alliance of Reformed Churches. Precisely in order to confess *why* this declaration was done and to explain *how* the gospel is not an abstract and ineffective power, a new confessional document, the *Confession of Belhar* (1982, 1986) was born.[37] That this act of confession, however, was done without Moltmann's alternative in mind as a serious option becomes clear from his subsequent comments: "If we only have the church's internal unity in view, we will push these questions off into the field of ethics. If we are looking towards messianic unity, they are questions of faith as well."[38]

According to South African Christians, it was—and still is—possible to take the "internal" unity of the real church seriously *without* regarding the challenges of society as merely ethical concerns. It was—and still is—possible to take the unity of the real church seriously *precisely* because we are called by and committed to the messianic unity of Christ and the Spirit, *precisely* because the real church is called to be a sign and instrument of the unity of Christ and the Spirit, *precisely* because this witness in the world is indeed a question of faith, not merely of ethics. It was—and still is—possible to understand the real church in spite of its weaknesses and failures, its own divisions and injustices, and its own vulnerability and betrayals as an integral part of the history of the triune God. It is *not* necessary to construe an alternative and to make a choice between the real church and a new, still vague, invisible, ahistoric, messianic community because of our disappointments with the real church. It is possible—and probably our calling—to struggle in, with, and through the real church for the witness and the embodiment to which we are called (and which Moltmann so movingly describes in his whole and ongoing theological project of retelling the history of the triune God) precisely because the sad, tragic, shameful story of the real church (and in South Africa we know this aspect of our story only too well) is part of the history of the triune God with the world.

Is it fair to suspect that Moltmann's ecclesiology was ultimately based on such an alternative and such a choice? Is that, indeed, the reason both why he paid scant attention to the traditional ecclesiological themes and issues and why his ecclesiology received less reception and response than the rest of his work? It is not very clear. He does not really spell this out. Even his concluding comments do not finally resolve the issue.

> If we only look at the unity without taking account of the freedom, reconciliation for fellowship easily becomes a policy of appeasement—a mere prevention of conflicts without any search for a solution. If we only look at the freedom without taking account of the unity, then we easily overlook the irreparable sacrifice required by conflict as a means to liberation and peace. Neither the unity as such nor the conflict as such is creative. The only creative thing is the strength that accepts the conflicts and seeks for unity in freedom, and freedom in unity. As far as the practical and personal questions in these conflicts are concerned, the primary question is not whether fellowship with the church or fellowship with the oppressed and persecuted is more important. The question of really pre-eminent importance is where the assured and consistent *fellowship of Christ* is to be found. For this alone is, after all, the foundation of the fellowship with our Christian brethren, and with the least of men. It will therefore also be the yardstick for church fellowship and political fellowship. Unity and division, conflict and reconciliation, confrontation and co-operation must be tested against the cross of Christ; for his cross is the first and last sign of the one kingdom.[39]

So, the primary question is *not* deciding between "fellowship with the church" or "fellowship with the persecuted and oppressed," but "where fellowship with Christ" is to be found. Indeed, but where? Does this criterion suggest a choice between "church" and "oppressed," or is it possible to search for fellowship with the persecuted and oppressed precisely *because* of fellowship in and through the one, united and uniting church and precisely *because* we have no other choice since his cross is indeed "the first and last sign of the kingdom"?[40]

STATEMENTS OF FAITH, HOPE AND ACTION—A SOUTH AFRICAN RECEPTION

Introducing his discussion of the four *marks* of the church, Moltmann explains that as integrated components of the confession of the triune God, they have to be understood as statements of faith, hope, and action.

These *marks* are not so much characteristics that the church possesses as characteristics of Christ's own activity and, therefore, are statements of faith. The unity, the holiness, the catholicity, and the apostolic character are all primarily statements of faith about what Christ is doing—in, with, and through the church. They are at the same time statements about "Christ's messianic mission and the eschatological gift of the Spirit," and, therefore, "messianic predicates of the church in the perspective of the coming kingdom, for which it exists and which in the church acquires form and testimony." Whether one speaks of unity, holiness, catholicity, or apostolicity, these are not so much descriptions of possession as statements of hope. They are, therefore, also statements of action. Precisely as statements of faith (in Christ's work) and hope (in God's coming kingdom), they call the church *to be* one, holy, catholic, and apostolic. Taken together in this way, these *marks*, therefore, make the visibility, the presence, and the real life of the church so important.

> The church's essential nature is given, promised and laid upon it in the characteristics. Faith, hope and action are the genesis of the form of the church visible to the world in unity, holiness, catholicity and apostolicity. That is why theology cannot withdraw to "the invisible church", "the church of the future", or "the church of pure demands". The church lives in the one, holy, catholic and apostolic rule of Christ through faith, hope and action.[41]

For us, this excerpt offers a very helpful way of understanding the church. These statements—together expressing what we believe, what we hope for, and that to which we are called—therefore create a critical tension with the real church, with what we are, and with how we live.

Under normal circumstances, this tension always calls for self-critical reflection, continuous discernment, and ongoing renewal in the spirit of the Reformed motto *ecclesia reformata semper reformanda* ("Church reformed always reforming"), an expression often quoted by Moltmann himself.

Under abnormal circumstances, this tension between what we are and what we believe, hope for, and are called to be can become so serious and strong that we may feel called to radical transformation, to total renewal, to conversion and commitment—in Moltmann's words, to consider that we may be facing questions of faith. This tension may involve facing resistance, also from without but especially from within. Since it may be called forth by the church's involvement in the divisions, injustices, and conflicts of society itself, it may raise the question, when does a political situation become so acute that it becomes a matter of creed? Such moments will be painful; but, at least according to many South African Reformed Christians during the time of apartheid, they do not have to force us to leave the institutional church and to seek an alternative in some form of social movement. They could, in fact, challenge us *in* the church to confess anew for this particular historical moment and then to seek to embody our confession in the order, the practices, and the everyday life of the church as a witness to the world of the power and truth of the good news of the triune God. For these churches, practicing visibly the living unity in freedom of the real church was—and is—indeed integral to the Christian confession of the history of the triune God.

When during the apartheid struggle the South African *Confession of Belhar* confessed this faith, hope, and commitment to action concerning the unity of the church, it explicitly used the phrase from Moltmann's work that this unity should be a unity in freedom.[42]

Within the South African context, this meant that the visible unity of the church is served neither by the ruthless pluralism of apartheid nor by any attempt to establish uniformity within the church. The wonderful riches of God's gifts should rather be celebrated in the one, living church as a witness to the world in a then deeply divided society. This was, in fact, the only direct quotation from any theologian or theological work in the *Confession*, although many other theologians, theological traditions, and even church documents influenced the *Confession* in major ways.

By using this phrase, *Belhar* was taking over neither the totally different context of the phrase in Moltmann's theology nor the whole thrust and all the implications of his ecclesiology as these reflections have hopefully indicated, albeit briefly.[43] At the time, these words were taken over with gratitude from a theological contemporary and friend from afar concerned with many of the struggles also threatening and challenging the South African churches.

CHAPTER 8

MAKE WAY FOR THE SPIRIT

Harvey G. Cox Jr.

I believe in the Holy Spirit, the Lord and giver of life.

Toward the end of the twelfth century C.E., an Italian Cistercian abbot named Joachim of Floris propounded an inventive doctrine of the Holy Trinity. The venerable monk suggested in a number of learned tractates that the three persons of the Trinity, although they lived in eternal mutuality, have actually manifested themselves in history in a sequential fashion. Thus, he conjectured, the period of the Old Testament had been the *Age of the Father*. The first millennium of church history had been the *Age of the Son*. In his own time, the abbot taught, humanity was entering the age of the third person of the Trinity. History, thus, was at the dawn of the *Age of the Spirit*.

In this new age just coming to birth, said Joachim, it would no longer be necessary for the church to have a hierarchy, because the luminous presence of God the Spirit would suffuse all people and all creation. Understandably, this idea did not win immediate acclaim from the pope and the bishops; but there was more. During this *Age of the Spirit*, the strife and hostility that had divided Christians from infidels would disappear; and all peoples and tribes would be joined in a single harmonious body. This harmonious life was another idea that was not greeted with universal acceptance, especially among those who were engaged in bloody but sometimes profitable crusades against those very infidels in Palestine and Syria. Joachim of Floris's imaginative teachings enjoyed a brief popularity for a century or two, especially among the Spiritual Franciscans, some of whom saw St. Francis himself as the figure who had introduced this new *Age of the Spirit*. Eventually, church authorities declared Joachim's teachings heretical and burned some of the Spiritual Franciscans at the stake for good measure.

Developments in world Christianity during the twentieth century, especially during the last few decades, might prompt us at least to ask whether the *Age of the Spirit* that Joachim foresaw, but appears not to have dawned in his own time, is making a late entrance into our own. Rather than witnessing the *death of God* that some theologians pronounced not too many years ago, we are experiencing what might be called the rebirth of the Spirit or, to borrow a term from Freud, "the return of the repressed"[1] in Christendom. One should quickly add, however, that evidence also suggests that the *Age of the Spirit*—or *Spirits*—that is now dawning may not be the period of unqualified bliss and harmony that Joachim predicted.

The phrase "the return of the repressed" seems appropriate because, as any careful reader of the New Testament can see, a lively belief in the unfettered presence of the Spirit was vividly present and already causing conflict and concern in early Christianity. The Epistles of St. Paul make the presence of this conflict about the Spirit quite clear. Then, over the centuries, for reasons that often had more to do with political and institutional considerations than with theological ones, Christian belief in the freedom of the Spirit was discouraged and even outlawed, though never fully extinguished. After all, it still survives in the Christian doctrine of the Trinity that holds that the Holy Spirit is just as much God as God the Father and God the Son are. The return of the repressed Spirit, as the twenty-first century begins, has become both a religious reality and a theological issue.

I have long believed that the chasm between those who study manifestations of religions from the perspective of ethnology, psychology, and the other sciences on the one hand, and those who study it from the perspective of theology on the other, is too wide and too deep. Theological doctrines, although they may at times seem remote from real life, frequently exercise an enormous influence on how the underlying culture, which all intellectual pursuits share, constructs and perceives issues.

This chapter will argue two points. First, new religious movements often seem threatening to existing churches because of a defective theology of the Spirit that has become institutionalized, especially in the Christian West. This defective understanding stems in turn both from centuries of underdevelopment of the doctrine of the Holy Spirit and from a tendency, again especially in the Western churches, to erect safeguards and channels to control, monopolize, and mediate this most dangerous of all realities: the Spirit.

My second thesis is that those who tried to channel the energy of the Spirit, though they often did so in a narrow and self-serving way, had good reasons to try. They realized that spirit can be toxic as well as salutary. They were attempting to introduce a norm, a norm that is still needed today. Did their efforts quench and repress the Spirit instead of channeling it? Do we need a newly configured norm today?

Perhaps it would be useful to ask at the outset why Christians first came to believe in the divinity of the Spirit, or in the classical language, the Holy Spirit. The answer is not obvious. There is nothing essential or magical about the number three. Why not believe in four persons of the Godhead? Or in seven? It might have been different. After all, the early Christians believed in the Creator God who had also called and liberated the people of Israel. They believed not only in the Jesus Christ who had lived and died in Palestine but also in the risen Christ. Why did they need a third manifestation of God?

The only answer is that their belief in what later came to be called the Trinity grew out of their undeniable experience of the variety of ways in which they had encountered God. They had not only met the Holy One in ways that were not reducible to the Creator God and the Christ, but—and this observation is the most important one—they were convinced that the God they met in these other ways was just as much and just as fully God as the first two. Given the gnostic environment in which early Christianity developed, they might well have made this third way some lesser or derivative one; but they did not. They refused to speak of a quasi-divine spirit. They insisted that the Spirit was also fully God.

How and why, then, did the repression set in? As we have seen, certain of Paul's letters, especially those to the Corinthians, suggest that the freedom of the Spirit was already a problem for church leaders in the first decades of Christianity. In 325 c.e. the same question was addressed by the Council of Nicea that the newly (and allegedly) converted Emperor Constantine I had called. There the church leaders first composed and promulgated what we now call the Nicene Creed. In it the church fathers said, "We believe in God the Father," in "Jesus Christ his only begotten Son." With each of these so-called articles of the creed, they also attached an explanatory paragraph; but then in what is almost a kind of appendix with no other explanation, they added, "*and* we believe in the Holy Spirit." That appendix is all they said—nothing more. Why was there no further description?

Perhaps the lack of further elaboration means there was not much controversy about the Spirit at the time. Creeds, after all, are meant to respond to controversies. But a controversy did develop rather quickly so that by the time of the Council of Constantinople, only fifty years later, the fathers amplified this third part of the creed by including the phrase "Lord and Giver of life" and adding "who proceeds from the Father and who with the Father and the Son is glorified, one God. . . . "

The phrase with which we are familiar in our current Western creeds, "who proceeds from the Father *and the Son*," was not included in the original Nicene Creed in its Constantinople version. In fact, it was not included for hundreds of years. How this later insertion happened is quite a saga.

Gradually, between about 800 and 1000 c.e., the Western churches unilaterally *added* the *filioque* phrase to the creed without due process of theology, that is, without the action of an ecumenical council and without the approval of the Eastern churches. Consequently, the Eastern churches to this day stalwartly refuse to accept this phrase in the creed, both on procedural and theological grounds; so the venerable old *filoque* controversy is not over. It is still very much alive in the minds of Russian and Greek Orthodox Christians. Why was such a troublesome and divisive phrase added?

Dozens of theories and libraries of argumentation discuss this point. We do know that the great champion of the *filioque* clause was Charlemagne who, as newly crowned emperor, wanted to solidify his rule, in part over Arian Christians who did not appreciate what they saw as an unwarranted elevation of Christ (the second person of the Trinity) over the Holy Spirit (the third person). We also know that several popes resisted this insertion, but that the papacy eventually conceded in the face of a variety of pressures and included it in the creed. We also know that it was resisted nearly from the outset by the Eastern churches and became the controversy that contributed to the schism between the two branches of Christianity in 1054, a break, however, that was precipitated just as much by political as by theological causes and that was also made irreparable when the Crusader armies took a very long detour from Jerusalem in order to sack Constantinople.

But what does the phrase *filioque* actually mean? To say that the Holy Spirit "proceeds" from both the Father "and" the Son, as the Western churches (Roman and most Protestant creedal churches) do, is to imply that the presence of the Spirit of God must in some way be subsumed under Jesus Christ. This view has usually meant that the Spirit can be present only where there is an explicit confession of Jesus Christ. In turn, this affirmation suggests that the Spirit of God, which according to John 3:8 "blows where it wills," must now restrict itself, as it were, to ecclesiastically approved channels. Its freedom is delimited, whereas in the Eastern and more mystical version of Christianity, the experience of God the Spirit is at least theoretically available in a wider, less refined, and less controlled way. A few years ago some Episcopal and Anglican churches decided to remove the *filioque* clause from the creed; consequently, the creed as it is now used in those churches, does not include it.

In tracing the history of the *filioque* addition, however, it is important not to overlook its theological purpose. Inevitably, questions such as these began to arise: How could one be sure this or that spiritual or religious upsurge was really of God? How could one "test the spirits" (1 John 4:1)? The *filioque* became a kind of litmus test, but history has shown that it turned out to be an inept and misguided attempt to guarantee some norm for religious movements. Where does the *filioque* controversy stand presently?

At the World Council of Churches Assembly held in 1991 in Canberra, Australia, the delegates gathered under the phrase "Come Holy Spirit, Renew Thy Whole Creation." For the first time the World Council of Churches had used an allusion to the Holy Spirit in its invitations to an assembly—this one based on "*Veni Creator Spiritus*," one of the oldest prayers of the church. It seemed appropriate enough, even harmless, but the Assembly found the issue far more explosive and divisive than anyone had anticipated. Exploring it caused deep resentments, divided the so-called older churches from the younger churches, and split Eastern and Western ones. The lack of consensus on this critical issue proves that the Greek Orthodox theologian Nicholas Nissiotis was correct when he once said—long before the Assembly convened—that neither the East nor the West has a sufficiently ample doctrine of the Holy Spirit.[2]

Clearly in future years we will see much more attention devoted to the theology of the Holy Spirit. Jürgen Moltmann is one of the pioneers in the new endeavor. I believe that this discussion may also open up some heretofore unexplored common ground between theology and the social scientific study of religion. How might this happen?

Joachim of Fiore foresaw a new *age of the Spirit*. That age did not come and maybe never will. The fate of his thought teaches us how difficult it is for the Spirit to range freely, to move wherever and whenever it will when its activities are hemmed in so severely by the doctrines and institutions of Western Christianity. Still, the Spirit cannot be stifled forever; and now eight centuries after Joachim's prediction, we are witnessing a worldwide outburst of religious energy that belies most secularization theories and makes us wonder if the gods are as dead as those death-of-God theologians of the 1960s supposed.

We are seeing what Sigmund Freud might call "the return of the repressed"; but we overlook that this raw spiritual energy was once a central element in Christian faith, one that has been repressed often and denied for many centuries. Now it is coming back—with a vengeance. First, the global scope of religious pluralism is forcing Christianity to find the basis for discerning the grace of God in faiths that do not explicitly confess Jesus Christ. That challenge is serious and real. I am suggesting that most Christian theological mechanisms are inadequate for affirming this graceful presence. Thus, to speak of the "anticipatory presence of God" or "the hidden presence of Christ" or of "anonymous Christians" in characterizing these religious traditions now seems condescending. But both theological relativism and theological triumphalism also seem unacceptable. How is it possible for Christians who are neither partial Christians nor half-hearted Christians to affirm the presence of God in other religious traditions?

The key is the ancient doctrine of the Holy Spirit. The great theologian Athanasius explained the doctrine this way, that the Holy Spirit is all that the Father is and all that the Son is, but the Holy Spirit is not the Father and is not the Son.[3] This statement may sound like a conundrum, but it means that the Spirit is wholly and fully God. It affirms the full divinity of the Spirit that "blows where it wills" (John 3:8), that cannot be boxed in. The other side of the issue, however, is the question of how one can legitimately claim that the Holy Spirit is *not* present in any given religious expression—Christian, non-Christian, or whatever.

A second evidence of the return of the repressed Spirit in our day is the spectacular increase in the participation of women in religious leadership—as priests, pastors, and theologians. This change has begun to raise unanticipated questions for all of us about the gender of God; the feminine qualities inherent in God; and ways to express these qualities in worship, liturgy, hymns, praise and prayer. Here is a development that might even have startled Joachim of Floris. Within our lifetime we have the first women rabbis after thousands of years of Jewish tradition and the first Anglican women priests and bishops. This is an epochal change in the life of the church. I was present in Boston for the consecration of Rev. Barbara Harris as a bishop in the American Episcopal church and as the first woman consecrated in the Anglican tradition worldwide. It was a moving and important event in the symbolical awareness of millions of people, especially in liturgical traditions in which the priest symbolizes to some extent the qualities of God.

The emergence of women in the Christian churches signals the "return of the repressed Spirit." Christian feminists like Rosemary Ruether and others understandably emphasize the Spirit as the preferred way of referring to God, and they link it with women's continuing endeavors to weave together and maintain the web of life. Here I think Christians have much to learn from other religious traditions, including Judaism. Often Judaism is mistakenly blamed for an overemphasis on the patriarchal side of God, the Father side. The people who make this accusation conveniently overlook the centuries of attention in Jewish theology to the *Shekinah* (the "glory of God"), the feminine aspect of God that, at least in some Jewish traditions, is diffused throughout the entire world and is symbolically united in the masculine God as the Sabbath queen arrives every week with the lighting of the candles.

God the Spirit clearly transcends gender; therefore, there is no good reason why Christians should not refer to God in song, prayer, and theology with feminine qualities as well. In various languages (e.g., Latin, Spanish, Italian, German, etc.), the word Spirit turns out to be masculine, feminine, or neuter. Passages from Genesis through Revelation speak of God with feminine qualities. Thus, employing feminine imagery for God in worship seems not only possible but urgent.

Third, the fastest-growing Christian movement in the world today is by all odds Pentecostalism. This growth is something else about which Professor Moltmann has written with critical appreciation. In the United States, South America, and the Third World generally, both small and large congregations of people are gathering round their immediate experience of the Spirit of God who comes with the gift of healing or of "speaking in unknown tongues." This movement is growing especially, though not exclusively, among poor and disprivileged people who feel uncomfortable or alienated from the established churches. How can this movement be understood, criticized where necessary, and welcomed where appropriate with a deepened appreciation both for the freedom of the Holy Spirit and for the Spirit's mutual relationality to the Creator God and to Christ?

Finally, if the Spirit is the source of *both* biological life and spiritual life, this perspective pushes us in the direction of developing an *ecological* ethic. The preliminary document for the World Council of Churches' Assembly in 1991 notes:

When we pray to the Holy Spirit to sustain the whole creation, we acknowledge that God is the source of life both biologically and spiritually and we affirm the intrinsic goodness of all creation as it is fashioned by the will of God. The ever-continuing activity of the Holy Spirit is the wellspring of creation. This life is one inner-connected whole uniting human survival and lively-hood with the fulfillment of the creative world. Yes, we live in a moment of extreme jeopardy made more poignant by the presence of the gift of life. For the first time in history the planet's major life support systems are being destroyed by human activity. Never before have humans threatened the ecological survival of the entire planet.[4]

The liberation of the Spirit from its bondage over the centuries might make it possible to transcend the obsession with history and history-making that has held the West in its grip for so long. It might enable us to imagine a religious ethic that would embrace the soil and the stars, the animals and the plants, along with all God's human creatures.

All these events and situations are evidences of the return of the ecclesiastically repressed Spirit, now seemingly bursting loose of its restraints and expressing itself outside duly recognized channels. But they also make evident that the return of the repressed creates some serious problems. Not all spiritual movements are life-giving or life-enhancing. Not all religious movements, new ones or old ones, institutional or popular, are healthy ones. How does one discriminate between those movements of the Spirit that are of God, that stem from the "source of life" and justice and human well-being, and those that are destructive, crippling, and noxious?

May I suggest here that those who imposed the *filioque* clause over a thousand years ago, despite the damage and vision they sowed, may have had a point? They were reminding both the theologians of their day and perhaps even social scientists of ours that we cannot analyze religious movements, including popular ones, without explicit norms. We cannot pretend to be *wertfrei* (value-free). Religious movements exert a powerful influence on individuals and on societies and cultures. They can have enormous life-giving and life-denying consequences. We cannot be satisfied as human beings with a method that is allegedly only descriptive.

What shall the criteria be? We have a hint, although a badly obscured one, in the *filioque* clause. At its best, the inner intention of this doctrinal idea is that those spiritual movements that are not in conformity with the values incarnate in Jesus and in the reign of God that he embodied and announced must be viewed with some suspicion. Jesus cast his lot with the poor. Using his commitment as a reference point, we have the right to question the claims of those movements (some of these claims associated with the so-called New Age Movement) that appeal so much to the rich and comfortable. Jesus made illegitimate the sacred claims of the tyrants. We must wonder about spiritual movements and religious groups that lend sacral authority to oppression. Jesus's message and actions threatened those religious leaders of his day who misused their office to make life more difficult for the unlearned, the abused, and the disprivileged. Religious hierarchies and spiritual movements today continue this misuse of religious power. Merely to study, document, and analyze spiritual movements that are a menace to the weakest and most vulnerable members of society without ever making judgments can surely never be good science; and it is certainly bad theology.

Precisely here, theology and the other ways of reflecting on religious and spiritual movements can begin to find each other again. If social science has been guilty of false objectivity and pseudo-neutrality, theology has often been obsessively normative without giving much sympathetic attention to what it is criticizing. The social sciences need to become much more explicit about the values on which their enterprise is based and on how they arrive at and defend those values. Theologians need to develop the skill of sympathetic observation and careful description.

As long as human sin and finitude persist, we will never see a pure and unspoiled age of the Spirit. We will need, as found in 1 John 4:1, to "test the spirits and see whether they belong to God." In this testing we must have something, however provisional, *against which* the testing takes place. Christian theology suggests that the life of Jesus provides such a touchstone, and this is where the advocates of the *filioque* clause had some insight. Since history has also shown that foul deeds can also be done in Jesus's name, we must insist, against the *filioque* clause, that the criterion of Jesus's life project and his life values must be applied just as rigorously to the evaluation of movements that do bear his name as to those that do not. The Spirit "blows where it will" (John 3:8). No one can control its movements; but that Spirit is the Lord and giver of life, not of death. We must learn how to tell the difference.

CHAPTER 9

THE TRINITY AND THE THEOLOGY OF RELIGIONS

Daniel L. Migliore

Rethinking the relationship between Christian faith and other religions is one of the most important tasks facing the church and theology in the twenty-first century. With the relentless advance of globalization in economy, science, communications, and culture and with the increasing awareness of the religious factor in national and international tensions and conflicts in the post–September 11 world, the need for Christian theology to attend to the task of a theology of the religions is both real and urgent.[1]

A Christian theology of the religions has the particular task of asking about the place of the plurality of world religions within the purposes of God made known in Jesus Christ. Is this plurality to be seen strictly negatively or does it also have a positive meaning? In recent years a number of theologians have taken up this question with particular emphasis on the significance of the Christian understanding of God as triune for a theology of the religions.[2] In this chapter I will first note how the positions long accepted as constituting the standard types of theologies of religion have generally overlooked the importance of the doctrine of the Trinity. Then I will briefly review the work of Jacques Dupuis and Mark Heim, whose explicit developments of trinitarian theology of the religions offer two of the most impressive efforts to move beyond the conventional typology. With this background I will then explore what the writings of Jürgen Moltmann might contribute to this new area of trinitarian theology.

THE STANDARD TYPOLOGY

Many surveys of the relationship of Christianity to the other religions employ the familiar typology of exclusivism, inclusivism, and pluralism. According to this typology, *exclusivism* is the view that there can be no salvation other than through explicit faith in Jesus Christ. In more moderate versions of the exclusivist type, other religions may possess some knowledge of the truth of God; but they are not ways of salvation. *Inclusivism* teaches that Jesus Christ is the definitive revelation of God, that the salvation accomplished in him embraces all people, and that it is somehow made available to all. *Pluralism* holds that all religions mediate true, if partial, knowledge of the mystery of God and that all are equally valid ways of salvation.

While attractive for its simplicity, this widely used typology of theologies of religions has serious limitations. One obvious weakness is that important differences among theologians ostensibly belonging to the same type are obscured. Noting a more important weakness, Christoph Schwöbel argues that because the inclusivist category is the most elusive, the standard typology tends to polarize the discussion between exclusivism and pluralism. For critics of inclusivism on the right, its suspected universalist leanings show that it is simply a covert form of pluralism; for critics of inclusivism on the left, its Christocentric commitments suggest that it is merely a camouflaged form of exclusivism. Schwöbel rightly contends that the resulting polarization between exclusivism and pluralism fails to take seriously the concern of Christian faith for both the particularity and the universality of God's grace, a concern that finds notable expression in the church's doctrine of the Trinity.[3]

In a recent work, Paul Knitter proposes a more ample typology of theologies of the religions that attempts to give a more adequate picture of the range and complexity of the different positions.[4] He identifies four models: Christianity as the complete or partial replacement of the other religions (the evangelical model); Christianity as the fulfillment of the other religions (the Vatican II Roman Catholic model); mutuality of the religions (the liberal Protestant and liberal Roman Catholic model); and acceptance of the irreducible particularity and incommensurability of the religions (the post-liberal model). Knitter's careful and informed study is clearly an advance on the conventional threefold typology.

Among the strengths of Knitter's work from the vantage point of the present essay is the attention he gives to the proposals of a trinitarian theology of the religions offered by Gavin D'Costa, Jacques Dupuis, and Mark Heim. Knitter recognizes, for example, that Dupuis offers a new approach to the theology of religions in which the work of the Spirit of the triune God in other religions may be viewed as distinctive and even different from God's Word in Jesus yet not contradictory to that Word. Knitter's brief summaries of newer trinitarian approaches to the theology of religions only underscore the need for greater attention to this topic than is usually given to it in the standard typology or even in Knitter's more sophisticated typology. The judgment of Carl Braaten written some years ago still remains true: "the significance of the doctrine of the Trinity for Christian theology of the world religions remains vastly underdeveloped."[5] In particular, the work of the Holy Spirit is often neglected in dealing with the question of religious pluralism; or if included, the relationship of the work of the Spirit and the work of Christ remains unclear. We are still in the early stages of the new interest in developing trinitarian perspectives on religious pluralism. The results are varied and uneven, and much remains to be done.

TOWARD A TRINITARIAN THEOLOGY OF THE RELIGIONS

In two recent seminal studies, Jacques Dupuis and Mark Heim offer distinctively trinitarian approaches to the theology of religions.[6] Dupuis, a Roman Catholic, and Heim, a Protestant, are both committed to the uniqueness and centrality of God's work of salvation in Jesus Christ. At the same time, they also share the conviction that the other religions have a positive place within the providence of God. Both argue that all religious traditions must be considered in their particularity and concreteness. Consistent with these emphases, both believe that a trinitarian understanding of God must be the doctrinal centerpiece of a Christian theology of the religions.

Under the influence of Karl Rahner, Dupuis builds on the achievements of Vatican II that recognized elements of truth and grace in the other religious traditions to an unprecedented degree. Whereas the Council of Florence in 1442 declared that all who are outside the Catholic Church—whether heathen, Jew, or unbeliever—will be consigned to the everlasting fire if they do not adhere to the church before they die, Vatican II acknowledged the rays of truth and the secret presence of God in the other religions. Yet Vatican II also affirmed that Jesus Christ is the fulfillment or definitive completion of all that is true and good in the world's religions.

After Vatican II, some Roman Catholic theologians have asked whether salvation might be mediated to non-Christians through their respective religious traditions, not in spite of them. Dupuis pursues this question further by asking what place the other religions have in God's overall plan of salvation. In responding to this question, Dupuis aims at "holding fast to faith in Jesus Christ as traditionally understood by mainstream Christianity" while at the same time assigning to other religious traditions "a positive role and significance in the overall plan of God for humankind, as it unfolds through salvation history."[7]

Dupuis thus emphasizes the constitutive and universal significance of what happened once and for all in Jesus Christ on the one hand and what the universal presence of the Word-to-become-flesh and the Spirit of God in persons, cultures, and religions is on the other. According to Dupuis, the Spirit's action is "unbound."[8] The work of the Spirit "spreads throughout the world, vivifying all things."[9] Acknowledging that the Spirit of God is at work in a special way in the church and its members, Dupuis nevertheless emphasizes that the same Spirit is universally present and active. The Spirit prepares for the event of Jesus Christ, enables believers to participate in his saving work, and is active both within and beyond the bounds of the church. Holding fast to the claim that the incarnation of the Word of God in Jesus Christ is decisive for salvation, Dupuis contends that this claim in no way contradicts "the universal presence and action of the Word and the Spirit."[10]

Dupuis emphatically distinguishes his position from a doctrine of God's saving grace that is centered on the Spirit separated from Christ. The universality of the work of the Spirit is understood as the Spirit's preceding, accompanying, and following the work of Christ. For Christian faith "the action of the Spirit and that of Jesus Christ, though distinct, are nevertheless complementary and inseparable."[11] From ancient times trinitarian doctrine has recognized this twofold activity of God by Word and Spirit. As the only Son of God, the work of Christ has constitutive saving significance for all of humanity. Without wishing to diminish this truth in the least, Dupuis contends that the Christ event does not "exhaust" God's saving power inasmuch as the eternal logos and the unbound Spirit are active both before and after the Incarnation.[12]

According to Dupuis, we must avoid both an abstract *pneumatocentrism* and an abstract *Christomonism*. The former separates the work of the Spirit from Christ, and the latter separates the work of Christ from the Spirit. We must not think of two independent or parallel economies of salvation. On the contrary, the work of Christ and the work of the Spirit are two inseparable and complementary aspects of the one economy of salvation of the one triune God. Dupuis favors the imagery of Irenaeus: Christ and the Spirit are the "two hands" of the triune God.[13]

Dupuis supports his argument by noting that for the biblical witness the covenants that God establishes with humanity are unified but take different historical forms. Dupuis appeals to Irenaeus's doctrine of God's four covenants (in Adam, in Noah, in Abraham and Moses, and in Jesus Christ) and lays particular emphasis on God's covenant with Noah, which he thinks has "far-reaching significance for a theology of the religious traditions of peoples belonging to the 'extra-biblical' tradition."[14] Dupuis further finds what he calls a "trinitarian rhythm" in all stages of the history of God's covenants with humanity. "Every divine covenant with humankind necessarily involves the active presence of God, of his Word, and of his Spirit."[15] We are, therefore, authorized to search for traces of the Trinity (*vestigia trinitatis*) in the religious life of individual persons and in religious traditions outside the biblical tradition.

For Dupuis, the actuality and legitimacy of religious pluralism rests neither simply on the plurality of persons in the one God nor on the plural character of created reality itself. Instead, it rests on "the superabundant richness and diversity of God's self-manifestations to humankind. . . . [It rests on] the immensity of a God who is love."[16] In God's providence and through the various religious traditions, all human beings tend to the ultimate goal of communion with the triune God.[17] Christ is the culminating point of the economy of salvation, but the grace and judgment of God are also present in the history of the religions. In particular, the work of the Spirit is indispensable in leading the world to its ultimate goal in Christ as well as in guiding believers into the riches of Christ.[18] Accordingly, Dupuis sees no contradiction between affirming both that the grace of God in Jesus Christ is "constitutive" for the salvation of all and that other religious traditions and their practices "can mediate secretly the grace offered by God in Jesus Christ and express the human response to God's gratuitous gift in him."[19]

Dupuis' proposal prompts many questions. One is whether his position bears many resemblances to Rahner's theory of *anonymous Christianity* despite Dupuis' acknowledgment of weighty criticisms of this theory. A related question is whether the project of a trinitarian theology of religions should not be more sharply distinguished from at least some versions of the heavily burdened doctrine of *vestigia trinitatis*. More promising, perhaps, is Dupuis' use of the Irenaean imagery of the "two hands" of God and his appeal to the trinitarian theology of Gregory of Nazianzus to describe the "trinitarian rhythm" of God's self-communication: but these ideas remain tantalizingly underdeveloped by Dupuis.

The questions raised by Dupuis' work converge on the issue of criteria. By what criteria are Christians to discern the secret grace of God in other religions? Dupuis expresses agreement with Hans Küng that congruence with the spirit of Jesus Christ and the presence of the gifts of the Spirit must be foremost among these criteria.[20] While Dupuis would no doubt understand his reference to the spirit of Jesus Christ to include the message of the cross, the importance of this topic for clarifying the Christian understanding of the identity of God is, in fact, surprisingly underdeveloped in Dupuis' discussion of specifically Christian criteria in the dialogue of Christianity and other religions.

Like Dupuis, Heim seeks to uphold the universal and constitutive significance of Jesus Christ for salvation while offering a theological rationale for attending to the particularity of the religious traditions and for affirming the work of God in them. Again like Dupuis, Heim sees the Trinity as the key to a Christian theology of the religions. Contending that a trinitarian inclusivism is the best alternative to a narrow exclusivism on the one hand and a relativistic pluralism on the other, Heim states, "The Trinity is Christianity's 'pluralistic theology.'"[21] He further argues that to some degree this has always been the case within the Christian theological tradition. At least implicitly, the doctrine of the Trinity has always provided the larger framework for thinking about other religions, whether in terms of a general revelation through creation (focus on the Father), of a universal presence and activity of God (focus on the Spirit), or of a hidden activity of the eternal Word incarnate in Jesus (focus on the Son). A trinitarian theology of the religions should recognize the validity of all three of these approaches.[22]

But Heim's trinitarian theology of the religions is distinctive. It focuses on the plurality of persons in the triune life and on their unity in communion. According to Heim, *salvation* is a distinctively Christian understanding of human fulfillment. The life of the triune God is in communion; and *salvation* is a tri-dimensional relationship of communion "with God, with other humans, and with the rest of creation."[23] Consistent with his emphasis on the distinctiveness of the Christian understanding of salvation, Heim argues that other religious traditions also have their own distinctive religious ends and that these too can be understood from a Christian perspective as rooted in the richness of the triune life. Because there is personal communion in difference within the triune unity, religions other than Christianity may offer ways to realize a particular dimension of the triune reality of God even if they do not offer the distinctively Christian understanding of salvation as participation in the triune life of communion. As Heim states, "Each religion's end involves relation to a particular aspect of the triune divine life."[24]

Accordingly, Heim contends that the inexhaustible plentitude of the triune God—the "depth of the riches" (as Paul would say) of the triune life—is the basis of a theology of religious pluralism.

A summary of the principles of Heim's trinitarian theology of the religions would include the following: the rich and diverse relationships within the triune life; God's universal saving will; the constitutive place of Christ as savior; and the freedom of persons to value the dimensions of divinity on their own terms and to select the human end they wish. By viewing the religions in this particular trinitarian framework, Heim can conclude that the plurality of religions belongs to the providential will of God. The religions offer an eternal pluralism of religious ends that befits the depth of the riches of the divine life and that honors the freedom of persons in their quest for fulfillment. At the same time, when seen from the vantage point of Christian faith, other religious traditions constitute penultimate paths to salvation in the distinctively Christian sense of communion with the triune God.

Heim's argument honors the value and integrity of different religious traditions and the need for "thick description" of their essential qualities; it also underscores the importance of the testimony of other religions for "internal Christian life."[25] Heim further contends that, far from undermining Christian mission and evangelism, his approach encourages greater clarity among Christians about the distinctive nature of the good news of salvation in Christ and strengthens the motivation to share the good news with others.

Perhaps the central questions raised by Heim's work are whether the idea of an eternal pluralism of religious ends is consistent with the unity of the triune life, whether the inclusivity of God's will to save (1 Tim. 2:4) is jeopardized or at least obscured, and whether the unity of humanity with its destiny is sufficiently acknowledged. In addition, Heim's argument for religious pluralism leans rather heavily on human autonomy and freedom of choice ("God allows each of us to become what we wish to become").[26] This emphasis stands in some tension with the biblical witness that consistently assigns priority to the freedom of God's grace in creation, revelation, and redemption. Another question is whether Heim's attempted justification of religious pluralism by appeal to the differences in the triune life of God is overly abstract. As already noted, for Dupuis, a trinitarian theology of the religions is anchored not directly in the plentitude of the divine life in itself but in the richness of the divine economy, in the wealth of God's covenantal engagements with the world.

Finally, the question of criteria looms large. Heim's theology of religious pluralism lifts up relationality and communion as important criteria of Christianity's self-definition and its assessment of other religious ends. Unfortunately, Heim does not sufficiently root these criteria in the economy of salvation centered in the ministry, crucifixion, and resurrection of Jesus Christ. The danger here is that talk of relationality and communion in the triune life may float free of the particularities of the self-communicating love of God in Jesus and in the outpouring of God's Spirit.

Dupuis's and Heim's proposals for a trinitarian approach to a theology of religions are still in process of development. In spite of the questions I have raised, I think their efforts offer important routes of exploration in this still mostly uncharted area of theological study. They both seek to avoid the sort of Christomonism that mostly ignores the triune reality of God just as they both try to avoid a vague and amorphous theocentrism. They both attempt to hold fast to the constitutive significance of the particular person and work of Jesus Christ for salvation while at the same time seeking solid trinitarian foundations for relating to other faith traditions with respect and openness. With their pioneering efforts as background, what follows are brief reflections on contributions that the trinitarian theology of Jürgen Moltmann might make to the development of a trinitarian theology of religions.

TRINITY, CROSS, AND THE RELIGIONS

Moltmann's theological journey has taken him down a long road "with many surprises and many bends."[27] Certain themes have nonetheless remained constant on this journey: the centrality of hope in the coming reign of God rooted in the divine promises to the elect people of Israel and ratified to the world in the resurrection of the crucified Jesus; the theology of the cross as the central criterion of Christian faith and life; the solidarity of God in Christ with the poor and the oppressed; the biblical story of the self-giving love of the triune God that defines the identity and purpose of God and provides the basis and norm of Christian faith and life; and the universal work of the Holy Spirit who is the life-giving, community-creative, and future-opening power of God.

If one surveys Moltmann's writings looking for a fully developed theology of the religions, one will be disappointed. Nowhere does he bring together the dominant themes of his theology to construct a full-scale theology of religious pluralism.

Consequently, it is not easy to bring his work into direct conversation with recent theologies of the religions such as those of Dupuis and Heim. Still, the distinctive themes of Moltmann's theology have important implications for a Christian theology of the religions. When gathered together, they comprise an identifiable approach to the reality of religious pluralism and to the difficulties and prospects of dialogue among the religions.

Moltmann's theological method is dialectical. He writes from an explicitly Christian faith perspective rooted in the biblical witness. At the same time he is remarkably open to the insights that come from diverse cultures and different areas of human experience. He understands the revelation of God attested in Scripture and the concrete life experiences of people as reciprocally related rather than mutually exclusive.[28] Moltmann's writings on the topic of Christianity and the other religions basically exhibit his characteristic dual concern for both Christian identity and contextual relevance. On the one hand, he rejects closed and domineering attitudes toward the *other*, including the religious *other*. On the other hand, he has no interest in locating a common essence of religion as a basis for interreligious dialogue. He calls for serious listening to and conversation with other religious traditions but at the same time warns of the danger of sacrificing or ignoring the distinctiveness of the Christian gospel under the pressure of a cultural or political ideology.

For Moltmann, the irreducible particularity of Christian faith and theology finds expression above all in the proclamation of Jesus Christ, the crucified and risen Lord; in the trinitarian understanding of God as an eternal communion of love whose history with the world is narrated in scripture and above all in the gospel story; and in the passionate and prophetic hope for the reconciliation of the nations and the redemption of the whole creation that the church shares with the messianic tradition of Israel.

Basic to Moltmann's trinitarian theology is that it is inseparable from the theology of the cross. As stated most eloquently in *The Crucified God*, the gospel narrative and its culmination in the crucifixion and resurrection of Christ drive inexorably to the trinitarian understanding of God as the history of the self-giving love of Father, Son, and Spirit. In Moltmann's formulation, the love of God, manifest supremely in the event of the cross, is the central content of the doctrine of the Trinity; and the doctrine of the Trinity is the form or comprehensive framework for understanding the event of the cross.[29] The triune God is the living God whose history of self-giving love embraces the whole of the groaning and yearning creation, struggles against the powers of sin and death, and opens the way to fullness of life in communion with God and others.

Moltmann's trinitarian history of God, centered in the ministry, crucifixion, and resurrection of Christ, forms the background and determines the direction of his understanding of Christianity's engagement with other religions. If the history of the triune God is cruciform and life-affirming, then Christians must also recognize the religions of the world as somehow included in this history. For Moltmann, the universal scope of the trinitarian history of God in no way lessens the uniqueness of the Christ event. He repeatedly emphasizes that the distinctively Christian understanding of God and salvation rests on the scandalous particularity of Christ and his cross. This scandal must not be downplayed in a Christian theology of the religions in order to conform to an ideology of pluralism or an anemic doctrine of tolerance. True dialogue among the religions does not rest on the discovery of a lowest common denominator. It rests instead on recognition of and respect for the particularity and integrity of the dialogue partners. Moltmann asks: "Can there be a Christianity without the cross? Islam without Shariah? Judaism without the Land?"[30] When pluralism becomes a form of reductionism and an ideologically driven disregard of the particularities of the religions, Moltmann rejects it because it offers not a real beginning but an abortive ending of honest dialogue.

The implications of a trinitarian theology of the cross for Christianity's engagement with other religions is perhaps most clearly stated in *The Church in the Power of the Spirit*. There Moltmann argues: "The right thing is not to carry on the dialogue according to superficial rules of communication, but to enter into it out of the depths of the understanding of God."[31] For Christian faith, the "depths" of God are decisively revealed in the event of the cross, in the self-giving love of the Son of God, in the Father's love that surrenders the Son, and in the life-giving love of the Spirit who comes from the Father and is sent by the Son. When the triune God is seen in this trinitarian history of self-giving love for the sake of the renewal of the world, it becomes clear that God is not an unchanging, apathetic, tyrannical deity but a God "who wins power in the world through the helplessness of his Son, who liberates through his self-giving, and whose strength is mighty in weakness."[32]

According to Moltmann, the openness and vulnerability of the triune God confessed by Christians should be reflected in the attitude they bring to their encounter with people of other faiths. Arrogance, aloofness, and fear have no place in the life and witness of Christians in their relationships to believers of other faiths or to nonbelievers. If they are true to the identity of the triune God known in Jesus Christ by the power of the Spirit, Christians will express openness and vulnerability to what is initially experienced as threatening, other, and alien. They will be willing to bear the otherness of the others without becoming defensive and hardening their hearts. "In that way we show God's passion through our living interest in the other. In that way we manifest God's vulnerability in the vulnerability of our love and our readiness for change."[33]

Moltmann's emphasis on the importance of respecting the otherness of the other in interreligious encounter rests neither on a modern doctrine of tolerance, nor on an abstract dialectic of identity and difference, nor on speculation about the copresence of unity and diversity in the triune life. Instead, it rests on the triune God's openness to and embrace of radical otherness—sinners and the lost—expressed in the entire ministry of Jesus and supremely in his crucifixion and resurrection. Thus, for Moltmann, the message of the cross is an essential aspect of any trinitarian theology of the religions that has to confront the confusion of power with domination present in all areas of human life, including the religious. Indeed, religious traditions have a disturbingly ambiguous history regarding attitudes toward the stranger and practices of violence toward the other.

TRINITY, REIGN OF GOD, AND THE RELIGIONS

Moltmann's trinitarian theology is not only a theology of the cross but also a messianic, eschatological theology. *Messianic*, as Moltmann uses the term, refers to "the promise of the Messiah in the Old Testament and the Jewish hope which is founded on the Hebrew Bible."[34] Christian hope in God's coming reign of freedom, justice, and peace in the whole creation is an heir of the messianic hope of Israel. For Moltmann messianic hope and the trinitarian understanding of God are interlocked. The triune God "realizes the kingdom of his glory in a history of creation, liberation, and glorification" that presses forward to the freedom of the children of God and the freedom of the whole creation.[35] In Jesus Christ, God has reconciled the world and has sent his life-giving Spirit as the firstfruits of the new creation, but the history of the triune God will come to its goal only with the final redemption and consummation of the creation. Christians are called to remember the activity of God in the past and to celebrate moments of the presence and renewal of life here and now by the power of the Spirit; but Christians primarily look forward. They live within a horizon of hope rooted in the promises of God to the people of Israel, decisively ratified in the proclamation, crucifixion, and resurrection of Jesus, and reconfirmed in the presence and activity of his world-renewing and future-opening Spirit of life.

A distinctive feature of Moltmann's theology of the trinitarian history of God is that the hope of the church and the hope of Israel are bound together. The church should recognize in Israel "its enduring origin, its partner in history, and its brother in hope."[36] There are, of course, important differences in the hope of Israel and the hope of the church. The church hopes for the return in glory of Jesus the crucified and risen Messiah. Israel hopes for the coming of the Messiah to redeem a still unredeemed world. In spite of these differences, the hopes of Israel and the church are not antithetical. In important ways they require each other. "Only in the eternal kingdom will the hopes of Israel and of the church be fulfilled. The promissory surplus of the Old Testament extends beyond the coming of Christ and of the Spirit and directs both toward God's future."[37]

In Moltmann's view, the resolution of the differences between the church and Israel cannot be reached on this side of the eschaton. Nevertheless, both church and Israel can acknowledge the necessity of their distinctive missions and can enter into cooperation in both theology and practice. God's covenant with Israel includes a great promise to the nations. The gospel of Jesus Christ opens this promise to all people. According to Moltmann, Israel and church together bear witness to the coming reign of God: "The theology of the kingdom of God in its complete scope and depth can be developed only in productive cooperation between Jews and Christians, between the church and Israel."[38] Moltmann further states that "in this process, neither Christians nor Jews will level their abiding differences, but rather will make full creative use of them. If both sides were to say the same thing, one would be superfluous."[39]

What Moltmann says of the relationship of church and Israel has an important bearing on his understanding of the relationship of Christianity and the other religions. On more than one occasion, Moltmann prefaces his discussion of the church's relationship to the other religions with a consideration of the church's indissoluble relationship to Israel. He would agree with Dupuis that the church's relationship with Israel, while unique, casts important light on the relationship of Christianity and the other religions. If the mission of the church includes the responsibility to be a bearer of the messianic hope of Israel to the nations, this responsibility has far-reaching ecclesiological and missiological implications.

One ecclesiological implication is that neither the state nor the church should be seen as the object of Christian hope. Neither church nor state is the instrument of the world's redemption. Rather, Christian hope is centered on the reign of God inaugurated in the ministry, death, and resurrection of Jesus Christ. God's reign is given provisional and anticipatory actualization here and now in the new beginnings of life by the power of the Holy Spirit. This life-giving work of the Spirit is not imprisoned in the church, but to say this is not to say that Moltmann's trinitarian theology of the reign of God is antichurch. When true to its calling, the church is a concrete witness to and an anticipatory presence of God's coming reign. This witness takes the form of the proclamation of the gospel, fellowship in faith, solidarity and loving service of those in need, and the planting of seeds of hope in God's coming reign. Because Christian theology is a theology of the coming reign of God and not simply a theology of the church, theology must be a public theology and not exclusively a church theology.

While Moltmann's theology of the coming reign of the triune God privileges Israel as Christianity's primary partner in interfaith dialogue, this privileging does not entail for him disinterest in, let alone hostility toward, other communities of faith. The point is that the church should constantly examine its relationships with other world religions in the light of its relationship with Israel. "The church's abiding origin in Israel, its permanent orientation to Israel's hope, Christianity's resulting special vocation to prepare the way for the coming kingdom in history—all this will give its stamp to the dialogue with the world religions."[40]

For Moltmann both Israel and the church, when faithful to their respective missions, become concrete yet provisional signs of God's reign in the world. Does Moltmann see the other religions as provisional signs of God's reign as well? In my judgment the answer to this question must be affirmative. It is consistent with

Moltmann's theology of the coming reign of God that other religious communities, as well as movements for justice and peace in secular society, can also be anticipatory signs or parables of the reign of God. They are so to the extent that they foster aspects of the fullness of life decisively made known in the gospel of Jesus Christ and manifest gifts of the Spirit of life that include commitment to justice and peace and resistance to the forces of violence and death in the world.

TRINITY, SPIRIT OF LIFE, AND THE RELIGIONS

If Moltmann's theology is both a trinitarian theology of the cross of Christ rooted in the gospel story and a trinitarian theology oriented to the future of God's reign of righteousness and peace throughout the creation, it must also be added that his trinitarian theology characteristically places special emphasis on the free activity and manifold gifts of the Holy Spirit. As is well known, Moltmann criticizes the tendencies in the Western theological tradition to subordinate the person and work of the Spirit. An important part of this critique is his rejection of the classical Western *filioque* doctrine that the Spirit proceeds from the Father "and from the Son." Moltmann places himself largely on the Eastern Orthodox side of this ancient debate, but he thinks both Eastern and Western churches should be able to agree on a substitute formulation, such as "the Spirit proceeds from the Father through the Son" or some similar mediating construction.

Moltmann's basic concern here is that the church free itself from the idea of an undialectical priority of the Son to the Spirit. Rather, Word and Spirit share full divinity with the Father and stand in reciprocal relationship with each other. Moltmann reads the biblical witness as giving abundant evidence of this reciprocity. On the one hand, the Spirit precedes and empowers the mission of Christ (Luke 4:18-21). On the other hand, Christ sends the Spirit to bear witness to him and to bring his work to completion (John 20:21-22).

Moltmann's theology of the Spirit is a thoroughly trinitarian pneumatology. The Spirit opens the eternal life of the triune God to the world. That the Trinity is an *open Trinity* means that the divine life has a surplus or overflow of love that gives life to creatures and enables them to become active participants in the triune life of love and the mission of God in the world.[41] Especially in *The Spirit of Life*, Moltmann attempts to retrieve an understanding of the Spirit as both the universal giver of life and the consummator of the redeeming work of Christ. According to Moltmann, a sound trinitarian pneumatology requires that proper attention be given both to the universal experience of the Spirit as the divine energy of life and to the work of the Spirit in the history of redemption centered in the incarnate Word. No economy of the Spirit is independent of the work of Christ; no economy of the Word is independent of the activity of the Spirit.

When the Spirit is viewed solely as the Spirit of redemption, pneumatology finds its location strictly in the church. In Moltmann's view, this location leads to a disastrous imprisonment of the Spirit. According to the witness of Scripture, the Spirit of God is free. The Spirit is universally present and active in the new creation of all things. Moreover, the Holy Spirit is more than simply the subjective side of the event of revelation, the primary role assigned to pneumatology in much modern theology. "The Holy Spirit is by no means merely a matter of revelation. It has to do with life and its source."[42] The Spirit of God is present both in the manifold sufferings of all creatures and in their hope for personal, communal, and cosmic transformation.

In the trinitarian history of God with the world, the Spirit is the giver of life, peace, and hope. The Spirit creates new life and enables its flourishing; brings hope in the midst of hopelessness; and establishes peace, justice, and harmony in the midst of division, injustice, and enmity. Glossing the Apostolic benediction, Moltmann writes that "'Community' seems to be the particular nature of the Holy Spirit and his creative energies, just as 'grace' determines the nature and specific action of the Son, and 'love' the nature and efficacy of the Father."[43]

The Trinity for Moltmann is divine life in communion. Father, Son, and Spirit abide and act in perichoretic union in a unique, mutually interpenetrating love that both distinguishes and unites. The perichoretic communion of the Trinity is the basis and goal of human life in relationship and community. We are created and redeemed for communion, and our life in relationship only becomes fully human as in some measure it corresponds to and participates in the communion of the triune life of God. Moltmann has applied the social trinitarian analogy primarily to various forms of human life in relationship and, in particular, to the communal life of the church. He has not, to my knowledge, used the triune life of God itself as a rationale for religious plurality nor invoked the triune life as a model of interreligious dialogue. One senses here a certain reserve in Moltmann's trinitarian theology in moving too directly from the perichoretic unity of the triune God to the complexities of interreligious dialogue.

Like his theology of the cross and his messianic eschatology, Moltmann's trinitarian pneumatology has implications for a theology of the religions. Stated briefly, Moltmann wants to place the question of the relationship of Christianity and the other religions in a strong trinitarian, christological, and pneumatological context. In his view the proper theological locus for understanding the plurality of the religions is neither the doctrine of original sin (where it was traditionally placed) nor the doctrine of revelation (where many modern theologians have dealt with it). For Moltmann, the proper locus is "*pneumatology*, and within pneumatology the doctrine of the *multiplicity of charismata*."[44] Moltmann explains:

Charisma is anything I can put into the service of building up the congregation and anything I can engage for the kingdom of God. . . . If the goal is not the church itself, but rather the kingdom of God, then anything commensurate with the righteousness and life of God can be taken along on this journey. Hence one can discover in other religions perspectives on the kingdom of God, on eternal life, and on the new earth, all of which are important for Christianity just as they are important for those other religions.[45]

For Moltmann, then, the real question posed by the plurality of the religions is neither whether other religions can be paths of salvation nor whether we may find an *anonymous Christianity* in other religious communities as Karl Rahner proposed. The important question is whether the presence of the Spirit of life can be discerned in the other religions. "*Missio Dei* means inviting all religious and non-religious persons to life, to an affirmation and guardianship of life. Anything that in other religions and cultures serves life in this sense is good, and must be appropriated into the 'culture of life.' Anything that hinders, destroys, or sacrifices life is bad, and must be overcome as the 'barbarism of death.' God's vivifying Spirit here is the beginning of the redemptive kingdom of God there."[46]

CONDITIONS OF INTERRELIGIOUS DIALOGUE

Moltmann, like Dupuis and Heim, emphasizes the particularity of the religions. All three agree that the religions are in important respects incommensurable. If we employed Knitter's typology, it would probably be best to understand all three as representatives of the *acceptance* model. Yet Moltmann would no doubt worry about the proximity of the term *acceptance* to the modern ideal of tolerance. Tolerance is far from enough.

While all three are trinitarian, Moltmann's theology, to a greater degree than Dupuis' and Heim's, displays his distinctive emphases on the centrality of the cross in his depiction of the work of God in the world, on the close relationship of church and Israel, on the messianic expectation of God's coming reign that church and Israel share, and on the universal activity of the life-giving Spirit of God. These emphases give Moltmann's approach to the theology of the religions a distinctive cast. Unlike Heim, Moltmann has not shown any interest in proposing the plenitude of the triune life of God in itself as a foundation and justification for the ultimate divergence of religious ends. Such an idea would not fit well with Moltmann's *universalist* way of thinking, his insistence on the coming reign of God as the transformation and renewal of all things. Here Moltmann's thinking seems closer to that of Dupuis's that also underscores the importance of the coming reign of God for the whole of creation and sees participation in the eternal triune life of love as the ultimate goal of all humanity. In addition, Moltmann shares with Dupuis the view that the relationship of Israel and the church has paradigmatic significance for the relationship of Christianity and the other religions. Moltmann shares with both Dupuis and Heim a strong practical orientation. All draw to some extent from the praxis method of liberation theology and would agree that a theology of the religions should not be produced in the abstract. It must be forged in concrete interaction and dialogue among the religions.

114

Again, like Dupuis and Heim, Moltmann is committed to dialogue. He has participated in many interreligious dialogues, has written much on the relationship of Jews and Christians, has engaged in conversations with Buddhists, and with Hans Küng has coedited a book on Christianity and Islam.[47] In Moltmann's judgement, "Truth is accessible to us only in dialogue with others."[48] Yet he also qualifies his commitment to dialogue because of its multiple meanings and forms. He observes that the modern program of interreligious dialogue has often been a fundamentally conservative program of reciprocal affirmation, lacking attention to the important critiques of religion found in such thinkers as Feuerbach, Marx, and Freud.[49] In contrast to uncritical understandings of dialogue, Moltmann holds that fruitful interreligious dialogue will be interested in the reform of the religions and not merely in their mutual affirmation.

By attending to whether Christianity and the other religions serve to guard and enhance life, Moltmann's view of the relationships of the religions emphasizes practice at least as much as doctrine. He explains that even where *direct dialogue* over doctrinal differences proves difficult, if not impossible, *indirect dialogue* can attempt to recognize common threats to the future of humanity (like nuclear weapons, destruction of the environment, and the neglect of the poor and the oppressed) and devise ways of cooperation. Here the questions become: "Which energies can these religions mobilize to avert these [mortal] dangers? What have the world religions done to destroy this world, and what can they do to save it? Where within these religions do we find life-negating and world-destructive forces, and how can these be changed into life-affirming, world-preserving forces?"[50] It is hypocritical for the religions to point their fingers at the outside world and see there the sources of misery, violence, and death. "Before religious communities can contribute something to world peace, they must themselves become religions of peace and overcome the invitation to enmity and the negation of enemies in their own traditions."[51]

As Moltmann sees the matter, several conditions will produce meaningful interreligious dialogue. First, "a life-threatening conflict must be present, a solution to which a dialogue offers hope."[52] He thinks that the life-threatening realities of our time are unmistakable. "Our common peril should force the religions of the world into dialogue: the nuclear threat, the ecological crisis, and the world's economic plight. The old liberal theology of pluralism, I fear, is based in the optimism of a pre-Hiroshima world. Today bringing about the unity of the world is not a metaphysical but a political question for all humanity."[53] For Moltmann, the urgency of dialogue among the religions today arises out of our present world crisis characterized by vicious circles of violence and death.

Moltmann's second condition is that "all participants must engage in the dialogue from within the context of their own faith or worldview" and must be responsible representatives of the communities for whom they speak.[54] Fruitful dialogue will not seek out the lowest common denominator but will recognize the real differences and particularities of the dialogue partners. As noted earlier, when speaking of the meeting of Christians and Jews, Moltmann states, "If both sides were to say the same thing, one would be superfluous." In relation to the particularity of the Christian faith tradition, he asks: "Can there be a Christianity without the cross?"

A third condition is that interreligious dialogue should be undertaken for the sake of truth that serves life, not simply for its own sake. The motivation should be to change the conditions that threaten life. Dialogue should aim at practical consequences. As the Marxist philosopher Roger Garaudy stated during the Christian-Marxist dialogues of the 1960s in which Moltmann was a prominent participant, the aim is to move "from anathema to dialogue, from dialogue to coexistence, and from coexistence to cooperation."[55]

Moltmann thinks of dialogue as a process of both giving and receiving. One cannot anticipate in advance what the primary questions will be or what one might receive from the dialogue. He thinks a theology of the religions would have to be shaped to a considerable extent by participation in the dialogue process itself. Yet Moltmann is no mere pragmatist. While the practical issue of the affirmation and enhancement of life is always important for him, he thinks that the task of critical engagement is an indispensable part of dialogue. The question of truth is always relevant. Of course, both sides should approach the other in a spirit of friendship, humility, openness, and receptivity; yet Christian theologians should not remain silent about the core affirmations of the Christian faith and the particular form of life and way of discipleship that are rooted in these affirmations. Christians will engage in testing other religious communities in the light of the gospel, even as Christians must be willing to have their doctrines and practices tested by others. For the Christian theologian in interreligious dialogue, important questions to be asked include these: What is compatible or incompatible with the gospel story of the crucified and risen Jesus Christ? What may challenge the church to recover forgotten or never before perceived dimensions of that story? What serves to deepen Christian hope in the consummation of God's coming reign? What helps to protect life and enables it to flourish? What opens new possibilities of a peaceful and just human community that offers parables or anticipations of the coming glorious reign of the triune God?

If Moltmann insists on rethinking the meaning of dialogue, he also insists on rethinking the meaning of mission. He refuses to choose between dialogue and mission. He calls for a better understanding of both. For Moltmann the goal of mission rightly understood is not the reestablishment of Christianity as the imperial religion, not the universal rule of the church, and not the saving of souls from the threatening judgment of God and the coming destruction of the world. Rather, mission is "the invitation to life," the "invitation to the future of God."[56] This invitation does not run roughshod over the religions and cultures of other peoples. Instead, it invites people of all religions to that life together that Christians speak of in the symbols of reign of God, eternal life, and a new creation of heaven and earth.

Moltmann summarizes his understanding of Christian mission as an invitation to life in this way:

> Human beings must be changed if the world is to be changed. If we want peace on earth, we must ourselves become peaceful human beings. If we want a future for our children and our children's children, then we must conquer our inertia and our egoism and be born anew to a living hope in the future. If life is to survive and mortal dangers be overcome, then faith must be awakened in us and others: a "faith that moves mountains." Unconditional love for life must be awakened in us, even for those assumed to be "superfluous." There is no future without hope. There is no life without love. There is no certitude without faith. It is the task of evangelism and the witness of Christian life to proclaim the living Christ and to awaken the Spirit of life.[57]

The only needed modification of Moltmann's summary is that politics and institutions must change as well as human beings. Equally urgent is the need for all religions to open themselves to renewal and reform. The religions must stand unequivocally for life. In the words of Jonathan Sachs, "When religion is invoked as a justification for conflict, religious voices must be raised in protest. We must withhold the robe of sanctity when it is sought as a cloak for violence and bloodshed."[58]

CHAPTER 10

BEYOND EXCLUSIVISM AND ABSOLUTISM

A Trinitarian Theology of the Cross

Ronald F. Thiemann

The cross is at the center of the Trinity. . . . No Trinity is conceivable without the Lamb, without the sacrifice of love, without the crucified Son.
　　　　　—The Trinity and the Kingdom: The Doctrine of God

If one conceives of the Trinity as an event of love in the suffering and the death of Jesus—and that is something which faith must do—then the Trinity is no self-contained group in heaven, but an eschatological process open for [all] on earth, which stems from the cross of Christ.
　　　　　—The Crucified God: The Cross of Christ as the Foundation
　　　　　　　　　　and Criticism of Christian Theology

One of the enduring contributions that Jürgen Moltmann has made to contemporary theology is his thoroughgoing integration of a *theologia crucis* (theology of the cross) into trinitarian reflection upon God. This bold and controversial effort to think through all aspects of Christian theology from the perspective of God's suffering in the cross of Christ has garnered both enthusiastic adherents and disdainful critics. Whether one finds Moltmann's trinitarian theology of the cross courageously innovative or dangerously speculative, his theology of the cross deserves serious engagement. While Moltmann developed his cruciform trinitarian thinking in the aftermath of the Holocaust and Hiroshima, his concern to put suffering at the center of Christian theological thinking takes on renewed importance in a world made more vulnerable in the aftermath of 9/11.

Moltmann's work draws upon a rich tradition of theological thinking about the Trinity, but his theology bears a particularly strong relation to the christocentric theologies of Martin Luther and Karl Barth. Like his forebears in the Reformation traditions, Moltmann seeks to reform Christian theological reflection through a consistent christological and soteriological focus on the reconciling work of God in the death and resurrection of Jesus Christ. In addition, he employs this christological and cruciform focus in strong political criticism of contemporary society. His thoroughgoing critique of political and clerical monotheism and their attendant forms of totalitarianism grows directly out of the christological and cruciological center of his theology, as does his critique of ecological destruction.

While many of Moltmann's strongest critics engage his radical reinterpretation of divine omnipotence or his apparent willingness to embrace *patripassionism*, his theology might just as easily be criticized for its exclusivist and absolutist christo-centrism. One might well ask whether a christological and cruciocentric theology, relying as it does on the most particular aspects of the Christian tradition, has continuing relevance in a religiously pluralistic and multifaith world. Can a trini-tarian theology of the cross possibly provide resources for critical engagement with religious pluralism and cultural diversity? Is such a theology inherently suspect because of its implicit commitment to Christian exclusivism and absolutism? Can a trinitarian theology of the cross retain its Christian particularism while still being genuinely open to the witness of other religions, including openness to their claims of truth?

In this chapter I explore the relation between a trinitarian theology of the cross and a Christian theology of religions, addressing the specific issue of whether claim-ing truth in Christianity can be construed in a way that distances the Christian tra-dition from its tendencies toward exclusivism and absolutism. Does a trinitarian theology of the cross possess resources for a Christian theology of religions that retains its particular Christian commitments while still being open to the differ-ent and even conflicting claims of other religious traditions to truth? I will not be developing or criticizing Moltmann's theological project in these reflections, but my own thinking remains indebted to his courageous and innovative struggle to integrate a theology of the cross into the heart of trinitarian theology. I understand my attempt to develop a Christian theology of religions out of the resources of a trinitarian theology of the cross as compatible with many of the deepest convic-tions of Moltmann's theology.

TRUTH AND JUSTIFICATION: AGAINST EXCLUSIVISM AND ABSOLUTISM

A common charge made against Christian doctrines of revelation is that they define truth as uniquely available to those who profess the Christian faith, thereby deny-ing access to truth to all those who do not confess the name of Christ. While these charges are most often directed against forms of Christian fundamentalism, they appear to apply equally to christocentric forms of theology, such as those advocated by Barth and Moltmann.

> Barth fumbles badly when he turns to the question of God's revelation other than
> that which is made known in Jesus Christ. . . . "That He is the one Word of God
> means further that His truth and prophecy cannot be combined with any other,

---

nor can it be enclosed with other words in a system superior to both Him and them." (CD IV/3, 100-101) . . . All other words, in fact, derive their truth only from the fact that the true Word indwells in them . . . [I]n Barth's analysis God is not finally free. . . . God stands limited in her freedom to one tradition born at one time and in one place in the world.[1]

The question to be explored in this chapter is whether a trinitarian theology of the cross can yield a Christian theology of religions that does not fall victim to *exclusivism* and *absolutism*.

Obviously, the first task facing this effort is to define the two terms *exclusivism* and *absolutism*. It is often difficult to fix precise meanings to these terms, since in the literature addressing Christianity and world religions, they are often used in various and rather loose ways. Exclusivism is, one of its opponents argues,

> a distortion of Christianity, resting on an exclusive claim by some Christians that theirs is the only "true" religion. . . . It is this sort of exclusivist claim that has been at the heart of much of the sorry Christian history of religious wars among Christians, crusades against Muslims, and continued persecution of Jews. . . . Unfortunately, the belief that one particular vision of Christianity can be equated with the one "true" Christianity has become deeply ingrained in American Christianity. . . . [I]t is likely that a majority of American Christians today still believe that "salvation" is possible only by faith in Jesus Christ. And for the most exclusionary, only a particular version of faith in Jesus Christ makes salvation possible.[2]

Clearly, a number of different claims are inherent in this statement about Christian exclusivism. According to the quoted passage, *exclusivism* seems to comprise at least the following claims: exclusivism asserts that Christianity is the only true religion; exclusivism leads to religious wars, crusades, and persecution; exclusivists identify true Christianity with "one particular vision of Christianity"; exclusivists believe that salvation is possible only by faith in Jesus Christ; exclusivists identify "only a particular version of faith in Jesus Christ" as enabling salvation.

Greater clarity is needed before we can assess the meaning and function of Christian *exclusivism*. Whether *exclusivism* has consequences, such as war, crusades, and persecution, can only be determined once we have precisely defined the phenomenon. Once we have defined *exclusivism* with precision, then we will able to see why and/or whether it leads to such terrible and tragic consequences. The assertions about *particularity* seem peculiar since claims to truth are necessarily particular, that is, about specific beliefs and objects of belief. There must be some special aspect of *particularity* that leads to the problems of *exclusivism*. The affirmation that salvation is possible only by faith in Jesus Christ is certainly a central claim of Christianity (*sola fide* is one of the fundamental principles of Reformation

120

Christianity); but clearly the term *only* can receive different construals, so this claim deserves our further attention. Indeed, the claims to *singularity* and the use of the term *only* seem to define the most troubling aspects of *exclusivism*. If Christians claim *Christ alone* as their source of salvation and reconciliation, is that affirmation inherently exclusivistic?

Some critics suggest that any assertion of singularity for one's own community necessarily entails the exclusion of other communities' claims to truth. Indeed, these critics often claim that religious pluralism undermines the very notion of truth-claiming in religion. Truth-claiming is, of course, an inherently exclusivist venture. To say something is true means that everything else that conflicts with that assertion must by definition be false. That is the meaning of *true*. Or, to put the matter differently: If I hold a belief to be true, I am thereby committed to denying the truth of beliefs that directly conflict with my own. That which conflicts with truth is by definition *false*. In this very restrictive and formal sense, then, truth is an absolute and exclusive concept.[3]

If one wants to maintain the place of claiming truth in religion as I do, then some assertions made by adherents of religious traditions will inevitably conflict with all other sentences that explicitly contradict those assertions. Surely the mere fact of claiming truth in religion cannot constitute exclusivism, at least not the sort that leads to wars, crusades, and persecution. The problem with Christian exclusivism in my judgment is not that it functions with a notion of truth that is exclusive, but that it *applies* the notion of truth incorrectly. In the first instance, truth is a property of propositions, beliefs, and assertions.[4] To say that something is "true" is to express commitment to the content of a proposition. What Elie Wiesel says about the evil of the persecution of Jews is true. In addition, however, to say something is *true* is to assert that "*it is the case that* the persecution of Jews is evil." "*S* is true if and only if *S*" is one standard way of expressing this second sense of the word *true*. Truth then is a property of propositions precisely when propositions correctly state "what is the case." In stating "what is the case," true propositions also contradict, or determine as false, propositions that directly conflict with true statements. To say that the sentence "The persecution of the Jews is evil" is true, is *necessarily* to assert that the sentence "The persecution of the Jews is good" is false. In that sense truth always excludes what is false. Our moral language could not function if that were not the case. If we are not to fall into a mindless and self-defeating form of relativism, we must acknowledge that true propositions do indeed exclude false propositions and their associated states of affairs.

Exclusivists are wrong, however, and dangerously so, because they take a notion of truth that belongs to propositions and their associated states of affairs and apply it to entire conceptual frameworks, worldviews, or religions. It would be impossible ever to gather together all the propositions within a worldview and show that without exception every proposition within it is true (or false). But that approach is the only intelligible way in which one can apply the notion of *truth* to a religion or comprehensive scheme, i.e., to the entire set of propositions comprised within that conceptual framework. The problem with many exclusivists is that they apply the term *true* to their entire framework and then believe that they have the warrant to dismiss all other frameworks as false as well. It is precisely this double intellectual and moral mistake that leads so easily to fanaticism.[5]

Another equally important issue for any Christian theology of religions is that of *absolutism*. If *exclusivism* is the form fanaticism takes with reference to truth, *absolutism* is the form fanaticism takes with reference to justification. *Justification*, in the sense I am using it here, refers to the way in which we argue in support of our beliefs and the manner in which we adduce reasons in favor of our commitments. Absolutists believe that they have indubitable grounds for their statements of religious faith. Often they appeal to revelation or doctrines of inspiration, inerrancy, and/or infallibility to support their claims to indubitability. It is precisely this conviction about the infallibility of Christian beliefs that breeds the attitude of arrogance and disdain that characterizes far too many Christians today. I have argued at length in earlier writings against this notion of *epistemological foundationalism* on both philosophical and theological grounds.[6] *Foundationalism*, especially in its Christian theological form, is deeply incompatible with religious pluralism and leads almost inevitably to the exclusivism that we should rightly excoriate.

We must be careful, once more, to develop precision in the argument against *absolutism*. Absolutist claims assert indubitability based on the self-evident, revelatory grounds adduced for those claims. Certain sentences are indubitable because the grounds for those claims are derived from the self-evidence of divine revelation.[7] In opposing absolutism one need oppose neither claims to revelation[8] nor strongly held robust truth-claims.[9] Absolutism grounded in a foundationalist epistemology cannot ultimately be given self-consistent formulation. The foundationalist asserts that true claims must be justified through an appeal to self-evident and incorrigible grounds but can adduce no such grounds for the foundationalist thesis itself. The claim that all rationally justified beliefs must ultimately be grounded in self-evident and incorrigible evidence cannot itself be justified by such evidence; thus, on its own account of rational justification, the foundationalist claim is found wanting. Wilfred Sellars identifies this problem as "the myth of the given" and develops an inconsistent triad to show the inability of foundationalist positions to be given self-consistent articulation.[10] Donald Davidson develops these ideas further to suggest that the epistemic division between scheme and content cannot itself be sustained.[11] In the light of such strong anti-foundationalist arguments, a consensus has formed within much theology and philosophy that absolutist claims grounded in foundational epistemologies simply cannot be sustained. Nonetheless, in practice many Christians and Christian communities continue to employ foundationalist, absolutist understandings of their doctrines of revelation. Many believe that without such assertions of indubitable foundations, Christian claims to truth lack their grounding in the revelation of God; thus, foundationalist accounts of revelation have shown remarkable resilience in the face of philosophical and theological critique.

If, however, one is convinced by the anti-foundationalist critique, what becomes of Christian claims to truth? Once the foundationalist basis for absolutism has been swept away, what remains then for the Christian adherent to assert? Does the fall of absolutism require the embrace of relativism? Do Christian theological assertions now reside in a realm where skepticism and even nihilism threaten the truth status of those claims? Such worries exemplify what Richard Bernstein has termed *the Cartesian anxiety*, that "grand and seductive Either/Or," meaning that "*Either* there is some fixed foundation for our knowledge *or* we cannot escape the forces of darkness that envelop us with madness, with intellectual and moral chaos."[12] The demise of foundationalism and its associated demons, exclusivism and absolutism, by no means entails the demise of robust truth-claiming in theology. The challenge remains, however, to show how nonexclusivist and nonabsolutist (but also nonrelativist) truth claims can be sustained in a religiously plural context.

A Trinitarian Theology of the Cross and Religious Pluralism

At stake here is the question of whether there is compatibility between deep and abiding commitment to the claims of truth in one's tradition and an openness to and respect for the claims of another tradition. In the remainder of this chapter, I argue that claims of truth and an acceptance of religious pluralism are not inconsistent. Nicolas Rescher has stated this issue with special eloquence:

> Pluralism holds that it is rationally intelligible and acceptable that others can hold positions at variance with one's own. But it does not maintain that a given individual need endorse a plurality of positions—that the fact that others hold a certain position somehow constitutes a reason for doing so oneself. . . .Pluralism is a feature of the collective group; it turns on the fact that different experiences engender different views. But from the standpoint of the individual this cuts no ice. We have no alternative to proceeding as best we can on the basis of what is available to us. That others agree with us is not proof of correctness; that they disagree, no sign of error.[13]

Fundamental to the acceptance of pluralism is the conviction that we have no self-evident, incorrigible means of establishing the truth of our positions. Thus, the same grounds that lead us to reject foundationalist absolutism also make it possible for us to embrace pluralism. That we have no way at all to establish the truth of our assertions does not follow; however, the means at our disposal will not necessarily convince those with whom we disagree. Consequently, we must hold open the possibility that those who disagree with us do so rationally. This position implies neither relativism nor indifferentism to truth but simply suggests that we cannot coerce others into believing as we do. We can offer our reasons for so believing; but these reasons, even if sufficient to support our claims, will not compel others to accept our beliefs. Thus, now we need to turn to a consideration of those "reasons for so believing" and an assessment of whether such beliefs can be formulated so as to avoid the twin dangers of exclusivism and absolutism.

Ludwig Wittgenstein has taught us that "the meaning of a word is its use in the language."[14] If you want to find meaning, look to use. If you want to find the meaning of beliefs, in this case Christian claims about truth, then you need to see how those beliefs are used in the context of Christian practice. I agree with George Lindbeck's argument:

> Christian ontological truth-claims [are made] in the activities of adoration, proclamation, obedience, promise-hearing and promise-keeping which shape individuals and communities into conformity with Christ. . . . Truth and falsity characterize ordinary religious language when it is used to mold lives through prayer, praise, and exhortation. It is only on this level that human beings linguistically exhibit their truth or falsity, their correspondence or lack of correspondence to the Ultimate Mystery.[15]

Christian truth claims are located within the complex web of beliefs and practices that constitute the Christian community. Christian identity is shaped and nurtured by belief-ful participation in the communal life of Christianity. While truth claims can be found throughout the Christian web of belief, some beliefs and practices are clearly more decisive for Christian identity than others. Beliefs that are decisive for forming and maintaining Christian communal identity might be called *fundamental beliefs*.[16] If they were discarded or radically changed, these beliefs would so fundamentally alter the identity of the community that it would no longer be recognizable as Christian. Or to put it another way, these are beliefs that the community should be least willing to discard in face of opposition or adversity; for if they were discarded, it would become unclear whether the community would remain any longer in significant continuity with the historic Christian tradition.

Bruce Marshall has introduced the helpful language of *epistemic primacy* to identify the function of fundamental beliefs when faced with conflicting or incompatible beliefs.

> [A] community regards belief A as central with respect to belief B if and only if, should conflict arise between A and B, the community persists in holding A true, and rejects or modifies B. But this is simply to say that the community regards A as a criterion for deciding about the truth of B. Faced with the incompatibility of the two beliefs—that is, the inconsistency which belongs to logical contradictions—it

holds A true, and finds that it must therefore hold B false. The community, we can say, regards A as *epistemically primary* with respect to B.[17]

The beliefs that the Christian community holds as epistemically primary include christological and trinitarian beliefs that Jürgen Moltmann has so vigorously defended as constituting the heart of the Christian vision through the assertion that the cross is at the center of the Trinity. Indeed, the claim that in the death and resurrection of Jesus Christ, the truth about the relation between the triune God and the cosmos has been revealed is the most central and fundamental claim of the Christian faith.[18] Can such a fundamental, identity-shaping, epistemically primary belief be compatible with religious pluralism? Can a trinitarian theology of the cross be developed in such a way as to avoid the dangers of exclusivism and absolutism? What might a Christian theology of religions focused on a trinitarian theology of the cross look like? To that question we now turn.

I believe that the appropriate goal of a Christian theology of religions is to understand those religions in and for themselves and to give an account of the grounds within Christian theology itself for being open to the witness of truth that might come from carefully listening to those religions. Careful listening done in a respectful manner requires a genuine openness to the claims of other religions, an openness that does not prejudge whether those claims confirm, conflict with, or simply differ from the Christian witness. Genuine respect for the religious Other requires Christians to hold open the manifold possibilities that might emerge from genuine interreligious dialogue and mutual examination. Generalizations about the truth of all religions seem no more plausible than generalizations about the falsity of all religions. Genuine respect for the religious Other requires, in my estimation, holding open the possibility that claims of the Other might be true, false, relevant, irrelevant, wise, or foolish. Empty generalizations about the necessary truth within the Other is no more respectful (though probably considerably less dangerous) than empty generalizations about the falsity of the religious Other.[19]

Rather than seeking grounds within the Christian faith that the Other is necessarily in possession of the truth or has necessarily embraced the One or the Way, Christian theology should simply give the grounds within the Christian faith for a respectful hearing of the Other that might alert us to claims of truth should we encounter them in the witness of other religions. I believe that the grounds for this openness are found at the heart of Christian trinitarian and christological doctrine. Thus, a Christian theology of religions, modest though it may be,[20] should emerge from the very heart of the Christian witness to the triune God revealed in the person and work of Jesus Christ.

Martin Luther has given the classic statement of *theologia crucis*:

He deserves to be called a theologian . . . who comprehends the visible and manifest things of God, seen through suffering and the cross. The "back" and visible things of God are placed in opposition to the invisible, namely, his human nature, weakness, and foolishness. . . . Now it is not sufficient for anyone, and it does him no good to recognize God in his glory and majesty, unless he recognizes him in the humility and shame of the cross. . . . For this reason true theology and recognition of God are in the crucified Christ. . . . He who does not know Christ does not know God hidden in suffering. . . . God can be found only in suffering and the cross.[21]

Christian doctrines of God's triune reality have traditionally asserted a dialectical relationship between the apophatic and cataphatic aspects of God's revelation. While some theologians stress the mystery at the heart of God and others emphasize the genuine availability of God's revelation to human knowing, all such doctrines claim a complex relation between God's hiddenness and revelation. Even Karl Barth, the great Protestant theologian of revelation, emphasizes God's inescapable hiddenness. For Barth, God is fundamentally defined as the "One Who Loves in Freedom."[22] For Barth, God's freedom is never *absolute freedom*; rather, it is the freedom of divine self-determination. The wonder of grace is that God uses that unconstrained self-determination to bind Godself eternally to human beings through the person of Jesus Christ. This act of binding does not constrain God's freedom, because God freely determined so to bind Godself. To suggest, as Joseph Hough does in his criticism of Barth quoted earlier in this chapter, that general notions of *absolute freedom* or *absolute sovereignty* are superior to the free self-determination by which God binds God's very being-in-act to the created world in Jesus Christ is to strike at the very heart of the Christian gospel. Understanding God's freedom as the self-determination by which God identifies with the human condition in Christ is not, I would argue, a denial of God's freedom but an affirmation of God's freedom under the conditions of a *theologia crucis*.

As one who stands in the tradition of theologians of the cross, Barth claims simultaneously that God has bound Godself eternally in Jesus Christ, is thereby available to be known by us, and remains sovereign Lord always and everywhere in control of God's own self-revelation. Finally, God's self-revelation is nothing more or less than the presence of God among us, Immanuel, the divine in human flesh; but the encounter with God's revelation is always itself an "event," an act in which God remains solely in control of God's own self-disclosure. Thus, while we do have confidence that God is truly present for us in Jesus Christ, we must recognize that God's presence always exceeds any ability we might have for knowing or grasping it. God's mystery is every bit as much a part of God's self-giving in Jesus Christ as is God's self-revelation. Consequently, a genuine modesty about what we claim to know must be yoked to an appropriate confidence that we do, nonetheless, genuinely know God in the person of Jesus Christ. Barth is characteristically better at asserting confidence than modesty, but both are an essential part of his doctrine of God.

Nonetheless, one can work within the context of a doctrine of God like Barth's and have ample grounds for asserting the continuing majesty of God's self-giving, a majesty that relies always and only on God's self-determination and never on our feeble attempts to understand. Only the scope of God's own unconstrained self-determination limits the scope and availability of God's self-revelation.

Other grounds, more centrally christological, assert Christian openness to the witness to truth within other religions.

> The Almighty exists and acts and speaks here in the form of One who is weak and impotent, the eternal as One who is temporal and perishing, the Most High in the deepest humility. The Holy One stands in the place and under the accusation of a sinner with other sinners. The glorious one is covered with shame. The One who lives forever has fallen prey to death. The Creator is subjected to and overcome by the onslaught of that which is not. In short, the Lord is a servant, a slave.[23]

At the heart of the Gospel narratives is a controversy concerning the identity of Jesus Christ. In the Synoptic Gospels, those closest to Jesus regularly misidentify him. I have shown in previous work how the Gospel of Matthew is structured around the distinction between *disciples* (*mathētēs*) and *those who follow* (*akolouthein* and its variations).[24] Often the disciples are physically in close proximity to Jesus, yet they often misunderstand his words and actions. An epithet Jesus uses of the disciples on a number of occasions in the narrative is "those of little faith" (*oligopistoi*). The ones who most often recognize Jesus' true identity are apparently minor characters in the stories: a leper, a Roman centurion, the Gadarene demoniacs, a paralytic, a hemorrhaging woman, two blind men, a Canaanite woman, and the centurion at the foot of the cross. Within the passion narrative itself the only true followers, the ones who recognize that Jesus' mission and ministry must follow the road to crucifixion, are Joseph of Arimathea and, most important, Jesus' female followers. So the Gospels themselves witness to the fact that Jesus' own identity is most likely to be recognized by those who live on the boundaries, beyond the pale, and on the margins. These stories give no support to those who would assert that *insiders* have a unique and incorrigible grasp of the Gospels' truth. On the contrary, those who are apparent *outsiders* recognize Jesus' identity and thereby witness to the truth.[25] *Mutatis mutandis* we should hardly be surprised if, in our own times, authentic witness to the truth comes not from those who are the apparent insiders within Christianity, but precisely from those religious others who too often have been consigned a place beyond the pale of truth but may in fact be carriers of it.[26]

Finally, the fundamental drama at the heart of the Christian story gives the strongest warrant for Christian openness to the witness to truth of other religious traditions. Christianity basically claims that the truth about God and the world is to be found in the story of the execution of a political prisoner at the hands of the

Romans. This itinerant preacher who now becomes the crucified victim of the state is, nonetheless, declared by Christians to reveal the loving being of God. Moreover, Christians further assert that this crucified man now lives through the resurrecting power of God—that the one who died by crucifixion now lives as exalted Lord of the universe. In its more radical christological traditions, Christianity claims that in the death of Jesus Christ, God engaged in a remarkable exchange, that in Jesus' death God became a curse for us in order that we might become righteous like God.[27] Even more astounding is that Christians go on to claim that through this extraordinary act of exchange God takes on our fate, the destiny of death, and transforms it into life everlasting in God's own presence.

Now if ever there were a religion founded upon a series of counterintuitive, some might say paradoxical, claims, it is surely Christianity. No simple act of reason can possibly incline Christian believers to commit themselves to the belief that Jesus the crucified now lives and that we, too, will live in him. Such a commitment entails an act of faith that contradicts ordinary experience concerning the finality of death. That is why Christians confess in the words of the book of Hebrews that "faith is the substance of things hoped for, the evidence of things not seen" (Heb. 11:1). That is why Christians confess with St. Paul that "now we see in a mirror, dimly" (1 Cor. 13:12) and cannot know with absolute certainty that the path of discipleship leads to its promised end. Still believers follow on in hope, awaiting that day when "we will see face to face" (1 Cor. 13:12). But for now, Christians have only faith, the demands of discipleship, and the beckoning presence of one who bids us to come and follow. For some, that faith, those demands, and that presence are enough.

Such following in faith, hope, and love should instill an attitude of modesty, humility, and gratitude. Far from grasping the truth and extolling the sufficiency and finality of the Christian revelation, followers of the cross recognize that in Luther's words, God always reveals Godself *sub contrario* (under God's opposite). Faith in the Christian gospel yields a *theologia crucis* (a theology of the cross) that seeks the truth of God's revelation wherever the loving self-determining God seeks to make Godself known. The path of Christian discipleship is one of hopeful following; the life of Christian discipleship is one of loving commitment to the neighbor in need. The theological virtues of faith, hope, and love ought thus to quicken the Christian's awareness of the manifold sources of God's glorious and gracious self-revelation. Knowing God as we do in Jesus Christ, Christians should be the first to acknowledge that God's self-revelation, indeed, appears in some surprising places.

Not only does the Christian gospel make no a priori denial of the possibility of God's self-revelation to persons in different times and places, it alerts Christians to the continuous possibility that God's revelation is likely to appear where we least expect it. In order to recognize such moments, we must engage in careful and modest listening to the religious Other, neither consigning the Other to eternal perdition nor claiming without careful examination that the Other has found the Way or the Truth. Listening carefully and making modest, careful, and thoughtful judgments about truth and falsity is the best way to be faithful to the Christian gospel and to respect the freedom and integrity of the religious Other. Through that process a genuine Christian theology of religions might finally emerge.

Part THREE

TRINITY
AND GOD-TALK

CHAPTER II

THE TRINITY AND GENDER RECONSIDERED

Sarah A. Coakley

Oone of the less celebrated dimensions of Jürgen Moltmann's thought as a systematic theologian is the significance that he has granted the category of gender, not only in the anthropological realm but also increasingly over the years in relation to his doctrine of God.[1] Moltmann's distinctive treatment of the theme of gender has attracted interest, as one might expect, from a variety of feminist theologians;[2] but it is doubtful whether other (malestream) theologians who comment on his work have taken these strands in his thought with adequate seriousness. Considerably more forward-looking than many of his followers in this sense, Moltmann has been a forerunner whom few have dared, or wanted, to emulate (and perhaps especially in the German context). Moltmann himself, with characteristic honesty and self-effacement, insists that his insights in this area could not have arisen without the all-important influence of his wife, Elisabeth Moltmann-Wendel.[3] Indeed, the gender themes, in particular, that are woven into his celebrated trinitarian theology are almost certainly the direct result of his cooperative work with her.[4] To laud him, therefore, for his pioneering undertakings in this regard is to laud them both: without their combined effort, we would not have the example of a world-class theological endeavor granting fundamental, and not merely peripheral, significance to gender as a matter intrinsic to the systematic task. Together they have made gender a new doctrinal *locus*, we might say.

In offering the Moltmanns this *Laudatio*, therefore, I first of all want to thank them for this prophetic move, one that (alas, even now) cannot yet be assumed to have left a permanent mark on the project of systematics. I want to recapitulate then, briefly and succinctly, the main points at which Jürgen Moltmann (as I read him) sees gender to have a form of paradigmatic standing in inner-trinitarian relations. I shall highlight here, in particular, the chief points at which "masculinity" and "femininity" (so-called) are said by Moltmann to be encoded in the *hypostatic* existence of the divine "persons" and their *perichoretic* interaction; but I shall then query the extent to which these gender ascriptions are fully compatible with what the Moltmanns write elsewhere about gender stereotyping and its cultural dangers. (This task will necessarily involve some brief reflection on the age-old question of how God-talk can be related—whether analogically or metaphorically—to our other human forms of linguistic interaction.) From here I shall move, finally, to my own systematic proposal—a suggestion for a rather different sort of grounding of gender in God than that suggested by the Moltmanns. I shall here argue that feminist theology up to now has been unduly influenced by secular theories of gender, theories that are then either wielded critically against the Christian tradition or smuggled in some form into the Christian doctrinal corpus (or both). This double ploy is certainly not without illuminating results and is also evident in the Moltmanns' work. However, I shall propose, in contrast, an alternative, and more radical, solution: that of construing "gender" *theologically* from the outset and precisely out of the resources of trinitarian and incarnational thought. Such an approach, I shall suggest, reveals "gender" as ultimately fluid, or labile, to a more fundamental category—that of divine "desire" (a "desire," however, not of lack but of loving plenitude). To make oneself radically subject to such desire, however, involves a profound rupture of the world's expectations of gender—more profound, I shall argue, than the Moltmanns have suggested up till now. I shall end by indicating more precisely where my proposal still links with the Moltmanns' theological goals, even as it departs from their particular mode of gender ascription. I trust it will be clear all along that this critique and extension of the Moltmanns' rendition of the theme of God and gender is offered to them both (with warmest salutation and admiration) for their own critical review and response.

WHERE IS GENDER IN GOD?

The question with which we start is one that Jürgen Moltmann is fully aware has many potential pitfalls and traps for the unwary.[5] How are we to speak of "gender" at all in relation to God, given that God, *qua God*, has no body? Indeed, is the question proper at all in purely theistic terms? How does the human (male) body of Jesus, as *hypostatically* conjoined with the Word, the second person of the Trinity, relate to, or give substance to, the question of gender in God? How are we to negotiate the difference between gender stereotypes in a fallen world and "gender" as it might potentially be construed in some perfect form in God? More fundamentally, how are we to define, or think of, "gender" in the first place, especially in relation to, or in distinction from, the physiological or chromosomal differentiations of "sex"?

This last and basic question is a crucial one to be faced at the outset; it is also a question that in recent years has been subject to notable swings of fashion, particularly in the United States, as successive waves of gender theory have come to the fore and dominated discussion.[6] Further (as I know only too well as one who lives perennially in two cultures, American and European), the cultural overtones of the words "gender," "sex," "sexuality," "femininity," and "masculinity" are simply not the same even in British and American English, let alone in German, French, or Italian. Gaining cross-cultural clarification of these terms semantically is a task of some subtlety, the more so because it is inextricably entangled with implicit questions of theory (or ideology) about their proper relation to one another. If we then add to the mix the specifically *theological* question of how "gender" relates to God (whether ontologically in some sense, or merely by verbal ascription), we have a multilayered complex of problems. It is the systematic theologian's task to address these problems and clarify them.

I must say here at the outset that I am not wholly convinced that Jürgen Moltmann has untangled this problematic theoretical knot to my satisfaction. To my knowledge, he has never given a precise analytic account of the relation of the terms "gender," "sex," or "sexuality"; and he sometimes uses the terms "feminine"/ "femininity" and "masculine"/"masculinity" as if they had natural or obvious cultural associations that are unproblematic.[7] At the same time, he will equally often expatiate on the deep problems, both cultural and psychological, that the burden of *damaging* gender stereotypes has caused for men as well as women.[8] On the one hand, then, we find in his work an acute critique of the distorting potential, at the anthropological level, of what we might call "fallen" gender prescriptions; but we also have a remaining sense that "gender" (*qua* mode of differentiated relationship)[9] is distilled in a binary of "femininity" and "masculinity" that is not intrinsically problematic, as long as rightly construed and leading to justice, mutuality, and wholeness.[10] (Indeed, reference to the complementarity of genders is not absent from Moltmann's repertoire, along with positive allusions to a "feminine principle" that must be accommodated for such a balance to occur.)[11] Finally, then, when he comes to the metaphysical question of God and gender, Moltmann rightly expostulates against the naïve feminist claim that all that is needed is some (Feuerbachian) projection of motherhood into the image of God, a straightforward reversal of the pathology of patriarchy:

> if men call God "Father" in order to be able to find an identity and now women call God "Mother" in order to discover themselves in religious terms, what would donkeys call God? Is the Godhead just a screen for all possible projections, with the slogan "What's your fancy?" Is Christian faith a religious supermarket?[12]

However, it is to be wondered—I suggest—to what extent Moltmann has fully guarded against his own critique on this front. Let me now explain by indicating the two vital places that gender features in his mature trinitarianism.

Key to Moltmann's whole trinitarian theology is the idea that "the Trinity is our social programme."[13] For trinitarianism (properly understood as perfect divine relationship in "community")[14] is deemed to be the means of overcoming "patriar-chal monotheism," a perversion that according to Moltmann arose from "Roman" thought and has particularly afflicted Western trinitarianism.[15] How then does gen-der enter into (or, better, constitute part of the eternal reality of) the life of the Trinity? Seemingly, it does so in two ways, as Moltmann sees it.

First, the so-called "feminine principle" at the divine level is above all accom-modated in the form of the person of the Holy Spirit (as divine "Mother"). Indeed, Moltmann goes so far as to say at one point that it is *only* possible to understand the "social" nature of the Trinity if the "femininity"/"Motherhood of the Spirit" is recognized:

> [The] discovery of the Motherhood of the Holy Spirit leads to a social understanding
> of the image of God. To express that in the opposite way, it will be possible to arrive
> at a real social understanding of the image of God only when the feminine character
> of the Spirit is recognized. This is not simply a matter of changing metaphors; it
> concerns, far more, the restitution of femininity in the dignity of the image of
> God. Only then will also actual masculinity be seen in its original dignity, and this
> masculinity will no longer appear with the distorting character of domination.[16]

Crucial here is Moltmann's reading of the significance of Genesis 1:26-27 for human gender and the *imago dei* implanted in it: only as two (v. 27), fully "equal" before God yet also differentiated, is humanity reflective of God's glory.[17] In this sense the binary of gender is indeed a manifestation of the being of God; and so too, in Godself, we expect to find both "masculinity" and "femininity," he claims. Thus, to speak of the Spirit as "Mother" (in the tradition of the Syriac fathers, as rein-stated by Count Zinzendorf and the Moravian Brethren and to whom Moltmann makes constant allusion)[18] is not to embrace straightforwardly a "matriarchy," nor yet, supposedly, merely to plaster a new metaphor into the collage of acceptable projections (*à la* Feuerbach), but rather to speak *truly* of God's reality, as bringer of a new "messianic community" of "free" and "equal" people.[19] Although this may suggest an overcoming, or erasure, of the gender binary, Moltmann will speak as if "masculine" and "feminine" dimensions in God mutually balance one another *hypostatically*; and unlike his wife, Elisabeth, who includes this topic at one point in her writing,[20] he will not choose to describe the Son in any sense as "feminine" too, but rather speaks of Word and Spirit as "complementary" to one another.[21]

The motherhood of the Spirit, then, is definitely the chief locus at which "femininity" is accommodated into the Trinity, according to Moltmann. The sec-ond place is not in the person of Christ per se, but in the *relation* between Father and Son. Here we are in the heart of the distinctive and controversial trinitarian-ism of the cross that Moltmann originally outlined in *The Crucified God* but later supplemented with a particular gender gloss. What was described in *The Crucified God* as a relationship of "mutual surrender" or of Father and Son "surrendering themselves" in abandonment, "though not in the same way," is, in an important later essay, expressed in terms of the Father's "motherliness."[22] Here is a Father, according to Moltmann, who both "begets" and "gives birth," whose omnipotence is the power not of "monarchical" authority but of "suffering love."[23] Elsewhere, Moltmann—evidently now aware that to call the Father motherly could be seen merely as a *co-option* of motherhood into patriarchy—speaks of the Father being just as much a "fatherly mother" as a "motherly father"[24]; so the striking oxymoronic phrase of the Council of Toledo (675) that the Son "came forth from the womb of the Father" is precisely an indication for Moltmann of how gender is, in some significant way, recast in and through the Trinity: God, he says, becomes "bisexual or transsexual."[25]

Underlying this approach is a strong, Barthian conviction (very far, though, from Barth's own biblical view of gender!) that the Trinity entirely recasts a pre-Christian, or philosophical, notion of God's power:

> Belief in God the Father starts from recognition of the Son, not from God's omnipotence and creation. . . . Through the doctrine of the Trinity God's name "Father" is indissolubly linked to Jesus the Son. The doctrine of the Trinity does not deify Christ but "christifies" God, because it pulls the Father into the life-story of the Son.[26]

Thus, according to Moltmann, we can rightly talk of *trinitarian* "Fatherhood" in a mode that is "literal" because it appropriately describes a true divine Fatherhood that is motherly—loving, compassionate, pitying—a Fatherhood of the Son in and through the Spirit.[27] This "literal" (because truly "generative")[28] ascription of "Fatherhood" is to be contrasted with a merely "metaphorical" rendition of the same title, which in Moltmann's understanding is at best about "kindly rule," but has all the underlying "monarchical" assumptions of "patriarchy."[29]

We have seen, then, how, in at least three ways, Moltmann's understanding of gender-in-God is purportedly *distinguished* from gender as entertained in the world. First, and most important, it is gender found in the trinitarian God, which (it is argued) will not allow the repressive mechanisms of patriarchy: it must be a vision of gender guaranteeing compassion, mutuality, and equality. Second, it is a view of gender that is supported by a particular view of religious language: true, divine Fatherhood is motherly, and this we can take as "literal" (by which Moltmann evidently means—in Thomistic mode—as true, or appropriate, rather than univocal with other human Father ascriptions). "Metaphorical" talk of God is, in contrast, seen as projective in the Feuerbachian sense and thus as inherently tending to idolatry.[30] Third (although this is only a minor and undeveloped strand in Moltmann's full braid of arguments about gender), gender in God does not merely *re-exemplify* the human gender binary, but somehow transcends it: God in Godself is "bisexual" or "transsexual."

Now if this last line of argument were more developed and clarified, the critique I am about to offer would possibly have less force. But my main worry, as intimated at the start of this essay, is that despite what is argued to the contrary, Moltmann's views on gender come primarily from secular sources in the first instance, not from a radical questioning, even rupturing, of those secular views as found in God. It is true that the trinitarian reading of the Father (as "motherly") offers a critique of the crudely monotheistic "patriarchal" God and reveals its idolatry as such. In this sense the gender theory that Moltmann holds is indeed utilized to critique a Christian tradition that has become besmirched and debased by patriarchy. It is less clear whether the attributions of "compassion," "pity," and (especially) "eternal suffering" to this divine motherliness do not merely then *reinscribe* a gender stereotyping of a particular Romantic heritage (which Moltmann admits at one point also inspired Count Zinzendorf in his rediscovery of the maternal Spirit of the Macarian homilies).[31] In short, as I see it, Moltmann's trinitarian gender strategies have a tension between, on the one hand, reading into God a "complementarity" between prescribed notions of the binary "masculine" and "feminine" (a view that has its roots in German Romanticism, but with different forms of afterlife in Jung, Neumann, and the "androgynous" feminisms of the 1970s and 1980s),[32] and, on the other hand, arguing that the Trinity altogether upends or transcends such a binary. (This tension is particularly evident when we see that Moltmann can sometimes underscore the psychological dangers for men of retaining an unresolved connection to the power of the mother, yet seemingly be unaware of that same ambiguous feature of maternality when he waxes enthusiastically on divine "motherhood" in the Spirit.)[33] Moreover, when he does express the view that the Trinity somehow goes beyond the existing gender binary, the terms "bisexuality" and "transexuality" are used of God as if they were equivalent—a matter that is at least strongly debatable and seemingly reopens the question of whether a gender binary is inherently God-given at all. Of course, if there is a covert eisegesis of secular gender views going on in Moltmann's trinitarianism, then his neat disjunction between "literal" (true) and "metaphoric" (projective) verbal ascriptions to God will also be called into question.

Perhaps it can now be seen why, at the start of this essay, I made the charge of a "double strategy" in much contemporary feminist theology, a strategy—as we now detect—also in Moltmann's, on gender theory and God-talk. On the one hand, Moltmann can explicitly appeal to both Enlightenment and Romantic views of gender—visions of equality and mutuality-in-differentiation—when outlining how important it is to correct prevailing current gender stereotypes. Here he will argue that such disjunctive stereotypes as male "mastery" or "machismo" and female "sensuality" or "feeling" are debasing and oppressive to both men and women and have deeply infected the church's tradition no less than secular culture.[34] (On this front, Moltmann uses secular theories of gender as critical weapons against a corrupted culture and church.) On the other hand, when Moltmann comes to indicate how only a trinitarian view of God can correct these tendencies from the divine and theological angle (top-down, as it were, and therefore "literally" rather than "metaphorically"), there remains, as we have seen, a strong suspicion that certain secular views of gender are still normatively in play. Moreover, as Moltmann himself admits at times, a mere insistence on orthodox trinitarianism (whether "Eastern" or "Western," so-called) is no guarantee *in itself* of a nonpatriarchal, or nonhierarchical, vision of God. Even trinitarianism can be corrupted.[35]

What, then, is the alternative, systematically speaking? How could we rescue and extend those dimensions of Moltmann's thought that seem to reach beyond a secular or worldly view of the gender binary, especially in their appeal to the particular significance of the Spirit? If Moltmann's trinitarianism—of a "motherly" Father and of the Spirit as the "feminine principle"—does not adequately deliver us from the hold of Romantic, "complementary" views of gender (which are themselves implicated, as the Moltmanns recognize, in damaging gender stereotyping), what vision of the Trinity and its relations would do so?

GENDER AND GOD: BEYOND THE BINARY OF WORLDLY GENDER?

Moltmann's brief, unexplained, talk of "transexuality" in God (and what that might mean) is what I wish to explore further in this final section. But I also want to keep close to his insistence (if only partially carried out in his own case) that the matter of gender should find theological, not secular, resolution. In particular, I want to suggest that Moltmann's own distinctive reemphasis on the Spirit as "primary," in what he calls the "eucharistic" ordering of the trinitarian processions, should be a guiding principle in this task.[36] Strangely, he never explicitly raises this question: What "difference" does it make to the issue of gender that God is *three*? Also, what difference does it make to gender that in the Incarnation the Son crosses (and we might say *transgresses*) the ultimate ontological binary "difference"—that between God and humanity, Creator and created?

I am aware that the secular gender theory that is currently dominant in my own context in North America is tilting the discussion in a quite different direction from that in which Jürgen Moltmann and Elisabeth Moltmann-Wendel forged their gender critique of Christian patriarchalism in the 1980s in Germany. In particular, the work of Judith Butler has made questions of the "gender binary," as itself potentially repressive and "normatively heterosexist," central to current American debates about homosexuality, freedom, and personal rights.[37] I too, then, am subject to the same riposte that I have just leveled against Moltmann, and could be accused of merely being the purveyor of current secular gender fashion in theological disguise.

Although I admittedly bring these current "interests" to the theological discussion, I also wish to appeal to Christian spiritual *practices* that can claim to aid a radical dispossession to the Spirit's power to reformulate and redirect our worldly thinking about gender. Precisely by the regular discipline of silently listening to the

Spirit in prayer and of meditating on the Bible, precisely by the invocation of the Spirit's "epicletic" power over bread and wine, precisely by the handing over—in these pneumatological interactions—of my *human* desire to control, order, and categorize my world, I am already inviting what is "third" in God to break the hold of my binary thinking.[38] The Spirit, then, is from this perspective no longer seen—as in so much Western medieval iconography of the Trinity—as the wafting "feminine" adjunct to an all-male negotiation of salvation; but the Spirit becomes the very source and power of a transformed understanding of gender, one rendered labile to the workings of *divine* desire in us. No longer do I start with the binary building blocks of "male" and "female," but instead with a primary submission in prayer to a form of love that necessarily transcends, and even ruptures, my normal forms of gender understanding. To speak thus, and admittedly boldly, is no mere subjective appeal to "experience" (for if such a repeated activity of prayer can be called an "experience," it is a highly paradoxical one, a sort of blanking of noetic certainties). It is, however, tied to a very close rendition of the textual authority of Paul in Romans 8, where he speaks simultaneously of prayer as divinely done *in us* by the Spirit "with sighs too deep for words" (Rom. 8:26), and yet as also forging us—through this painful process of nescience and loss of control—into the very likeness of Christ, into "the glorious liberty of the children of God" (Rom. 8:21).[39] Such too, as I read Paul (rather differently on this point from Moltmann), is the significance of the celebrated saying "neither male *and* female'" in Gal 3:28; it is not, as I see it, that maleness and femaleness are necessarily *obliterated* by what Paul envisages, either now or eschatologically, but rather that they are rendered spiritually insignificant, or (as we might now put it) nonbinary in their possibilities, in the face of the Spirit's work and our transformations into Christ's body.[40]

If we think of the Trinity, then, not as a set of perfect mutual relations into which the (known) gender binary somehow has been interposed in a cleansed form, but rather as an irreducible threeness that always *refuses* a mere mutuality of two, then we reemphasize the importance of the Spirit precisely as Moltmann has always urged, yet with a significantly different theological outcome for gender. Here we do not allocate the binary of "masculinity" and "femininity" to different "persons," or even to their relation, but instead step into a circle of divine desire (the "sighs too deep for words" that signal the Spirit's gift of loving plenitude, drawing us to the "Father") which is necessarily beyond our comprehension and categorization, but is drawing us by degrees into the "likeness" of the "Son." And since the Son himself, in the very act of incarnation, has transgressed the difference between the *fundamental* metaphysical binary of divinity and humanity, we may rightly see the incarnation, also, as a destabilization of basic binaries. Indeed, when the writer of the letter to the Ephesians (Eph. 5:21-33) explicitly genders this binary and speaks of Christ as the bridegroom or husband of the ("feminine") church, and yet the church as his very *own* body we again see—in my suggested reading—not necessarily the simple reinstantiation of an existing patriarchal or subordinationist view of gender (although it *seems* to be such!), but instead the beginnings of an alluring questioning of it.[41] Christ, and the life in him that we share, is—as Gregory of Nyssa later stated—a very "mingling" of divinity and humanity, an *erotic* transformation of apparently settled roles and statuses precisely in their intersection.[42] The same Gregory, of course, also—and famously—read Genesis 1:26-27 (in his *de opificio hominis*) as implying a maleness and femaleness that is not fixed and permanent, but rather (initially) *en route* to the fall, yet capable thereafter of ascetical upending and constant transformation in the crucible of intensified longing for God.[43] For Gregory, as much later also for John of the Cross in the West, it is the purification of our desire in God's desire which is the acid test of our human "differentiated relationality" (as I earlier defined "gender"). In this sense human "gender" is rendered both labile and fluid to something more fundamental: the workings of the divine desire in us through the power and operation of the "third" that is the Holy Spirit, a transformation that is strictly speaking ineffable in human terms. As John of the Cross says of the height of union in *The Spiritual Canticle*:

> By his divine breath-like spiration, the Holy Spirit elevates the soul sublimely and informs her and makes her capable of breathing in God the same spiration of love that the Father breathes in the Son and the Son in the Father. This spiration of love is the Holy Spirit himself, who in the Father and the Son breathes out to her in this transformation in order to unite her to himself. There would not be a true and total transformation if the soul were not transformed in the three Persons of the Most Holy Trinity in an open and manifest degree.
>
> And this kind of spiration of the Holy Spirit in the soul, by which God transforms her in himself, is so sublime, delicate, and deep a delight that a mortal tongue finds it indescribable, nor can the human intellect, as such, in any way grasp it. . . . This is transformation in the three Persons in power and wisdom and love, and thus the soul is like God through this transformation. He created her in his image and likeness that she might attain such resemblance.[44]

Conclusions

In these last few brief paragraphs, I have been trying to give a mere sketch of a view of gender that would satisfy, I suggest, many of the Moltmanns' admirable *desiderata* in relation to theological anthropology, and be equally founded in trinitarian theology, as theirs is. Where my systematic strategy fundamentally differs from theirs is in my much greater sense of the *rupture* of the world's gender binary by the transformative intervention of the Spirit, and its ultimate knitting of us into the threefoldness of God. Such a rupture, if John of the Cross is right, involves not only sensual but spiritual darkening: the self's normal crutches of support, of purportedly ordering or controlling the world, one by one fall away. Thus, like Augustine, and unlike Gregory of Nazianzen, I question the advisability—recommended more than once by Jürgen Moltmann—of symbolizing the Trinity as the triad of the human family—two parents with a child;[45] this symbol, I believe, domesticates the Trinity and tends to reinstantiate the power of existing sexual stereotypes even as it attempts to cleanse or change them. Rather, I have pointed briefly to ascetical and monastic literature (in both East and West) that sees "incorporation" into the life of the Trinity very differently: as a process in which a *radical* interruption by the Spirit (if asked for, welcomed by grace) calls settled views of binary "gender" into question, and makes the flow of trinitarian "desire" the ultimate means of a sharing in a Christic life, which itself defies secular gender characterization.

It will have become clear in this short chapter of salutation to Jürgen Moltmann and Elisabeth Moltmann-Wendel, that their pioneering work on the Trinity and gender in systematic theology has been among the most significant—one might say the most generative!—on the topic in the late twentieth century. In the discussion and critique of their views I have provided here, it will have become equally clear how much hangs, in our assessments in this area, on the ever subtle matter of the relation of biblical authority, exegetical reflection, examination of doctrinal tradition (in all its variety), the lessons of spiritual and ascetical practice, and the particular challenges of contemporary life. In choosing to press the radicality of the Moltmanns' thought in the area of gender a little further here than they themselves have done, I can truthfully say, with deep gratitude and appreciation, that I am merely following their own principle that a serious engagement with the life of the Trinity involves, perforce, nothing less than "the new creation of *all things* through the Spirit of God."[46]

Chapter 12

God's Perfect Life

John Webster

To speak of God's perfection is to speak of the fullness with which he is and acts as the one he is. God's perfection is not first and foremost a negative concept, denoting the absence of restriction or fulfillment in the being of God; these entailments may follow, but perfection chiefly refers to the sheer positive plenitude of God's being. Further, like the closely parallel concepts of God as *a se* or *causa sui*, the concept of divine perfection is not primarily a formal concept but a material one. "We call that perfect which lacks nothing of the mode of its perfection," says Aquinas.[1] A theology of divine perfection must, therefore, have as its chief task to specify the particular *modus perfectionis* that is proper to God. As *causa sui*, the perfect God owes his being to no other reality than himself. His being is self-originating, self-moving, self-explicating, self-fulfilling; but what God originates, moves, explicates, and fulfills as *causa sui* is *himself*. The perfect God is *causa sui*, this one. Perfection indicates God's unqualified and wholly realized identity; it does not so much speak of a quality that God instantiates to the highest degree, as to make an identifying reference to the one who declares himself: "I am first" (Isa. 41:4).

Because the concept of perfection is in this way an indicator of God's identity, it is not to be filled out by a process of comparative description. That is, we do not arrive at a sufficiently robust and theologically determinate understanding of divine perfection by denying of God what are taken to be creaturely deficiencies or by magnifying what are taken to be properties of greatness.[2] Such operations may perhaps gesture in the direction of God's perfection; but when they are left to do all the work in a doctrine of God, they commonly wander off onto one of two false trails. First, at the formal level, they can promote the mistaken notion that

Christian theological talk about God is a synthetic statement, not an analytic one. A concept of perfection synthesized from observations on creaturely realities is, however, not a conception of divine perfection; to speak of God on the basis of or as a result of speaking of other realities is not to speak of God. God's perfection is his singular, incomparable, and wholly nonderivative identity and so is a matter for confession rather than construction. The concern of a Christian theology of God's perfection is God's singularity—what Barth called "*Gott selber, sein eines, einfaches, eigenes Wesen*";[3] and what Dorner earlier called God's "*Einheit, Einzigheit, und Einfachheit.*"[4] Second, more materially, attempting to reach a conception of God's perfection by way of comparison leads to a neglect of the unfathomable strangeness of God. The prophetic question, "To whom will you liken me and make me equal, and compare me, as though we were alike?" (Isa. 46:5), is not simply a prohibition of those comparisons that render God familiar, but of all comparisons. Because God is categorically different, the only adequate, trustworthy basis for talk of God's perfection is this tautology: God is God.

If these false trails are to be avoided and the law of God's particular being is to guide theological thought, then an account of God's perfection must undertake its work under a specific command from which there flows a specific prohibition. The command is that theology must direct its attention to the places where God enacts and therefore declares his perfect being: to the free, spontaneous presence of the Holy Trinity in majestic condescension. (This is a command because the mind is corrupt and fallen nature will not bend itself to attend to the self-presentation of truth.) The corresponding prohibition is that we may not look elsewhere. For the concept of God's perfection to indicate his identity fittingly, much will hang on the deference with which theological reason heeds this *command* and repudiates its own longing for a less narrow gate by which to enter. A good deal might be said at this point about the practices of theological reason; but this point, at least, must be said: those who seek to articulate a theology of divine perfection attentive at its heart to the divine self-manifestation will undergo a certain mortification as concepts are torn from our grasp and discarded; only in this way will we enter into the joy of theological service.

Creaturely knowledge of God's perfection derives from God; it is revealed knowledge whose origin and realization are out of our hands. As revealer, the perfect God makes himself present to creatures as the one he is. If theological reason properly follows this movement of God's self-presentation, two things must be borne in mind. First, the ground of God's revelation of himself in the economy is the free antecedent perfection that God is in himself as Father, Son, and Spirit. God does not first become himself as he presents himself to creatures; his immanent being is not mere potentiality, a "being-towards-revelation" that becomes actual in the economy of God's works *ad extra*. In revelation, God makes himself present to and known by creatures only as he is from all eternity present to and known by himself. Revelation does not perfect God; it is, rather, a reiteration in created space and time of God's perfection *in se*. On this first statement (much neglected in contemporary trinitarian theology), everything hangs; without it, God's works drift free from God *in se*, becoming groundless. As with the corresponding affirmation in incarnational theology of the eternal deity of the Word who *becomes* flesh, so here the intention is not to propose some abstract deity apart from God's works, but to state with finality that the works of God are, indeed, the works of God.

Second, in revelation God reiterates and re-presents his perfect being in his *opera exeuntia*, his outgoing works. On the basis of and with the sovereign energy of his immanent perfection, God wills, sustains, and completes fellowship with his creatures. He presents himself as the perfect one and does so authoritatively, with commanding power and genuineness that he has as *auctor* of all things. As this one, God turns to creatures, making himself present not only to himself but also to them. Further, this divine presence is not mutely objective, a mere state of affairs to be observed; it is summons, word, love that brings into being creaturely knowledge that corresponds to God's reality and is itself active as faith, hope, and love. Where and how does this turning or reiteration of God's perfection take place? In the *operationes trinitatis externae*, that breathtaking history of God with us, God the Father wills fellowship with that which is not God, determining and forming the creature out of nothing to exist as his child. God the Son sustains this fellowship, above all by stepping into the place of the ruined creature, bearing its alienation from the Father, and repairing the deadly breach that has opened up between the Creator and the objects of his love. God the Holy Spirit completes this fellowship, realizing it in the present by drawing the creature into the sphere of Christ's filial relation to the Father and by promising to perfect the creature in the heavenly fellowship of the redeemed.

ASPECTS OF GOD'S PERFECTION

So far then, God's perfection is the excellence with which he is what he is; it is *perfectio integralis*, integral perfection in the sense of fullness of identity. This perfection is both *in se* and *ad extra*. Or, to put it more precisely, God's integral perfection does not exclude but rather includes the movement of his perfect being toward creatures in the works of love. God's excellence is complete in itself; but even as such, it is luminous, self-communicating, and self-distributing. As the perfect one, God sheds himself abroad. His perfection is unhindered self-possession and self-enjoyment that includes (but is not exhausted by) infinite generosity.

A successful theological presentation of the matter will then depend on, among other things, a fully integrated and yet properly ordered account of *immanent* and *economic* perfection. The double temptation to which theology is exposed at this point is to allow one aspect or mode of God's perfection to assume the upper hand, or to relate them in a way that fails to correspond to the given order and sequence that is proper to the being and works of God. In recent theology, the temptation to collapse God's *ad extra* perfection into his immanent being seems by and large to be in recession. Probably the last account along these lines of any real substance was Gollwitzer's *The Existence of God as Confessed by Faith*.[5] Although the alarming lack of objectivity in German Protestant existentialism justifiably motivated Gollwitzer (with Herbert Braun as a primary target), his appeal to the idea of God in-and-for-himself tended to produce a mirror image of what it was intended to overcome.[6] Much more pressing now is the temptation to neglect the immanent perfection of God. This temptation has afflicted a good deal of recent trinitarian theology, perhaps the most startling example being the *Systematic Theology* of Robert Jenson.[7] Combined with a potent theology of the *koinonia* between God and creatures, the effect of the claim that "God's self-identity lies in dramatic coherence,"[8] precisely because of its resistance to talk of God *in se*, can be the eclipse of any sense of immanent divine perfection, since that concept seems to be irredeemably tied to a metaphysics in which God's excellence is identified with stability and repose anterior to his work as the God of creatures.

An orderly account of the relation of God's *immanent* perfection and his *economic* perfection is required—orderly in the sense that it fits the particular character of God's being as Holy Scripture attests. In trying to construct such an account, it is worth noting that the terms *immanent* and *economic* can have only provisional significance. Like many theological concepts, these terms function as abstractions that condense or summarize more primary theological descriptions, partly for the purpose of clarity and regularity and partly in order to display systematic relations between different aspects of Christian teaching. As such, they are necessary; but the cogency of a presentation of this or of any other matter in theology will be primarily a matter of *descriptive* adequacy, which is to be served—but not dominated—by concepts. Because of this necessity, it may be better to make greater use of concepts that are less formal and more material. Barth exemplifies this approach when he organizes his arrangement of the divine attributes around the notions of *freedom* and *love*. Both, it should be noted, are only one step removed from event and action, and both are filled out descriptively rather than by formal analysis of terms. Before Barth, however, Dorner had already seen the point with customary penetration (although without Barth's fluency) in his presentation of the being of God as the unity of God's acts of "self-preservation [*Selbstbehauptung*] and self-communication [*Selbstmittheilung*]."[9] Although not so kerygmatically resonant, Dorner's terminology is in some respects preferable to Barth's, especially because it is somewhat more precise, and so correspondingly less likely to attract the wrong kind of expectations or to be filled out with improper content, than more general terms such as freedom or love. Barth certainly has to expend much energy in specifying a *usus theologicus* of his terms. Although Barth's results are magnificent, Dorner's more restricted terms may prove more fruitful in our present discussion. Taken together and in the right order, these two concepts, *self-preservation* and *self-communication*, may help to shape a description of God's perfection in its double character.

God preserves himself. His self-preservation is the effortless activity in which he maintains the eternal and undisturbed harmony, blessedness, and excellence of his life as Father, Son, and Spirit. God is effortlessly perfect. He preserves himself, not in opposition to threats, whether from beyond or from within the circle of his life, but in the enactment of his utter aliveness. Divine self-preservation is not to be conceived as a countermove, a defense of God's perfection against that which might corrupt it or break it down. God is eternally perfect and, therefore, beyond agony; he contends with no one because there is no one who may contend with him. Rather, God's self-preservation is his celebration and the reiteration of the plenitude that he is in himself. Similarly, God's self-preservation is not to be conceived as that by which God realizes a perfection for which he waits, for his perfection is integral, never lacking in fullness. This fullness does not mean that God's perfection is simple stasis. God *enacts* his perfection. This enactment, however, is not his self-production, God emerging out of the possibility of his own nonbeing. Rather, as in Barth's conception of God's freedom:

> When we say that God is free to exist, we do not say that God lifts himself, as it were, out of non-existence into existence, that he makes himself free to exist. What we say is that the mode of existence is proper to him which is exempt from any limitation by the possibility of its non-existence. He is the one who is himself the Existent.[10]

As perfect God, he is the one who is self-existent, reaffirming or confirming his being as God *a se*.

Again, God's perfection as the self-existent one is not mere immobility, rest conceived as simple absence of motion. To say God "is" *a se* is to say God "live" *a se*. God is, and therefore God lives, and therefore God moves; and in this being, his life and movement, he is perfect. In this restricted, nonspeculative, and dogmatically determinate sense, we may speak of God's being in becoming. The "becoming" that is proper to God's being does not presuppose some state of defect as if the plenitude of God's identity were the product of God's self-enactment. To speak in such terms would be to make nonsense of both God's eternity and perfection *in se*:

> It is true that, compared with pure motionless being, movement is given in becoming. But we cannot use becoming as a commencement, for instead of stiff, lifeless being we should have in "becoming" a principle of movement, but one that was restless and aimless. Such a principle might provide for an eternal mutation, but not a firm ground for a more concrete idea of God. If God . . . is only becoming, then absolute spirit, in order to carry on the becoming, must subside into his other form of being (nature), out of which he will raise himself again to absolute spirit in an eternal round. In absolute becoming of itself we should have

a commencement, which could never reach a goal, but only Heraclitic flux, the restless transition from one thing to another.[11]

Theological language about God's becoming indicates the particular character of his perfection. God's perfection is not a state resulting from an original act of self-constitution, but an eternal, ever-fresh act of self-reiteration and of being self-realized. As Donner explains, "God has not, so to speak, once, in the past, constituted himself the absolutely and actually existent" but "has thus constituted himself eternally" so that he "is and remains the real ground of his absolute reality" and on "that basis he is eternally the absolute and real potentiality or causality of himself, the real possibility of his reality."[12] More concretely, Dorner claims that "*God is absolute life*" . . . in himself, not by his being realized once for all, but by eternal self-realization" and that "the absolute potentiality or possibility of himself is not lost in action, but securely preserved therein."[13] Dorner fills out that conceptual statement thus:

> *God is living.* God may not allowably be thought of as mere being in repose, or merely as ideal and thinking. As absolute life, he has a πλήρωμα, a world of real forces in himself. He bears within him an inexhaustible spring, by virtue of which he is life eternally streaming forth, but also eternally streaming back into himself. Still he is not to be defined as transient life; he is before everything essentially absolute life; he neither empties nor loses himself in his vital activity. He is a sea of self-revolving life; an infinite fullness of forces moves, so to speak, and undulates therein.[14]

In short, the perfect God is in himself "the living God and the everlasting King" (Jer. 10:10). His perfection is the self-originating, self-moving, self-extending, and self-returning life of Father, Son, and Holy Spirit.

As God preserves, so he communicates himself. The perfection that is God's life, the "sea of self-revolving life" with its "infinite fullness of forces," includes a turning to that which is not God. The perfect God has his perfection in himself in the integrity of his own life; but he also has his perfection in relation to the life that he creates, reconciles, and brings to perfection. God the Father, whose fatherhood is complete in the perfect mutuality of Father and Son, is also the creator of heaven and earth. God the Son, the perfect counterpart to the Father in their eternal fellowship, is also the Lord of creatures; he has his deity also in the exercise of his saving rule over the realm of created being. God the Holy Spirit, the perfect bond of life and love between the Father and the Son, is also the giver of life to creatures, the perfect one who perfects all things. God is thus also himself in his self-communication to creatures and in the history of fellowship between himself and that which he has made.

This turn of God in self-communication is wholly gracious. This gracious self-communication includes election, reconciliation, and redemption, at the core of which lies the divine will. As God communicates himself, there is no compromise of the completeness of the life-act of God in which he preserves himself in the eternal joy of the triune persons. God communicates himself not out of lack but out of fullness; that to which he turns does not realize or extend his perfection, which is wholly self-constituted and self-maintaining. Yet in making such an affirmation, is there not a danger of deep disorder in the Christian doctrine of God? Is there not a temptation to cancel out the movement of God *ad extra* by insisting that God's perfection is anterior to the history of his fellowship with creatures? The danger might be that of ensnaring Christian theological assertions about God's eternal perfection with a metaphysics in which the only perfection that can be envisaged is one of static persistence.[15] In terms more directly trinitarian, the further danger might be that of determining the identities of the persons of the godhead simply in terms of relations of origin, such that the *opera ad extra* become merely epiphenomenal.[16] Alarm cries about these menaces (of varying degrees of sophistication and persuasiveness) are stock-in-trade of some conventional styles of trinitarian theology at present.[17] Can the perils to which they alert us be avoided?

An initial sketch of an answer might find some resources in the concepts of procession and mission to indicate the ordered unity of God *in se* and God *ad extra*, thus showing that God's spontaneity—the perfect liberty with which he enacts his life—is both anterior to his fellowship with creatures in the economy and also ratified in his works. This pure and perfect freedom, this self-sufficiency, is God's life in the processions or personal relations that constitute his absolute vitality *in se*. God is perfect as the Father who begets the Son. In this begetting, God repeats his own being—repetition here meaning not sameness but affirmation, confirmation, and fullness demonstrating itself as fullness of life and relation as *paternitas* and *filiatio*. The Son's generation is divine plenitude upholding itself as absolute life: God from God, light from light, very God from very God. This, of course, is one reason why the Son is confessed as "begotten, not made": the entire and eternal sufficiency of Father and Son forbids any *productive* understanding of their relation. God "from" God is no accumulation of deity: "from" signifies both origin and eternal, infinite abundance, the inexhaustible relation which is God's life. Further, God is perfect as the Father and the Son who together breathe the Spirit, and so as the Spirit who proceeds from them. Whatever content be given to the term *spiration* (trinitarian theology has been characteristically, even embarrassingly, oblique about the matter), the *spiratio* of the third person—his ineffable, eternal derivation from Father and Son—does not indicate any kind of hiatus or temporal interval between, on the one hand, the Father and the Son as agents of *spiratio activa* and, on the other hand, the Spirit as the one to whom *spiratio passiva* is proper. Active and passive, that from which the Spirit proceeds and the proceeding Spirit, are modes of God's perfection, not separable elements in a causal sequence (so that Aquinas comments that in the godhead relations of origin are *secundum aequalitatem*, according to equality).[18] All the perfect relations of the triune God are ἀγέννητος, unoriginate; but the negation "unoriginate" is only the reverse of the sheer positive wholeness and richness of life enacted as paternity, generation, and spiration.[19]

All this discussion suggests that to speak of God's immanent perfection is to indicate the boundlessness of God's life. It is to say that God preserves himself in the love that constitutes his eternal being in himself as Father, Son, and Spirit; but again, as God preserves, so he communicates himself. The missions of both the Son and the Spirit in obedience to the Father correspond to the personal relations in which God has his absolute life. The divine processions and the divine missions that flow from them are together the perfection of God.

God communicates his absolute life. This communication does not mean that creatures participate in the life that is proper to the Holy Trinity, for then God would be not only the giver of life *to* creatures but also the receiver of life *from* creatures; and so his life would no longer be absolute. God communicates his life by summoning creatures into being and by preserving, saving, and glorifying them so that they might attain their own creaturely integrity and perfection in fellowship with himself. *Fellowship* is a key term in explicating the divine missions because unlike the much more fluid term *communion*, which rather easily becomes *mutual coinherence*, *fellowship* indicates both the intimacy of God with creatures and the unbridgeable gulf between them that is the essential condition of their relations in time. *Fellowship* indicates the mutuality of grace, not of shared being. In the majestic exercise of his own freedom, God the Father determines that there should be a history of God with creatures and that this history should reach its goal in the missions of the Son and the Spirit.

In the sending of the Son and the Spirit, the triune God gives life. "As the Father has life in himself, so he has granted the Son also to have life in himself" (John 5:26). This procession of the Son from the Father, expressed in Johannine terms as the Father's granting of divine life to the Son, is the condition for the Son's saving work. By virtue of his relation to the Father, the Son is in himself "the life" (John 14:6) and, therefore, the one who comes to the world "that they may have life and have it abundantly" (John 10:10). Similarly, the Spirit is one who is sent by the Father in the name of the Son (John 14:26) and by the Son from the Father (John 15:26) and so acts toward creatures as the life-giving Spirit (Rom. 8:2; 2 Cor. 3:6). In attempting some kind of conceptual paraphrase of this matter, it is crucial that the life-communicating missions of God *ad extra* be fully integrated with the divine processions in which God preserves the life-filled abundance of his own immanent being. This integration means, on the one hand, that the temporal missions of the Son and the Spirit are not merely ancillary: abstracted from his self-communication, God's self-preservation is a closed circle, nothing more. If this problem is to be countered, then self-preservation and self-communication, though they are not identical, are equiprimordial. Yet, on the other hand, the missions *ad extra* are not somehow God's coming-to-perfection, but an integral element of the perfection that God eternally is as *actus purus*. In them, God confirms (but does not create) his being by making himself freely and personally present to creatures. In this connection, Aquinas is entirely correct to insist that the economic missions of the Son and the Spirit do not entail temporal succession or local motion, still less subordination or separation within the godhead. The missions are inseparable from the processions of God *in se*, in which they are grounded. Aquinas, again, notes that mission "includes the eternal procession, with the addition of a temporal effect," precisely because he does not want to concede that the temporal missions somehow complete God's perfect life. Thus, he argues that "the relation of a divine person to his principle must be eternal" and that therefore "the procession may be called a twin procession, eternal and temporal, not that there is a double relation to the principle, but a double term, temporal and eternal."[20]

The fact that there is a temporal, creaturely term of the immanent divine processions is of very great significance, not only for the way theology understands creaturely reality but also for the doctrine of God. To conceive of God's perfection exclusively as self-revolving plenitude is, in the end, to fall back into the ruinous assumption that we must choose between God's original and teleological perfection. The Christian doctrine of God insists that the choice is spurious. God is replete in the personal relations of the eternal Father, the eternal Son, and the eternal Spirit; but God's perfection is not such that it can only retain its purity and integrity by holding itself aloof from any presentation of itself among creatures. Self-preservation and self-communication are not competing moments. Self-preservation is the condition for and sustaining energy of God's movement outside himself; self-communication does not jeopardize the stability or achieved status of God's perfect life. In the same way that God's immensity is neither imperiled nor extended by his ubiquity, but confirmed by it, so also God's immanent perfection is reiterated in his *perfectio relativa*.

"Why," Jenson asks, "should commitment in a history not be . . . an ontological perfection?"[21] That it should indeed be so regarded is, I have suggested, a necessary corollary of the doctrine of the Trinity; but the assertion is only secure as one about God's *perfection* if it is matched by a parallel affirmation that God's "eventful actuality"[22] is predicated upon his immanent excellence. It is imperative that we do not force a choice between God's *Selbstbehauptung* and his *Selbstmittheilung*. At the end of his critical prolegomenon to the doctrine of the Trinity where he develops these terms, Dorner concludes that "it is imperative to so think of God that he transcends absolute transcendence and solitary majesty, which of itself would be exclusive" and then asks, "How is that transcending to come about without risk of new comminglings of God and the world?"[23] There is in the question, perhaps, something of the shadow cast by Hegel over modern theology; yet there is also something that points to a central issue in any Christian theology of God's perfection, namely, how can God's perfection include his relation to the world? The answer, Dorner suggests, lies in the deployment of "*the specifically Christian doctrine of God,*"[24] for it is that doctrine alone that "opens the prospect that God can communicate himself to the world without self-detriment, just as he is able to preserve his being without incommunicativeness."[25]

GOD'S PERFECTION AND OUR OWN

By way of a brief coda, we may return to the matter of the kind of knowledge of divine perfection that is proper to creatures. Creatures know God's perfection by revelation, that is, by God's gift of his presence in which he commands and enables acknowledgment of himself. Revelation is an aspect of the fellowship between the perfect God and those whom he engages in his works of love. Because this is so, the knowledge that we come to have of this God is an aspect of being drawn to stand in a certain relation to him, namely, the relation of reconciled creature on the way to perfection. That relation—we can call it the history of sanctification—includes a certain reordering of our cognitive life: falsehood and vanity are exposed and overwhelmed by the light of God's presence; reason is renewed as the Spirit instructs the reconciled by leading them into truth. Christian theological talk about God, and therefore about God's perfection, is merely an episode in reason's sanctification. It does no more than putter around the foothills of the knowledge of the perfect God. "There must," said Jonathan Edwards in a sermon from early 1730, "be a direct and immediate sense of God's glory and excellency. I say direct and immediate to distinguish from a mere acknowledging that God is glorious and excellent by ratiocination." To know God's perfection properly, creatures must themselves be perfected, brought to their proper end, so that they can see how fitting, how supremely *right*, the whole matter is. "He that has a blessed-making sight of God, he not only has a view of God's glory and excellency, but he views it as having a propriety in it."[26] Such sight of the perfection or excellence of God lies in our future; for the present, theological work remains *spes quaerens intellectum.*[27]

CHAPTER 13

DIVINE PROVIDENCE AND ACTION

David Fergusson

The doctrine of providence occupies a pivotal place in most theological systems. Its connection with creation, redemption, and eschatology demands an account of the relationship of God to the world. This relationship is often expounded through the distinction between general and special providence, the created and the present order of the universe together with the particular acts of God therein. Yet the standard presentation of providence as a subsection of the doctrine of creation frequently results in too rapid a consideration of the many problems and themes it traverses.[1] This consideration led to Karl Barth's complaint that providence was too easily identified with the prevailing world order. Mysterious, hidden, and often contrary to appearances, providence was required to be more closely attached to the covenantal purposes of God enacted in the history of Jesus Christ. As an aspect of faith, it should enable the believer to live with only a very partial and provisional worldview.[2]

PROVIDENCE IN BIBLICAL THEOLOGY

In treating themes of conservation and preservation, the doctrine of providence deals with the regularity of nature as a manifestation of divine faithfulness. This manifestation can be illustrated by reference to the Noahic covenant, the Psalms, and the Sermon on the Mount. One also finds contemporary appeal to anthropic considerations concerning those fundamental features of the cosmos, such as the law of gravity, that enable the emergence of galaxies, planets, and carbon-based life forms. The engagement with modern science, however, becomes more defensive in the face of neo-Darwinism, although here again discussion is confined to the nature of general providence. When limited to these themes, providence, as an aspect of creation, is a doctrine that may be compatible with several forms of theism. In this respect, its content contrasts unfavorably with the much thicker description of the God-world relationship in Scripture. Here providence is integrated with the story of divine involvement with creation throughout the economy of salvation.

Biblical constraints upon providence generate a set of rules for any adequate theological formulation. Although standing in some tension to one another, these rules require to be addressed. Included are the claims that creation is good; that the work of God is not exhausted by an initial act of creation; that the rhythms of nature and life are well ordered; and that struggle and an overriding of sin, suffering, and death are necessary for the fulfillment of the divine purpose. The need to accommodate themes of sin and redemption prevented any obvious identification of providence with natural or historical processes. The rejection of Gnostic patterns of thought, however, also compelled theology to discern in the established order, at least in some measure, the good purposes of God that would be brought to eschatological completion.

Consideration of the scriptural material suggests that these tensions are already captured in the canon. The serenity of the acts of creation in Genesis 1 contrasts with other myths that depict the making of the world through a struggle. Glimpses of this struggle lie elsewhere in Scripture (e.g., Ps. 74:12-17), while some commentators argue that the waters (*tehom*) in Genesis 1:2 retain some allusion to a surd force that is checked but not wholly overcome at the commencement of creation. In any case, Hebrew scholarship tends to support the view that for the Genesis writer creation is out of formless and disorderly waste, rather than nothing. In the Psalms, the providential rule of God is celebrated as universal and consistent; yet this rule is combined with a wrestling against the forces of evil as well as a struggle with the stubborn resistance of God's own people. What emerges from this combined struggle is the exercise of providence not as a simple predetermining of everything that happens; it is much more the exercise of a rule to be celebrated, but one that is never complete or lacking in conflict. "Preservation is often erroneously presented as a static state of affairs," as Berkhof argues and then claims, "In reality, it is filled with tension and drama."[3]

The biblical account of "creation as Yahweh's partner"[4] depicts the world as blessed. It is a fitting home for human and other creatures in which to flourish and multiply (e.g., Pss. 24 and 104). This flourishing requires wisdom to discern, attention to maintain, and worship that celebrates and reminds the people of the character of the world under God's rule. The affirmation of providence is less a philosophical hypothesis (although philosophical elements are present in the Wisdom literature) and more an act of faith set in the context of worship and ethics. At the same time, God's rule is threatened by forces of chaos that manifest themselves in a variety of forms, including sickness, injustice, misfortune, and untimely death. The language of combat, victory, and enthronement cannot be understood except in terms of forces active in creation that jeopardize God's reign and call forth resistance.[5] It is a recurrent criticism that Christian theology has for too long ignored this central feature of the configuration of the God-world relationship in the Hebrew Bible. The psalms of lament, Job, and passages from the prophets *inter alia* (among other things) return to the theme that there is resistance to God's reign. This resistance is not constructed in a Manichaean sense since there is no other creator. God ultimately commands the world order. Nonetheless, God is inexplicably delayed and too often silent in dealing with these palpable threats to the divine rule. This delay and silence are frequent sources of Israel's complaint that are resolved only by the action of God in reasserting the order of the world through the vindication of the righteous. It can hardly be stressed too often here that there is no attempt to expound a theodicy that explains why the world is the way it is. The solution rests in divine action that obliterates evil. Even in Jeremiah 12:1-3, where something like the classical dilemma of evil is posed, the desire of the prophet is not for explanation. It is for God's banishing the "workers of treachery."

The presence of quasi-dualist strains cannot be viewed merely as the hangover of elements of Near Eastern mythology otherwise overcome by Hebrew monotheism. These strains fulfill an important function in attesting forces that have not yet been destroyed or wholly overcome. They enable Israel, moreover, to construe the historical experience of a ruined temple (Ps. 74) and a people in exile (Isa. 51:9-11) in terms of cosmic threats to Yahweh's rule.

> Awake, as in days of old,
>   the generations of long ago!
> Was it not you who cut Rahab in pieces,
>   who pierced the dragon?
> Was it not you who dried up the sea,
>   the waters of the great deep;
> who made the depths of the sea a way
>   for the redeemed to cross over?
> So the ransomed of the LORD shall return,
>   and come to Zion with singing. (Isa. 51: 9-11)

Jon Levenson argues that the persistence of such themes in the Hebrew Bible attests the vitality of evil in a way that has been neglected in the history of both Jewish and Christian theology.[6] Other strands that confirm this include the presence of the serpent in the Garden of Eden (Gen. 3), and the role of Satan (Job 1–2, 1 Chron. 21). An absolute monotheism that posits God's total control over all world events is inadequate in the face of widespread and horrendous evils. The order of the world is manifested for the present only in partial and provisional ways. It requires God's constant action for its maintenance while it awaits fuller

establishment in the future. Other strands of the canon are arguably more resolutely monotheist, especially Second Isaiah. These strands perceive the forces of
evil as agencies fully controlled by, and even derived from, Yahweh. The monsters
described in the whirlwind speeches at the end of Job are God's creatures. So is
the benign Leviathan of Psalm 104. The floodwaters are ruled by God (Job 38),
while the cosmic flood of Genesis 6–7 is at the divine command and abates only
as God decides.[7]

> I am the LORD, and there is no other;
>> besides me there is no god.
>> I arm you, though you do not know me,
> so that they may know, from the rising of the sun
>> and from the west, that there is no one besides me;
>> I am the LORD, and there is no other.
> I form light and create darkness,
>> I make weal and create woe;
>> I the LORD do all these things. (Isa. 45:5-7)

The model of providence that emerges is one in which God's sovereignty is
surely proclaimed, yet as far as we can tell, that sovereignty does not function
unproblematically. Total control is deferred. There is no effortless outworking of
an initial plan immutable in every detail. Struggle, silence, and dramatic confronta-
tion are amid the vicissitudes of nature and history. God's role cannot be reduced to
either a general superintendence or a serene survey of this process. Moreover, while
human sin and error contribute significantly to the turmoil of creation, the problem is much wider. Unlike later Christian theology, the Hebrew Bible makes little
attempt to explain present turmoil on the basis of the events recorded in Genesis 3.
Chaos does not issue from the first primeval sin as Augustine tended to argue, but
precedes it. The psalms of lament are less preoccupied with sin and guilt than the
Christian penitential tradition might suggest. Frederik Linström argued this point
partly to dispel the thought (in relation to HIV-related concerns) that all suffering
was somehow attributable to sinful acts.[8]

One might see the Hebrew pattern of struggle and enthronement as intensified by what Paul calls the "foolishness" of the cross (1 Cor. 1:23). The divine world
rule is enacted through the crucifixion of God's only Son, a view that must appear
folly to Greek and Stoic accounts of providence. In accepting the constraints of
creaturely material, God's power and wisdom are displayed in a scandalous manner. This points not merely to our ignorance of God's ways but also to the divine
accommodation of our condition beset by sin, suffering, and evil. Never entirely
subdued, those threats to God's rule depicted in the imagery of the Old Testament
recur in the apocalyptic sections of the Gospels and Epistles, as also in the book of
Revelation with its frequent allusions to Hebrew images of evil. There the waters

of chaos continue to pose a threat. The beast in all its destructive violence arises from the waters to menace the world (Rev. 13:1). Not until Revelation 21:1 when "the sea is no more" is the threat of another catastrophe finally removed.[9] Divine sovereignty is undoubtedly a governing theme, but this sovereignty is exercised dramatically in a conquest of evil. For a time, the forces represented by the beast hold the upper hand over God's people. The rule of God, though genuine, is hidden. Realized finally in the new creation, this rule works for those on the underside of history.

AQUINAS AND CALVIN ON PROVIDENCE

A brief sketch of some classical theories of providence may indicate ways in which these theories have become detached from scriptural motifs, although I shall argue that this detachment is at most only partial. For example, the definition of providence offered by Thomas Aquinas reveals Platonic and Stoic influences although the extent to which these determine his account is disputed. God has providence as creator, as source of being and goodness, and as the one who directs all things to their final end. "It is not only in the substance of created things that goodness lies, but also in their being ordained to an end, above all to their final end, which, as we have seen, is the divine goodness."[10] This providence governs not only the general course of events but every single particular. Since each thing owes its existence to God, its final end is bound to be directed by God. Aquinas here employs the model of God as artist, an analogy favored by several recent writers. "Since his knowledge is related to things like that of an artist to his works of art . . . it must be that all things are set under his ordering."[11]

Subsequent exposition suggests an understanding of the divine rule in which every event is determined by the prior (or timeless) will of God. This understanding is confirmed by several features of his account, particularly where he follows Boethius. Nothing happens by chance, insofar as there are no uncaused or random events. The only sense in which chance can be said to occur within the created order is in the intersection of particular, unrelated, causal sequences. Nonetheless, these sequences are governed by the universal cause. "Thus the meeting of two servants, in their eyes unexpected because neither knew the other's errand, was foreseen by their master who intentionally sent them where their paths would cross."[12] The presence of evil in the creation is itself ruled by divine providence. Although evils may conflict with the nature of some particular thing, these evils contribute to the overall *telos* of nature. "Were all evils to be denied entrance, many good things would be lacking in the world: there would not be life for the lion were there no animals for its prey, and no patience of martyrs were there no persecution by tyrants."[13] The secondary causes that govern contingent entities are related to the primary cause of God's will which is both their necessary and sufficient condition. "Consequently the whole of their design down to every detail is anticipated in his mind."[14] Although the integrity of secondary causes is guaranteed by the primary cause, their direction and outcomes are always willed by the primary cause. While emphasizing the contingency of secondary causes, Aquinas is able to follow Boethius in describing everything as fixed by fate. In this sense providence can be regarded as the universal plan in God's mind, while destiny or fate is the realization of this plan in the world.[15] Furthermore, the Augustinian doctrine of predestination, as affirmed by Aquinas, reinforces the sense of an eternal foreordination of every temporal effect.[16] Predestination, as also reprobation, is an aspect of providence. It cannot be reduced to foreknowledge of free choices because it is gratuitous, fixed, and certain.[17]

Aquinas's view on one reading appears determinist and monistic. Everything moves according to an immutable divine plan. The primary cause of all effects, though removed from the creaturely arena through the mediation of secondary causes, remains all controlling. Here the apparent combination of divine absence with total determinism suggests an austere Stoic-like vision. This vision has occasioned severe criticism of Aquinas as, for example, in the following remarks of Keith Ward:

> The remorseless logic of Aquinas left the prime mover incapable of real relation to the world. . . . [But] it is possible to give freedom and responsibility a fundamental place in one's view of reality, and to admit a form of personal relationship to God in prayer which is impossible with the immutable, impassable God of Thomism.[18]

However, the context of the *Summa Theologiae*, its sustained engagement with Scripture, and other resultant features of Aquinas's theology indicate that this criticism is overstated. It results in part from readings of Aquinas that are dominated by the opening sections of the "Prima Pars." The third part of the *Summa Theologiae* and the goal of much of his writings in the prior parts is Christology. It is by the mystery of Christ's incarnation that we come to blessedness. Intimations of this blessedness occur throughout the *Summa Theologiae*, the parts of which cannot be understood except in relation to the overall intention and vision of Aquinas.[19] Elsewhere, the attention to human freedom, miracles, and petitionary prayer offers a more dramatic account of the God-world relationship in which divine initiative and creaturely response achieve a degree of mutuality.[20] This mutuality is reflected in Aquinas's insistence upon the friendship of God. Here mutual love forms the common life of God and human persons.[21]

On the subject of freedom, Aquinas appears to soften the Augustinian position by maintaining that divine agency guarantees rather than threatens our contingent freedom. God does not so much act upon human persons so causing them to act in the ways they do; but instead, God makes them to be what they are, thus enabling them to be free. In the exercise of human agency, divine and creaturely causes belong to different orders.[22] A similar justification of petitionary prayer is offered.

In response to ancient anxieties about the efficacy and propriety of prayer, Aquinas argues that divine providence has ordered the world in such a way that the will of God is sometimes made effective through the agency of human prayer. Thus prayer is a natural and universal activity: "In the case of prayer, we do not pray in order to change God's plan, but in order to obtain by our prayers those things which God planned to bring about by means of prayers, in order, as Gregory says, that our prayers should entitle us to receive what almighty God planned from all eternity to give us."[23] Such passages do at least illustrate the central place accorded human agency and divine response in Aquinas's account of the world order.

In his *Institutes,* John Calvin argues from the conviction that the teaching of Scripture claims that God ordains everything. Yet biblical notions of resistance, struggle, and threat to the divine rule are scarcely accorded a place in this treatment of the subject. Where these notions are present, they describe, at most, epistemological limitation. Behind what appears uncertain and confused lies the steady and immutable will of God. Where Scripture uses the language of repentance in relation to God, this language should be interpreted as an accommodation to human ways of thinking. The providence of God employs creaturely means for the fulfillment of the divine will. Here Calvin, as also Aquinas, is careful to note that the attribution of all events to God's will does not entail that God is the cause of sin and evil. Sin and evil are to be assigned to creaturely agencies that, although subordinate to the divine action, carry the sole responsibility for wrongdoing. The rays of the sun may cause the corpse to putrefy, but the stink is to be attributed to the corpse and not to the sun.[24]

The rhetoric of determinism informs Calvin's account, and it promotes a particular type of piety. Attacking Epicurean notions of chance with typical ferocity, he insists that God ordains everything. All things come to pass by the divine dispensation. This perspective elicits an attitude of trust that nothing can happen by fortune or chance. Everything is under the paternal care of God. There is good practical wisdom in this trust. A consideration of the evils that may befall can induce anxiety and paralysis. The ship may sink. There lurks danger on the streets and in the fields. One's house may burn. Even within a garden with a high wall, a serpent may lurk. In face of possible misfortune, we draw a feeble breath.[25] The remedy is to trust God and commit oneself to the knowledge that all things are ruled by a parental care. This trust doubtless affords comfort and promotes constancy throughout the Christian life. It may even energize one for secular action (we are not far from the Weber thesis here); yet in the face of life's fragility, it also has the questionable effect of suppressing complaint or questioning. There can be no interrogation of God. The psalms of lament do not feature positively in Calvin's treatment of providence in the *Institutes.* There is no trace of the importunate widow. He speaks instead of those words of beautiful solitude, "The LORD gave, and the LORD has taken away; blessed be the name of the LORD" (Job 1: 21). Summarizing the attitude of those who have made no little progress in their meditation on divine providence, he writes, "The Lord willed it, it must therefore be borne; not only because it is unlawful to strive with him, but because he wills nothing that is not just and befitting."[26]

Much in Calvin's *Commentary on the Psalms* confirms this form of piety, especially where it argues that faith, prayer, and all the duties of religion depend on the conviction that every single event happens by the personal rule of God.[27] Since God rules all things, we are required to view evils that befall us as signs of divine displeasure with our sins while yet perceiving anything good as a token of God's unmerited favor. In the Heidelberg Catechism (1563), a similar form of piety is advocated:

Q27. What do you understand by the providence of God?
A. The almighty and ever-present power of God whereby he still upholds, as it were by his own hand, heaven and earth together with all creatures, and rules in such a way that leaves and grass, rain and drought, fruitful and unfruitful years, food and drink, health and sickness, riches and poverty, and everything else, come to us not by chance but his fatherly hand.

Q28. What advantage comes from acknowledging God's creation and providence?
A. We learn that we are to be patient in adversity, grateful in the midst of blessing, and to trust our faithful God and Father for the future, assured that no creature shall separate us from his love, since all creatures are so completely in his hand that without his will they cannot even move.

Recent historical study of the development of Protestant identity in early modern England has revealed the practical effects of this lively belief in divine providence. Central to political, medical, and philosophical thought, providentialism is also an "ingrained parochial response to chaos and crisis, a practical source of consolation in a hazardous and inhospitable environment, and an idea which exercised practical, emotional and imaginative influence upon those who subscribed to it."[28]

If we turn to what Calvin says elsewhere in his scriptural commentaries and sermons, we can discern signs of a modified account. Here his attention to the details of the text and its unfolding of the gospel through contingent historical events offers some surprising reflections. The theme of accommodation, which is found everywhere in his theology, is employed to show that God chooses individuals, gives laws, and directs Israel in such a way as to accommodate human weakness and frailty.[29] Here the providence of God is presented as more reactive. It must wrestle with recalcitrant human material. The outcome is divine action, which in order to prevail, must improvise to a much greater degree than is conceded in the *Institutes*. Despite what Calvin says elsewhere in his Psalms commentary, there is a stronger sense of divine struggle, concession, and perseverance when he deals with the history of Israel as narrated in Psalm 106.[30] Furthermore, the doctrine of providence teaches the divine interaction with creation at the microlevel. Divine interaction cannot be reduced to an initial determining cause that enables it to run programmatically in accordance with the divine blueprint. God's hand is to be detected in the operation of the laws of nature and in historical forces. Providence is not the infusing of nature with general powers but the particular care of every created thing. As Christ taught, the benevolence of God extends to the level of little birds whose sustaining of themselves is "virtually a miracle."[31] John Leith argues in this context that Calvin's horror of deism leads him to the brink of pantheism, a position he only avoids by repeated stress on divine transcendence.[32]

Criticisms of the Thomist and Calvinist accounts as determinist, enthralled to philosophical influences, and inadequate to Scripture are at best partial. Such criticisms become more formidable when set against the rationalist accounts of providence of the early modern period. Here the search for positions that can be defended without prior commitment to a particular confessional tradition generates a view of providence more resolutely determinist. The boldest expression of this view is Leibniz's *Theodicy*, in which each event makes its distinctive contribution to the best of all possible worlds. In creating this world, the divine intellect is constrained by considerations of simplicity and variety. The highest simplicity yields the greatest variety with the maximum degree of order; so God must choose to actualize this world as the best possible.[33] David Blumenfeld points out that the austerity of this vision leads to a diminution of the earlier sense that Leibniz gives of God's parental care for creatures. "In the *Discourse* Leibniz describes God as a father who is infinitely solicitous of the needs of his children, but in the *Theodicy* he warns us not to view God as a 'mother . . . whose almost only care concerns . . . the happiness of [her child].'"[34] The rational demand that God create such a world imposes a necessity upon everything that happens. Thus mistakes, calamities, and crimes contribute in some way to the overall harmony of the cosmos. In its variety and order, the history of the world is held to express the divine will in every detail. Here biblical themes of struggle, resistance, and covenant partnership are increasingly remote from the philosophical justification offered of evil.

REVISIONING PROVIDENCE

Attempts to defend earlier forms of theological determinism are still to be found. Paul Helm argues trenchantly for the Augustinian-Reformed position that the rule of God requires that there be no indeterminacy in the created order.[35] A creation, it is argued, which is let loose from divine sovereignty is one in which future and final states cannot be guaranteed. The intrusion of radical risk and uncertainty into the cosmos is inconsistent with biblical claims about providence and eschatology. Indeterminacy must destabilize the rule of God in a way that is ruinous. As a child will tend to be undermined by an erratic and unpredictable parent, so a creation that eludes divine control will precipitate insecurity and eventual despair. In any case, the logic of sin and grace is such that, unless we are chosen first by God, our human decisions will inevitably lead us astray.

Yet the perceived determinism of this tradition, represented variously by Aquinas and Calvin, can be criticized on two related grounds. First, it is unable to make sufficient distinction between those events that God wills and those that are opposed to the divine intention; and, second, its account of human freedom is inadequate. The distinction between primary and secondary causes constructs all world events as caused and, therefore, determined absolutely by the primal will of God. This concept of providence, as Calvin is at pains to show, is not merely a matter of divine omniscience foreknowing everything that happens. Such a view would render God unacceptably passive. Divine foreknowledge is itself a function of the divine will, which is a necessary and sufficient condition for what comes to pass. The chain of worldly causes is here perceived as the means by which the divine will is executed. The tendency of the Reformed tradition (as opposed to the Lutheran) to maintain this position in the heat of the Amyrauldian and Arminian controversies produces a theology dominated by the divine decrees. The upshot, it is argued, is a fatalist mentality—what is for you will not go by you—and a religion that must perceive every contingent event as expressive of some divine purpose. Thus the misfortunes we endure are interpreted as tests to strengthen faith, chastisements to recall us to obedience, or simply retribution for sins committed. On this view, there is scope for human freedom, but this freedom is usually that of the compatibilist. Freedom is here described in terms of spontaneity and inner determination of the will. It is compatible with divine (and other) forms of determinism.[36] Yet where a stronger account of freedom is required, some abridgement of divine determinism will be sought.

Attempts to soften determinism and reconcile it with freedom sometimes appeal to Aquinas and point to the asymmetry of divine and creaturely causality. When attributed to God, the concept of cause can be used only analogically in ways that are not clear to us from a creaturely perspective. Without the chain of contingent events from which we derive our primary knowledge of causation, God cannot be located as a link in any spatio-temporal sequence. On the other hand, God is not absent or uninvolved in what happens. A causal role is exercised in bringing about, preserving, and securing the final end of everything that exists. This role confirms rather than destroys the contingency of creaturely causes. In assessing divine and creaturely causality, therefore, we should not perceive this assessment as a zero-sum game in which more of one entails less of the other. The analogical relation of the two forms of causality suggests a relationship of mutual entailment rather than exclusion. This relationship can be illustrated by the analogy of a play in which the characters are moved by a mixture of free choices, temperament, circumstances, and the actions of others.[37] We can assess the relative contribution of each of these to the outcome of the plot. At another level, however, we can understand the whole play as the creation of the playwright and perceive it in relation to his or her context, assumptions, and intentions. These perspectives are compatible; indeed, critics would do well to attend to both. As an illustration, this analogy is necessarily limited, yet it exposes the problem with all theories of double agency. They slide inexorably into determinism.[38] If contingent causes include scope for human freedom, then the effects cannot be sufficiently determined by anything other than the acts of freedom. Yet if these acts themselves, along with everything that happens, are foreordained (or timelessly ordained), then from God's perspective the outcome of our choices was necessarily and sufficiently determined, in which case freedom is not what we intuitively take it to be. On this reading, secondary causes, including free acts, are merely the instruments by which the primary cause is executed.[39]

Of greater significance in resisting the determinism of the Leibnizian position, however, are anxieties about the problem of evil. If everything happens by the will of God, can we make sense of the divine resistance and defeat of evil as depicted in Scripture? The need to see much of what happens around us as defiance of God's will is experienced both pastorally and politically. The refusal to interpret illness as sent by God may be part of any healthy strategy to combat it. Similarly, the struggle against forms of injustice is invigorated by the conviction that these are plainly contrary to the divine will. Resistance, not acquiescence, is required of us. This defiant resistance is not to deny that these attitudes were not present in much of classical theology, but accentuation of them now requires abridgement of its determinism.

In revisioning the doctrine of providence, one is presented with the process option as a standard alternative to the classical position. Here determinism and control are abandoned, while creation out of nothing and eschatology are radically revised. Instead, an account of the kenotic love of God is presented that requires, as the condition of its fulfillment, a world that is independent and uncontrolled, yet also receptive to the allurement of God. Providence is exercised only through endless attraction and persuasion of entities. The divine will is accomplished, if at all, by its influence on the free actions of creatures. In some respects, this account offers a way out of the difficulties noted above yet in other respects, as Daniel Migliore argues, it may be much further removed from the grammar of the biblical narrative. The loss of divine creation, incarnation, and eschatological redemption renders providence tentative and too precarious. God's resistance and promise of vindication are undermined with attendant practical consequences.[40]

Yet if the foregoing historical considerations are relevant, there may be some middle ground for the doctrine of providence. The classical model in Aquinas and Calvin requires its distinction from the rationalism of Leibniz by the presence of biblical themes that testify to divine struggle and victory. At the same time, revisionary models cannot be reduced to a single alternative standard, for example, process theology, since many of these models accommodate accounts, inherited from the classical theologians, of divine action in creation, incarnation, and eschatology. So-called *risk* theories of providence—these have gained ground in recent years—advance the view that creation is akin to a controlled experiment in which on account of contingent factors, especially human freedom, not every event is planned or determined.[41] This view generates a model of providence not as a plan immutable in every detail but as a project requiring divine improvisation in reaction to creaturely causes. The narratives of Scripture are read not as the outworking of an initial design determining every event. Instead, the emphasis upon covenant relationality yields an account with strange turns and twists as God reacts to events that are unwilled, if not unforeseen. The constitutive case is the crucifixion, in which the collusion of the forces of religion and law brings about the death of God's only Son; yet this same story is the occasion of the world's redemption. "If the cross is our guide, God is no determinist."[42] Here divine foreknowledge becomes defeasible. It can often be affirmed as future contingent events vindicate prior beliefs, but at other times it may be disconfirmed. God is more concerned, we must assume, with maintaining the covenantal relation than with preserving an immutable omniscience.[43]

In Aquinas and Calvin, it is surely significant that there is little discussion within the doctrine of providence of the sustained action of the Holy Spirit in bringing creation to perfection. The inward groaning of creation for redemption is closely linked to the work of the Spirit in Romans 8:22-25, yet this aspect of divine involvement is articulated neither in Aquinas's discussion of world government nor in Calvin's standard presentation of providence in the *Institutes*. B. B. Warfield may have rightly described Calvin as "the theologian of the Holy Spirit," yet pneumatology is not conspicuous in his remarks on providence. A fuller doctrine of the Spirit, however, may enable one to speak of creation as a project or a site under construction rather than as a perfect expression of a divine scheme. By treating this pneumatologically, one can avoid a breach between the rule of God and the autonomy of the world. In moving the world to its *telos* (end), the Spirit is active as decisively shaping the final outcomes, not in ways that are deterministic.[44]

The term *risk theory* is not entirely felicitous since the flanking of the world's story by creation out of nothing and eschatology indicates that the end is not in jeopardy even when the routes leading there are imprecise. Nonetheless, theories of this type can articulate a providential ruling of the world in which not everything that happens can be perceived as willed by God. The nature of divine love as limitless, precarious, and vulnerable creates a context in which the world is accorded its time and space as God's covenant partner, the object of faithfulness and loving kindness, yet without being wholly programmed in advance. The cosmos is created and redeemed, but it requires to be brought to perfection by the ongoing movement of the Spirit and the final eschatological action of the Father. Here frequent use is made of Vanstone's phenomenology of love.[45] A standard criticism is that the use of this phenomenology accords too much scope to human freedom, a freedom untrammeled by divine grace. However, it remains consistent with the view that only as God assails us with judgment and mercy can we be saved. Freedom neither lacks direction nor is it exercised in a void. The account of providence offered here is not one in which creatures could ever exercise any choice over whether to be loved by God.[46]

A modified objection to such a strategy is that it concedes too much. A risky creation in which not everything happens at the behest of God is one that is never fully under control. Final outcomes may become underdetermined. Our best efforts are threatened with eventual failure. Consequently, anxiety and loss of confidence have an enervating effect on the Christian life. This tension is already experienced in the different trajectories of the Hebrew Bible and its tendency to suppress all hints of dualism. Nonetheless, the sense that creation is not finally subdued until the end of time is one that runs through Scripture to its culmination in the book of Revelation. Where an eschatological perspective and a doctrine of the action of the Spirit complement an account of providence, that account can be retrieved from the standard criticisms of nondeterministic theories.

What has been presented is no more than a prolegomenon to a sustained treatment of the topic. But three further considerations may be offered in conclusion. The doctrine of providence here conceived need not restrict itself to any single model of divine action. Several types of divine involvement in the creation may be mutually compatible, and a differentiated account may enable clearer distinctions to be made between permission, will, influence, and effectiveness. Within this context, one can operate with a description of God's action in terms of persuasion and presence without eschewing other options. Consequently, an account of divine interaction in creation, incarnation, and eschatology can be promoted without neglecting the importance of action through influence. These forms of God's involvement with creation need not be disjoined as tends to happen in rival accounts of divine action.

In this regard, as Jürgen Moltmann has frequently reminded us, a description of divine action in trinitarian terms may enable us to perceive the works of God in a threefold pattern that can accommodate different models of engagement with the created order. Second, where providence works by influence, this engagement should not be underestimated. If God's Spirit is both omnipresent and possesses the fullest possible knowledge of the creation, then the scope for exercising influence is extensive. In this respect, the perceived weakening of God by revisionary theories of providence may be more apparent than real. Finally, the pastoral outcomes of a doctrine that does not need to attribute everything to the will of God should not be underestimated. It goes without saying that the problem of evil is not resolved by revising the doctrine of providence; yet if such revision leaves us with an alternative less intolerable, then embracing it will have some positive practical gains.[47]

CHAPTER 14

SPIRIT-CHRISTOLOGY AS ACCESS
TO TRINITARIAN THEOLOGY

Philip J. Rosato

This honorary chapter is both systematic in its argumentation and content and has a pastoral-ethical tone. It argues that the New Testament understanding of the conjoined divine missions of the Son and of the Spirit, which modern historical and systematic theology have revitalized and called Spirit-Christology, has recently become relevant as an access to a future-oriented and praxis-based Trinitarian theology. The characteristics of eschatology and ortho-praxy in the treatise *De Deo uno et trino* are derived from the teleological dimension of the missions of the Son and the Spirit, that is, from their role at the end of history to bring about the fulfillment of the human race through the resurrection of the dead, the universal judgment, and the definitive inauguration of the kingdom of the Father. Since this end-time dimension underscores the perennial interconnection between the mysteries of the incarnation and of grace, it also reveals the Father as the ultimate agent of human fulfillment; thus, the treatment of the teleological dimensions of Christology and pneumatology entails engaging precisely in trinitarian theology.[1]

Yet this chapter is pastoral-ethical as well since this teleological dimension of the mandates of the Son and the Spirit includes the participation of Christians in the ultimate reconciliation of all people, for according to the powerful symbolism of certain New Testament texts, they are invited by the Son and the Spirit to join them in bringing about the universally desired embrace of both the victims of history and their oppressors.[2] This future responsibility at the threshold of the kingdom urges contemporary Christians to embark on a new phase of their history, which can be designated as a pronounced commitment to the actual reconciliation of the unjustly treated and the unjustly motivated in their societies. By being noted for their sincere allegiance to nonviolence and to benevolence, the members of the church could provide tangible and credible evidence to others that they are now motivated, with greater consciousness and renewed vigor, by their primordial claim to be, first and foremost, a reconciling community (cf. 2 Cor. 5:18-21).

The three subdivisions of this essay concern the prospective, the retrospective, and the speculative functions that Spirit-Christology served in the early church, and that its revitalization should do at present.[3] The first subdivision concerns the prospective dimension of Spirit-Christology, that is, the mandates of the Son and the Spirit as they now exist and as they will be exercised on the threshold of the kingdom. In this subsection an initial reflection on the New Testament teaching about the role of the members of the church, along with roles of the Son and the Spirit, in the universal judgment has to be presented. The second subdivision deals with the retrospective functions of Spirit-Christology. Here emphasis is placed on the essential task of the Holy Spirit to prepare Jesus of Nazareth throughout his lifetime to become the just and persuasive judge and reconciler of history. Again in this subdivision, the spiritual formation of Jesus for this universal responsibility will shed light on the mode in which the church must ready itself for its future co-involvement with the Son and the Spirit in the final reconciliation of all people. From the unique point of view provided by Spirit-Christology, the third subdivision speculates about the eternal mandates that the Father bestowed on the Son and the Spirit, mandates that constitute not only the preincarnational basis, but also the post-kingdom elucidation, of the full meaning of the human history of salvation and of sanctification, and of the part played in it by the reconciling mission of the church. In this final subdivision, a future-oriented and praxis-related trinitarian theology, inspired by insights drawn from Spirit-Christology, can be understood as indispensable in guiding the contemporary church anew into a decidedly reconciliatory phase of self-awareness and activity.

THE PROSPECTIVE DIMENSION OF SPIRIT-CHRISTOLOGY

Along with other supporting biblical passages, the trinitarian text found in Revelation 3 provides the New Testament foundation of this essay since it both alludes to the eschatological task of judgment or that the Christ and the Spirit entrusted to the early church and epitomizes the renewed mission of reconciliation provided by the present ecclesial community. In this text, the risen Christ, who had become not only the bearer but also the sender of the Spirit, speaks in the first person singular to the members of the local church at Laodicea in Asia Minor.[4] He challenges them to repudiate their lukewarm response both to the temporal goal of announcing the good news of the kingdom in their sophisticated social ambience and to the end-time goal to rejoice with him once they have sat on the judgment throne with him, taken part in the definitive reconciliation of all people, and thus facilitated the complete glorification of the Creator-Father. Christ voices his final promise to his followers at the end of the letters to the seven churches and attests that the Spirit fully concords with his words: "Listen! I am standing at the door, knocking; if you hear my voice and open the door, I will come in to you and eat with you, and you with me. To the one who conquers I will give a place with me on my throne, just as I myself conquered and sat down with my Father on his throne. Let anyone who has an ear listen to what the Spirit is saying to the churches" (Rev. 3:20-22). A later text in the book of Revelation, which records the words of the prophetic narrator, supports this understanding that the risen Christ transfers the full power of his eschatological task to judge all people onto those who had conquered evil at the point when they had been freely reborn as sons and daughters with him and had become coheirs with him through baptism: "Then I saw thrones, and those seated on them were given authority to judge" (Rev. 20:4).

The antecedent New Testament passages in the Pauline letters and in the Synoptic Gospels, which ground these Johannine texts, can be found chiefly in 1 Corinthians and the Gospel of Luke. Paul declares to the Corinthians: "When any of you has a grievance against another, do you dare to take it to court before the unrighteous, instead of taking it before the saints? Do you not know that the saints will judge the world? And if the world is to be judged by you, are you incompetent to try trivial cases? Do you not know that we are to judge angels—to say nothing of ordinary matters?" (1 Cor 6:1-3). At the Last Supper Jesus announces this promise to his disciples: "You are those who have stood by me in my trials; and I confer on you, just as my Father has conferred on me, a kingdom, so that you may eat and drink at my table in my kingdom, and you will sit on thrones judging the twelve tribes of Israel" (Luke 22:28-30; cf. Matt. 19:28).[5] The notable similarity, particularly between Luke 22:28-30 and Revelation 3:21, but also between those texts and 1 Corinthians 6:1-3; Matthew 19:28; and Revelation 20:4, rests on their dependence on Psalm 110:1 and Daniel 7:9, 22, and 26, in which taking a place on the throne of God entails admittance to the function of judging as God does. Through his resurrection, Jesus was elevated to the status of universal lordship; yet he prefers not to exercise this honored and responsible task alone. He wills that his disciples and all their followers participate in the full authority of his judging function. In the New Testament, therefore, "the one who sits on the throne is the messianic King, along with God and with his victorious community."[6] Thus, the early Christians were urged to conduct prophetic lives in accordance with their objective forgiveness and glorification through baptism; this way of life meant that they were to have the same mind and the same goal as Christ, and in this way to prepare themselves for their eschatological role as co-judges with him before the full inauguration of the kingdom.[7]

At present, these texts could be read as a timely admonition to all the baptized to act against their tepidity by anticipating, now in history, the practice of responsibility that Christ and the Spirit will require of them before the ultimate realization of the kingdom. Far from entailing a complacent waiting in their environment, this responsibility consists in Christians freely allowing themselves to be steadily "conquered" by Christ through their dedication to nonviolence and benevolence and through their mission of reconciliation among actual victims and oppressors. Only such a stance will prepare them to join the Son and the Spirit on the Last Day in effectively convincing wrongdoers of their inhuman violence, in encouraging them benevolently to undergo a free conversion, and in voicing a spontaneous request of pardon. The members of the church must also assist the Christ and the Spirit in vindicating and consoling the wronged while gently urging the wronged to accept the repentance of their aggressors and to forgive them freely. Contemporary Christians might view themselves as weighed down by theological, moral, and practical problems far heavier than those of the seven churches in the book of Revelation, problems on which basis they could deem themselves too unworthy in the sight of God and others to have to assume such a serious task. Nonetheless Christ, who once and for all had made them conquerors with him in the power of the Spirit, does not negate his promise to include them in the community around his judgment seat.[8]

The accentuation on the word *freely* throughout this subsection is clearly meant to distinguish this description of what will occur before the full inauguration of the kingdom from the concept that underlies the term *apocataclasis*, that is, that all members of the human race will enter into eternal joy per force, given that the divine freedom in their regard far surpasses their own created autonomy. In the description proffered here, the Son and the Spirit who act for the Father fully respect the sincerity of the acceptance or the rejection of human beings. The Son and the Spirit invite Christians to share in the universal judgment, precisely so that reconciliatory, nonviolent, and benevolent fellow human beings persuade the victims of history to leave aside their bitterness and the oppressors to leave aside their brutality.[9] Moreover, in these pages it is acknowledged that the outcome of this persuasion on the part of the Son and the Spirit, along with the members of the church, is a mystery of faith associated with the sheer gratuity of divine creativity, for to what extent the victims can and will freely accept the pardon of their persecutors, and the latter can and will freely repent of having done evil and ask pardon of the former, cannot be known. Christian faith does not fully know the outcome, yet Christian hope fully expects that the final embrace will be universal.

THE RETROSPECTIVE DIMENSION OF SPIRIT-CHRISTOLOGY

Although the future implications of Spirit-Christology were not overclouded, its immediate usefulness to the early Christians was as a retrospective tool by which they could comprehend, with the aid of the light offered by Easter and Pentecost, the meaning of the horrific death of Jesus of Nazareth, and of the prior politico-religious condemnation of him after his brief public manifestation. These stark realities seemed to contrast with the hope-filled baptism of Jesus by John and with the previous discernment in which Jesus had engaged for years, so that he become conscious of, and willing to undertake, the clearly heard yet seemingly impossible mandate originating from *Abba* to save humankind by re-creating it. The Synoptic Gospels and the body of *The Gospel of John* after its prologue explicitly attest that this mandate conferred on the historical Jesus, in all the phases of its actualization, was facilitated by the collaborative and coextensive mandate of the Holy Spirit to guarantee its effectiveness.[10] Thus, beginning from the events at the end of the life of Jesus and proceeding backwards toward its mysterious beginning, the early Christians could gradually comprehend that his mandate appeared to be inseparable from that of the Spirit in terms of its collaboration and coextension, but not in terms of its inherent dynamism.

The specific dynamism inherent in the mandate of Jesus can be characterized as visible, kenotic, and oriented toward the darkness of death, while the specific dynamism of the accompanying mandate of the Holy Spirit can be described as invisible, victorious, and oriented toward the light of life. How can these different types of dynamism found in the Spirit-Christology of the early church be illustrated in this brief chapter centering primarily on its contemporary relevance? It seems that some paradigmatic examples should be chosen by which the interaction of the two dynamisms could be exemplified, while two other factors can be explained: first, the Holy Spirit's subtle yet thorough preparation of Jesus for his eschatological role as universal judge of humankind; and second, the nonviolence and the benevolence at the core of the moral message and activity of the Spirit-led Jesus, which has been hitherto accentuated in this chapter. All these criteria are met by the so-called *prophetic sign-actions* of Jesus, the specialized subcategory of his public ministry. Prominent exegetes claim that these consist in parables that he put into the symbolic form of street dramas and by which he indicated his reliance on the similar sign-actions of the prophets of Israel.[11]

Succinctly examining two of these prophetic sign-actions can, in fact, identify the specific dynamism at work in the otherwise collaborative and coextensive mandates of Jesus and the Spirit. This identification is possible since the prophetic sign-actions have apparently foolhardy and audacious characteristics and thus might lead those who enact them to become spurned; at the same time their potential efficacy, whether at the moment of their realization or afterwards, might lead their enactor to become regarded as having attained human salvation before God, expressed in signs and realized in moral actions consonant with them. The potentially ambiguous outcome of these prophetic sign-actions is rooted in their nature as (1) *extraordinary* gestures, which are meant to persuade their onlookers to incorporate the salvific and sanctifying design of God into history; (2) *creative* gestures, which form a strong allegiance, based either on acceptance or on rejection, among their onlookers; (3) *provocative* gestures, which demand their onlookers undergo moral conversion; and (4) *anticipatory* gestures, which announce to the onlookers the in-breaking of the impending messianic kingdom of God, the reality at the core of the normal discourse of this self-proclaimed prophet.[12] Even if Jesus might be led deeper into the darkness of sin, suffering, and death by enacting these sign-actions, this fact would not diminish the power of the Holy Spirit to cause him obliquely to enter into the redemption from sin, the victory over suffering, and the attainment of new life along with all who accepted his prophetic gestures.

The first example is found in Luke 7:36-50; and the second, in Luke 13:10-17. The first, featuring Jesus in the presence of Simon the Pharisee and a female public sinner, centers on a moral-theological argument; and the second, depicting him in the presence of the leader of a synagogue and a crippled elderly woman, turns on a moral-legalistic argument. Particularly significant for the theme of this chapter is the moral dimension of these prophetic sign-actions, in that they compose scenes of judgment in which Jesus attempts to convert a self-righteous, yet cynical, wrongdoer from his religious indifference toward the moral suffering of the prostrate sinful woman, or to convert the legalistic, yet indignant, wrongdoer from his religious blindness to the physical suffering of the bent-over daughter of Abraham.[13] Once converted, they might ask for forgiveness from their victims, if they would accept it. Moreover, Jesus calls the victims of prejudice and marginalization from attachment to bitterness to readiness to pardon their persecutors, should they sincerely request it of them. For these reasons, it can be said that the Spirit was leading Jesus to be both nonviolent and benevolent and at the same time just and persuasive as he reconciled both the victims and the wrongdoers in his culture, thereby providing a prelude to his eventual end-time judgment of all people along with his followers.

How did the breath or the finger of *Abba* accomplish this? It has been established that the specific dynamism of the mandate of Jesus from the Father to save humankind by re-creating it, without having patent instructions according to which it was to be fulfilled, called for his willingness to undertake self-emptying actions that might lead to his failure. The fact that Jesus freely adopted a form of completing his mandate, which was potentially as effective as it was life-threatening, obliquely reveals the specific dynamism of the mandate given by the Father to the Spirit: to accompany Jesus and to render his entire mission, and especially his divisive prophetic gestures, eschatologically effective or trans-creative, that is, victorious, liberating, and life-giving. The breath of God accounts for the inspiration through which Jesus discovered, in silent discerning prayer, the audacious genre of the prophetic sign-action to integrate into his ministry.[14]

In terms of this chapter, the main significance of these two prophetic sign-actions of Jesus for contemporary Christians is the role model he provides for their own task of discerning, with the guidance of the Holy Spirit, how best in their particular society to convince the victims to be open to granting pardon freely to those who have hurt them and to persuade the aggressors to ask for pardon from those whom they have hurt. In particular, the key verbal phrases enunciated by Jesus in the course of each of these symbolic actions indicate the wisdom and the holiness the Holy Spirit is presently working to instill in members of the ecclesial community so that, both now and on the Last Day, they can bear the responsibility with Jesus of convincing the victims and the aggressors of history to embrace this wisdom and holiness immediately before the final inauguration of the kingdom. The response "Therefore, I tell you, her sins, which were many, have been forgiven; hence she has shown great love. But the one to whom little is forgiven, loves little" (Luke 7:47) presages the arguments concerning the relationship between forgiveness and genuine love for others,[15] which Jesus has to present to the victims and the oppressors alike on the day of judgment. The response "And ought not this woman, a daughter of Abraham whom Satan bound for eighteen long years, be set free from this bondage on the sabbath day?" (Luke 13:16) foretells the arguments concerning the relationship between compassion and genuine humanity[16] that Jesus has to put forth on the Last Day to the same groups. Forgiveness and compassion are the ultimate motives that might lead the victims to move freely toward the aggressors who brutalized them by giving in to evil, and these are the motives that might lead the aggressors to move toward those who were brutalized by the evil they had done against them.

THE ETERNAL MANDATES OF THE FATHER TO THE SON AND THE SPIRIT

The question, that would logically project the reflections sketched in this chapter onto a far broader horizon is this: What particular nuances do Spirit-Christology, a mystery which is normally viewed as the historical self-manifestation of the economy of salvation and sanctification achieved by the Trinity, offer to the Christian comprehension of the immanent and eternal existence of the three divine persons? More particularly, how does the retrospective dimension of the collaborative and coextensive mandates of the Son and the Spirit illumine what, from the human viewpoint, can be called the preincarnational dimension of the divine eternity; and how does the prospective dimension of these mandates cast light on its *post regnum* dimension? These two questions can be posed even more pointedly: Does the Creator-Father eternally bestow the re-creative mandate on the Son and the trans-creative mandate on the Spirit in such a way that they could reveal his glory to a potentially free creation that would either retain fully or lose to some degree its original *being in freedom*? Does the Creator-Father eternally confer these same mandates in such a way that, after the full inauguration of the kingdom, the Son-Re-creator and the Spirit-Trans-creator would continue to exercise them?[17]

While not directly accessible either to perception or to reason, various answers to these questions have been given over the centuries by Christians who speculate about them on the basis of faith in divine self-revelation that opens up realities that were accomplished in the past, are being enacted in the present, and will come about in the future. What is offered here is a speculation that stems chiefly from a revitalized Spirit-Christology.[18] With regard to the dimension of the divine eternity *ante incarnationem*, the three persons of the Trinity can be said always to have possessed foreknowledge that a potential creation of intelligent and loving beings, made in their image and endowed with their autonomy, could become a reality and could either accept or reject the gratuitous grace at the core of their *being-as-image*. This leads to the insight that the three divine Persons were eternally capable of revealing themselves freely to a created race that would in various degrees either maintain or reject grace.

The Hebrew scriptures clearly attest that free creatures have ensued from a gratuitous decision of God and that they, while not having entirely rejected divine grace, have chosen to be evildoing and evil-enduring creatures. The Christian scriptures presuppose the scriptures of the Hebrews but confess that at the fullness of time God first brought about an initial reconciliation, and will bring about an ultimate reconciliation between himself and both the perpetrators and the recipients of evil, and between these as well. The Christian scriptures further presuppose that these two moments of reconciliation could be achieved only by the eternal commitment of the Son of the Creator-Father to re-create human beings by entering into their sin, suffering, and death, and by the concomitant eternal commitment of the Spirit of the Creator-Father to make this re-creation efficaciously pass into the state of trans-creation. In this way, the glory of the Creator-Father, objectively achieved by the Son, could be enhanced by the subjective willingness of redeemed creatures rendered wise and holy by the power of the Spirit. Thus, the conjoined mandates of the Son and the Spirit could fully glorify the sovereign and benign creativity of the Father only through the objectively redeemed and subjectively sanctified human race, the steward of all the works of his hand.

With the statement made above that God has first brought about an initial, and then will bring about an ultimate, reconciliation between himself and both the doers and the recipients of evil, and between these as well, the eternity of the mandates that the Son and the Spirit received from the Father is affirmed as the timeless, yet *antecedent*, precondition of the possibility that it could be decided to re-create and to trans-create gratuitously endowed *free-beings-in-the-world* who had collectively rejected not all, but many of, the benefits of divine grace.[19] This statement implies that the mandates of the Son and the Spirit have eternally existed *ante incarnationem*. By use of the terms employed in this chapter, the eternal mandate of the Son could be described as follows: The Father fully bestowed his nonviolent and benevolent being on the Son so that within the divine life he objectively could be its perfect image and beyond the divine life, could re-create it through an objective embodiment; thus the Son was eternally generated by the Father as the image and communicator of divine nonviolence and benevolence.[20]

Using the same terms, the eternal mandate of the Spirit can be envisioned as follows: the Father of the Son fully bestowed his nonviolent and benevolent being on the Spirit so that within the divine life, the Father subjectively could be its perfect image along with the Son. Beyond the divine life, the Father could trans-create it, or bring it to a heightened status, in those in whom it had been re-cre-ated by the Son. Thus, the Spirit eternally proceeded (had his divine nature, his being) from the Father of the Son and eternally received his form (his intra-divine profile, his specificity) from the Father and the Son so that he is the subjective embodiment and communicator of divine nonviolence and benevolence.[21] Such speculation would explain why in the economy of salvation and sanctification the Spirit taught Jesus of Nazareth, the Son sent on a kenotic mission, to judge others according to these values in his prophetic sign-actions, just as he still teaches the church, in the time between the first and final comings of the Son, to be a visible communion marked by these very same values. If this were not the case, neither the Son in the flesh nor those who exist mystically united with him would be capable of exercising properly, that is, according to the will of the Creator-Father, their roles of judging all people before the final inauguration of the kingdom.

Will the re-creative mandate of the Son and the trans-creative mandate of the Spirit eternally exist *post regnum*, that is, after the ultimate reconciliation has taken place? On what basis can a positive answer to this question be made? On this side of eternity as it were, Christian speculation cannot fathom how redeemed and sanctified human beings along with the wholly restored creation are to fill up this vast duration. Revelation implies, however, that the entire reconciled human race is to experience eternity as the only duration that is providentially sufficient so that together they can look back on their lives and perceive for the first time the myriad ways in which the mandates of the Son and the Spirit led them to be saved and sanctified. This means that the victims will be able to view their aggressors, and the latter, the former in an unimaginably different light.

Thus, with each explosive insight into the mystery of their corporate salvation and sanctification, the urge will arise to magnify all the more the glory of the Creator-Father, the Re-creator Son, and the Trans-creator Spirit. In order to be satisfied in an infinite manner, however, all would have to plumb the eternal existence of the divine Trinity in terms not only of their individual stories of salvation and sanctification, but also of the stories of those whom they both knew and loved as friends and knew and rejected as enemies. In effect, after the ultimate reconciliation, the continuance of the mandates of the Son and the Spirit, along with the particular dynamism appropriate to each, that is, the kenotic intention of the Re-creator and the life-giving intention of the Trans-creator, will have to continue.[22] Why? They have to serve all the redeemed as the totally translucent models by which they can not only know themselves just as they have been known, but also rejoice in their salvation and sanctification precisely as the Father eternally foresaw it by endowing the Son as their potential liberator and the Spirit as their potential sanctifier.

CONCLUDING REMARKS

Despite the hope that they may provide, the insights that have emerged in this chapter might strike most Christians both as novel and as disconcerting. These insights may seem novel, since Christians normally interpret the closing words of the second article of the Creed, which read, "And he will come again to judge the living and the dead," in terms of their being passively scrutinized, along with all people, by the Son, and not in terms of their having an active role in this mystery of faith. These insights may seem disconcerting, because Christians rightly consider themselves, as far as the totality of history is concerned, to be included both among the perpetrators of evil and among the victims of evil. Thus, they would be perplexed in attempting to understand how they are at the same time to be judged and to judge others on the threshold of the kingdom. A resolution to this perplexity could consist in diminishing the traditional reliance on Matthew 25:31-46, which emphasizes a starkly apocalyptical or retaliatory understanding of the Last Judgment and thus dangerously overshadows the saving gospel of Jesus, which announces that only the righteousness of God creates justice. In its place a genuinely eschatological understanding of the Last Judgment could be fostered, which accentuates the love of Jesus and his desire to put an end to enmity (cf. Eph. 2:16) and to establish a kingdom of justice and peace.[23] According to this eschatological understanding, Christians can indeed view themselves as converted perpetrators and victims whose wisdom and holiness persuasively qualify them to convince both these groups, along with the Son and the Spirit, ultimately to judge each other mercifully, that is, in such a way that they make a final reconciling gesture and so that the full realization of the kingdom of righteousness and nonviolence is begun.

Apart from this matter, it could seem to most contemporary Christians that the content of this chapter would cause those who are not baptized to read it as further evidence that Christianity makes far too many exalted claims about its unique role in the universal history of salvation and sanctification. In answering this serious objection, one could argue that such claims might beneficially cause the adherents of other religious traditions to ask themselves on the basis of their sacred texts what better goal their undisputed wisdom and holiness can have than to partake in the end-time fulfillment of the reconciliation of the divine and the human, and of the human with the human.[24]

If the reflections presented in this chapter raise divisive issues both in the church and beyond it, the wide consensus of Christian theologians might be that it is not opportune to emphasize any special role of the baptized at the final judgment. If this were to be decided, this powerful New Testament symbol and the reflections to which it leads might be deemed advantageous only as an intramural reminder to the members of all the contemporary local churches that they should safeguard two essential aspects of their communal life. The first is their prophetic, or messianic, identity as those who await in active hope the full manifestation of the eternal mandates of the Son and the Spirit when all human beings enter into the glorious kingdom of the Father. The second is their credible fidelity to their reconciliatory, nonviolent, and benevolent mission within history that the Spirit of the risen Son guides to the same end. Remaining oriented to the future fulfillment of divine self-revelation and faithful to the practice of historical reconciliation clearly depends on the gratuity of divine grace. As this chapter suggests, pondering on their participation in the mystery of the nonviolent and benevolent triune God is a constant source of grace and thus a perennial empowerment of their mission.[25] The Son-Re-creator and the Spirit-Trans-creator expect them to be ready to do whatever is required, now and in the future, to witness to the righteousness of the Creator-Father (cf. 2 Cor. 5:21) before the unjustly motivated and the unjustly treated within history.

CHAPTER 15

IS THERE JUSTICE IN THE TRINITY?

Nicholas Wolterstorff

Most Christians, ancient, medieval, and modern, but especially modern, if they heard of the topic justice in the Trinity would regard thinking and writing about it as appalling. How dare one even think of justice in the Trinity? Love is what resides within the Trinity. Love casts out justice.

Many, when they hear of justice, think of *meting out* justice. No meting out of justice occurs within the Trinity. Meting out justice means pronouncing and executing justice on the wrongdoer. There can be no meting out of justice within the Trinity because there is no wrongdoer within the Trinity. If the whole of justice is the meting out of justice, then there is no justice within the Trinity.

Others think of justice more broadly as *rendering judgment*. Rendering judgment comes in three forms: first, rendering a decision in cases of conflict; second, determining whether the accused is guilty of the accusation and declaring the accused guilty if that person is guilty and innocent if not guilty; and third, meting out judgment on one declared guilty. No rendering of judgment can occur within the Trinity because neither wrongdoing nor conflict occurs within the Trinity. If the whole of justice involves the rendering of judgment, then there is no justice within the Trinity.

Is there justice within human life in the eschaton? If one thinks of justice as rendering judgment, there is no justice. Since there is neither wrongdoing nor conflict in the eschaton, there can be no rendering of judgment. In the eschaton there is love, not justice. Would there be justice in this present age had things in God's creation gone as God intended them to go and wants them to go? If rendering judgment is the whole of justice, there would not be. Conflict and wrongdoing are contrary to God's will for creation.

It is a tightly integrated package: There is no justice within the Trinity, there is no justice among human beings in the eschaton, and there is no justice in this present life as this present life is meant to be. Life in the eschaton and life in this present age as it is meant to be mirror life within the Trinity. Justice is nowhere in view. Love rules. Where love rules, justice has no room. Justice has room only when love breaks down.

Justice has its home in this present age as it actually is. Here there is room—far too much room—for rendering judgment. What mirrors the Trinity in life in this present age is not justice but love finding its way into the cracks and fissures within conflict, wrongdoing, and rendering judgment.

JUSTICE AS RENDERING JUDGMENT

But does the rendering of judgment exhaust justice? Is it the whole of justice? Is justice to be equated with the rendering of judgment? That question is one of the principal ones to be discussed if we want to consider seriously whether there is justice in the Trinity and do not want to dismiss the thought as either mindless or heretical.

First, though, a word about the Trinity is needed. It will not be necessary for our purposes to delve deeply into doctrines of the Trinity. All orthodox Christians, whatever their doctrine of the Trinity (if any), hold that the differentiation among the individual persons of the Trinity is sufficient for them to love each other. That degree of differentiation will be sufficient for us to consider whether there is justice in the Trinity. Orthodox Christians also hold that the persons of the Trinity are not individually God but that only the threesome is God. There are not three gods but one. To understand this point, it may help to explicitly employ an analogy that is constantly present, either as foreground or background, in the speech of Jesus: the Trinity is like a family. A family has members, but a member of a family is not the family. The family consists of all the members together in their familial relationships.

The action of rendering judgment cannot comprise the whole of justice. Take that form of rendering judgment that consists of making a determination in cases of conflict. Not every act of rendering judgment is a case of justice. An act of rendering judgment is a case of justice only if it is a just judgment that has been justly rendered. What, then, is a *just judgment*? A *just judgment* is a judgment in which the judge, having made a determination of what it would be like for the parties to treat each other justly in the matter under dispute, issues a declaration to that effect. Treating each other justly, however, will not in turn consist of one of the parties rendering just judgment except for those unusual cases in which the dispute was over the rendering or not rendering of judgment by one of the parties. In those cases, the judgment, which, so it is determined, one of the parties has a right to render, will not in turn be a judgment about the rendering of judgment. Unless there were more to justice than rendering judgment, rendering judgment could not be a form of justice.

Or take that form of rendering judgment that consists of determining whether an accused is guilty of the accusation and of declaring that person guilty if the accused is and innocent if the accused is not. Of this form of rendering judgment, it is also true that only some examples are cases of justice; for it must be a just judgment justly rendered. To be a just judgment, the judge must bring to light whether or not the accused performed the act with which the accused is charged and, if the accused did, whether it was an infraction of justice—whether it was an unjust act. That act of which the accused is charged will seldom be an act of rendering judgment; and in those cases in which it is, that judgment will not in turn have been about an act of rendering judgment. Once again, we see that unless there were more to justice than rendering judgment, rendering judgment could not be a case of justice.

The same point is to be made for that form of rendering judgment that consists of meting out judgment. Only some cases of meting out judgment are cases of justice. If the judgment is not just and justly rendered, it is not. A just judgment will consist of declaring that such and such actions performed on the guilty party will be just actions, and of being correct in that declaration. The actions that the guilty party is sentenced to undergo will usually not consist, in turn, of someone rendering judgment on the guilty party; so once again, rendering judgment is a case of justice only if there is more to justice than rendering judgment.

Now consider the second form of rendering judgment, that of determining whether an accused is guilty of the accusation and of declaring the accused guilty if that person is and innocent if that person is not. To prevent our formulations from becoming unduly complicated, let me set off to the side those cases in which the accused is charged with unjustly rendering judgment. Suppose the judge determines that the accused is guilty as charged, and suppose the judge is correct in that determination. The accused acted unjustly toward someone and committed an infraction of justice. To declare that the accused treated someone unjustly is to imply that there was a way of treating the victim that would not have been unjust, a way of treating the victim that would not have been an infraction of justice. There was a way of treating the victim that would have been just. Let us call such justice *primary justice*. The justice that consists of rendering just judgment is *secondary justice*, in the sense that it deals with infractions of primary justice, accusations of infraction, or disputes over what would be an infraction.

The justice that consists of justly rendering just judgment deals with breakdowns in primary justice and with charged or threatening breakdowns. Such justice presupposes another form of justice, viz., primary justice. If there is justice in the Trinity, it will be primary justice. There can be no room in the Trinity for secondary justice; but from that claim it does not follow that there is no justice in the Trinity. So too, if there is justice in the eschaton, and in this present age as it was meant to be, it will be primary justice.

JUSTICE IN THE OLD TESTAMENT

In his book *The Desire of the Nations*,[1] Oliver O'Donovan says that the Old Testament understanding of justice

> is often obscured by the influence of a quite different conception of justice, classical and Aristotelian in inspiration, that is built on the twin notions of appropriateness and proportionate equality—justice as receiving one's own and being in social equilibrium. *Mishpat* is primarily a judicial *performance*. When "judgment" is present, it is not a state of affairs that obtains but an activity that is duly carried out. When it is absent, imbalance or maldistribution is not complained of but the lapsing of a judicial function that always needs to be exercised. So, for example, when Amos calls for *mishpat* to "roll on like a river," he means precisely that the stream of juridical activity should not be allowed to dry up. Elsewhere (5:16) he has demanded that it should be "set up" like a fixed monument in the town's public place, always to be found there.[2] Very comparably, Isaiah of Jerusalem demands that the citizens of Jerusalem should "seek *mishpat*," explaining this as a commitment to giving judgment in the cause of the fatherless and litigating on behalf of the widow (Isa. 1:17);[3] and he promises that YHWH will "bring back judges" to the city "as in the days of old," because Zion is to be "redeemed by *mishpat*" (Isa. 1:26f.).[4]

O'Donovan holds that although the noun *mishpat* has a secondary sense in the Old Testament, this secondary sense "has still not lost touch with the context of litigation. *Mishpat*, having been proper to the judge, now becomes proper to the plaintiff; it is his 'claim,' which the judge is bound to attend to."[5]

There can be no doubt that *mishpat* in the Old Testament—usually rendered as "justice" in our English translations—often refers to juridical judgments and pleadings and to what I have been calling *rendering judgment*. Thus, in the midst of a lengthy catalog of regulations for Israel's life, we find Moses saying:

> You shall appoint judges and officials throughout your tribes, in all your towns that the LORD your God is giving you, and they shall render just decisions for the people. You must not distort justice; you must not show partiality; and you must not accept bribes, for a bribe blinds the eyes of the wise and subverts the cause of those who are in the right. Justice, and only justice, you shall pursue, so that you may live and occupy the land that the LORD your God is giving you. (Deut.16:18-20)

Furthermore, even though as I have argued above, rendering judgment could not be a form of justice unless there was also primary justice, it is theoretically possible that primary justice never received verbal expression in the Hebrew of the Old Testament. Although unlikely, it is possible; but as we shall see, it is definitely the case that such verbal expression occurred.

Many examples could be cited; I will limit myself to one. In Deuteronomy 24:17, Moses says to Israel, "You shall not deprive a resident alien or an orphan of justice; you shall not take a widow's garment in pledge." The clause "you shall not take a widow's garment in pledge" already makes one prick up one's ears. It is hard to see how this could be construed as instruction for rendering judgment; it appears to be instruction for primary justice. Should there be any doubt on the matter, Deuteronomy 24:19-21 removes it:

> When you reap your harvest in your field and forget a sheaf in the field, you shall not go back to get it; it shall be left for the alien, the orphan, and the widow, so that the LORD your God may bless you in all your undertakings. When you beat your olive trees, do not strip what is left; it shall be for the alien, the orphan, and the widow. When you gather the grapes of your vineyard, do not glean what is left; it shall be for the alien, the orphan, and the widow.

There can be no mistake: these instructions are instructions for primary justice, not for rendering judgment.

Even the familiar passage Amos 5:24 that O'Donovan cites as an illustration of his thesis leaves room for doubt that it really is that. The prophet has been speaking on behalf of God to the people of Israel generally. Immediately before the passage in question, God says that he finds the cultic activities of the people offensive and unacceptable. Then we read the verse: "But let justice roll down like waters, And rectitude like an ever-flowing stream" (Amos 5:24).[6]

By itself, the first line is not implausibly interpreted as referring to judicial proceedings; the prophet might be enjoining his hearers to see to it that there are just laws and a judicial system producing just verdicts. The parallelism with the second line, however, makes it unlikely that the latter is what he means. The rectitude that the prophet enjoins his hearers to make "an ever-flowing stream" is surely the rectitude of each and every person, not only that of judges. That command makes it likely that the same is true for the justice of which he is speaking.

It is even more likely that the justice spoken of in the equally familiar verse from Micah is not simply the justice of judicial proceedings. "O mortal" is the prophet's address to his hearer before he tells them, "What the LORD requires of you is to do justice, and to love kindness, and to walk humbly with your God."[7] Given the address "O mortal," and given the parallelisms between "do justice," on the one hand, and "love kindness" and "walk humbly with your God," on the other, I find it implausible to suppose that "doing justice" is exclusively, or even primarily, a reference to judicial proceedings—although let it be noted that the passage occurs within the context of an imagined judicial proceeding with the people as accused and God as judge.

Somewhat ironically, O'Donovan himself is on the verge of taking note of my point, that rendering judgment could not be a form of justice unless there were another form of justice, primary justice, this latter being more basic in that rendering judgment deals with breakdowns in primary justice and with threats and charges of breakdown. After claiming that *mishpat* pertains to rendering judgment, referring primarily to juridical judgment and secondarily to juridical pleading, O'Donovan goes on to say that when *mishpat* "is present, it is not a state of affairs that obtains but an activity that is duly carried out." Then he goes on to describe the juridical activity: "To judge is to make a distinction between the just and the unjust, or, more precisely, to bring the distinction which already exists between them into the light of public observation."[8] When a judge determines that one party is guilty, that judge does more by going on to issue a sentence. But judging involves doing at least what O'Donovan says it does, and of making a declaration of innocent or guilty in which one announces one's determination.

The judge brings to light for each case the distinction between the just and the unjust. This distinction can be nothing else than a distinction within primary justice; it is not a distinction within rendering judgment. With an eye on the demands of primary justice, the judge brings to light whether or not the accused has violated those demands. The judge brings to light the state of affairs on the matter: is the state of affairs that of the accused having violated the demands of primary justice, or is the state of affairs that of the accused not having violated those demands? The performance of juridical judgment presupposes the existence of primary justice and injustice.

WHAT IS JUSTICE? WHAT IS RIGHT?

I said that for our earlier purposes we did not have to delve into doctrines of the Trinity. With regard to *primary justice*, some account will now have to be given. Since this account will have to be brief, most of the claims I make cannot be defended here.[9] The reader who disagrees will have to treat what follows hypothetically: If what I say about justice were true, what would follow about justice in the Trinity?

Since Greek and Roman antiquity, there have been two fundamentally different ways of thinking of justice in the Western tradition. In one way of thinking about justice, justice is right order; the just society is the rightly ordered society. The rules for the right ordering of society are then the rules of justice; and the just society is the society that conforms to the rules for justice. Among those who think along these lines, there is, as one would expect, a great deal of dispute over the origin and the content of those rules. Plato's discussion of justice in the *Republic* remains a paradigmatic example of thinking about justice as right order. The fundamental rule for the rightly ordered society, thus the fundamental rule of justice, is that everyone must occupy the social role for which he or she is best fitted. The origin of this rule is that it articulates the content of the form, the just itself.

The main alternative to thinking of justice in terms of the rightly ordered social whole is thinking of justice in terms of the rights of members of the social whole. The just society is the society whose members (and the social whole itself) enjoy those goods to which they have a right. The formula by the ancient Roman jurist Ulpian already caught the idea: justice is rendering to each his or her *ius*—his or her "right." Some of these rights will be conferred by social practice or legislation; but not all will, for the social conferral and nonconferral of rights is itself just or unjust. Justice and injustice at that point cannot in turn be determined by reference to socially conferred rights; or if they are, the justice and injustice of the latter cannot in turn be so determined, and so forth. We would be off on an infinite regress. There must be some rights that are *natural rights*.

I hold that thinking of justice as right order proves ultimately untenable. Justice, at bottom, consists of members of the social whole (and the social whole itself) enjoying those goods to which they have rights. I further hold that the conception of justice as rights articulates the moral vision of Scripture with respect to justice. A clue to this vision is the fact that the biblical writers see the recipients of injustice as wronged—not just harmed but wronged. Their moral status has been altered. The biblical writers think in terms of a passive as well as an active side of moral status: one can be wronged and one can be guilty. The ancient pagan eudaemonists, by contrast, did not believe that to be the recipient of an unjust action was to be wronged, thus to have one's moral status diminished. The recipient might well be harmed but not wronged. It is only the moral status of the person who acts unjustly that is diminished. The agent's own virtue is diminished.

I am well aware that this claim, that justice is understood in Scripture as justice as rights rather than justice as right order, will strike many readers as incredible. There is a powerful narrative abroad in the contemporary world to the effect that natural rights were an invention either of nominalist philosophers of the fourteenth century or of Enlightenment philosophers of the late seventeenth and eighteenth centuries. Whichever story is preferred, the moral is always the same: individualistic modes of philosophy spawned the idea of natural rights, and only within such philosophies does it have a home. This narrative has now been decisively refuted, most notably by the eminent medievalist Brian Tierney in *The Idea of Natural Rights*.[10] Tierney shows beyond the shadow of a doubt that the canon lawyers of the twelfth century were working with the explicitly formulated concept of natural rights. Of course, this study remains far short of tracing the idea back to the Old Testament; but it does show that the idea was born neither of late medieval nominalism nor of secular individualism in the Enlightenment.

What is a *right*? Recall that we are talking here only about *primary justice*; retributive rights, and whatever additional forms of rights wrongdoing may generate, are not in view. Also, we are talking about moral rights, not legal rights, not the rights one has as a participant in a certain game, and so forth. A *right* is a morally legitimate claim to some good, more specifically, to some good in one's life or history. To have a right to some good in life is to be entitled to have it come one's way, to be entitled to "enjoy" it. Or in yet other words, to have a right to some good in life is for that good to be due one.

I hold, furthermore, that the goods to which one has a right always consist of action or restraint from action on the part of persons or social entities such as institutions and organizations. Almost always it will be other persons, but in some cases, oneself. Examples include your right against me to my providing you the benefit of a correct answer to your question, your right against me to my cooperating with others in providing you the benefit of protection against assault, your right against me to my refraining from torturing you (freedom from), and your right against me to my refraining from preventing you from walking on the New Haven Green (freedom to). With the minor exception of such rights as one may have against oneself, rights are inherently social. They pertain to how we treat each other. It is commonly charged against "rights talk" that it is an expression of possessive individualism. One might as plausibly charge "duty talk" with being an expression of assertive individualism. It is true that I have rights against you, just as I have duties toward you; but it is also true that you have rights against me. You come into my presence bearing claims on me.

We have to dig deeper yet. What accounts for the fact that to some of the actions and restraints from action that would be goods in one's life, one has a right, whereas to others, one does not? You have a right to the good in your life of my not swindling you out of your life savings; you do not, however, have a right to the good in your life of my making a donation to your life savings. It would be nice if I did that, but you do not have a right to my doing it. What accounts for the difference? Why is the former life-good one to which you have a right, whereas the latter is not?

Once again, my answer will have to be offered without the argumentation necessary for defending it. I suggest that you have a right to the life-good of my acting or refraining from acting a certain way just in case I would be treating you with disrespect if I were to act that way—treating you in a way that would only fit someone or something of less worth than your worth. To swindle you out of your life savings would be to treat you with disrespect. Treating you in a way that fits your worth requires that I refrain from doing that.

One consideration that we all must and do take account of in determining how we shall act is the relative value of various life-goods: would this course of action bring about a greater total of life-goods, or would that alternative course of action bring about the greater total? If one is an egoist, one will consider only one's own life-goods; if one is not an egoist, one will consider the life-goods of others as well. If that sort of consideration is the only one that enters into one's deliberations, one is not taking account of rights. To take account of rights, one must bring a different sort of consideration into one's deliberations. One must bring the worth of persons into one's deliberations. Yes, it may be that doing X would bring about a greater total of life-goods than doing Y; but doing X would amount to treating someone with disrespect, treating the person as if that person had less worth than that person does. I must never do that. I must never treat a person as befits someone or something of less worth than that person is. So I must not do X.

One of Kant's famous formulae for the moral life was Always treat a person as an end, never merely as a means.[11] It is by no means evident on the face of it what the formula means. Ordinarily, we think of an *end* (*goal, telos*) as something that one brings about, or tries to bring about, and a *means* as something one brings about in order to bring about an end. On the basis of this understanding, a person can be neither an end nor a means, for a person is not something one brings about. So what did Kant mean when he spoke of treating persons as ends and refraining from treating them as means? Kant's discussion in *Groundwork for the Metaphysic of Morals* makes clear what he had in mind. To treat a person as means is to allow life-good considerations to be a determinant of how one treats the person. By contrast, to treat a person as an end is to allow the worth of the person to enter into one's deliberations. Kant's thought, then, is that one should never allow life-good considerations to be the sole determinant of how one treats a person, nor should one make those the final word. One should always see to it that one treats the person with due respect for that person's worth—that one never treats that person with disrespect, with under-respect. Kant's formula is thus another way of expressing the point I was making.

We can pull together the various strands of our discussion of primary justice like this: primary justice consists of treating persons with due respect for their worth.

JUSTICE AND LOVE

Is there justice within the Trinity? Suppose that primary justice is what I have suggested it is. How could there not be justice within the Trinity—primary justice, of course, not secondary or corrective justice? How could the members of the Trinity fail to treat each other with due respect for their worth?

Rather than letting the matter rest there, let us now bring love into the picture. Ever since the publication in the early 1930s of Anders Nygren's *Agape and Eros*, Christian theologians and ethicists have found the distinction between *agape* and *eros* almost irresistible in their thinking about love.

Agape is love as benevolence. It seeks the well-being of the other often to the extent of sacrificing one's own well-being. Agapic love is investment in the well-being of the other. Nygren describes *eros* as the opposite of *agape*. *Eros*, he says, is love that seeks one's own well-being. Erotic love treats the other as a means to the maintenance or enhancement of one's own well-being.

Given this understanding, one can see why Nygren is unremittingly hostile to erotic love, and why he thinks that all his fellow Christians should be so as well. When one sets to the side the contrastive description of erotic love that Nygren employs and looks at his examples, one sees, however, that the description is off target. *Eros* is love as attachment. The *agape/eros* contrast is not the contrast between love aimed at maintaining or promoting the well-being of the other and love aimed at maintaining or promoting one's own well-being; it is the contrast between love

185

as investment in the other's wellbeing and love as attachment. The person who finds oneself attached to some person, some institution, some cause, some house, some landscape, will perforce find this attachment to be a good; if the attachment is destroyed by the destruction of that to which the person is attached, that person will grieve over what has happened. But this attachment is not for the sake of some good in that person's life; it is not a means to some end beyond itself. The attachment is itself an intrinsic good, as are the experiences that ensue from the attachment: delight in the presence of the person or thing loved, and so forth. That person's well-being is in part constituted by this attachment and what ensues from it; but let us note that the person's well-being is also in part constituted by investment in the wellbeing of the other. That person's life is better, worthier, and more admirable on account of that investment.

Love as attachment to the other and love as investment in the wellbeing of the other often come together, inextricably intertwined. My love for my wife is constituted of both attachment to her and investment in her well-being, but they need not come together. One can invest oneself in someone's well-being without feeling any attachment to that person whatsoever; this is the love of the do-gooder who feels no grief when the person whose well-being the do-gooder has promoted dies. The do-gooder's negative emotion is confined to disappointment over the fact that this outlet for benevolent impulses has now been closed off and requires finding another. Conversely, one can be attached to things that do not have well-being and to things on whose well-being one can have no effect. One can have the love of attachment for Mount Rainier.

Nygren argued that, strictly speaking, it is never right to love God; the appropriate stance of a human toward God, speaking strictly, is faith, *pistis*. Given his characterization of *eros* and *agape*, one can see why he makes this argument. Agapic love, love as benevolence, love as investment in the well-being of the other, is inappropriate because we can do nothing to maintain or promote God's well-being. But erotic love, construed as engagement with the other for the sake of one's own well-being, is also inappropriate; God is not to be treated as a means to the end of maintaining or promoting one's own well-being. The same reasoning would lead to the conclusion that, strictly speaking, there is no love within the Trinity. The members of the Trinity neither seek to maintain or promote the well-being of the other; nor do they engage each other so as to maintain or promote their own well-being. Had Nygren thought of *eros* as the love of attachment rather than as engagement with the other for the sake of one's own well-being, he would not have found himself in the odd position of saying that it is wrong for us to love God and mistaken to speak of the members of the Trinity as loving each other.

It is tempting to think of erotic love, the love of attachment, as grounded in acknowledgment of the intrinsic worth of the entity to which one is attached: the wit and grace of the person, the stark assertive beauty of the mountain, and so forth. But it need not take that form. Attachment, bonding, works in mysterious ways, often having little if anything to do with the intrinsic worth of the thing to which one is attached. Children become intensely attached to stuffed animals that leave much to be desired in terms of intrinsic worth. If offered an alternative, they will often agree that the alternative is nicer but nonetheless reject it in favor of the one to which they are attached.

The love of attachment must, thus, be distinguished from acknowledgment of worth. The two often come together, with the former grounded in the latter; but that need not be the case. The latter may also come without the former: in one's actions one may acknowledge the worth of the other person without being attached to that person.

How are we to think of the love of the members of the Trinity for each other? Suppose it is correct to hold that it cannot take the form of *agape* ("love"): investment in maintaining or promoting the well-being of the other. Surely it does take the form of erotic love, the love of attachment: delight in being in the presence of the other, delight in the works of the other, and so forth. The question, then, is whether the love of attachment will take the form of incorporating, and being grounded in, acknowledgment of the worth of the other. How could it not take that form in this instance? But to acknowledge the worth of the other, so I have argued, is to treat the other with justice.

We come then to this conclusion: Not only is there justice in the relation of the persons of the Trinity to each other, justice in their relationship is caught up within love for each other. Justice within the Trinity is not a social relationship within the Trinity in addition to love within the Trinity. Justice in the Trinity is a constituent of love within the Trinity.

I began my discussion by characterizing a view that I find to be common among Christians. Justice in our world in no way reflects the Trinity. It could not since there is no justice in the Trinity. Scripture speaks of God as loving and doing justice. These words do not reflect the inner life of the Trinity. In doing and loving justice, God is not reflecting God's inner, trinitarian life. The members of the Trinity cannot treat each other justly, so they cannot love so doing.

I have argued that this view depends heavily on taking the action of rendering just judgment as the whole of justice. Reflection, however, shows that rendering judgment cannot be the whole of justice. Rendering just judgment presupposes another form of justice, *primary justice*. If primary justice is what I have suggested it is, then justice must be in the Trinity.

God's doing of justice in human affairs reflects the justice internal to God's own life; God's love of justice in human affairs reflects the justice that incorporates love that is internal to the Trinity. Accordingly, when we treat each other justly, we neither merely obey God's injunction to act justly nor merely imitate God's doing of justice within creation. We mirror the inner life of the Trinity.

Part FOUR

TRINITY
AND HISTORICAL THEOLOGY

CHAPTER 16

ESCHATOLOGY AND CHRISTOLOGY
Moltmann and the Greek Fathers

Nicholas Constas

Jürgen Moltmann has made sustained, creative, and often provocative use of theological insights from the Greek Fathers, especially Basil of Caesarea, Gregory Nazianzus, and Gregory of Nyssa, collectively known as the Cappadocians.[1] The most celebrated instance of such attention has surely been Moltmann's use of *perichoresis* in his social doctrine of the Trinity, in which the three persons "form their own unity by themselves in the circulation of the divine life."[2] Moreover, Moltmann's early experience of the elusiveness of God, who is forever in excess of what might be grasped, leaving one with an "inward drive, a longing which provides the impetus for hope," is a profoundly Cappadocian sentiment, an articulation of a lived, existential *apophasis*.[3] Those early "experiences of the inexpressible" drew Professor Moltmann to the study of theology, which for him is not merely an academic discipline, but a pilgrimage, a voyage of discovery into an unknown country, a notion that resonates deeply with the definition of theology offered by Gregory Nazianzus in his *Theological Orations*.[4] God is unknowable, and human beings can have no knowledge whatsoever of the divine essence. The experience of God is beyond our thoughts, and our thoughts are beyond our words. Thus, our language about God is like the "shadowy reflections of the sun in water, whereas the sun itself overwhelms our perception" (*Theological Orations* 28.3-4). The failure of signification drove Gregory Nazianzus to the mountain of theology, to the summit of *apophasis*, where we "gaze in impotence at what lies beyond our mind's powers." To do otherwise is to reify something in the world and, thus, to practice "idolatry" (*Theological Orations* 28.13).[5]

The mountain of theology, however, is not a place of despair, but one of hope, for the theological significance of language is found precisely in its inability to signify. If created symbols (including the world itself) are ultimately inadequate to the task of theological predication, that very nullity provides the condition for the possibility to participate more deeply in the mysterious life of God. If the immediacy of the world can threaten us with epistemological incarceration, it also holds forth the promise of freedom. The key to liberation, according to Moltmann, is a future-oriented *epektasis* (cf. Phil. 3:13), in which the impenetrable immanence of the world is rendered transparent in and through eschatological transcendence.[6]

As a result of that important insight, cosmology and eschatology moved to the center of Moltmann's systematic project.[7] In contrast to earlier definitions, eschatology is understood not as a future state of completion, but rather as a process of continuing openness, in which all creatures increasingly participate in God's unending and open eternity, even as God participates in their temporality. God not only transcends the world but is also immanent in the world, acting in and through it by means of *perichoretic* self-donation.[8] Above all, Moltmann's vision of an eschatologically transformed creation is ultimately rooted in Christology, for it is a theology of hope in the coming kingdom of God, based on the cross and resurrection of Christ.

Eschatology and Christology are two critical elements in what Professor Moltmann has called the "ecological doctrine of creation." These same categories, which are also the experiential realities of Christian life, figure prominently in Greek patristic cosmologies and in the commentary tradition associated with the first chapter of Genesis. The following chapter, which I am pleased to offer to Professor Moltmann, considers the eschatological and christological tendencies of what is arguably the founding work of all Christian cosmology, Basil of Caesarea's *Hexaemeron*.

BASIL OF CAESAREA, *HEXAEMERON*

One of the most significant attempts to locate creation within the interconnected frameworks of eschatology and Christology was undertaken by Basil of Caesarea (d. 379) in a work known as the *Hexaemeron*, a series of nine exegetical homilies on the first chapter of Genesis (Gen. 1:1-25).[9] Traditionally assigned to the period of Basil's priesthood, they are now dated to the last year of his life and considered to be works of theological maturity. Originally delivered before a working-class congregation during Great Lent, the homilies were subsequently read and studied throughout the Christian world. Ambrose of Milan read them in the original Greek (as did Robert Grosseteste); and by the mid-fifth century, they had been translated into Latin and Syriac.[10]

Modern commentators have tended to focus on either Basil's use of secular scientific sources or his allegedly literalist exegesis, which is typically set in facile opposition to that of the earlier Alexandrians. These scholarly foci, however, have created something of a false impression regarding the purpose of the *Hexaemeron*, which is to present a robust Christian cosmology. This purpose was certainly the understanding of Gregory Nazianzus, who at Basil's funeral revealed that "whenever I take up his *Hexaemeron*, and feel its words roll off my tongue, I find myself in the presence of the creator; and I understand the inner principles (*logoi*) of creation, and marvel at the world around me, more than I had before, when mere sight was my teacher" (*Oration* 43.67).[11]

In reading through the homilies, which are ostensibly explications of the biblical narrative of nonhuman creation, one is immediately struck by Basil's overwhelming interest in the place and purpose of human beings within that creation. The connection between exegesis, cosmology, and anthropology is so important that Basil introduces it at the outset of the first homily (*Hom.* 1.1), where it appears in the form of a hermeneutical caveat. As a reflexive challenge to the congregation, Basil affirms that one cannot properly understand either the text of scripture or the text of creation apart from a life of virtue oriented to God. In contrast to a reductive historical-critical treatment, an objective scientific study, or a disinterested phenomenological analysis, Basil calls for an exegetical practice that engages the reader at the fundamental level of will and desire, "for our minds have no other way of seeing themselves, unless they attend closely to the scriptures" (*Hexameron* 10.1).[12] As a result of such a dialectical exercise, the discovery of meaning in the narrative of creation simultaneously discloses humanity's calling to develop a moral activity in relationship to the world.[13]

CREATION AS THEOPHANY

Implicit in both Basil's method and argument is a belief in the intelligibility of the natural order, that is, in the inherent "rationality" (*logos*) of creation. Beginning with Origen, the intelligible structures of creation were said to be revealed to the mind during a stage of spiritual progress known as "natural contemplation" (*physike theoria*).[14] As an active, devotional meditation on objects within the created order, natural contemplation was typically associated with the book of Ecclesiastes, a view that Basil himself had advocated.[15] In the *Hexaemeron*, however, Basil applies the tropes of natural contemplation directly to the textual study of the natural world described in the book of Genesis. Such a shift was partly encouraged by the larger cultural context in which the cosmos was understood as a kind of text (or related symbolic structure, such as a musical instrument or work of art), and thus constructed as a vast and variegated system of meaningful signifiers. Moreover, the Greek word for the "elements" of creation (*stoicheia*) was the same word used to designate the "letters" of the alphabet, a linguistic coincidence that supported the notion that the phonemes of language were analogous to the elements of the physical world.[16]

Basil's doctrine of creation, however, is not simply an example of Hellenistic cosmic piety. For the Bishop of Caesarea, as for the Greek patristic tradition more generally, the world is understood as a *theophany* of God, that is, as a real presence of the deity manifest within the fabric of the material world. As a result, the metaphor of the divinely written book is given a critical twist: God and the world are related, not like an author and a book, but rather like a text and its meaning, the latter pair being intimately and perhaps inextricably interrelated. In the sixth century, Dionysius the Areopagite crystallized the patristic view of the cosmos as a manifestation of the divine. It will be worth reviewing his doctrine of creation in order to bring out the theological tendencies of Basil's interpretation of Genesis.

In *On the Divine Names* 4.13, a key passage, Dionysius describes creation as the self-manifestation of the uncreated deity: "In a moment of ecstasy, the cause of all comes to be outside itself by its providences for all beings; and being, as it were, seduced by goodness and affection and love (*eros*), is led down from being above all and transcending all is brought down to being in all."[17] This movement of erotic ecstasy is God's creative gift to the world, in which the absolutely nameless and unknowable becomes knowable through all things and subject to all names. Even in this ecstatic self-impartation, God nevertheless remains radically unknowable in essence. In God's own nature, God is neither a being nor even being itself, but in the ecstasy of creation becomes "all things in all things and nothing in any" (*On the Divine Names* 7.3).[18] Because creation is God's own self-revelation, Dionysius regards all creatures as "symbols" of intelligible reality in so far as they are symbols of God as imparted and revealed. Creation, then, is a form of incarnation because it is a true theophany of the divine, the paradoxical visibility of the invisible, the sensuous apprehension of that which cannot otherwise be known.

We have, then, a cosmology in which creation is not simply the stage for a theological drama, but the very medium and form of divine-human communication, a threshold across which the transcendent hopes of earth meet the increasing densifications of heaven. Creation is thus the movement of reflexivity between God and human beings, in which two infinitely different realms of existence perichoretically unite. These anthropological and theological commitments convinced Basil to reject the atheistic materialism of secular science and philosophy that had defined the world as a closed system, a self-contained unit without relations, a unit divorced from both God and humanity.[19] At the same time, arguing for the world's constitutive relation to God was a pointed response to the Arians, especially Eunomius, whose extreme emphasis on the radical transcendence of God had not simply subordinated the Word to the status of a creature, but had made the Creator remote from creation, undermining the relationship of gratitude proper to creatures saved by an incarnate Savior.[20]

CREATION AND ESCHATOLOGY

The relational character of creation leads Basil to a second insight: If creation is not autonomous, neither is it eternal; for it has both its beginning and its end in God. According to Basil's reading of Genesis, the auspicious use of the word *arche* (cf. Gen. 1:1, "In the beginning") is intimately linked with the notion of a *telos*, a final moment to be marked by a just judgment, through which the world will be definitively transfigured. Basil affirms that both human and nonhuman creation are moving inexorably toward an encounter, not with an abstract principle of justice, but with the person of the Just Judge. Where the philosopher sees static fixity (including the cyclical movement of nature), the bishop sees relation, direction, and intentionality. In a letter to a friend, Basil remarked that the aim of Christian life is to "keep one's mind on God, and to keep it directed steadily on the future" (Letter 293).[21] We find the same momentum in the *Hexaemeron*. Thus it is not protology, but rather eschatology, that provides the major hermeneutical principle for Basil's reading of Genesis.

An example of Basil's eschatological hermeneutic is found in the third homily, where he addresses the words of Genesis 1:8 (LXX): "And God saw that it was beautiful (*kalon*)." If those who heard this verse recited by the preacher imagined that God somehow experiences aesthetic pleasure, or that the deity held within its view a particular object, such expectations were quickly overturned:

> It is not to the eyes of God that the things created by him afford pleasure, nor is God's appreciation of beautiful objects such as it is with us. Rather, beauty is that which is brought to perfection and which conforms to the usefulness of its end (*telos*). God, therefore, established a clear aim (*skopos*) for his works, and approved them individually as fulfilling that end (*telos*). In fact, a hand by itself, or an eye alone, or any other pieces of a statue lying about in fragments, would not appear beautiful to the viewer. But, when set in their proper place, they exhibit the beauty of relationship (*analogia*), the artist having organized them by directing his judgment to their final end (*telos*).[22]

Basil begins by distinguishing God from creatures who differ markedly in their recognition and assessment of the beautiful. From the perspective of the creator, the "beautiful" is not discerned within a static, isolated object, but rather as a subject in process, in organic relation to the end for which it was created. (It is intriguing to note that Basil's disciples associated such fragmentation with libidinal obsession and its tendency to reduce human subjects to objects of self-gratification.)[23] To illustrate his point, the preacher makes use of an artistic metaphor and contrasts the meaninglessness of the broken, disconnected parts of a statue to the beauty that shines forth (*emphanes*) when the same fragments are brought together and ordered to the creative intention of the artist. In the first homily, Basil affirmed that the "whole world is a work of art, displayed by the creator for universal contemplation" (*Hexaemeron* 1.7), thereby lending a critical resonance to his image of a statue broken and restored.[24]

Basil returns to these themes in the fourth homily where he considers the "creation of the seas" (Gen. 1:10):

"And God saw that they were beautiful" (Gen. 1.10). But this does not mean that a certain delightful vision of the sea presented itself to God, for the creator does not look upon the beauty of creation with eyes like ours. Rather, he contemplates the things he has made by means of his ineffable Wisdom. A pleasant sight indeed is the sparkling sea, when deep tranquility possesses it; and pleasant also when, ruffled on the surface by gentle breezes, it reflects colors of purple and iridescent blue to the spectator. However, we must not think that the meaning of Scripture here is that the sea appeared pleasant and beautiful to God in this way. Instead, its beauty is determined by the inner purpose (*logos*) of the creative activity.[25]

In this passage, Basil suggests that creation by itself yields no ultimately meaningful horizon for reflection or contemplation. Neither does the created order acquire significance by the imposition of human perspectives and values. Instead, as we saw in the passage cited above from the third homily, it is the perspective of the future, the perspective of God's purposes, which places all things in their proper light. Basil once again challenges his audience to see creation, not through the sentimental lens of romanticized aesthetics, but rather through the eyes of God, to see it, that is, in terms of the purpose for which it was created.

It should be underlined that Basil has not denigrated creation, but rather placed it within a wider, eschatological horizon of value. Creation is neither autonomous nor absolute; it is relative to the permanence and meaningfulness of that which is beyond creation. Here Basil continues to work with the principles of *natural contemplation* associated with the book of Ecclesiastes mentioned above. Origen, for example, exploiting the rhetorical force of that book's opening and concluding exhortation (cf. Eccles. 1:2; 12:8: "Vanity of vanities, all is vanity"), argued that Solomon's purpose was to teach "that all visible and corporeal things are fleeting and brittle; and . . . once the seeker after Wisdom has grasped that these things are so, he is bound to spurn and despise them; renouncing the world . . . he will reach out for the things unseen and eternal."[26] Origen's understanding of the "vanity of creation" as relative to the transcendence of that which is beyond creation became the standard gloss on Ecclesiastes and, as such, was variously developed by Gregory of Nyssa, Evagrius of Pontus (d. ca. 399), and Basil himself who rather uniquely applies it to a reading of Genesis.[27]

CREATION AND CHRISTOLOGY

Let us return to the passage from the fourth homily of the *Hexaemeron* cited above (4.6). As was noted, Basil defined divine appreciation of creaturely beauty by means of a future-oriented exegesis based on the tradition of *natural contemplation*. Here, however, and unlike the excerpt from homily 3 (3.10), the agent of God's primordial contemplation of creation is plainly disclosed. "God contemplates the things he has made," Basil avers, "by means of his ineffable Wisdom." God, in other words, contemplates creation in Christ, that is, in its union with Christ; thus, already "in the beginning," God sees creation as having realized the purposed plan for the union of all things in the person of Wisdom incarnate. In *Hom.* 1.7, Basil had already alluded to the presence of Wisdom within creation when he proclaimed that "the world was a work of art." Here is the quotation in full: "The world is a work of art displayed by God for universal contemplation, so that through it, all may come to know the Wisdom of the creator."[28]

References to the figure of Divine Wisdom occur throughout the *Hexaemeron*, and Basil's christological interpretation of creation is largely sophiological.[29] In the first homily, Wisdom's creative art is said to be imaged in the work of the architect Beseleel, who fashioned the tabernacle of Moses as a microcosm of creation (*Hom.* 1.5, p. 10, lines 14-15; cf. Exod. 31:3, 7). In what is likely a rejoinder to the Eunomian disparagement of creative Wisdom as a secondary deity, Basil exalts her with a host of *apophatic* epithets, such as "unapproachable" (*aprositos: Hom.* 1.2, p. 5, line 18); "unspoken" (*arrhetos: Hom.* 3.6, p. 49, line 3; cf. *Hom.* 4.6, p. 66, line 11); "ineffable" (*aporretos: Hom.* 5.8, p. 83, line 9; cf. *Hom.* 6.1, p. 87, line 7); and "unsearchable" (*anexichniastos: Hom.* 9.5, p. 157, line 1), to mention only a few.

Altogether, the presence of Wisdom in creation subtly but significantly alters the nature of Basil's argument. Moreover, consistent with his eschatological interests, sophiology is not limited to the demiurgic function of preexisting Wisdom. Indeed, the marked christological turn of the fourth homily was anticipated by the argument of the third homily (3.10), where Basil affirmed that the movement of both human and nonhuman creation was toward a final reckoning with Christ himself, the "just judge." We may, therefore, conclude that Basil's eschatology is pointedly christological (and not simply a form of natural teleology) and that both eschatology and Christology are deeply embedded within the fabric of creation.

THE BOOK OF WISDOM

The convergence of eschatology and Christology in the context of creation has important consequences for ethics and the life of virtue. Wisdom has inscribed the book of the cosmos with sage doctrines, extensions of her own proper righteousness on the plane of matter, which render creation a "school for souls" (*didaskaleion*) and a "place of training" (*paideuterion*).[30] When properly read, the book of creation offers cogent examples of moral, social, and political justice. Turning the pages of that great book, Basil everywhere sees traces of harmony, equity, order, and cooperation. He discerns, for instance, the presence of Wisdom in the social organization and peaceful coexistence of various animal kingdoms, which he takes as a paradigm for human relations. Perhaps the best example of this harmony among creatures occurs in his discussion of Genesis 1:20: "And God blessed the creatures of the sea and said, 'Increase and multiply and fill the waters of the seas.'" As Basil writes:

How is it that all the different species of fish, having been allotted a place suitable for them, do not intrude upon one another, but stay within their own bounds? No surveyor established the limits of their dwelling places, they do not build fences and walls around themselves, nor do they mark off boundaries, but what was useful for each was clearly and spontaneously settled among them. We, however, are not at all like them. We cut up and divide the land into parts, we enlarge and expand our possessions and take the things that belong to our neighbors. A fish does not oppose the law of God, but we men cannot endure the teaching which is for our own salvation. Do not despise the fish because they cannot speak or reason, but beware lest you become even more unreasonable than they are by resisting the command of your creator.[31]

The creatures of the sea provide Basil with an image of human society for his audience to enact mimetically; however, the same creatures could also serve as a cautionary model to be scrupulously avoided:

Different foods are assigned for different fish according to their species. While some eat plants most of them eat one another, and the smaller among them are food for the larger. Sometimes it happens that both the smaller and the larger are in turn swallowed into the stomach of one larger still. Is this not what you do when you oppress your inferiors? How do you differ from that last fish, who with a greedy love of riches swallows up the weak in the bowels of his avarice? One man holds the possessions of a poor man, and you with your greater power seize them both. You have clearly shown yourself more unjust than the unjust man and more grasping than the greedy. Beware lest you befall the fate of the fish caught by a hook or in a net. Surely, if we have committed such unjust deeds, we shall not escape the final retribution.[32]

As these passages suggest, Basil's reading of scripture is a moral rather than an intellectual endeavor, with an implicit agenda of social justice ordered to an eschatological end. Creation is woven together as a continuous, narrative whole, whose plain sense provides abundant models for affection in family life, the adequate support of simple nourishment, the just distribution of property, and the advantage of harmony with neighbors. Basil invites his audience to admire, imitate, and learn from the book of creation, for God has "placed even within the smallest living creature the visible traces of his own Wisdom."[33]

The theological principles underlining Basil's interpretation of the first chapter of Genesis appear throughout his works. In one of his ascetical sermons, he provides us with a summary sketch of creation, anthropology, ethics, and eschatology:

This is the human being: mind united to a fitting and useful body. This union was fashioned in the womb by the all-wise Artisan (*pansophos technites*) of the universe, and was brought to light from those dark inner chambers by the pangs of birth. This being has been appointed the steward of all things on earth, and before him creation unfolds as an arena (*gymnasion*) of virtue. For him, the law has been laid down to imitate the creator in accordance with his powers, and to sketch upon the earth the good order of heaven. When summoned, this being departs from the world to stand before the judgment seat of the God who sent him forth. This being is accountable and will receive a recompense for his life and conduct.[34]

CONCLUSION

Creation bears the burdens of human history, freighted with our memories, myths, and meanings, all of which constitute an elaborately carved framework through which we survey the world around us. From the moment of the divine command to cultivate the garden of paradise (Gen. 2:15), the human mind has deeply shaped nature. The "face of the earth" (Gen. 2:6) has been formed as much from the topography of human desire and hope as from layers of soil and rock.

If it is true that there is no nature without culture, it is also true that there is nothing inherently shameful about our cultural occupation of the environment. As Basil's own theological annexation of creation has shown us, not all approaches to the environment are cause for guilt and sorrow but may give reason for celebration and praise. While we acknowledge (as we must) that the impact of humanity on the earth's ecology has not been an unmixed blessing, neither has the long relationship between nature and culture been an unrelieved and predetermined calamity. Now more than ever we need a new poetics of nature, new eyes with which to see, and a new hermeneutic with which to read the book of creation. But what we also need are silence, inner stillness, and the recognition that our world is the threshold of "unspeakable, unsearchable" wisdom. In Professor Moltmann's eschatological and christological approach to creation, we have a new, nondominant way of looking and acting indebted to the legacy of the Greek fathers, who likewise sought to restore the balance between ourselves, God, and the wisely made creatures with which we share the planet.

CHAPTER 17

JOHN DONNE ON THE TRINITY

Gerald O'Collins, SJ

In writing his essay "Priest and Poet,"[1] Karl Rahner knew that one and the same person could be both priest and poet or, for that matter, theologian and poet. Obvious examples come from early Christianity (e.g., St. Ephraem the Syrian and St. Gregory of Nazianzus) and from later centuries (e.g., St. John of the Cross and Gerard Manley Hopkins). In a special way, the word is entrusted to both poets and priests (theologians). It could be argued that theology has suffered because its practitioners have become more prosaic and because poets are few among the ranks of theologians and priests. In this chapter I reflect on an English writer who is remembered as both a poet and a preacher of genius, John Donne (1571/2–1631), and examine what his trinitarian theology has to offer. His highly personal approach clearly differs from the social doctrine of the Trinity that Jürgen Molt-mann developed in several major works.[2] Are there any resemblances to be found between Donne and Moltmann in their presentation of the distinctively Christian doctrine of the Trinity?

Donne is famous for his love poetry that he wrote both before and after his marriage to Ann More. Their love drew from him some of the finest love poetry in the English language; but God was powerfully present to his imagination, even more than any wife or mistress, in his love poems. One might describe his and other religious poetry as "overhearing human beings at prayer."[3] Religious poets pray out loud, so to speak. Some of them, one must add, are committed to showing themselves as they want to be rather than as they are. Donne has been criticized on this score as an exhibitionist when compared with his deeply devout contemporary, the poet and priest George Herbert (1593–1633).[4]

Donne was not remarkable for spiritual gifts and graces that went beyond the experience of the majority of human beings. He was no mystic as John of the Cross (1542–91) was. Unlike Gerard Manley Hopkins (1844–89), he seemed blind to the beauty of the natural world and the traces of the Trinity to be found there. Where the introspective and self-critical Donne excelled was in his capacity to express in memorable ways and through natural speech common Christian beliefs and common human experiences. Donne's true subject was the human heart in its relationship to the tripersonal God, to whom and about whom he spoke with an intensity of religious feeling that few poets have surpassed or even rivaled. Let us look first at one of his *Holy Sonnets* and then at "A Hymn to God the Father."

"BATTER MY HEART"

In what is normally listed as number 14 in his *Holy Sonnets*, Donne engages in a violent colloquy with the Holy Trinity. Speaking as a sinner who needs mercy and has found mercy, he writes with deep feeling and an emphasis on his personal experience that make it easy for others to associate themselves with what they read. Personal pronouns abound in this sonnet: six times the Trinity is addressed with "you"; and three times, with "your." Donne speaks of himself once with "my," four times with "I," and six times with "me." The preference for "you" and "me" emerges as theologically appropriate: What matters above all is what the Trinity ("you") can do for Donne ("me"). Let us see the sonnet:

> Batter my heart, three-personed God, for you
> As yet but knock, breathe, shine, and seek to mend;
> That I may rise and stand, o'erthrow me and bend
> Your force, to break, blow, burn and make me new.
> I, like a usurped town to another due,
> Labour to admit you, but Oh, to no end.
> Reason your viceroy in me, me should defend,
> But is captived, and proves weak or untrue.
> Yet dearly I love you, and would be loved fain [gladly, with joy],
> But am betrothed unto your enemy.
> Divorce me, untie, or break that knot again.
> Take me to you, imprison me, for I,
> Except you enthrall me, never shall be free,
> Nor ever chaste, except you ravish me.

Rich with verbs (from "batter my heart" to "ravish me"), the sonnet declares Donne's need to be redeemed. Vigorous verbs come in two sets of triplets when he implores help from the Trinity: "*Divorce* me, *untie*, or *break* that knot again. / *Take* me to you, *imprison* me, for I, / Except you *enthrall* me." His situation is helpless, and it will take strong action from the "three-personed God" to deliver him. He depicts the Trinity as for us rather than the Trinity as in itself—very much the economic rather than the immanent Trinity. The poem includes rhetorical paradoxes: To rise and stand, he prays to be overthrown. If he is to be free, the Trinity must imprison and enslave ("enthrall") him. If he is to be chaste, God must "ravish" him.

Three images portray the process of divine redemption that can dramatically transform Donne's desperate situation: a metal smith repairing a faulty vessel (lines 2 and 4); the rightful lord besieging a captured town; and the true lover delivering someone subjected to a false lover. The first image has some background in the Old Testament picture of God as the master potter who molds the clay as he wills (e.g., Isa. 45:9, 64:7; see Rom. 9:20-21). The Old Testament tells of Jericho and Jerusalem under siege but provides no story of God's besieging a town like a king wanting to win back what has been "usurped" or wrongly taken away from him. The third image enjoys a full biblical background when the prophets write of Jerusalem or the chosen people of God as an unfaithful spouse with whom God lovingly wishes to renew the covenant relationship (e.g., Hos. 2:14-23). The line that introduces this image ("dearly I love you, and would [gladly] be loved") could be intended to recall the triple protestation of love from St. Peter that ends with "Lord, you know everything; you know that I love you" (John 21:15-17).

Donne follows orthodox theology by writing of the Trinity as acting together in "battering" his heart; as the traditional axiom put it, the actions of the "three-personed God" are common. Donne hints at the personal distinction within the Trinity with his three verbs for the divine action: "knock," "breathe," and "shine." "Knock" may evoke the Son in the Book of Revelation: "Listen! I am standing at the door, knocking" (3:20). "Breathe," of course, points to the Holy Spirit. "Shine" may be intended to bring to mind God as light (1 John 1:5), "the Father of lights" (James 1:17), or the shining glory of God so often found in the Old Testament scriptures. Merely knocking, breathing, and shining will not be enough to mend the broken vase that Donne is; beyond repair, he needs to be remade. Hence he implores God to act much more forcefully; he calls on the Trinity to "bend your force to break" (not merely knock), to "blow" (not merely breathe) and "burn" (not merely shine), and so to make him into a "new" being. The Pauline language about divine redemption through Christ making us a "new creation" (2 Cor. 5:17) supports Donne's prayer, and so too does the divine declaration, "I am making all things new" (Rev. 21:5).

The violent action needed to redeem Donne's sinful state emerges in the very first words of the poem: "Batter my heart." One can readily think of the battering rams used against the gates of a besieged town. Such an image of a town under siege (Donne's second image) is also subtly anticipated when he develops the first image for the redemption he wants: "That I may rise and stand, *o'erthrow* me." During the incessant wars in the Low Countries, Germany, and elsewhere that marked Donne's lifetime, the forces of one ruler often captured a town that right-fully belonged to another ruler ("to another due"). Donne belongs to the King of heaven but has been seized by Satan, God's enemy. When the rightful king arrived and besieged the town, the citizens within the town who had remained loyal to him would try to open the gates and let in the liberating forces. That is Donne's situation: he belongs to the King of heaven but has been captured by the enemy. He tries to open the gates from the inside, but his efforts are "to no end." His reason, which is the "viceroy" or representative of God within him, should resist Satan but proves too "weak" or has even proved "untrue" or unfaithful by switching to Satan's side. Since not even reason will open the gates, the Trinity will have to batter down the gates and recapture its own town (Donne).

The image of being subject to a wrongful ruler leads easily to the third and final image, that of being subject to a false lover, "your enemy." At the time of Donne, parents arranged betrothals for their children. In Donne's case, his ances-tral parents, Adam and Eve, fell into sin and so "betrothed" him to God's "enemy," Satan; but Donne wishes to be united with his true, divine lover. For that union to happen, the Trinity must act with vigor and even violence: "Divorce me, untie, or break that knot again." Since betrothals in the seventeenth century entailed a union more like modern marriage than engagement, Donne uses strong terms: "divorce" and "break that knot." When he says, "break that knot *again*," he has in mind the way that Christ's incarnation and crucifixion broke the original betrothal that the sin of Adam and Eve brought about for their descendants—in a "breaking" that was of eternal benefit to all human beings. Since, like other baptized believers, Donne has committed sins of his own and so has renewed his betrothal to Satan, God must once again use force to rescue Donne if Donne is to be "taken" into the arms of his rightful lover.

Paradox marks the violent deliverance that Donne yearns for: "imprison me, for I, / Except you enthrall me, never shall be free." Ideally, human beings should freely choose to give themselves totally to the tripersonal God who has created them and given them their freedom. Donne, however, knows his own weakness; he could too easily submit himself again to sin and Satan. He will not remain truly free unless God keeps him "enthralled" or enslaved in the divine service. The teach-ing of St. Paul about the two slaveries stands behind this language. Salvation brings freedom from sin and a new "slavery" to God; those who have been "slaves of sin" become "slaves of righteousness" (Rom. 6:15-23).

Along with the sense of "to enslave," "enthrall" also enjoys a romantic mean-ing that opens the way for Donne's final line: "Nor ever chaste except you ravish me." Donne can remain "chaste" or loyal to his divine spouse only if God "ravishes" him or takes him by force. The New Testament (e.g., Eph. 5:23-27) and subse-quent Christian tradition picture Christ as the bridegroom of the whole church or final community of the redeemed. Donne adapts this image: the Trinity is the bridegroom and Donne himself the bride. The poet employs erotic love to express his yearning for a total, exclusive union with his divine lover, the "three-personed God." Thus, the sonnet comes full circle—from Donne's *heart* being battered by God to his whole person being *ravished* by God.

However one finally evaluates the theology of the Trinity expressed in this "Holy Sonnet," Donne certainly does not rationally reduce trinitarian faith to little more than a logical puzzle for experts—a development that encouraged Immanuel Kant to state in *Conflict of the Faculties*, "The doctrine of the Trinity, taken literally, has *no practical relevance at all*, even if we think we understand it; and it is even more clearly irrelevant if we realize that it transcends all our concepts. Whether we are to worship three or ten persons in the Deity makes no difference."[5] In his struggle with his weakness and sin, Donne found the "three-personed God" highly relevant; in fact, the Trinity "for us" (*pro nobis*, in traditional theology, the economic Trinity) is our only possible hope of salvation. The next poem provides an even more passionate prayer for forgiveness and salvation.

"A Hymn to God the Father"

The content and language of this poem is even more personal than that of the "Holy Sonnet" we have just examined. The address to God involves "thy, thyself" twice and "thou" nine times. Donne uses "my" four times and "I" eleven times. These pronouns all help to make the poem very personal, giving a powerful blend of feelings with theological argument:

> Wilt thou forgive that sin where I begun,
> Which is my sin, though it were done before?
> Wilt thou forgive those sins through which I run,
> And do them still, though still I do deplore?
> When thou hast done, thou hast not done,
> For I have more.
> Wilt thou forgive that sin by which I won
> Others to sin, and made my sin their door?
> Wilt thou forgive that sin which I did shun
> A year or two, but wallowed in a score?
> When thou hast done, thou hast not done
> For I have more.
> I have a sin of fear, that when I've spun
> My last thread, I shall perish on the shore;
> Swear by thyself that at my death thy Sun
> Shall shine as it shines now, and heretofore;
> And having done that, thou hast done,
> I have no more.

The poet could have taken his sins and plea for forgiveness to Christ but seems to choose the first person of the Trinity as his father confessor to make a kind of general confession that, as we will see, takes Donne from his conception right through to his death. This confession enables Donne to pray: "Swear by thyself that at my death thy Sun / Shall shine as it shines now, and heretofore." The pun on "Sun" as "Son" is clear. Talk of Donne's coming death easily suggests Christ's own death, which lets God's merciful love shine forth toward human beings. Elsewhere the poet often uses "the Sun" as a symbol of the divine mercy and moves easily between "the Sun" and "the Son." Thus one sermon draws the parallel in expressing his hope: "I shall see the Son of God, the Sun of glory, and shine myself, as that sun shines" (Sermon 4.162).[6]

Painfully, even obsessively conscious of the seriousness of sin and death, Donne makes no appeal to any alleged merits of his own but throws himself on God's mercy. In doing so, he subtly touches at several points on the biblical story. He opens with a plea for forgiveness for the taint of sin which through his own parents he has inherited from Adam and Eve: "Wilt thou forgive that sin where I begun, / Which is my sin, though it were done before?" He may understand in these terms the confession of the psalmist: "Indeed, I was born guilty, a sinner when my mother conceived me" (Ps. 51:5). By choosing "wallowed" in reference to his sins, Donne possibly wants his reader to recall Christ's parable of the prodigal son degraded by working for swine who wallowed in filth as they gulped down their food.

The poet expresses anguish at the thought of death: "I have a sin of fear, that when I've spun / My last thread, I shall perish on the shore." Does he think here of Charon, the aged ferryman in Greek mythology who for a price carried the shades of the dead across two rivers in the underworld? Is Donne afraid that he will not "make it across to the other side"? His fear might draw on the story of the Exodus and the flight from Egypt. At death will he pass through the Red Sea to freedom and the promised land of eternal life with God? Or perhaps he refers to the story of Abraham and the "deep sleep . . . and a deep and terrifying darkness" which fell upon him (Gen. 15:12). Donne is deeply concerned that when he has lived his last moment ("when I've spun / My last thread"), he might "perish" forever and not journey to heaven. His plea to God "swear by thyself" evokes God's promise to Abraham: "By myself I have sworn . . . I will indeed bless you, and I will make your offspring as numerous as the stars of heaven and as the sand that is on the seashore . . . and by your offspring shall all the nations of the earth gain blessing for themselves" (Gen. 22:10-18; see Heb. 6:13-19). Lastly, Donne very concisely brings up the past, present, and future in the prayer: "Swear by thyself that at my death thy Sun / Shall shine [future] as it shines now [present], and heretofore [past]." The divine mercy is effectively manifested through the Son of God, "the same yesterday and today and forever" (Heb. 13:8). Donne's prayer, albeit in a highly personal way, evokes the past, present, and future dimensions in the whole sweep of salvation history.

"A Hymn to God the Father" is not fully trinitarian since the Holy Spirit does not make an appearance. Once again, however, we see how passionately intense Donne's faith in God is and what he begs from God: the forgiveness of his sins and final deliverance from death. When those prayers are granted, then Donne will have nothing more to ask from God; he says to God in a pun on his name, "And having done that, thou hast done." At the end he also hints again at his sinful idolizing of his wife Ann More. The first and the second stanzas have both ended with the confession "I have more." If the poet is delivered at death, God will "have done"; and Donne will be freed from his guilty worship of his wife: "I have no more."

Let me complete this account of Donne's version of the Trinity by next examining "A Litany" to "The Father," "The Son," and "The Holy Ghost" in his *Divine Poems*. Once again, we will see how faith in the "three-personed God" was a vital doctrine for Donne, a matter of life and death.

"A Litany"

Naturally, Donne begins his litany[7] with God the Father:

> Father of heaven, and him by whom
> It and us for it, and all else for us
> Thou madest and governest ever, come
> And re-create me, now grown ruinous:
> My heart is by dejection, clay,
> And by self-murder, red.
> From this red earth, O Father, purge away
> All vicious tinctures, that new fashioned
> I may rise up from death, before I'm dead.

Even though Donne writes twice in the third line about "us," his deep concern for his own personal fate comes through strongly with "me" and "my" (once each) and "I" (twice). As the Christian tradition normally did, the poet appropriates to the Father the work of creation and conservation (the making and "governing ever"); but right from the start, the future of redeemed humanity turns up. The "Father of heaven" has made it (heaven) and "us for it [heaven]."

Donne longs for redemption because he has "grown ruinous." His heart suffers from "dejection" or melancholy, reckoned at that time as the cold, dry humor that corresponds to "clay" or earth. "Self-murder" has wounded the poet's heart, let its blood flow, and made it "red earth." Hence the being "new fashioned" or "re-creating" that he needs must first take the form of a purging away of impurities that adhere to him: "From this red earth, O Father, purge away / All vicious tinctures." Since the Hebrew for red is *adom*, from the time of St. Jerome some Christians like Donne interpreted *Adam* as made from "red earth" or earth dyed with blood. Redemption will bring Donne not only a cleansing from "vicious tinctures" inherited from the *first Adam* but also, through Christ the *Second* or *Last Adam*, spiritual resurrection from the dead, even before he dies physically. Thus the poet begins his litany by picturing the Father as "for us," not only through the work of creation but also, and even more, through that of redemption (in its negative and positive aspects).

The redemptive work of the Son is then associated with his suffering and death. The resurrection does not feature in this poetic account of salvation.

> O Son of God, who seeing two things,
> Sin and death, crept in, which were never made,
> By bearing one, triedest with what stings
> The other could thine heritage invade.
> O be thou nailed unto my heart,
> And crucified again.
> Part not from it, though it from thee would part,
> But let it be, by applying so thy pain,
> Drowned in thy blood and in thy passion slain.

Christ's redeeming work aims at overcoming "two things" that "were never made" by God in the original creation but "crept in" subsequently: sin and death. The Son of God bore "one" (death by crucifixion) and "triedest" (experienced) "the other" (sin) with all the "stings" with which it "could . . . invade" his "heritage" of human nature.

After spending four lines on what has been called the *objective redemption*, Donne turns back to himself and his fickle faith. He fears that his "heart" wants to "part" from Christ, and he begs him: "part not from it." He pleads with Christ to be "nailed unto my heart, / And crucified again." Thus, "by applying so thy pain," he pleads let "my heart" be "drowned in thy blood and in thy passion slain." This bold language not only echoes St. Paul's declaration about being "crucified with Christ" (Gal. 2:19), but makes a paradoxical use of the somber way in which the Letter to the Hebrews characterizes Christians who fall away: "They are crucifying again the Son of God and are holding him up to contempt" (Heb. 6:6). Donne can avoid such sinful failure only if Christ *is crucified again*, but this time by being nailed to the poet's heart. Any apostasy on the part of Donne will then prove impossible; he will be drowned in Christ's blood and slain in his passion.

When he turns to the Holy Ghost, Donne looks exclusively at himself and the spiritual damage his sinful youth has caused and that only God can repair.

> O Holy Ghost, whose temple I
> Am, but of muddy walls and condensed dust;

> And being sacrilegiously
> Half wasted with youth's fires of pride and lust,
> Must with new storms be weatherbeat.
> Double in my heart thy flame,
> Which let devout sad tears intend; and let
> (Though this glass lanthorn, flesh, do suffer maim)
> Fire, sacrifice, priest, altar be the same.

Donne believes that through baptism his body has become a temple of the Holy Spirit (1 Cor. 3:16-17; 6:19), yet he knows that "mud walls" and "condensed dust" (see Gen. 3:19) make his body perishable, that body which he has "sacrilegiously" profaned with sins of pride and lust.

Donne knows that he must be purified by being beaten by the weather of "new storms," presumably those of sickness and old age. The "flame" of the Holy Spirit must be doubled in his heart. Paradoxically, the poet's devout tears of repentance will not quench this flame but "intend" or intensify it. Donne's human body, a glass lantern through which the candle of the soul and the divine light shine, suffers "maim" or injury by his sins of pride and lust. Even so, he prays that the fire of the Holy Spirit will remain unchanged ("be the same") in its burning on the altar of the heart of this priest/poet, who offers sacrifice—arguably the sacrifice of "a broken spirit" (Ps. 51:17).

After addressing poems to the Father, the Son, and the Holy Spirit, Donne directs a fourth poem to the Trinity. While throughout the first three poems the poet reveals a deep sense of his sinfulness and a relentless quest for divine mercy, the fourth poem begins with the *immanent Trinity* and moves only in the last three lines to the *economic Trinity*—in this case, the tripersonal God revealed and at work for Donne in his own personal history of revelation and salvation.

> O blessed, glorious Trinity,
> Bones to philosophy but milk to faith,
> Which, as wise serpents, diversely
> Most slipperiness, yet most entanglings hath,
> As you distinguished undistinct
> By power, love, knowledge be,
> Give me a such self different instinct,
> Of these, let all me elemented be,
> Of power to love, to know you unnumbered three.

The doctrine of the Trinity may be baffling to human reason, a hard bone to philosophy; but it is, as Donne recognizes, "milk to faith." In one of his sermons he declares that "these notions . . . of God, as a Father, as a Son, as a Holy Ghost . . . are . . . so many breasts, by which we may suck such a knowledge of God, as that by it we may grow up into him" (*Sermons* 3.263). Then the poet boldly compares the three divine persons to serpents, albeit "wise serpents." John's Gospel drew from the book of Numbers to picture Christ as a serpent lifted up on the cross to bring faith and life to the world (John 3:13-15; Num 21:9); but Donne daringly goes further and attributes to his "wise serpents" qualities that art, literature, and common human lore conventionally associate with a serpent as a type of evil: being slippery and entangled.

Presumably, he thinks of the doctrine of the Trinity as involving diverse or opposite challenges: it eludes or slips out of our grasp, and yet it involves us in endless entanglements or complications. The language of the Trinity being slippery yet entangled is to be understood through the line that follows. On the one hand, the three persons are to be "distinguished" as three persons; but, on the other hand, they remain "undistinct" inasmuch as they form one God with only one divine nature.

In completing this poem, Donne attributes "power, love [and] knowledge" to the Father, Son, and Holy Spirit, respectively. Appropriating to the Father the "power" deployed in creating the world is normal practice. "Love," however, is normally associated with the Holy Spirit, the gift of "Love" between Father and Son; moreover, it would seem more suitable to appropriate "knowledge" to the Son, who is the Word of God and the Wisdom of God. In short, "power, knowledge, love" would correspond more closely to the way attributes are usually appropriated to the three divine persons. At the same time, Donne could claim scriptural warrant for associating "love" with the Son (e.g., Gal. 2:20; 2 Cor. 5:14) and "knowledge" with the Holy Spirit (e.g., 1 Cor. 2:10-13). Or perhaps the order follows the prayer Donne at once makes. He wants to be given such a different "self-instinct" or identity that he will become in himself totally ("all me") "elemented" or composed of the power to know and love the "unnumbered three." Like Thomas Aquinas and many other leading Christian writers, Donne may be endorsing the principle that love leads to knowledge and insight.[8] He needs love in order to know the Trinity and to be truly aware of their distinct but related attributes. The poet ends by worshiping the mystery of the Trinity with an "elemented" or integrated self. The divine persons are "unnumbered" or not to be placed in a numerical series. Paradoxically, we call them "three"; but they remain "unnumbered."

A COMPARISON

More than three centuries separate Donne and Moltmann. Their lives, worlds, and particular concerns differ dramatically when they expound their faith in the tripersonal God. Donne does not anticipate Moltmann by developing a post-Auschwitz, trinitarian theology of the cross; he does not ask: What do the suffering and death of Christ mean for God? Neither does the poet ever explore the theme of trinitarian fellowship and become well known for a social doctrine of the Trinity.

Donne's personal needs and his hope for loving mercy from the Trinity dominate the six poems we examined. He is preoccupied with his own sins and his need for God's mercy. He never thinks of drawing from the three divine persons-in-relation a fundamental social doctrine for the ordering of Christian and human life. But, for all their differences, both Donne and Moltmann write about the Trinity with an intense conviction that nothing matters more than the Trinity in the distinctively Christian adventure to which they both witness.

CHAPTER 18

TRINITARIAN BELIEF AND WORSHIP
A Historical Case

Bryan D. Spinks

In Book I of the 1559 *Institutes of the Christian Religion*, John Calvin observed of the nature of God:

> When he proclaims his unity, he distinctly sets it before us as existing in three persons. These we must hold, unless the bare and empty name of Deity merely is a flutter in our brain without any genuine knowledge.[1]

After Calvin had written the first edition of the *Institutes* in 1536, his treatment of the doctrine of the Trinity had led to accusations of Arianism. In subsequent editions, he provided a much fuller treatment of the doctrine to counter such accusations; and in the 1559 edition the Trinity was treated after the knowledge of God. Indeed, Philip Butin has cogently argued that it is, in fact, the doctrine of the Trinity that undergirds the whole of the later editions of the *Institutes*.[2] More recently, Richard Muller has drawn attention to the purpose and structural development of the *Institutes* and their relationship to Calvin's biblical commentaries; and Stephen Edmondson has emphasized the role of the biblical narrative and Christology in the first two books.[3] It would seem, therefore, that Calvin saw his trinitarian doctrine as a legitimate understanding and exegesis of the biblical narrative as a whole. He fiercely defended the full divinity of the Son, arguing that although the person of the Son was begotten, the essence of the Son, being the one common essence of the divinity, was not. The Son could thus be described as *autotheos*, God of himself: "Therefore, when we speak of the Son simply, without reference to the Father, we truly and properly affirm that he is of himself, and, accordingly, call him the only beginning; but when we denote the relation which he bears to the Father, we correctly make the Father the beginning of the Son."[4] Calvin seems to have regarded *autotheos* as sufficiently safeguarding the *homoousios* of the Son.

In his recent work *Reformed Scholasticism and the Battle for Orthodoxy in the Later Stuart Church*, Stephen Hampton noted that although Calvin's terminology was accepted in most Reformed circles, and even received some endorsement from the Catholic Robert Bellarmine, in England his terminology caused negative reaction and, when influenced by Episcopius and the Dutch Remonstrants, gave rise to a growing trend of subordinationism in Trinitarian discussion.[5] Hampton finds the first traces in the writings of Ralph Cudworth, George Bull, and John Pearson. As documented by Philip Dixon, in the last decades of the seventeenth century it gave rise to a succession of books with accusation and counteraccusation of heresy, most notably in the heated exchange between Robert South and William Sherlock.[6] Battle recommenced in the early decades of the eighteenth century, sparked by two Newtonian theologians, William Whiston and Samuel Clarke. William Whiston succeeded Isaac Newton in the Lucasian Chair of Mathematics at Cambridge; he was a polymath, who wrote on a wide range of mathematical, scientific, and religious subjects. He believed that Athanasius had led the whole Church astray and that Arius had held the true biblical teaching. For his pains Whiston was deprived of his chair and lived privately in London, finally leaving the Church of England for the Baptist Church.[7] The focus of this essay, however, is the other Newtonian, Dr. Samuel Clarke.

Clarke was born in 1675 in the city of Norwich, where he attended the local free grammar school. He went up to Cambridge in 1690,[8] took his B.A. in 1695, was ordained in 1698, and was Fellow of Gonville and Caius, and chaplain to the Bishop of Norwich. At Cambridge he acquainted himself with both the work and person of Sir Isaac Newton, who engaged him to translate his *Opticks* of 1704 into Latin. He defended Newton against Cartesianism in correspondence with Leibniz. Clarke, regarded as one of the most brilliant minds of the Church of England, gave the Boyle lectures in 1704 and in 1705. It is said that after his examination for the Doctorate of Divinity, the Regius Professor of Divinity, Dr. Henry James, emended the usual "I will now finish, as I have tested you enough" to "You have taxed me enough."[9] In 1709 he was appointed Rector of St. James, Westminster, which was frequently a stepping-stone to a bishopric; however, the publication of *Scripture-Doctrine of the Trinity* in 1712, in which Clarke boldly presented what was perceived to be a heterodox understanding of the Trinity, effectively brought to an end all chances of preferment. Clarke's contemporary, Thomas Emlyn, though, was not surprised by the book and claimed to have deduced from Clarke's earlier Boyle lectures that he could not hold an orthodox view of the Trinity.[10]

CLARKE ON THE TRINITY

Clarke's doctrine was set out in three parts and prefaced by fifty-five propositions. In the introductory pages he stated that Scripture alone must be used to determine and explain doctrine:

> For, Matters of Speculation indeed, of Philosophy, or Art; things of humane invention, experience, or disquisition; improve generally from small beginnings, to greater and greater Certainty, and arrive at Perfection by degrees: But matters of Revelation and divine Testimony, are on the contrary complete at first; and Christian Religion, was most perfect at the Beginning; and the words of God, are the most proper significations of his Will, and adequate expressions of his own Invention; and the Forms of Worship set down in Scripture, by way either of Precept or Example, are the best and most unexceptional Manner of serving him.[11]

Clarke appealed to Tillotson, Wake, and Chillingworth; and with approval he quoted Chillingworth:

> The Bible, I say, the BIBLE only, is the Religion of Protestants. Whatsoever else they believe besides it, and the plain, irrefragable, indubitable consequences of it; well may they hold as a Matter of Opinion.[12]

Already, Clarke had differentiated between what may be deduced from the plain text of Scripture and what was simply private opinion.

In the first part Clarke presented all the Scripture passages relating to God the Father, the Son of God, and the Holy Spirit of God. Even in the choice of these titles, a subordination can be detected—Son of God rather than God the Son. In the chapter relating to God the Father, the first section pertained to those passages where God is One or Only God; and the second section pertained to passages where God is styled God absolutely by way of eminence and supremacy. The last section pertained to passages where all prayers and praises are to be offered only to God the Father. In the chapter relating to the Son, although he gathers those where Jesus is styled God and where honor and worship ought to be paid to him, his main interest seems to be in the passages where the Son "is declared to be subordinate to the Father, deriving his being from the Father."[13] Again, although he lists passages that show the Spirit as the author and worker of miracles and that declare that honor and worship are due to him, he also collects passages where the Spirit is subordinate to the Father and to the Son. A fourth chapter lists passages where the three persons are mentioned together.

After having set out a total of 1,251 passages, in part 2 Clarke then expounded the doctrine that the passages set forth. He concluded that in Scripture, "There is

One Supreme Cause and Original of Things; *One* simple, uncompounded, undivided, intelligent Being, or Person; who is the Author of all Being, and the Fountain of all Power."[14] Clarke went on to explain that with the first and supreme cause or Father, there has existed from the beginning a second divine person, who is the Word or Son, and that with both Father and Son, there has existed from the beginning a third divine person, the Spirit of the Father and of the Son. Clarke warned, however, that Scripture nowhere says what the metaphysical nature, essence, or substance of these is. Thus, he argued that "All Reasonings therefore, deduced from their *supposed metaphysical Nature, Essence, or Substance,* instead of their *Personal Characters, Offices, Powers and Attributes* delivered in *Scripture,* are but Philosophical and probable Hypotheses."[15]

According to Clarke, the Father alone is unoriginate and thus the author and Principal of whatever is done by the Son; moreover, the Father is the God of the universe—both the God of Abraham, Isaac, and Jacob and the God and Father of our Lord Jesus Christ.[16] The Father alone is unoriginate because "the Scripture, when it mentions the *One God,* or the *Only God,* always means the Supreme *Person of the Father.*"[17] This assertion Clarke repeated several times: "Whenever the Word, *God,* is mentioned in Scripture, with any High *Epithet, Title,* or *Attribute* annex'd to it; it generally (if not always) means the *Person of the Father*"; and "The Scripture, when it mentions *GOD,* absolutely and by way of Eminence, always means the *Person* of the *Father.*"[18] These statements already indicate Clarke's deductions, namely, that the Son and Spirit are subordinate and inferior to God/Father. Thus, Clarke points out that the Son is not self-existent, but derives his being or essence and all his attributes from the Father, as from the supreme cause.[19] The Spirit is derived from the Father and so is subordinate although Scripture is silent on how either the Son or the Spirit are derived from the Father.[20] The Son is sometimes called God, not on account of metaphysical substance, but because of his authority over us. Clarke further concludes that all prayers and praises ought primarily to be directed to the person of the Father as "the Original and Primary Author of all Good."[21] Honor rendered to the Son and Spirit redound to the glory of God; and no scriptural warrant exists, adds Clarke, for putting prayers directly to the Holy Spirit.

In the third part of his treatise, Clarke first of all lists passages from the 1662 *Book of Common Prayer* that styled the Father alone as the one and only God, or where prayer is through the mediation (subordination) of the Son; however, he also lists passages that "seem to differ from the foregoing Doctrine,"[22] such as in the Gloria Patri added to the psalms and canticles, the Athanasian Creed, and the opening sentences of the Litany, as well as various collects and other prayers. He suggests how they might be reconciled with the correct (i.e., his own) doctrine of the Trinity.

Although Clarke managed to dampen down the controversy he caused, he regarded his doctrine as logical and correct. Having outlined possible liturgical changes to the Prayer Book rites in his 1712 work, at a later date he privately recorded what the changes would look like in a revised liturgy. The British Library holds an interleaved *Book of Common Prayer*, printed in 1724, in which Clarke wrote out his emendations.[23] The book includes some emendations that are simply a matter of style; for example, in the confession in Morning Prayer, "left undone those things" is corrected to "left undone *many* things." Perhaps a more theological reason is found for the change from "and there is no health in us" to "from ourselves we have no hope of salvation."[24] However, passages that suggested three equal persons of the Trinity were heavily emended. Thus, in place of the Gloria Patri, Clarke suggested either "Glory be to God, by Jesus Christ, through the heavenly assistance by the Holy Ghost," or "Unto God be glory in the Church, by Christ Jesus; Throughout all Ages, world without end, Amen." The christological section of the Te Deum, which begins with "Thine honorable, true: and only Son" and ends with "didst open the gate of heaven to all believers" becomes as follows:

> Who hast manifested thy self to us, by thy true & only Son,
> And by the Holy Ghost, the Comforter.
> We acknowledge thy Christ to be the King of glory;
> The only-begotten Son of the Father.
> Who when he took upon him to deliver man,
> He did not abhor the Virgin's womb.
> And when he had overcome the sharp=
> =ness of Death, he did open. . . .[25]

The Athanasian Creed was crossed through in its entirety. The Apostles' Creed was repunctuated, "I believe in God, the Father," and "Sitteth on the right hand of God, the Father Almighty," thus making sure that God is equated with Father. The threefold Kyrie was omitted; and the Prayer of St. John Chrysostom was emended so as to attribute the promise of being present to the Son, not "God," which is reserved for the Father. In the Litany, petitions to the Son are altered or removed. It is significant that in these suggested liturgical emendations, Clarke was prepared to call Jesus "Our Lord" but not address him as "Lord." Although Clarke was fully aware that Jesus is addressed as Lord in Scripture, his desire was to preserve this title for God the Father. Thus, *God*, *Father*, and *Lord* are terms that indicate for Clarke the supremacy of the first person of the Trinity over the other two persons.

NEWTONIAN AND ENLIGHTENMENT INFLUENCE

In his study of Clarke's life and work, James Ferguson regarded Clarke as an Arian in doctrine. Thomas Pfizenmaier's more recent study argues for a more nuanced treatment, for he claims that *Scripture: Doctrine of the Trinity* "represents a reassertion of the trajectory of thought found in Eusebius of Caeserea. Eusebius received from Origen's school a certain subordinationism, primarily related to the derived nature of the Son. Both Clarke and Eusebius affirmed that the generation of the Son was ultimately beyond human knowledge."[26]

Pfizenmaier suggests that Clarke should more accurately be labeled a *homoiousian* or a Eusebian.[27] Of course, many debates have questioned whether Arius was an Arian, or whether Arianism ever existed apart from Athanasius's construction, and how the fourth-century rhetoric should be interpreted.[28] Furthermore, many of Clarke's statements are quite in keeping with those of the Nicenes. Clarke himself was well aware of the *homoiousian* position but never claimed it; and he was also well aware that the views he put forward fell short of traditional orthodoxy. He seemed to promote his own rigorous logic and methodology above traditional orthodoxy. Furthermore, his a priori views of what constituted deity were certainly not borrowed from either Scripture or his patristic sources. They owed their origin more to Enlightenment philosophy and, as James Force and others have convincingly shown, from his friend and mentor Sir Isaac Newton.[29]

Newton was eventually exempted from both ordination and subscription to the Thirty-nine Articles of the Church of England; but in the 1670s before his exemption by the king, Newton had begun to write down his ideas on the nature of God and Christ. His tenth proposition states:

> It is a proper epithete of ye father to be called almighty. For by God almighty we always understand ye Father. Yet this is not to limit the power of ye Son, for he doth what soever he seeth ye Father do; but to acknowledge yt all power is originally in ye Father & that ye son hath no power in him but wt derives from ye father for he professed that of himself he can do nothing.[30]

Newton had himself compiled a list of Scripture proofs—or, more accurately, disproofs—on the Trinity, that he shared with Locke and were to be published anonymously by Locke's friend LeClerc; but at the last moment Newton withdrew them. As with Clarke, Newton was hostile to Athanasius and felt that the *homoiousian* party represented the true convictions of the Nicene Fathers.[31] Newton rejected metaphysical speculation on substances. In his *Principia* Newton writes:

> We have ideas of his attributes, but what the real substance of anything is we know not. In bodies, we see only their figures and colours. We hear only the sounds. We touch only their outward surfaces, we smell only the smells, and taste the savours; but their inward substances are not to be known either by our senses, or by any reflex act of our minds: much less, then, have we any idea of the substance of God.[32]

Clarke shared Newton's commitment to natural philosophy. From this natural philosophy Scripture was interpreted and judged, together with an understanding of general world history.[33] For Newton, this natural philosophy included the belief in an original rational monotheism, which, because of human irrationality and fallibility, moved toward polytheism and hence the need for revelation. Clarke writes:

> Indeed in the original uncorrupted State of Humane Nature, before the Mind of Man was depraved with prejudiced Opinions, corrupt Affections, and vitious Inclinations, Customs and Habits; right Reason may justly supposed to have been a sufficient Guide, and a Principle powerful enough to preserve Men in the constant Practice of their Duty. But in the present Circumstances and Condition of Mankind, the wisest and most sensible of the Philosophers themselves have not been backward to complain, that they found the *Understandings* of Men so *dark and cloudy*, their Wills so *biased and inclined to evil*, their *Passions* so *outrageous and rebelling against Reason*; that they lookt upon the Rules and Laws of right Reason, as very hardly practicable, and which they had very little Hopes of being able to persuade the world to submit: In a Word, they confessed that Humane nature was strangely *corrupted*; and acknowledged this *Corruption* to be a Disease whereof they knew not the true *Cause*, and could not find out a sufficient Remedy. So that the great Duties of Religion, were laid down by them as Matters of *speculation and dispute*, rather than as the *Rules of Action*. . . . To remedy all these Disorders, and conquer all these Corruptions; there was plainly wanting some extraordinary and supernatural *Assistance*; which was above the reach of bare Reason and Philosophy to procure.[34]

Although this might suggest that reason was subject to revelation, for both Newton and Clarke revelation was itself governed by their own reasoning.

Newton's understanding of space and time to God led him to posit the absolutes of self-existence and nonorigination to God/the Father alone. This was focused in God's unity and dominion, which meant that Christ and the Spirit must be subordinate beings. In the *General Scholium* in the second edition of the *Principia*, Newton asserts:

> The Supreme God is a Being eternal, infinite, absolutely perfect; but a being, however perfect, without dominion, cannot be said to be Lord God; for we say, my God, your God, the God of *Israel*, the God of Gods, and Lord of Lords; but we do not say, my Eternal, your Eternal, the Eternal of *Israel*, the Eternal of Gods; we do not say, my Infinite, or my Perfect: these are titles which have no respect to servants. The word God usually signifies *Lord*; but every lord is not a God. It is the dominion of a spiritual being which constitutes a God: a true, supreme, or imaginary dominion makes a true, supreme, or imaginary God.[35]

Newton relied on the view of Dr. Edward Pococke, a professor of Arabic at Oxford, that the Latin word *Deus* derived from the Arabic *du* and means Lord. As

James Force concludes, for Newton, only a God of true and supreme dominion is a supreme and true God.[36] God's dominion was also the fundamental principle underlying Newtonian mechanics; in the *Opticks* (which Clarke translated into Latin), Newton writes that because

> Matter is not necessarily in all places, it may be also allow'd that God is able to create Particles of Matter of several Sizes and Figures, and in several Proportions to Space, and perhaps of different Densities and Forces, and thereby to vary the Laws of Nature, and make Worlds of several Sorts in several Parts of the Universe.[37]

God is the Pantocrator who chooses one material system by a willful act, that is, by the exercise of dominion. In the *General Scholium*, Newton writes, "We know [God] only by his most wise and excellent contrivances of things, and final causes; we admire him for his perfections; but we reverence and adore him on account of his dominion: for we adore him as his servants; and a god without dominion, providence, and final causes, is nothing else but Fate and Nature."[38]

Newton's understanding of God meant that Jesus could only be derived from God's dominion, "the Son receiving all things from the Father, being subject to him executing his will, sitting in his throne and calling him his God, and so is but one God with the Father as a King and viceroy are but one King. For the word God relates not to the metaphysical nature of God but to dominion."[39]

Clarke could write in similar fashion:

> The reason why the Scripture, though it stiles the *Father* God, and also stiles the *Son* God, yet at the same time always declares there is but *One God*; is because in the *Monarchy* of the Universe, there is but *One Authority*, original in the *Father*, derivative in the *Son*: The *Power of the Son* being, not *Another* Power *opposite* to That of the *Father*, nor *Another* Power *co-ordinate* to That of the *Father*; but it self *The Power and Authority of the Father*, communicated *to*, manifested *in*, and exercised *by* the Son.[40]

If Clarke echoes Newton's conception of God, he seems to echo the Enlightenment understanding of *person* as defined by John Locke in the late seventeenth century. Most of Locke's contemporaries accepted Boethius's definition that a person was an individual substance of rational nature. Whereas Thomas Hobbes had focused more on actors and actions,[41] John Locke, in his *An Essay Concerning Human Understanding*, concentrated on defining person in terms of the self. A person is "a thinking intelligent Being, that has reason and reflection, and can consider itself as itself, the same thinking thing, in different times and places; which it does only by that Consciousness which is inseparable from thinking . . . consciousness always accompanies thinking . . . and 'tis that, that makes everyone to be, what he calls *self*."[42]

Newton had defined *Person* as *substantia intellectualis*; but, applying strict logic, he held that the three persons are three substances.[43] Throughout *Scripture-Doctrine of the Trinity*, Clarke consistently defined *Person* as intelligent agent; and in God, three such persons would yield three Gods. In a reply to one of his critics, Robert Mayo, Clarke asserted:

> By the Word God, when used absolutely, I mean that supreme intelligent Agent which governs all things; and the Words Intelligent Agent are the definition of a Person. . . . Your conclusion therefore, (if meant literally) one God IN Persons three, is a Language of which I understand not the terms. One Intelligent Agent in Three intelligent agents, or three intelligent Agents in one intelligent Agent, are English words, but have no English signification.[44]

Here Clarke's hermeneutic is out in the open. He had no interest in how the Fathers may have attempted to press and bend the word *hypostasis/idiotes/persona* to explain the mystery of the Trinity. His definition in the English language governs the discussion, as did his Newtonian deity, for he argued, saying, "I have no other Notion of God, but his being Supreme Governor of the Universe, and that He derived this Power from none, but had it eternally of Himself, being Self-existent" and concluding that "this is the Notion of God by the Light of Nature."[45]

MUSINGS ON CLARKE'S METHODS

With benefit of hindsight from the vantage point of twenty-first-century theological methods, it is easy to spot some of Clarke's weaknesses. Philip Dixon has rightly observed that the God that Clarke describes seems far from the loving creator, redeemer, and sanctifier revealed in the very Scriptures Clarke claims to be explaining.[46] The reasons are not too difficult to discern. Faith seeking understanding requires theologians to make sense of the Christian gospel in the framework of their world picture; but the axiomatic priority is not that world picture, but God's initiative in church proclamation and theology. Human history of philosophical and religious attainment is a predicate of revelation, not vice versa.

First, Clarke begins, not with YHWH, but with God as Being, where Being is as conceived in Newtonian thought. Although there continues to be difference of opinions among Old Testament scholars as to both the uniqueness of the name YHWH to Israel and the precise meaning of the name, it would seem that "I am" or "I am that I am" is best understood, not so much as "Being," but more in terms of "I cause to be." Being is defined by the action of this God; YHWH is known through saving actions. To posit dominion as the main attribute of God is to prefer an a priori concept and definition of the word *God* over against YHWH Elohim as revealed in Scripture.

Second, Clarke imposes a modern (Enlightenment) concept of person on the term used by the Fathers. As Dixon notes, the term used by the Fathers was at best analogical; and they realized that they were pressing it beyond what it might bear to indicate that the divine nature is known to us only through three hypostases. Clarke takes the modern definition of person and presses it univocally to a point where the doctrine of the Trinity is reduced to an absurdity.

Third, although Clarke displays his remarkable knowledge of the Scripture text, his book *Scripture-Doctrine of the Trinity* is entirely devoid of any narrative concept of Scripture, an omission fatally flawing his approach. For example, C. Kavin Rowe has drawn attention to the fact that in Luke 1:5-38, *kyrios* clearly refers only to YHWH, the God of the Old Testament. Between 1:38 and 1:39 there is a narrative gap during which time the conception of Jesus occurs. In light of 1:43, the gap can be seen as the incarnation of YHWH, passed over in silence but captured when Elizabeth greets Mary as the Mother of my *kyrios* and at which time Jesus is given the title *kyrios*.[47] The Johannine Jesus's claim of the title "I am," and the possible utterance of the divine name before the high priest in the Markan passion narrative might have suggested that an identity between YHWH and Jesus should not be so hastily dismissed.[48] Clarke was keen to note that sometimes "lord" might mean no more than "sir," but was silent on the fact that elsewhere it clearly carries overtones of the LXX rendering of YHWH. Contra Clarke, what Jesus is given is not lordship or honorary dominion, but the name (Phil. 2:9).[49] As Augustine says:

> [We must believe] that Trinity is one God. Not that Father, Son and Spirit are identically the same. But Father is Father, Son is Son and the Holy Spirit is Holy Spirit, and this Trinity is one God, as it is written "Hear O Israel, the *Lord* thy God is one God."[50]

By avoiding discussing Scripture as narrative, Clarke's claim to have presented a "Scripture-doctrine" of the Trinity rings a little hollow.

Lastly, the liturgies of the *Book of Common Prayer*, in continuity with the Romano-African Western liturgical tradition, sit light to the doctrine of the Trinity other than by formulae.[51] Nevertheless, they retained sufficient narrative in proclamation, prayer, and creed, for Clarke to know that the *lex orandi* contradicted his own *lex credendi*. Hence his discomfort with the received liturgical text. Both his recommendations in *Scripture-Doctrine of the Trinity* (1712) and his emendations to the 1724 edition of the *Book of Common Prayer* appear to have been expansions of the ad hoc emendations he was already making when he officiated at services in St. James Church, Westminster, so that his prayers did not contradict his belief. Enlightenment rationality demanded consistency. Indeed, it is Clarke's liturgical emendations that ultimately confirm his departure from received orthodoxy—both Nicene Christology and Constantinopolitan trinitarian theology.

FURTHER MUSINGS

In some ways what Clarke did in the first decades of the flowering of the Enlightenment has counterparts in the last decades of modernity as it yields to postmodernity, especially counterparts in some strands of feminist critique of the language of the Trinity in worship and liturgical alternatives sometimes proposed. Like any collective term, feminist theology covers many very different and nuanced views; and generalizations run the risk of caricature. My musings here are limited to some brief remarks on views set forward by Ruth Duck.[52]

In her *Gender and the Name of God*, Duck adopts Elizabeth Schüssler Fiorenza's definition of patriarchy, and Tillich's definition of God as "Being itself."[53] She argued that all language for God is metaphorical, where metaphors give meaning by similarity and dissimilarity. The New Testament and liturgical term *Father* is a metaphor, but a dead metaphor, and even unsuitable in the light of child abuse by fathers. It is interesting that she appeals to Eusebius of Caesarea to justify suspicion over the text of Matthew 28:19, rather than considering whether Eusebius's Christology had led him to paraphrase the Matthean text. She also appeals to the late Western adoption of the Matthean text as a baptismal formula, totally ignoring the Eastern evidence.

Duck builds on this earlier study in the book coauthored with Patricia Wilson-Kastner, *Praising God the Trinity in Christian Worship*.[54] Here, in her particular chapters, Duck argues that God is profoundly relational but that the traditional terms *Father*, *Son*, and *Holy Spirit* are patriarchal. She proposes to speak of Source, Christ, and Spirit. Since *person* is problematical in modern thought, but Duck is concerned to express that the Christian deity is relational, she opts to replace *person* with the term *partner*. Father is a metaphor alongside Mother, Source, Creator, Holy One, Living God, and Mystery, although Father is one she chooses not to use. Unlike Clarke, she does briefly discuss YHWH, but only in the sense that it is translated "Lord," which is judged a further example of patriarchy. There is no discussion of the link among YHWH, Adonai, and Kurios/Dominus that gives us *Lord*. She also discusses possible problems with the term God: How can one distinguish between God in general and the triune God? She justifies its use on the grounds that liturgical contexts will make it clear. Problems with traditional texts include, as with Clarke, the traditional creed, which, on the authority of Michael Downey, she asserts should be praise and thanksgiving rather than doctrinal, the Gloria in Excelsis, and the Gloria Patri. She finds the pre-Nicene doxology, espoused by the Arians, congenial. Her version of a baptismal creed is as follows:

Do you believe in God, the Source, the fountain of life?
Do you believe in Christ, the offspring of God embodied in Jesus of Nazareth
     and in the church?
Do you believe in the liberating Spirit of God, the wellspring of new life?[55]

Of course, Duck, an American feminist theologian writing at the end of the twentieth century is not the same as Clarke, a British Enlightenment theologian writing in the first decades of the eighteenth century; and any comparison may seem as absurd as comparing a game of checkers to a game of chess. My suggestion is, however, that they are both like chess players who use some rules imported from another game. Despite being separated by both time and agenda, there are similarities in their approaches to Scripture and the liturgical text. Like Clarke, Duck has no concern for a narrative framework and does not pursue YHWH as the name of God and its resonances in the narrative of the New Testament. In the liturgical texts Duck provides, God is the preferred term and almost invariably reserved for the Creator and Source; Christ/Jesus/Word and Spirit are rarely found joined with the word *God*. This preference is similar to that of Clarke, who reserves the term *God* for the Father only. Though suggesting that the understanding of the term *God* will derive its meaning from context, ironically Duck does not allow the possibility that in Scripture this context is in relation to Father, Son, or Lord and that the narrative of Scripture in turn gives those words their meaning.[56] For Duck, the meaning is imported from outside the narrative. Like Clarke, she dislikes the term *person*. Given that her term *partner* cannot begin to convey the patristic term *hypostasis/idiotes/persona*, it is difficult not to see Trinitarian subordination in many of her liturgical texts. Like Clarke, the *homoousios* of the three persons is simply abandoned in favor of a generic God. As Karen Westerfield Tucker has noted, when God is taken as designating only the first person of the Trinity, making the second and third persons less or other than God, the result is Arianism *redivivus*.[57]

The case of Samuel Clarke might have suggested to twentieth-century writers the dangers when starting with presuppositions and definitions taken from outside the framework of the narrative of Scripture. To commence with the generic term *God*, whether defined as Unity having dominion, or Being and "Source," seems to lead all too easily to a Trinitarian subordination in belief and worship. Duck asserts that she firmly believes in the Trinity, though not in its traditional liturgical usage or understanding. Clarke too maintained that his views were perfectly orthodox, but his liturgical suggestions were enthusiastically taken up and adopted by Unitarians.[58] In the end, Clark's case confirms that, as Thomas Marsh writes: "In their prayer human beings name and address their God. The structure of human prayer, therefore, discloses the God that is here believed in, who and what this God is. One can truly say: Tell me your prayer and I will tell you your God."[59]

NOTES

1. BEING AS GOD IS

1. Dante Alighieri, *The Divine Comedy: Paradiso*, trans. Allen Mandelbaum (New York: Alfred A. Knopf, 1995), canto xxxiii, 540.

2. The most famous formulation of this position is Kant's. See, for instance, Immanuel Kant, *Critique of Practical Reason*, trans. T. K. Abbott (Amherst, N.Y.: Prometheus, 1996), 160–61.

3. See Gregory of Nyssa, *Contra Eunomium*, 7.5 (198–99). (All citations from Gregory of Nyssa are from vol. 5 of *The Nicene and Post-Nicene Fathers*, 2nd ser. [Grand Rapids, Mich.: Eerdmans, 1979].) Gregory of Nyssa's argument was that we know the divine persons (along with their relations and their attributes) but that the divine nature remains radically hidden from us because "no form, no place, no size, no reckoning of time, or anything else knowable is there" in the divine nature (1.26 [69]).

4. On the other hand, to claim that God simply *is* as God shows Godself in the economy of salvation—to affirm the complete identity of the economic and immanent Trinity—would amount to making the world a necessary condition of divine life. For instance, God would then be such that taking on human flesh and suffering on the cross would belong to God's very nature.

5. Jürgen Moltmann has rightly drawn attention to the need to add a third category to the categories of the *immanent* and the *economic Trinity*, namely, the *Trinity in glory*. Additionally, he has suggested that the relation between these need to be understood as part of the "history" of God (see Jürgen Moltmann, *The Trinity and the Kingdom: The Doctrine of God*, trans. Margaret Kohl [New York: Harper & Row, 1980], 153, 176, 177–78).

6. See, for instance, Ted Peters, who follows Wolfhart Pannenberg and Robert Jenson in locating the immanent Trinity in the eschaton (Ted Peters, *God as Trinity: Relationality and Temporality in Divine Life* [Louisville, Ky.: Westminster John Knox, 1993], 20–24, especially 23. He argues that the kingdom of God rather than the Trinity should serve as the ethical standard according to which Christians operate. For Peters, the Trinity is a *second-order symbol* that is already dependent on the ideas of personhood and relationality that it supposedly explicates (184–85). In other words, the doctrine of the Trinity is not the kind of knowledge of God that can serve as the basis upon which humans can act. Instead, the idea of the kingdom of God contains within itself a radical critique of all human authority, which leaves people free to attempt to transform society without allowing temporal social structures to usurp the eternal status that belongs only to the kingdom of God (185–86).

7. These two qualifications of correspondences between the Trinity and the character of human life echo Karl Barth's claim that all speech about God is characterized by "twofold indirectness"—it takes form in a medium that is both "creaturely" and that "contradicts God" (Karl Barth, *Church Dogmatics*, trans. G. W. Bromiley [Edinburgh: T & T Clark, 1975], I/1:168).

8. On both of these methodological observations—the two limits of correspondence and the claim that the construction of correspondences has to go from divine to human as well as from human to divine—see Miroslav Volf, *After Our Likeness: The Church as the Image of the Trinity* (Grand Rapids, Mich.: Eerdmans, 1988), 198–200.

9. Brian Leftow, "Anti-Social Trinitarianism," in *The Trinity: An Interdisciplinary Symposium on the Trinity*, ed. Stephen T. Davis et al., 203–49 (Oxford: Oxford University Press, 1999), levels his critique on rather naïve versions of social trinitarianism.

10. In Sarah Coakley's persuasive reading of Gregory of Nyssa's trinitarian theology, she rightly protests against flat appropriations of Gregory's "three men" analogy by some contemporary social trinitarians (Sarah Coakley, "'Persons' in the 'Social' Doctrine of the Trinity: A

Critique of Current Analytic Discussion," in *The Trinity: An Interdisciplinary Symposium on the Trinity*, ed. Stephen T. Davis, Daniel Kendall, and Gerald O'Collins, [Oxford: Oxford University Press, 1999], 132–33. See also Sarah Coakley, "Re-thinking Gregory of Nyssa: Introduction—Gender, Trinitarian Analogies, and the Pedagogy of *the Song*," *Modern Theology* 18 [October 2002]: 433–34). Her polemic is one-sided, for she does not seem to consider texts in which Gregory develops a rationale for multiple models, including a social model. Gregory argues, for instance, that, on account of our creaturely incapacity, the Scripture "employs the numerous forms of generation to present to us, from the inspired teaching, the unspeakable existence of the Only-begotten, taking just so much from each as may be reverently admitted into our conceptions concerning God" (*Contra Eunomium*, 8.4 [204]). Second, although it should be beyond dispute that Gregory does not speak of three persons and self-consciousness in the Trinity in the modern sense of the term, still the question needs to be answered as to how he cannot argue that "the will of the Father, of the Son, and of the Holy Ghost is one" (*Contra Eunomium*, 2.15 [132]), but can claim that the Son, "*by his own agency* brought all things into being" (*Contra Eunomium* 5.4 [179]), or that "the Holy Spirit wills that which seems good to the Son" (*Contra Eunomium* 2.15 [132]), or insist that "the Word, who both wills and is able to effect the good, . . . is other then He of whom He is the Word (*Oratio Catechetica*, 1 [476]). The language of the "will" as applied to the Trinity breaks down at some level, of course (see also Coakley, "'Persons' in the 'Social' Doctrine," 133). According to Gregory, we cannot either say, for instance, that the Father "had a Son without choice, by some necessity of His Nature" nor affirm that "the 'willing' separate(s) the Son from the Father, coming in between them as a kind of interval" (8.2 [202]). But so does all language. At the same time, such language is necessary to account for the economy of salvation, which is what gave rise to Trinitarian reflection in the first place.

11. Augustine, *De Trinitate*, VII, 2 (220): "If the Father is not also something with reference to himself, there is absolutely nothing there to be talked about with reference to something else."

12. Augustine, *De Trinitate*, XV, 11–12: "And because the Son too is wisdom, begotten of wisdom, it means that the Father does not do his remembering for him or the Holy Spirit his loving any more than the Father or the Holy Spirit do his understanding, but he does it all for himself; he is his own memory, his own understanding, his own love, but his being all this comes to him from the Father of whom he is born. Holy Spirit too does not have the Father for memory and the Son for understanding and himself for love, because he is wisdom proceeding from wisdom; and he would not be wisdom if another did his remembering and another his understanding for him, and he himself only did his own loving. No, he himself has these three, and he has them in such a way that he is them" (404). See also *De Trinitate*, XV, 28 (419).

13. See Karl Barth, *Church Dogmatics* I/1:296–98.

14. See Karl Rahner, *The Trinity*, trans. Joseph Donceel (New York: Crossroad, 1999), 34–37.

15. Moltmann also rightly points this out in *The Trinity and the Kingdom*, 64.

16. Martin Luther, *The Bondage of the Will*, in *Luther's Works*, ed. Helmut T. Lehman (Philadelphia: Fortress Press, 1972), 33:243, hereafter cited as *LW*.

17. See, for instance, Immanuel Kant, *Critique of Pure Reason*, ed. Vasilis Politis (London: Everyman, 1993), 519 [A807/B835].

18. See, for instance, Karl Marx, "Moralizing Criticism and Critical Morality," in *Karl Marx: Selected Writings*, ed. David McLellan (Oxford: Oxford University Press, 1977), 216–18.

19. On reconciliation and identity in relation to the Trinity, see Miroslav Volf's three works: *Exclusion and Embrace: Theological Exploration of Identity, Otherness and Reconciliation* (Nashville: Abingdon, 1996); "'The Trinity Is Our Social Program': The Doctrine of the Trinity and the Shape of Social Engagement," *Modern Theology* 14, no. 3 (1998): 403–23; and *Free of Charge: Giving and Forgiving in a Culture Stripped of Grace* (Grand Rapids, Mich.: Zondervan, 2006), chaps. 4–6.

20. In what follows, I draw heavily on *Free of Charge*, chaps. 1–3.

21. We can view creation under the aspect of divine creativity and under the aspect of divine gift giving. Creativity concerns the fact that, by creating, God brings into being states of affairs that were not there without God's activity. Gift giving concerns the fact that God brings into being states of affairs that enhance the good of another (for instance, human beings). The presumption behind this distinction is that an entity must first *be* in order to be given a gift. It is on the basis of this latter presumption that I will treat God's creative activity.

22. Etienne Gilson, *God and Philosophy* (New Haven, Conn.: Yale University Press, 1941), 49–50.

23. See Jürgen Moltmann, *Trinity and the Kingdom*, 107–8.

24. Seneca, *On Benefits*, trans. John W. Basore (Cambridge: Harvard University Press, 2001), 2.1.2 (51).

25. Ibid., 3.15.4 (151).

26. Many today think that no other kind of giving is possible for humans. Anything else is an illusion—a useful illusion but illusion nonetheless. We are self-interested givers. In giving a gift, we are just playing a game in which, as Bourdieu put it, "everyone knows (and does not want to know) that everyone knows (and does not want to know) the true nature of the exchange" (Pierre Bourdieu, "Marginalia—Some Additional Notes on the Gift," in *The Logic of the Gift: Toward an Ethic of Generosity*, ed. Alan D. Schrift [New York: Routledge, 1997], 232).

27. Seneca, *On Benefits*, 1.3.2 (13).

28. Jürgen Moltmann, *Trinity and the Kingdom*, 94–95.

29. See Karol Wojtila, *Love and Responsibility*, trans. H. T. Willetts (New York: Farrar, Straus and Giroux, 1981).

30. Jacques Derrida, *The Gift of Death*, trans. David Wills (Chicago: University of Chicago Press, 1995), 68.

31. Ibid., 96.

32. Martin Luther, *Luther's Works* 31 (Philadelphia: Fortress Press, 1957), 351. See p. 224, n. 16.

2. The Social Trinity and Property

1. A representative instance of such critique is Randall E. Ott, "Moltmann and the Anti-Monotheism Movement," *International Journal of Systematic Theology* 3, no. 3 (2002): 293–308; see also Ott, "The Use and Abuse of Perichoresis in Recent Theology," *Scottish Journal of Theology* 54, no. 3 (2001): 366–84.

2. An extreme form of the use of the immanent Trinity to protect God's freedom is found in Paul D. Molnar, *Divine Freedom and the Doctrine of the Immanent Trinity* (London: T&T Clark, 2002), 197–233.

3. See, for example, Jürgen Moltmann, *God in Creation* (San Francisco: Harper & Row, 1985), 234–43.

4. Bruce Marshall, "Putting Shadows to Flight: The Trinity, Faith, and Reason," in *Reason and the Reasons of Faith*, ed. Paul J. Griffiths and Reinhard Hütter (London: T&T Clark, 2005), 77.

5. Thus Moltmann has held firm against the sectarian critiques of some postliberal and radical orthodox theologians.

6. See Moltmann's discussion of the monarchical, historical, eucharistic, and doxological dimensions of the Trinity in *The Spirit of Life: A Universal Affirmation* (Minneapolis: Fortress Press, 1992), 289–306.

7. M. Douglas Meeks, *Origins of the Theology of Hope* (Minneapolis: Fortress Press, 1989).

8. As Moltmann's view of the Trinity developed, he took up to a significant extent Barth's challenge to develop the doctrine of the immanent Trinity in order to give the *eschata* grounding

while including creation and grace; but he did this within his consistent search for an ontology of God's love and grace. Karl Barth, *Letters 1961–1968*, trans. Geoffrey Bromiley (Edinburgh: T&T Clark, 1981), 176.

9. "[T]he knowledge and the representation of the immanent Trinity is to be found in the sphere of doxology, which corresponds to the experience of salvation and anticipates the kingdom of glory." Moltmann, *The Trinity and the Kingdom*, trans. Margaret Kohl (San Francisco: Harper & Row, 1980), 161.

10. Leonardo Boff followed Moltmann in developing the doctrine of the social Trinity, but Boff saw the social Trinity primarily as a utopian model for social construction and thus missed Moltmann's constant trinitarian concern for conversion and empowerment. See Boff, *Trinity and Society* (Maryknoll, N.Y.: Orbis, 1986), 6, 8. Boff finds the Trinity extremely rich in the "context of oppression and desire for liberation. . . . For those who have faith, the Trinitarian communion between the divine Three, the union between them in love and vital interpenetration, can serve as a source of inspiration, as a utopian ideal. . . . The community of the Father, Son and Holy Spirit become a prototype of the human community dreamed by those who wish to improve society and build it in such a way as to make it an image and likeness of the Trinity."

11. Cf. for this Moltmann, *The Trinity and the Kingdom*, 191–200.

12. The etymological root of property (*proprius* = one's own) points to the *relationship* between a person or thing and what is properly possessed. Whether property is humane and just depends on the quality of the relationship.

13. Portions of the following are taken from M. Douglas Meeks, *God the Economist: The Doctrine of God and Political Economy* (Minneapolis: Fortress Press, 1989), chap. 5, and from my article, "The Economy of Grace: Human Dignity in the Market System," forthcoming in *God and Human Dignity*, ed. R. Kendall Soulen and Linda Woodhead (Grand Rapids, Mich.: Eerdmans, 2006).

14. Lawrence C. Becker, "The Moral Basis of Property Rights," in *Property*, ed. J. Roland Pennock and John W. Chapman (New York: New York University Press, 1980), 193–94. Becker has discerned four general theories justifying private property: (1) the Locke-Mill version of the labor theory in which entitlement comes from the laborer producing something that would not otherwise have existed; (2) the labor-desert version of the labor theory in which a laborer who produces something of value to others is said to deserve some benefit for it; (3) complex arguments of utility in terms of economic efficiency or political and social stability; and (4) the argument from political liberty that claims that the inevitable acquisitiveness of human beings cannot be prohibited without ruining all liberties but nevertheless should be regulated, a system of private property rights being the only justifiable way of regulating acquisitiveness so as to maintain liberty. On the basis of these general theories of justification, absolute exclusive property became a fundamental assumption of social organization.

15. While some theories of property portray it as a universal reality, ontologically given and never changing, property is historically determined. Property has a history and must be made open to history. Its meaning and function have varied widely. If in human history there have always been kinds of property, there has certainly not always been what is thought of in modernity as absolute exclusive private property.

16. Moltmann, *The Trinity and the Kingdom*, 54–55.

17. This does not mean that market participants are not in relation but rather that they are free to choose and be chosen by any possible offer or transaction.

18. "The individual in market society *is* human as proprietor of his own person. . . . His humanity . . . depends on his freedom from any but self-interested . . . relations with others." C. B. Macpherson, *The Political Theory of Possessive Individualism* (Oxford: Clarendon, 1982).

19. "The Author of nature and the Provider of all things exercises his absolute dominion by continually giving us all the riches of the earth." This paraphrase of Basil, is mentioned by Charles Avila, *Ownership: Early Christian Teaching* (Maryknoll, N.Y.: Orbis, 1983), 53.

20. Karl Polanyi, *The Great Transformation* (Boston: Beacon, 1957). According to Polanyi, both barter and money economies are taken to be great advances over gift economies since "gifts obligate the recipient to make a reciprocal gift"; but "since the receiver decides how and when to reciprocate and can delay," reciprocal gift giving "offers little opportunity to obtain a specified benefit by my offer of benefits." Charles E. Lindblom (*The Market System* [New Haven, Conn.: Yale University Press, 2001], 54–55), comments: "Money had to be introduced as a way of moving beyond barter, according to which the meeting of my needs is blocked unless I can find someone with the object or skill or performance I want who simultaneously wants what I have to offer. The only solution is an object everyone is pleased to have: money. Now I offer a universally desired object and therefore do not have to search for someone who wants what I can offer. Money is a sufficient inducement for all transactions." Money as a universal means of exchange is a great tool, but as a sign of unlimited human desire it leads to enormous imbalances in the market system. It makes possible the unrestrained, unregulated rule of financial markets in the global economy. All limits to the accumulation of wealth and the display of opulence are lost. Bringing global financial markets under control is made all the more difficult by the fetish character of money.

21. Michael Walzer, *Spheres of Justice* (New York: Basic, 1983).

22. Robin Cook, "Will Genetics Alter Health Insurance?" *New York Times*, May 22, 2005.

23. Ibid.

24. See the helpful distinction of kinds of property made by David E. Klemm, "Material Grace: The Paradox of Property and Possession," in *Having: Property and Possession in Religions and Social Life,* ed. William Schweiker and Charles Matthewes, 222–45 (Grand Rapids, Mich.: Eerdmans, 2004). His definition of "material grace," however, tends to be individualistic.

25. For the following, cf. Kathryn Tanner, *Jesus, Humanity and the Trinity: A Brief Systematic Theology* (Minneapolis: Fortress Press, 2001), 82–95.

26. "We are ransomed on the cross from the suffering and oppression in which a debt economy has thrown us; taken from the cross we are returned to our original owner God, to God's kingdom of unconditional giving, snatched out of the world of deprivation and injustice from which we suffer because of our poverty, our inability to pay what others demand of us." Tanner, *Jesus, Humanity and the Trinity*, 88.

---

3. THE SPIRIT OF LIFE AND THE REVERENCE FOR LIFE

1. Jürgen Moltmann, *The Source of Life: The Holy Spirit and the Theology of Life*, trans. Margaret Kohl (Minneapolis: Fortress Press, 1997), 49.

2. On the structure of Moltmann's thought and also the theme of "why there is no ethics," see Geiko Müller-Fahrenholz, *Phantasie für das Reich Gottes: Die Theologie Jürgen Moltmanns Eine Einführung* (Gütersloh: Chr. Kaiser Gütersloher Verlag, 2000).

3. Moltmann, *The Source of Life*, 49.

4. Albert Schweitzer, "The Ethics of Reverence for Life," *Christendom* 1 (1936): 225–39. It is also reprinted in Henry Clark, *The Ethical Mysticism of Albert Schweitzer: A Study of the Sources and Significance of Schweitzer's Philosophy of Civilization* (Boston: Beacon, 1962), 180–94. It has been posted at www1.chapman.edu/schweitzer/sch.reading4.html, 13. This quotation and subsequent ones are from a printed online version.

5. Thich Nhat Hanh, "The First Precept: Reverence for Life" at www.ncf.carleton.ca/rootdir/menus/sigs/religion/buddhist.

6. On this see, Larry L. Rasmussen, *Earth Community, Earth Ethics* (Maryknoll, N.Y.: Orbis, 1998).

7. Albert Schweitzer, *The Philosophy of Civilization*, trans. C. T. Campion (Buffalo, N.Y.: Prometheus, 1987), xiv.

8. Schweitzer, "The Ethics of Reverence for Life," 4. Although I cannot explore the topic here, it should be noted that after Freud it is difficult to imagine that the immediate datum of

consciousness is a will-to-live somehow free from the death instinct. In a word, consciousness is more complex, overdetermined, and chaotic than Schweitzer seems to have admitted.

9. Schweitzer, *The Philosophy of Civilization*, 312.

10. Ibid., 311.

11. Ibid., 310.

12. Ibid., 312. One should remember that Schweitzer studied Schopenhauer and also Asian traditions, including Jainism. The claim that ultimate reality (creative will) is creative and destructive is consistent with these forms of thought.

13. Ibid., 313.

14. Albert Schweitzer, *Christianity and the Religions of the World*, trans. Johanna Powers (New York: Henry Holt, 1939), 81. Also see Lois K. Daly, "Ecofeminism, Reverence for Life, and Feminist Theological Ethics," in *Liberating Life: Contemporary Approaches in Ecological Theology*, ed. Charles Birch, William Eaken, and Jay B. McDaniel, 86–110 (Maryknoll, N.Y.: Orbis, 1990).

15. Jürgen Moltmann, *The Coming God: Christian Eschatology*, trans. Margaret Kohl (Minneapolis: Fortress Press, 1996), xi.

16. Ibid., x–xvii. Also see *Experience in Theology: Ways and Forms of Christian Theology*, trans. Margaret Kohl (Minneapolis: Fortress Press, 2000). For a discussion of the methodology, see Benedict H. B. Kwon, "Moltmann's Method of Theological Construction," in *Sin-Theology and the Thinking of Jürgen Moltmann*, ed. Jürgen Moltmann and Thomas Tseng, International Theology 10, 1–22 (Frankfurt: Peter Lang, 2004).

17. Jürgen Moltmann, *The Spirit of Life: A Universal Affirmation*, trans. Margaret Kohl (Minneapolis: Fortress Press, 2001), 34.

18. Moltmann, *The Source of Life*, 68.

19. Ibid., 111–12.

20. Ibid., 124.

21. Ibid., 48.

22. I should note here for the sake of precision in moral theory that I am offering a responsibility ethics that seeks to provide guidance for how one responds to actions and relations in terms of a complex mixed imperative that links duties and ends (we are to *respect* and to *enhance*) with respect to a good related to, but distinct from, responsible action, the *integrity of life*. On this argument see my books *Responsibility and Christian Ethics* (Cambridge, UK: Cambridge University Press, 1995) and *Theological Ethics and Global Dynamics: In The Time of Many Worlds* (Oxford, UK: Blackwell, 2004).

23. The claim here is distinct from, but related to, other basic frameworks in theology. Paul Tillich, for instance, argued that being has a polar structure as well as its depth (self-world and the depth of the power of being). Life is the dynamic affirmation of this structure in self amid time and against the threat of nonbeing. Kierkegaard talked about a self-relating dynamics that is also related to the divine. Hegel spoke of the dialectic of spirit, whereas Kant and Fichte explored the synthetic power of the transcendental subject. Schleiermacher explored consciousness with respect to an oscillation between abiding in self and passing beyond self. The idea, then, that "life" is a dynamic power is hardly new, for the idea reaches back, one might say, to ancient ideas about "anima" and soul. My worry about these other positions is that talk about polarities or existential self-relation can be empty and seems driven more by the problem of self-certainty than how to exercise power. The innovation of my argument, if that can be said, is to explore the multiplicity of needs and capacities that must be integrated and how that integration helps to fill out a conception of goodness. While my argument has resonance with classical and modern ideas, it avoids reducing life to a polar structure or the power of self-relation.

24. H. Richard Niebuhr helpfully called this a "relational theory of value." I have drawn on this idea and yet modified it in order to explore the complexity of the integrity of life at its various levels. On this theory, see H. Richard Niebuhr, *The Responsible Self: An Essay in Christian Moral Philosophy*, introduction by James M. Gustafson, foreword by William Schweiker (Library of Theological Ethics; Louisville, Ky.: Westminster John Knox, 1999).

25. The point here is about the distinction between moral and amoral. The amoral person on this account could engage in actions that are, in fact, responsible, but the intentionality of an act would not be truly moral. The question of what is immoral requires for its intelligibility clarity about the domain of the moral, of what is just, right, good, and fitting as well as the proper intentionality of action. On this account, I judge that Kant was simply right and, in fact, merely articulated a principle of Jewish and Christian thought. The point of the moral life cannot be simply to achieve happiness as Aristotle thought. The moral life entails an intentionality, a proper maxim of action as Kant put it, and so is bound to the rectitude of will. This is absolutely basic in classical Protestantism. Luther, for instance, always drew the distinction between "doing works of the law" and "fulfilling the law." Only the later, rooted in grace, is truly "moral" or "spiritual." See Martin Luther, "On the Bondage of the Will," in *Luther and Erasmus: Free Will and Salvation*, ed. E. Gordon Rupp and Philip S. Watson, Library of Christian Classics (Philadelphia: Westminster, 1969), 302–18.

26. Reinhold Niebuhr, *An Interpretation of Christian Ethics* (New York: Seabury, 1979), 33. Many thinkers in various religious traditions have noted this paradox.

27. Interestingly, at several points Moltmann cites Wesley, especially in *The Spirit of Life*, on the relation between happiness and holiness. My own reflections here are deeply Wesleyan. Importantly, Wesley thought that the Sermon on the Mount, and not natural law and virtues, as with Roman Catholics, or the Decalogue, as among the sixteenth-century Reformers, presented the proper construal of the Christian life. See John Wesley, *Sermons on Several Occasions* (London: Epworth, 1975).

---

4. "Speak, 'Friend,' and Enter"

1. This is my translation of Rosario Castellanos, *La muerte del tigre y otros cuentos* (México: Alfaguara, 2000), 45–64.

2. Ibid., 64.

3. For example, see Sharon H. Ringe's reading of the Gospel of John in *Wisdom's Friends: Community and Christology in the Fourth Gospel* (Louisville, Ky.: Westminster John Knox, 1999).

4. See Luke Timothy Johnson, "Making Connections: The Material Expression of Friendship in the New Testament," *Interpretation* 58 (2004): 158–71; and also Rainer Metzner, "In aller Freundschaft. Ein frühchristlicher Fall freundschaftlicher Gemeinschaft (Phil 2.25–30)," *New Testament Studies* 48 (2002): 111–31.

5. The words of this nineteenth-century hymn were written by Joseph Scriven, with music by Charles C. Converse; the Spanish translation is by L. Garza Mora. See *Himnos Selectos Evangélicos*, 16th ed. (Buenos Aires: Junta Bautista de Publicaciones, 1970), no. 255.

6. More so in the English than in the Spanish version, which does at least state in the final stanza that "Jesus is *our* friend; this he proved *to us*" ("*Jesucristo es nuestro amigo, de esto pruebas nos mostró*").

7. H. W. Longfellow translates this quatrain poetically but excises the explicit reference to friendship and the intimacy of the appellation "My Jesus" and renders the "door" (*puerta*) reminiscent of Rev. 3:20 as "gate": "Lord, what am I, that with unceasing care / Thou did'st seek after me, that Thou did'st wait / Wet with unhealthy dews before my gate, / And pass the gloomy nights of winter there?" See Thomas Walsh, comp., *Hispanic Anthology: Poems Translated from the Spanish by English and North American Poets* (New York: G. P. Putnam's Sons, 1920).

8. In the monastic tradition, which speaks highly of friendship, it is clear that the classics are read through a Johannine lens and not the other way around; on this see Adele Fiske, "Paradisus Homo Amicus," *Speculum* 40 (1965): 436–59.

9. Wes Howard-Brock, *Becoming Children of God: John's Gospel and Radical Discipleship* (Maryknoll, N.Y.: Orbis, 1994), 336.

10. See Ringe, *Wisdom's Friends*, 67–68.

11. See ibid.

12. Jürgen Moltmann, *In der Geschichte der dreieinigen Gottes. Beiträge zur trinitarischen Theology* (München: Chr. Kaiser Verlag, 1991), 52 (my translation, emphasis added).

13. Conversation both as method and as metaphor for theology seems to be of interest to many theologians at present. For instance, when the organizers of the Leuven Encounters on Systematic Theology proposed the topic of "Theology and Conversation" for a conference for late 2001, the response was impressive: and a long list of optional lectures was added to those by the main speakers. For a list of the topics, see www.theo.kuleuven.ac.be/lest/LEST%20III/0LEST-papers.html

14. *Confessions* 8.6.14. This English translation by Albert C. Outler (*Confessions and Enchiridion*, LCC 7 [Philadelphia: Westminster, 1955]), now in the public domain, is available at www.fordham.edu/halsall/basisconfessions-bod.thml. The critical Latin edition, with text and commentary by James O'Donnell (New York: Oxford University Press, 1992) can be accessed at www.stoa.org/hippo/.

15. Michel de Certeau, *The Practice of Everyday Life* (Berkeley: University of California Press, 1984), 176.

16. Walter Mignolo, *Local Histories/Global Designs: Coloniality, Subaltern Knowledges, and Border Thinking* (Princeton, N.J.: Princeton University Press, 2000), xi. All the quotations from Mignolo in this paragraph stem from that page.

17. For feminists, this concern is of particular importance: neither to replicate oppressive practices of speaking for other women by putting one's own words in their mouths nor to take advantage of their words and ideas for advancing one's own ends. I find Kathleen Logan's review article "Personal Testimony: Latin American Women Telling Their Lives," *Latin American Research Review* 32 (1997): 199–211 still quite eye-opening in this regard.

18. Virginia R. Azcuy, "Entreveros biográficos como lugares teológicos. Aportes para un *ethos* de mutualidad eclesial y social," lecture given in Wolfsburg, Germany on October 5, 2004, and accessible at http://www.die-wolfsburg.de/pdf/scriptspanisch.pdf.

19. See his *Ética y creatividad*, which can be accessed at http://www.cnice.mecd.es/tematicas/etica/modulo1/modulo1.html.

20. Ambrose, *Off.* 3.22.135 (NPNF²). On this question see David Konstan, "Problems in the History of Christian Friendship," *Journal of Early Christian Studies* 4 (1993): 87–113.

21. I say the person "to whom we want to be a friend" thinking of how Jesus phrases his question about who was "a neighbor to" the man on the road to Jericho (Luke 10:36).

22. Trinh T. Minh-ha, *Woman, Native, Other* (Bloomington: Indiana University Press, 1989), 28.

23. June Jordan writes wonderfully about both situations in "Report from the Bahamas," in *Feminist Theory Reader: Local and Global Perspectives*, ed. Carole McCann and Seung Kyung Kim (New York: Routledge, 2003), 438–46 .

24. See Aili Mari Tripa, "Rethinking Difference: Comparative Perspectives from Africa," *Signs: Journal of Women in Culture and Society* 25 (2000): 649–75. She makes the point that in societies that are very fractured along particularistic lines, feminists often make tactical moves that appear to minimize "difference" and challenge the politicization of race, gender, or religion and that U.S. discussions of "difference" do not serve the analysis of such societies well.

25. Néstor García Canclini, *Diferentes, desiguales y desconectados. Mapas de la interculturalidad* (Barcelona: Gedisa, 2004), 169–70.

26. On this see Raúl Fornet Betancourt, *Transformación intercultural de la filosofía* (Bilbao: Desclée de Brouwer, 2001), 280–81.

27. Canclini, *Diferentes, desiguales y desconectados,* 166.

28. Homi Bhabha, *The Location of Culture* (New York: Routledge, 1994), 235.

29. *Eth. Nic.* 8.4; here I quote the translation by David Ross (*The Nicomachean Ethics*, The World's Classics [New York: Oxford University Press, 1980]), which can be accessed at http://classics.mit.edu/Aristotle/nicomachaen.8.viii.html.

30. See Jürgen Moltmann, *Der Geist des Lebens: eine ganzheitliche Pneumatologie* [The Spirit of Life: A Universal Affirmation] (Munich: Chr. Kaiser Verlag, 1991), 230–32; and

Erfahrungen theologischen Denkens: Wege und Formen christlicher Theologie [Experiences in Theology: Ways and Forms of Christian Theology] (Munich: Chr. Kaiser/Gütersloher Verlagshaus, 1999), 140–42. Closely related to this are his comments on the church as a "fellowship of friends"; see *The Church in the Power of the Spirit* (Minneapolis: Fortress Press, 1993 [1977]), 314–16.

31. Jürgen Moltmann, *Experiences in Theology: Ways and Forms of Christian Theology*, trans. Margaret Kohl (Minneapolis: Fortress Press, 2000), 183–299.

32. J. R. R. Tolkien, *The Fellowship of the Ring* (New York: Ballantine, 1973), 396–402.

33. Castellanos, *La muerte del tigre*, 62.

---

5. WISDOM, THEOLOGICAL ANTHROPOLOGY, AND MODERN SECULAR INTERPRETATION OF HUMANITY

1. Jürgen Moltmann, *Science and Wisdom*, trans. Margaret Kohl (Minneapolis: Fortress Press, 2003), chap. 10.

2. Claus Westermann, *Genesis 1–11: A Commentary*, trans. John J. Scullion, SJ (Minneapolis: Augsburg, 1984); *Beginning and End in the Bible* (Philadelphia: Fortress Press, 1971); *Blessing in the Bible and the Life of the Church*, trans. Keith Crimm (Philadelphia: Fortress Press, 1978); *Creation*, trans. John J. Scullion (Philadelphia: Fortress Press, 1974).

3. Westermann, *Creation*, 16.

4. Westermann, *Genesis 1–11*, 2.

5. Ibid., 2.

6. Ibid., 17.

7. Westermann, *Creation*, 55.

8. Ibid., 65.

9. Ibid.

10. Westermann, *Genesis 1–11*, 7.

11. Ibid., 6.

12. Ibid., 67.

13. Westermann, *Blessing*, 61.

14. Westermann, *Blessing*, 61.

15. Westermann, *Beginning and End in the Bible*, 6.

16. Ibid., 3–4; cf. also Westermann, *Creation*, 41–65.

17. Westermann, *Creation*, 41.

18. Ibid., 65

19. Jürgen Moltmann, *Theology of Hope: On the Ground and Implications of a Christian Eschatology*, trans. James W. Leitch (London: SCM, 1967), especially introduction and chap. 2.

20. Gerhard Von Rad, *Old Testament Theology*, trans. D. M. G. Stalker (Edinburgh: Oliver and Boyd, 1963), 1:175–79.

21. Westermann, *Beginning and End in the Bible*, 6.

22. Ibid., 7.

23. Walther Zimmerli, "Concerning the Structure of Old Testament Wisdom," in *Studies in Ancient Israelite Wisdom*, ed. Harry M. Orlinsky (New York: KTAV, 1976), 316.

24. Brevard Childs, *Biblical Theology of the Old and New Testaments* (Minneapolis: Fortress Press, 1992), 189.

25. Zimmerli, "Concerning the Structure of Old Testament Wisdom," 315.

26. Childs, *Biblical Theology*, 189.

27. On the ways in which Priestly editors "bent" the genealogies they appropriated, see Westermann, *Genesis 1–11*, 16.

28. Wesley Wildman, "A Theological Challenge: Coordinating Biological, Social, and Religious Visions of Humanity," *Zygon* 33, no. 4 (1998): 571–99.

29. Ibid., 583.

30. Ibid., 575.

31. Ibid., 578.

32. Ibid., 579.

33. Ibid., 576.

34. Ibid., 581.

35. Ibid.

36. Ibid., 582.

37. James Gustafson, *An Examined Faith: The Grace of Self-Doubt* (Minneapolis: Fortress Press, 2004), especially chaps. 1–3.

38. Moltmann, *Science and Wisdom*, 24.

39. Wildman, "A Theological Challenge," 595.

40. Ibid., 595.

41. On "primitive concept," see P. F. Strawson, *Individuals* (Methuen: London, 1959), chap. 3.

6. Jürgen Moltmann's Engagement with the Natural Sciences

1. Jürgen Moltmann, *Science and Wisdom*, trans. Margaret Kohl (Minneapolis: Fortress Press, 2003), 34.

2. John C. Polkinghorne, *Reason and Reality: The Relationship between Science and Theology* (Philadelphia: Trinity Press International, 1991).

3. See John C. Polkinghorne, *The God of Hope and the End of the World* (New Haven, Conn.: Yale University Press, 2002).

4. Moltmann, *Science and Wisdom*, 79.

5. Ibid., 101.

6. Jürgen Moltmann, *God in Creation: A New Theology of Creation and the Spirit of God*, trans. Margaret Kohl (San Francisco: Harper & Row, 1985), 133.

7. John C. Polkinghorne, *Quantum Theory: A Very Short Introduction* (Oxford: Oxford University Press, 2002).

8. See John C. Polkinghorne, *Belief in God in an Age of Science* (New Haven, Conn.: Yale University Press, 1998).

9. Moltmann, *Science and Wisdom*, 91.

10. Ibid., 66.

11. Arthur R. Peacocke, *Creation and the World of Science* (Oxford: Oxford University Press, 1979), 105–6.

12. Stuart Kauffman, *At Home in the Universe: The Search for Laws of Self-organization and Complexity* (Oxford: Oxford University Press, 1995), chap. 4.

13. Moltmann, *God in Creation*, 100.

14. Ibid., 212.

15. Polkinghorne, *God of Hope*, 117–22.

16. Moltmann, *Science and Wisdom*, 46.

17. Ibid., 79.

18. It is interesting to recall that Kurt Goedel showed that there are solutions to the equations of general relativity corresponding to closed timelike curves. Because of problems of consistent causal ordering, they are commonly regarded as not being of physical significance.

19. Polkinghorne, *God of Hope*, 117–22.

20. See John C. Polkinghorne and Michael Welker, eds., *The End of the World and the Ends of God: Science and Theology on Eschatology* (Harrisburg, Pa.: Trinity Press International, 2000), passim.

21. Moltmann, *God in Creation*, 213.

22. See the essays in John C. Polkinghorne, ed., *The Work of Love: Creation as Kenosis* (Grand Rapids, Mich.: Eerdmans, 2001).

23. Moltmann, *God in Creation*, 86–87.

24. Ibid., 88–89.

25. For dissent from panentheism, see John C. Polkinghorne, *Faith, Science and Understanding* (New Haven, Conn.: Yale University Press, 2000), 89–95.

26. Moltmann, *Science and Wisdom*, 66.
27. Moltmann, *God in Creation*, xii.
28. Ibid., 36.
29. Ibid., xii.
30. Ibid., 100.
31. Ibid., 63.
32. See Polkinghorne, *Quantum Theory*.
33. Moltmann, *God in Creation*, 32.
34. Ibid., 70.
35. Ibid., xi.
36. Moltmann, *Science and Wisdom*, 26.
37. See, for example, Celia Deane-Drummond, *Creation through Wisdom: Theology and the New Biology* (Edinburgh: T&T Clark, 2000); John C. Polkinghorne, *Science and Creation: The Search for Understanding* (London: SPCK, 1988).
38. Moltmann, *Science and Wisdom*, 7.
39. Ibid., 24.
40. Ibid.
41. See John C. Polkinghorne, *Scientists as Theologians: A Comparison of the Writings of Ian Barbour, Arthur Peacocke and John Polkinghorne* (London: SPCK, 1996).

---

7. Church Unity in Freedom

1. Jürgen Moltmann, *The Church in the Power of the Spirit: A Contribution to Messianic Ecclesiology* (Minneapolis: Fortress Press, 1993 [1977]), 337.
2. Ibid., 337–61.
3. The first chapter already argues that a doctrine of the church today should include these dimensions, namely, that it is the church of Jesus Christ and that the church is missionary, ecumenical, and political (*The Church in the Power of the Spirit*, 1–18). Interestingly enough, he explicitly indicates here that these foundational ideas about the church are based on the Reformed confessional writings and the convictions of the Confessing Church as formulated in the *Theological Declaration of Barmen*, especially Thesis 1.
4. These phrases represent the successive themes of chapters 3 to 6, which form the heart of *The Church in the Power of the Spirit* before he concludes with the final chapter on the four marks of the church.
5. *The Church in the Power*, 340–41. Of course, he does not merely make these claims; he argues at length to motivate and to substantiate these qualifications for today.
6. The question how to understand the marks of the church is, of course, very complex and controversial, historically, systematically, and practically. For an interesting discussion that includes a challenging historical interpretation, see, e.g., Gordon W. Lathrop and Timothy J. Wengert, *Christian Assembly: Marks of the Church in a Pluralistic Age* (Minneapolis: Fortress Press, 2004).
7. W.-D. Marsch, ed., *Diskussion über die "Theologie der Hoffnung" von Jürgen Moltmann* (Munich, 1967); M. Welker, ed., *Diskussion über Jürgen Moltmanns Buch "Der gekreuzigte Gott,"* (Munich, 1979).
8. For helpful discussions, see Geiko Müller-Fahrenholz, *The Kingdom and the Power: The Theology of Jürgen Moltmann* (Minneapolis: Fortress Press, 2001), 100–106; Richard Bauckham, *Moltmann: Messianic Theology in the Making* (Hants, UK: Marshall Pickering, 1987), 114–39.
9. Müller-Fahrenholz, *The Kingdom and the Power*, 171.
10. The one exception, the volume of essays written during the time when *The Church in the Power of the Spirit* itself was published, reflects the same general ideas: *The Passion for Life: A Messianic Lifestyle*, trans. M. Douglas Meeks (Philadelphia: Fortress Press, 1978). It is instructive that the original German edition was entitled "a new lifestyle, steps towards the congregation": *Neuer Lebensstil. Schritte zur Gemeinde* (Munich: Kaiser, 1977). It was also

instructive that the book was dedicated to the Moravian Seminary "as a sign of friendship with The Herrnhuter Brüdergemeinde." Most of these studies, although very instructive to gain insight in his theology, deal more with the Christian lifestyle than with the church. Only the last chapter, "The Congregation 'From Below,'" provides some focused discussion of the reformation of the church.

Other well-known volumes with collected essays include *The Experiment Hope*, trans. and ed. M. Douglas Meeks (Philadelphia: Fortress Press, 1975); *The Future of Creation: Collected Essays*, trans. Margaret Kohl (Philadelphia: Fortress Press, 1979); *Experiences of God*, trans. Margaret Kohl (Philadelphia: Fortress Press, 1980); *On Human Dignity: Political Theology and Ethics*, trans. M. Douglas Meeks (Philadelphia: Fortress Press, 1984); *History and the Triune God: Contributions to Trinitarian Theology* (New York: Crossroad, 1991); *God for a Secular Society: The Public Relevance of Theology* (Minneapolis: Fortress Press, 1999). Other works scarcely contain essays specifically dealing with the church.

Also, few studies of his ecclesiology are available. Perhaps the most helpful is the informative, carefully argued study by Arne Rasmusson, *The Church as Polis: From Political Theology to Theological Politics as Exemplified by Jürgen Moltmann and Stanley Hauerwas* (Lund: Lund University Press, 1994). Rasmusson refers to an unpublished dissertation by M. L. Brink, "The Ecclesiological Dimensions of Jürgen Moltmann's Theology: Vision of a Future Church?" (Fordham University, 1990), but shows that she describes Moltmann, as well as Barth, Anabaptists, and Mennonites all as Lutherans, and concludes that most of her criticisms of Moltmann are "rather absurd" (Rasmusson, *The Church as Polis*, 22, 88).

Even the two volumes dedicated to Moltmann on the occasions respectively of his sixtieth and seventieth birthdays do not take his ecclesiology very seriously. *Gottes Zukunft—Zukunft der Welt*, ed. H. Deuser, G. M. Martin, K. Stock, and M. Welker (Munich: Kaiser, 1986), follows the sequence of his major publications until then and, therefore, include nine essays under the theme of "Kirche in der Kraft des Geistes." Most of these essays, however, do not really engage Moltmann's thought, but rather develop their own arguments around themes suggested by his work. Miroslav Volf, Carmen Krieg, and Thomas Kucharz, eds., *The Future of Theology: Essays in Honor of Jürgen Moltmann* (Grand Rapids, Mich.: Eerdmans, 1996), focus, indeed, on the future of theology; and only Wolfhart Pannenberg's essay "The Teaching Office and the Unity of the Church," 221–32, deals with an explicit ecclesiological theme, yet without even mentioning Moltmann or any of his works.

11. This raises very interesting and important questions about Moltmann's own understanding of *congregation* and *community* and about the background and tradition against which he should be understood. Müller-Fahrenholz is convinced that Moltmann's "community principle . . . is clearly rooted in the Reformed congregationalist tradition." He adds that in the relevant sections in Moltmann "almost always only Reformed theologians are quoted, above all Moltmann's teacher Otto Weber" (Müller-Fahrenholz, *The Kingdom and the Power*, 104, 253). Arne Rasmusson, however, is convinced that Moltmann's congregationalist ecclesiology is informed by roots in the Radical Reformation. He argues this position often and in many ways, also quoting key passages of Moltmann himself, and interestingly enough points out that "Weber's *Versammelte Gemeinde* from 1949 (republished with an introduction by Moltmann in 1975) has a strong Radical Reformation character" (Rasmusson, *The Church as Polis*, 23).

12. For example, the local impact of his emphasis on the congregational form of the church has been one very interesting development. In Reformed church circles in South Africa, the emphasis on the congregation has become widespread and very popular after the demise of apartheid in society and church, particularly in the so-called white Dutch Reformed Church. The present moderator of the DRC, C. W. Burger, a very influential church leader and theologian, has published several very popular and ground-breaking works on the nature and the role of the congregation. The most recent and comprehensive one is *Gemeentes in die kragveld van die Gees* [Congregations in the Force-field of the Spirit] (Wellington: Lux Verbi, 1999), a title directly attributed to Moltmann's work. A remarkable aspect of this development is the way in which post-Constantinian language, so typical of Moltmann, is also used in these church

circles in South Africa today to focus the attention on the local congregation and often away from broader denominational and ecumenical church concerns and public issues.

13. Especially the early work on the theology of hope played a major role here. Several South African theological students studied during the seventies in Tübingen and attended his lectures. Daniël J. Louw wrote his unpublished doctoral dissertation, *Toekoms tussen hoop en angs*, on Bloch and Moltmann and later became professor and dean at the Stellenbosch Faculty of Theology. The widely respected systematic theologian and public figure at the University of the Western Cape, J. J. F. Durand, gave his inaugural lecture on the question of the suffering God, dealing at length with Moltmann's work. Durand and Jonker published a very influential series of works in Christian doctrine in which contemporary theology in general but also Moltmann became serious discussion partners. From his side, Moltmann remained informed about and interested in the South African issues of racism, human dignity, and human rights; the struggle against apartheid; the difficult question of peace and nonviolence; and the issues of social injustice and oppression. In several of his papers, especially in the context of the ecumenical movement and the German academies, he often addressed those issues.

14. For the role of different churches in the South African history, see e.g., Richard Elphick and Rodney Davenport, eds., *Christianity in South Africa: A Political, Social and Cultural History* (Cape Town: David Philip, 1997); John W. de Gruchy, *The Church Struggle in South Africa*, 25th anniversary ed. (Minneapolis: Fortress Press, 2005).

15. For apartheid in church and theology, see e.g., J. C. Adonis, *Die afgebreekte skeidsmuur weer opgebou* (Amsterdam: Rodopi, 1982); Allan A. Boesak, *Black and Reformed: Apartheid, Liberation, and the Calvinist Tradition* (Maryknoll, N.Y.: Orbis, 1984); H. R. Botman, "'Black' and Reformed and 'Dutch' and Reformed in South Africa," in *Keeping the Faith*, ed. R. Wells, 85–105 (Grand Rapids, Mich.: Eerdmans, 1997); J. Cochrane, *Servants of Power: The Role of the English-speaking Churches 1903–1930* (Johannesburg: Ravan, 1987); Charles Villa-Vicencio, *Trapped in Apartheid: A Socio-Theological History of the English-Speaking Churches* (Maryknoll, N.Y.: Orbis, 1988); J. Kinghorn, *Die Ned. Geref. Kerk en apartheid* (Johannesburg: Macmillan, 1986); C. J. A. Loff, *Bevryding tot eenwording* (Kampen: Theologische Universiteit, 1997); Takatso Alfred Mofokeng, *The Crucified among the Crossbearers: Towards a Black Christology* (Kampen: Kok, 1983); Lebakeng Ramotshabai Lekula Ntoane, *A Cry for Life: An Interpretation of "Calvinism" and Calvin* (Kampen: Kok, 1983).

16. Friendship is, of course, a key idea running throughout his whole work. It is also very important for his understanding of the church as community and congregation. In *Church in the Power*, he even discusses the traditionally Reformed understanding of the threefold office of Christ and then suggests that friend as a fourth aspect of the work of Christ is even more important today than the other three, 76–114 and then 114–21.

17. Moltmann, *Church in the Power*, 342.

18. For South African Reformed Christians, biblical references and arguments are very important; but they are also important for Moltmann. In many of his scholarly writings, in addition to his published sermons and more meditative works, he deals at length with some of the biblical pericopes that also played crucial roles in the debates about apartheid. See e.g., as a typical treatment, his essay "Community with Others," in *The Passion of Life: A Messianic Lifestyle* (Philadelphia: Fortress Press, 1978), 27–36, which reflects on Rom. 15:7, "accept one another as Christ accepted us."

19. See J. J. F. Durand, "Church Unity and the Reformed Churches in Southern Africa," in *Farewell to Apartheid? Church Relations in South Africa: The WARC Consultation in South Africa*, ed. P. Réamonn, 60–66 (Geneva: WARC, 1994).

20. Particularly in and since *The Way of Jesus Christ*, Moltmann has described the church as "a contrast society," "an alternative community," "the great alternative," "a public alternative," "an instrument of the kingdom." So, for example, Rasmusson, *The Church as Polis*, 76–78. The well-known South African missiologist David Bosch, but also the Reformed systematic theologian P. F. Theron, made major contributions in this regard, precisely regarding the unity of the church within the apartheid society. See, e.g., Theron, *Die*

kerk as kosmies-eskatologiese teken—Die eenheid van die kerk as "profesie" van die eskatologiese vrede (Pretoria: NGKU, 1978).

21. Moltmann, *Church in the Power*, 343.

22. Interestingly, *weaknesses* was a loaded term within the South African debates on the unity of the church. The infamous decision by the Synod of the Dutch Reformed Church in 1857 that eventually led to apartheid in church and society had been based on allowance for "the weaknesses" of some, which at the time meant the sinful unwillingness of some members to share the Lord's Supper with members not from their class, race, or social and economic status.

23. Moltmann, *Church in the Power*, 343.

24. See Dirk J. Smit, "Spirituality, Worship, Confession, and Church Unity: A Story from South Africa," in *Ecumenical Theology in Worship, Doctrine, and Life*, ed. David S. Cunningham et al., 271–81 (New York: Oxford University Press, 1999).

25. Moltmann, *Church in the Power*, 343–44.

26. For Moltmann's use of friendship in this way, see Rasmusson, *The Church as Polis*, 82–83: "brotherhood entails a relationship that is not chosen, while friendship is voluntary."

27. Moltmann, *Church in the Power*, 344.

28. Ibid., 344–45.

29. Ibid., 345.

30. Ibid.

31. Ibid.

32. Ibid., 345–46.

33. Ibid., 346.

34. Ibid.

35. Ibid.

36. Ibid., 346–47.

37. For the text and some discussion of the historical context, see e.g., G. D. Cloete and D. J. Smit, eds., *A Moment of Truth: The Confession of the Dutch Reformed Mission Church* ['n Oomblik van waarheid] (Grand Rapids Mich: Eerdmans, 1984).

38. Moltmann, *Church in the Power*, 347.

39. Ibid.

40. This choice appears repeatedly throughout his oeuvre and in many different contexts and forms. In *The Experiment Hope*, 116–18, for example, he says that according to "an old sentence," the true church is where Christ is, *ubi Christus, ibi Ecclesia*. But where is Christ? The New Testament, he continues, provides two promises of Christ's presence, namely in word, sacrament, and the community of the faithful and in the least of the brothers (Matt. 25). This second form of presence, he argues, does not belong in social ethics, but in ecclesiology. According to him, this promise leads to "a double brotherhood of Christ: the one is the manifest brotherhood of the believers; the other is the latent brotherhood of the poor." In fact, in this context the thrust of his argument is again in the direction of a choice for the second form of Christ's presence and being the church. "Race, class, status, and national churches smack of heresy in their structures"—a sentiment with which the South African believers struggling with apartheid would tend to agree. Then he again seems to see an alternative that is not fully convincing or very concrete and clear, in that he calls for "concretely dissolving their alliances" with those who seem to belong to the "false church."

Rasmusson shows that Moltmann, in fact, works with a threefold form of the presence of Christ, with his presence in the parousia as the third form (*The Church as Polis*, 76–78): "The important question is then not, concludes Moltmann, how people outside it related themselves to the church, but how the church relates itself to the presence of Christ among the poor. He has later reformulated the same ideas in terms of how Jesus proclaimed the gospel. To the poor it is proclaimed unconditionally. They are not called to the kingdom, as it already belongs to them, a truth that gives their life true dignity. To the rich, the message of liberation, on the contrary, includes the call to conversion and discipleship. From this follows that the new messianic people consist of the converted together with the poor. The practical consequence for the life and mission of the church is that "this mission should neither bring people again into the church nor the church into the people, but rather discover the church *of* the people and live the brotherhood of Jesus in the brotherhood of the 'least of these.'" Rasmusson comments that "it is not too easy to know how this should be understood in practical terms," since "the sort of sharp contrasts" that Moltmann makes "makes it very difficult to understand in practical terms what he might possibly mean."

It is probably the same stark alternative, the same sharp contrasts in his ecclesiology that M. Welker also criticizes in his "Gottes freie Gnade ausrichten an alles Volk," *epd-Dokumentation,* No. 29, 6 (July 2004). During the 1984 anniversary of the *Theological Declaration of Barmen,* Moltmann, in his "Zum Abschluss," interpreted the phrase "to the whole people" in Thesis 6 in the sense of the New Testament *ochlos* and therefore in the sense of the poor, the marginalized, and the suffering ("Zum Abschluss," in *Bekennende Kirche wagen,* ed. Jürgen Moltmann, 260–61 [Munich: Kaiser, 1984]). The gospel is for them, and they are the real church. Welker is very critical of that interpretation, arguing that this perspective suggests a false alternative and, in fact, presupposes that the church *is* not the church (that should *remain* the church, although it should be radically renewed and even converted), but should first *become* the church (in a vague and unclear way).

41. Moltmann, *Church in the Power,* 340.

42. The *Confession* has an introduction and conclusion, with three sections dealing with living unity, real reconciliation, and compassionate justice—the three Christian convictions ultimately at stake in the theology of apartheid, according to the (then) Dutch Reformed Mission Church. The section on the unity of the church reads: "We believe in one holy, universal Christian Church, the communion of saints called from the entire human family. We believe that Christ's work of reconciliation is made manifest in the Church as the community of believers who have been reconciled with God and with one another; that unity is, therefore, both a gift and an obligation for the Church of Jesus Christ; that through the working of God's Spirit it is a binding force, yet simultaneously a reality which must be earnestly pursued and sought: one which the people of God must continually be built up to attain; that this unity must become visible so that the world may believe that separation, enmity, and hatred between people and groups is sin which Christ has already conquered, and accordingly that anything which threatens this unity may have no place in the Church and must be resisted; that this unity of the people of God must be manifested and be active in a variety of ways: in that we love one another; that we experience, practice and pursue community with one another; that we are obligated to give ourselves willingly and joyfully to be of benefit and blessing to one another; that we share one faith, have one calling, are of one soul and one mind; have one God and Father, are filled with one Spirit, are baptized with one baptism, eat of one bread and drink of one cup, confess one Name, are obedient to one Lord, work for one cause, and share one hope; together come to know the height and the breadth and the depth of the love of Christ; together are built up to the stature of Christ, to the new humanity; together know and bear one another's burdens, thereby fulfilling the law of Christ that we need one another and upbuild one another, admonishing and comforting one another; that we suffer with one another for the sake of righteousness; pray together; together serve God in this world; and together fight against all which may threaten or hinder this unity; *that this unity can be established only in freedom* and not under constraint; that the variety of spiritual gifts, opportunities, backgrounds, convictions, as well as the various languages and cultures, are by virtue of the reconciliation in Christ, opportunities for mutual service and enrichment within the one visible people of God; that true faith in Jesus Christ is the only condition for membership of this Church.

"Therefore, we reject any doctrine which absolutises either natural diversity or the sinful separation of people in such a way that this absolutisation hinders or breaks the visible and active unity of the church, or even leads to the establishment of a separate church formation; which professes that this spiritual unity is truly being maintained in the bond of peace whilst believers of the same confession are in effect alienated from one another for the sake of diversity and in despair of reconciliation; which denies that a refusal earnestly to pursue this visible unity as a priceless gift is sin; which explicitly or implicitly maintains that descent or any other human or social factor should be a consideration in determining membership of the Church."

43. It is immediately clear from the section from the *Confession* that the notion of "freedom" is not used in the technical sense in which Moltmann develops freedom in his theology. For him, freedom is indeed a crucial term since it plays a central role in almost every work and in every systematic locus and captures much of his theological project. See e.g., Rasmusson, *The Church as Polis*, 90–99, for a helpful introduction. In the *Confession of Belhar*, it is not used in such a technical and philosophical sense, but is used as a practical term, underlining that the unity of the church should not be equated with uniformity or be forced upon believers in ways that practically deny their diversity and otherness and the richness of gifts to the church.

8. MAKE WAY FOR THE SPIRIT

1. Sigmund Frued, *Moses and Monotheism* (Hogarth Press and the Institute of Psycho-Analysis, 1939), 197.
2. From a private conversation with the author in 1964.
3. See Athanasius, *Ep. ad Serapionem* I, and discussion in J. N. D. Kelly, *Early Christian Doctrines* (New York: Harper & Row, 1978), 255–58.
4. Michael Kinnamon, ed., *Signs of the Spirit: Official Report, Seventh Assembly, Canberra, Australia, 7–20 February 1991* (Geneva: WCC Publications; Grand Rapids, Mich.: Eerdmans, 1991).

9. THE TRINITY AND THE THEOLOGY OF RELIGIONS

1. For an eloquent appeal to the religions of the world to respect difference and to be part of the solution rather than part of the problem of global conflict and violence, see Jonathan Sacks, *The Dignity of Difference* (London: Continuum, 2003).
2. See Gavin D'Costa, *The Meeting of the Religions and the Trinity* (Maryknoll, N.Y.: Orbis, 2000); Jacques Dupuis, *Toward a Christian Theology of Religious Pluralism* (Maryknoll, N.Y.: Orbis, 1997); Stanley J. Grenz, "Toward an Evangelical Theology of the Religions," *Journal of Ecumenical Studies* 31, no. 2 (1994): 49–65; Mark Heim, *The Depths of the Riches: A Trinitarian Theology of Religious Ends* (Grand Rapids, Mich.: Eerdmans, 2001); Veli-Matti Kärkkäinen, *Trinity and Religious Pluralism* (Burlington, Vt.: Ashgate, 2004); Kevin J. Vanhoozer, *The Trinity in a Pluralistic Age: Theological Essays on Culture and Religion* (Grand Rapids, Mich.: Eerdmans, 1997).
3. Christoph Schwöbel, "Particularity, Universality, and the Religions: Toward a Christian Theology of the Religions," in *Christian Uniqueness Reconsidered*, ed. Gavin D'Costa, 30–46 (Maryknoll, N.Y.: Orbis, 1990).
4. Paul Knitter, *Introducing Theologies of Religion* (Maryknoll, N.Y.: Orbis, 2002).
5. Carl Braaten, *No Other Gospel! Christianity among the World Religions* (Minneapolis: Fortress Press, 1992), 7.
6. Dupuis, *Toward a Christian Theology of Religious Pluralism*; Heim, *The Depth of the Riches*.
7. Dupuis, *Toward a Christian Theology of Religious Pluralism*, 1.
8. Ibid., 321.
9. Ibid., 243.
10. Ibid., 387.
11. Ibid., 197.
12. Ibid., 298.
13. Ibid., 195, 300, 321.
14. Ibid., 226.
15. Ibid., 227.

16. Ibid., 387.

17. Ibid., 313.

18. Ibid., 300.

19. Ibid., 283, 303.

20. Ibid., 322

21. Heim, *The Depths of the Riches,* 133.

22. Ibid., 136.

23. Ibid., 75.

24. Ibid., 268.

25. Ibid., 291.

26. Ibid., 263.

27. Jürgen Moltmann, *The Coming of God* (Minneapolis: Fortress Press, 1996), xii.

28. See Jürgen Moltmann, *Experiences in Theology* (Minneapolis: Fortress Press, 2000).

29. Jürgen Moltmann, *The Crucified God: The Cross of Christ as the Foundation and Criterion of Christian Theology* (New York: Harper & Row, 1974), 246.

30. Jürgen Moltmann, "Is 'Pluralist Theology' Useful for the Dialogue of World Religions?" in *Christian Uniqueness Reconsidered,* ed. Gavin D'Costa, 152 (Maryknoll, N.Y.: Orbis, 1990).

31. Jürgen Moltmann, *The Church in the Power of the Spirit* (New York: Harper & Row, 1977), 161.

32. Ibid.

33. Ibid.

34. Jürgen Moltmann, "Jesus between Jews and Christians," in *ARC: The Journal of the Faculty of Religious Studies, McGill University* 24 (1996): 63.

35. Jürgen Moltmann, *The Trinity and the Kingdom* (San Francisco: Harper and Row, 1981), 218.

36. Moltmann, *Church in the Power,* 136.

37. Jürgen Moltmann, Nicholas Wolterstorff, and Ellen T. Charry, *A Passion for God's Reign* (Grand Rapids, Mich.: Eerdmans, 1998), 57.

38. Ibid.

39. Ibid., 57.

40. Moltmann, *Church in the Power,* 150.

41. Moltmann, *Experiences in Theology,* 323.

42. Jürgen Moltmann, *The Spirit of Life: A Universal Affirmation* (Minneapolis: Fortress Press, 1992), 7.

43. Moltmann, *Experiences in Theology,* 326.

44. Moltmann et al., *A Passion for God's Reign,* 62.

45. Ibid., 63–64.

46. Ibid., 62.

47. See Jürgen Moltmann, "God Is Unselfish Love," in *The Emptying God: A Buddhist-Christian Conversation,* ed. John B. Cobb Jr. and Christopher Ives, 116–24 (Maryknoll, N.Y.: Orbis, 1991); Hans Küng and Jürgen Moltmann, eds., *Islam: A Challenge for Christianity* (Maryknoll, N.Y.: Orbis, 1994).

48. Moltmann, "Jesus between Jews and Christians," 61.

49. See Jürgen Moltmann, "Dialog oder Mission?" in *Bekenntnis zu dem einen Gott? hg.* Rudolf Weth, 36–49 (Neukirchen-Vluyn: Neukirchener Verlag, 2000).

50. Moltmann, *The Passion for God's Reign,* 59.

51. Jürgen Moltmann, "Friedenstiften und Drachentöten im Christentum," in *Evangelische Theologie* 64 (2004): 285.

52. Moltmann, "Is 'Pluralist Theology' Useful for the Dialogue of World Religions?" 154.

53. Ibid., 155.

54. Ibid., 154.

55. Ibid.

56. Moltmann, "Dialog oder Mission?" 44–46.

57. Ibid., 49.

58. Sacks, *The Dignity of Difference*, 9.

---

10. BEYOND EXCLUSIVISM AND ABSOLUTISM

1. Joseph Hough, "Christian Revelation and Religious Pluralism," *Union Seminary Quarterly Review* 56, no. 3–4 (2002): 70–71. I first sketched my thoughts on this topic in my reply to Hough, "Toward a Christian Theology of Religions: Some Philosophical and Theological Reflections," *USQR* 56, no. 3–4 (2002): 157–66.

2. Hough, "Christian Revelation and Religious Pluralism," 65–66.

3. The most thorough discussion of truth-claiming in theology is Bruce Marshall, *Trinity and Truth* (Cambridge: Cambridge University Press, 2000), 234: "We do have a stable grasp of the concept of truth, [Donald] Davidson argues, for every sentence in our language. Supposing that language is English, our grasp of the concept 'true' as applied to the sentence 'Grass is green,' for example, is expressed in our untroubled assent to the sentence 'Grass is green' is true if and only if grass is green . . . that is . . . *s* is true-in-*L* if and only if *p*.'"

4. I have been helped enormously in my understanding of this issue by Jeffrey Stout's seminal book *Democracy and Tradition* (Princeton: Princeton University Press, 2004).

5. Donald Davidson has argued that the very distinction between *scheme* and *content,* a distinction presupposed by the notion of a *framework,* is logically flawed, in "On the Very Idea of a Conceptual Scheme," *Inquiries into Truth and Interpretation* (Oxford: Clarendon, 1984), 183–98.

6. See *Revelation and Theology: The Gospel as Narrated Promise* (Notre Dame: University of Notre Dame Press, 1985); and *Religion in American Public Life: A Dilemma for Democracy* (Georgetown: Century Fund/Georgetown University Press, 1996).

7. Among the many accounts of *foundationalism,* Bruce Marshall's (*Truth and Trinity,* 54) is one of the most succinct. "By 'foundationalism' I mean a set of three claims tightly connected by adherents of the thesis: (F1) that with regard to at least some of the sentences we hold true, we have direct or immediate access to states of affairs, events, or experiences in virtue of which those sentences are true; (F2) that this direct access guarantees the truth of these sentences, and so justifies us in, or serves as the ultimate evidence for, holding them true; (F3) that the rest of our beliefs must be justified by establishing some suitable kind of warranting link with those which are directly tied to the world (and thereby serve as the justificatory 'foundations' for the rest)."

8. I seek to develop a *nonfoundational* understanding of revelation in *Revelation and Theology.*

9. Bruce Marshall, who shares my critique of *foundationalism,* nonetheless, affirms the "incorrigibility" of "the Church's central beliefs." "The Christian tradition, however, has generally taken the church's central beliefs to be certain and incorrigible, while explicitly denying that those beliefs are self-evident, empirically evident, or even very widely held. . . . We who hold these beliefs should therefore regard them as certain and incorrigible—incapable of turning out to be false." *Trinity and Truth,* 168–69.

10. Wilfrid Sellars, "Empiricism and the Philosophy of Mind," *Science, Perception, and Reality* (London: Routledge & Kegan Paul, 1963), 127–96.

11. Donald Davidson, "On the Very Idea of a Conceptual Scheme," *Inquiries into Truth and Interpretation* (Oxford: Oxford University Press, 1984), 183–98.

12. Richard Bernstein, *Beyond Objectivism and Relativism: Science, Hermeneutics, and Praxis* (Philadelphia: University of Pennsylvania Press, 1983), 18.

13. Nicolas Rescher, *Pluralism: Against the Demand for Consensus* (Oxford: Clarendon, 1993), 89.

14. Ludwig Wittgenstein, *Philosophical Investigations,* vol. 1, no. 43 (Oxford: Basil Blackwell, 1958), 20.

15. George Lindbeck, *The Nature of Doctrine* (Philadelphia: Westminster, 1984), 68.

16. In *Revelation and Theology* I spoke of these beliefs as *basic*, but I now think that this term does not sufficiently signal the strong resistance a community should have to revising such beliefs. Bruce Marshall in *Trinity and Truth* terms such beliefs *essential* and is willing to claim that some of these beliefs are incorrigible. Because I am unwilling to make the latter claim, I prefer the less essentialist language of *fundamental*.

17. Marshall, *Trinity and Truth*, 45.

18. Marshall claims for this belief and indeed all fundamental Christian beliefs "unrestricted epistemic primacy": "To say that central Christian beliefs have unrestricted epistemic primacy means that any possible belief which contradicts them must be false. Ascribing genuinely *unrestricted* primacy to these particular beliefs, moreover, preempts the application of the category; no other beliefs will be able to enjoy this logical status. From this it follows that no true belief can contradict the narratives which identify Jesus and the Trinity." Ibid., 120.

19. Religious traditions will almost certainly possess different, and possibly incompatible, fundamental epistemic priorities. Religious dialogue should not, in my estimation, have as its goal the attempt to resolve these differences between fundamental identity-shaping epistemic priorities; rather, dialogue should seek to find the many places in the complex bodies of beliefs held by different communities where these traditions have resolvable disagreements. Recent advances in understanding between Roman Catholic and Lutherans on the doctrine of justification give ample evidence that such an approach to dialogue works in the intra-Christian ecumenical discussion. The fundamental changes in Christian beliefs regarding the election of Jews and the rejection of all forms of *supercessionist* doctrines give another instance of such powerfully important dialogical work. While Roman Catholics and Lutherans and Christians and Jews have the advantage of sharing some fundamental epistemic priorities, their differences have been theologically profound. This approach to dialogue can also serve as a model for discussions among religious traditions that share neither fundamental epistemic priorities nor a common history.

20. The kind of theology of religions I am offering here is modest primarily in the sense that it eschews the attempt to provide an overarching theory of religions which claims that all religions have either the same aim or share a common experience.

21. Martin Luther, "Heidelberg Disputation," *Luther's Works* 31 (Philadelphia: Fortress Press, 1957), 52–53.

22. Karl Barth, *Church Dogmatics* (Edinburgh: T&T Clark, 1957), II/1:257–321.

23. Ibid., IV/1:185.

24. Ronald F. Thiemann, *Revelation and Theology: The Gospel as Narrated Promise*, 112–40; and Thiemann, "The Unnamed Woman at Bethany: A Model for Discipleship," *Constructing a Public Theology: The Church in a Pluralistic Culture* (Louisville, Ky.: Westminster John Knox, 1991), 63–74.

25. For a discussion of the relationship between insiders and outsiders in narrative interpretation, see, Thiemann, "Radiance and Obscurity in Biblical Narratives," *Constructing a Public Theology*, 45–62.

26. I do not intend here to assert the identity of the adherents of non-Christian religions as *outsiders*. I am using the term ironically to remind Christians, who have often marginalized the non-Christian *Other*, that so-called *outsiders* in the Gospel narratives are the bearers of truth. If non-Christians are bearers of such truth, too, then their marginalization by Christians can no longer be sustained.

27. See especially, Martin Luther, *Lectures on Galatians 1535, Luther's Works* 26 (St. Louis: Concordia, 1963), 248–90. See also, Eberhard Jüngel, *God as the Mystery of the World* (Grand Rapids, Mich.: Eerdmanns, 1986).

11. The Trinity and Gender Reconsidered

1. The materials by Jürgen Moltmann and Elisabeth Moltmann-Wendel on theology and gender that I am particularly drawing on for this essay are as follows (for this English-speaking *Festschrift*, I have utilized the relevant English translations): Jürgen Moltmann, "The Motherly Father: Is Trinitarian Patripassianism Replacing Theological Patriarchalism?" in *God as Father?* ed. J.-B. Metz and E. Schillebeeckx, 51–56 (Edinburgh: T & T Clark, 1981); Jürgen Moltmann, *The Trinity and the Kingdom: The Doctrine of God* (London: SCM, 1981); Elisabeth Moltmann-Wendel and Jürgen Moltmann, *Humanity in God* (New York: Pilgrim, 1983); Elisabeth Moltmann-Wendel and Jürgen Moltmann, *God—His and Hers* (New York: Crossroad, 1991); Jürgen Moltmann, *History and the Triune God: Contributions to Trinitarian Theology* (London: SCM, 1991); Elisabeth Moltmann-Wendel, *Autobiography* (London: SCM, 1997); Jürgen Moltmann, *The Source of Life: The Holy Spirit and the Theology of Life* (London: SCM, 1997); Jürgen Moltmann, *Experiences in Theology: Ways and Forms of Christian Theology* (Minneapolis: Fortress Press, 2000). I am grateful to my doctoral student Faye Bodley-Dangelo for helping me collect these sources and for several informative discussions.

2. See, most notoriously, the charge of theological "sadism" by Dorothee Soelle, *Suffering* (Philadelphia: Fortress Press, 1975), 26–27, to which critique Moltmann has responded with clarity. See, e.g., *Experiences in Theology*, 375–76; Mary Louise Bringle, "Leaving the Cocoon: Moltmann's Anthropology and Feminist Theology," *Andover Newton Quarterly* 20 (1980): 153–61; Catherine Mowry LaCugna, "The Baptismal Formula, Feminist Objections, and Trinitarian Theology," *Journal of Ecumenical Studies* 26 (1989): 235–50; Elizabeth A. Johnson, "The Incomprehensibility of God and the Image of God Male and Female," *Theological Studies* 45 (1984): 441–65; Rebecca S. Chopp, *The Praxis of Suffering* (New York: Orbis, 1986), chap. 6; Elizabeth A. Johnson, *She Who Is: The Mystery of God in Feminist Theological Discourse* (New York: Crossroad, 1992), especially 207–37; Catherine Keller, *Apocalypse Now and Then: A Feminist Guide to the End of the World* (Boston: Beacon, 1996), chap. 7; Catherine Keller, "Pneumatic Nudges: The Theology of Moltmann, Feminism, and the Future," in *The Future of Theology: Essays in Honor of Jürgen Moltmann*, ed. M. Volf, C. Krieg, and T. Kucharz 142–53 (Grand Rapids, Mich.: Eerdmans, 1996); Darby K. Ray, *Deceiving the Devil: Atonement, Abuse, and Ransom* (Cleveland: Pilgrim, 1998), chap. 5; J. A. McDougall, "The Return of Trinitarian Praxis? Moltmann on the Trinity and the Christian Life," *Journal of Religion* 83 (2003): 177–203.

3. On this point, see especially Moltmann, "Feminist Theology for Men," in *Experiences in Theology*, chap. 5.

4. See especially their joint work, Moltmann and Moltmann-Wendel, *Humanity in God*, chap. 6.

5. See, e.g., Moltmann, *History and the Triune God*, xiii–xvi, which even anticipates some of the critical points I raise afresh in this essay. However, the position I adumbrate below is not one, I think, that can be easily subsumed into any of the "steps" of earlier feminist thought that Moltmann discusses here.

6. Attempts at providing typologies for successive waves have been attempted in older, but still useful, textbooks, such as Alison M. Jaggar, *Feminist Politics and Human Nature* (Totowa, N.J.: Rowman and Littlefield, 1988), and Rosemarie Tong, *Feminist Thought: A Comprehensive Introduction* (Boulder, Colo.: Westview, 1989). The work of Judith Butler, in particular, has since then queried the confident distinction between the categories "sex" and "gender" that characterized the theoretical discussion in the late 1970s and the 1980s. See Judith Butler, *Gender Trouble* (New York: Routledge, 1990), for a now classic problematization of the distinction.

7. This tension is particularly evident if we compare, for example, his earlier article, "The Motherly Father," where "femininity" and "masculinity" are used as if their descriptive use were unproblematic, with his more recent *Experiences in Theology*, chap. 5 ("Feminist Theology for Men"), where more guarded phrases much as "so-called femininity"(275) and "allegedly

feminine" (276) are used. Yet even in the latter chapter, there can still be the recommendation that women and men need to "arrive at their different, feminine or masculine identities," since "they are in [God's] image in their sexual difference and their community with one another" (285).

8. E.g., in Moltmann, *Experiences in Theology*, 274–78.

9. This is my own preferred definition of "gender," for it does not predetermine whether there are, or can be, only two "genders." It is also open to a richly theological rendition. The (rather different) phenomena of intersexuality and of transsexuality both suggest that a straightforward gender binary is misleading; yet *some* sort of distinction between "sex" and "gender" surely must still be maintained precisely if we are to do justice to the transsexual's conviction that s/he has been falsely attributed to a *sex* to which s/he does not really belong. On these issues, see most recently Judith Butler, *Undoing Gender* (New York: Routledge, 2004).

10. These are the *desiderata* stressed by Moltmann in *Experiences in Theology*, chap. 5. (See n. 34, below, for my comments on the conjoined intellectual heritage of Enlightenment and Romantic views of gender in Moltmann's writing.)

11. For "complementarity," see, e.g., Moltmann, *The Source of Life*, 116, where Moltmann is discussing how "Word and Spirit complement each other. The Word specifies and differentiates; the Spirit binds and forms the harmony." (Yet interestingly in Moltmann and Moltmann-Wendel, *His and Hers*, 33, in response to points made by his wife [ibid., 10], Moltmann can acknowledge that a merely "supplemental" view of "femininity" is insufficient.) For Moltmann's refererence, in Romantic mode, to a "feminine principle," see, e.g., Moltmann, *The Trinity and the Kingdom*, 57: "The theology of love is a theology of the Shekinah, a theology of the Holy Spirit. This means that it is not patriarchal, but rather feministic. For the Shekinah and the Holy Spirit are 'the feminine principle of the Godhead.'" Also cf. Moltmann, *Humanity in God*, 101; Moltmann and Moltmann-Wendel, *God—His and Hers*, 9.

12. Moltmann and Moltmann-Wendel, *God—His and Hers*, 35.

13. See, e.g., the discussion of this characteristically Moltmannian theme in *Humanity in God*, 104–6.

14. The translation of the Greek *koinonia* as "community" does beg the question of whether "communion" would not be a more appropriate rendition. Many have criticized Moltmann for a tritheistic emphasis in his trinitarianism, and also for a drift toward a dangerous anthropomorphism (raising new problems of idolatry) in his construal of the divine "persons" as distinct *centers of consciousness*. I share these anxieties but will not develop the particular point in this *Festschrift* chapter. For some astute criticisms of Moltmann on this issue, see K. Kilby, "Perichoresis and Projection: Problems with Social Doctrines of the Trinity," *New Blackfriars* 81 (2000): 432–45.

15. For the charge against so-called "Roman" patriarchal views of divinity, see, e.g., Moltmann, *God—His and Hers*, 33; Moltmann, *The Source of Life*, 35; and for a more general blaming of "Western," and specifically Augustinian, views of the Trinity for such ills, see Moltmann, *Humanity in God*, 100–106, especially 100–101; and Moltmann, *The Trinity and the Kingdom*, x. Such claims about so-called "Western" versus (in Moltmann's case, preferred) "Eastern" views of the Trinity are in my view now up for critical reassessment and seem to go back to a misdirected historiography of doctrine initiated by de Régnon. Among others, see M. R. Barnes, "De Régnon Reconsidered," *Augustinian Studies* 26 (1995): 51–79.

16. Moltmann, *Humanity in God*, 103.

17. For this interpretation, see, most recently, Moltmann, *Experiences in Theology*, 285.

18. See, e.g., Moltmann, *Humanity in God*, 103; Moltmann and Moltmann-Wendel, *God—His and Hers*, 8–9, 36–37; Moltmann, *The History of the Triune God*, 64–65; Moltmann, *The Source of Life*, 36.

19. See Moltmann and Moltmann-Wendel, *God—His and Hers*, 33–38, especially 37; cf. also Moltmann, *The Source of Life*, 27.

20. See Moltmann and Moltmann-Wendel, *God—His and Hers*, 10, where Elisabeth Moltmann-Wendel suggests that some women may want to "trust their fantasies more than

tradition" and to speak of Jesus as a "sister." She here also expresses criticism of any view of "'femininity" that merely "supplements" an existing "masculinity" (cf. again n. 11, above).

21. See again Moltmann, *The Source of Life*, 116, and n. 11 above.

22. Jürgen Moltmann, *The Crucified God* (London: SCM, 1974), 243; compare Moltmann, "The Motherly Father," 52–53.

23. Ibid., 53–54.

24. See Moltmann, *The Trinity and the Kingdom*, 164, to be compared with Moltmann, "The Motherly Father," where only the phrases "motherly Father" and "fatherly Father" are used.

25. Moltmann, "The Motherly Father," 53; cf. also Moltmann, *History and the Triune God*, 22–23.

26. Moltmann, "The Motherly Father," 53.

27. Ibid., 52–55; cf. also Moltmann, *Humanity in God*, 103.

28. Moltmann, "The Motherly Father," 51. Of course the "generation" here is not thought of in a physical sense, but in the ontological sense of fundamental dependence on the Creator. See also ibid., 53: "It is only in his relationship with his Son that God can *literally* be called 'Father'" (my emphasis).

29. Ibid., 51, 52.

30. See again ibid., 51–52. Moltmann does not spell out here the theological history of using the term literal in the sense of appropriate to God: for a discussion of the importance of Thomas's distinction between the "literal"/analogical and the "metaphorical" in connection with the naming of God as Father, see J. A. DiNoia, "Knowing and Naming the Triune God: The Grammar of Trinitarian Confession," in *Speaking the Christian God*, ed. Alvin F. Kimel, 162–87 (Grand Rapids, Mich., Eerdmans, 1992). For an entirely different rendition of the notion of "literal" speech for God (meaning univocal with ordinary use, rather than appropriate to God), see Richard Swinburne, *Revelation: From Metaphor to Analogy* (Oxford: Oxford Universtity Press, 1990), a work that also argues convincingly for the fluidity *over time* of "metaphorical," "analogical," and "literal" uses of terms for God. Moltmann does not consider the possibility that the same term could, diachronically, move from one category to another in its usage; nor does he reflect on the position (argued persuasively by Janet Martin Soskice, *Metaphor and Religious Language* (Oxford: Clarendon, 1985) that metaphors may in principle—and precisely *because* inappropriate to their subject—make robustly realistic claims about God without falling into idolatry.

31. See Moltmann, *The Source of Life*, 36: "Zinzendorf . . . describes the influence of the Spirit on the soul in romantic terms of great tenderness."

32. The history of this cluster of associations, and its contemporary application to feminist theory of the late 1970s and the 1980s, respectively, are well described in Sara Friedrichsmeyer, *The Androgyne in Early German Romanticism* (Bern: Peter Lang, 1983), and Mary Vetterling-Braggin, ed., *Femininity, Masculinity, and Androgyny: A Modern Philosophical Discussion* (Totowa, N.J.: Littlefield, Adams, 1982).

33. This tension is particularly evident in Moltmann, "Feminist Theology for Men," in *Experiences in Theology*: on the one hand, the "split" "male self" produces a problematic view of the mother, such that "mothering," just as much as "dominating," "must cease" in a post-patriarchal society (289); on the other hand, "feminine traditions" must be recuperated (278), so that one can feel "like a child in its mother's arms" (291).

34. See ibid., especially 273, 275, for discussion of the stereotypical gender disjunction. Note that in that essay Moltmann equally lauds the Enlightenment goals of freedom and equal rights and the Romantic notion of difference, claiming that there should be a "balance between likeness and difference" (ibid., 287).

35. See, e.g., Moltmann, *Humanity in God*, 94, where he admits that both Eastern and Western views of the Trinity have been utilized to represent the "Lordship of God—as dominion in super-power." Yet ibid., 100–106, could be read as suggesting that "the secret of the Triune God" (100) inexorably delivers a nonpatriarchal view of the deity.

36. This has been a distinctive theme in Moltmann's work since *The Church in the Power of the Spirit* (London: SCM, 1977), but see especially on this point his *History and the Triune God*, 68–69.

37. See again Butler, *Gender Trouble*, and also her *Bodies that Matter* (New York: Routledge, 1993); *Excitable Speech* (New York: Routledge, 1997); *The Psychic Life of Power* (Stanford, Calif.: Stanford University Press, 1997); and *Undoing Gender*.

38. What follows here is a very condensed form of an argument on gender and trinitarianism spelled out further in my *God, Sexuality and the Self: An Essay "On the Trinity"* (Cambridge, Cambridge University Press, forthcoming), especially chap. 1.

39. I have argued elsewhere for the significance of the prayer-based, incorporative logic of Romans 8 (as the only convincing model for the Trinity to protect the primary significance of the Spirit) in Sarah Coakley, "Why Three? Some Further Reflections on the Doctrine of the Trinity," in *The Making and Remaking of Christian Doctrine*, ed. S. Coakley and D. A. Pailin, 29–56 (Oxford: Oxford University Press, 1993).

40. Compare what Moltmann says about Gal. 3:28 in, e.g., *The Trinity and the Kingdom*, 165. He takes the passage to point beyond sexual subordination to fellowship between men and women; my stress is more on the rendering of the binary insignificant altogether (though without obliterating bodiliness or personal "difference"/distinctiveness). Cf., too, Moltmann, *History and the Triune God*, xiv–xv: It is important to distinguish both Moltmann's and my positions from the desire either to transcend the body altogether, or to suggest an "androgynous" personality.

41. Cf. Moltmann on Ephesians 5 ("The Motherly Father," 52), where he rightly reads v. 23 as a hierarchical ordering and so a "patriarchal pattern." My point, however, is that this order seems implicitly to undo itself in the same passage when we press the analogy of Christ's head and body as *jointly* and *inseparably* making up the church. In other words, while one cannot deny that this deutero-Pauline passage gives a New Testament mandate for the subordination of women to their husbands, it also contains the potential for an argument precisely to destabilize such a view.

42. Gregory of Nyssa's favored language of "mingling" for the unity of the divine and human in Christ has sometimes been read as a covert Apollinarianism. I argue against that reading and point out the erotic, as well as philosophical, allusions that Gregory is utilizing in this metaphor, in a forthcoming essay, "Desire and 'Mingling' in Gregory of Nyssa: A New Appraisal of His Anti-Apollinarian Christology." The point of the christological metaphor of "mingling," as I read Gregory, is to insist on the radical *transformation* of the human in the divine in Christ; when he applies this incarnational idea analogously to the *mingling* of sexual intercourse (*In Cant. 1.16*), it cannot therefore be read as an endorsement of a subordinationist view of woman, but rather as her opportunity for an equally radical transformation.

43. See Gregory of Nyssa, *de opificio hominis* 16.7–18. The interpretation of this intriguing passage has been much debated of late; suffice it to say, we should not be misled by an earlier, but influential, feminist assessment that reads Gregory as rendering body and gender *insignificant* by his argument here. (For this view see Rosemary Radford Ruether, "Virginal Feminism in the Fathers of the Church," in *Religion and Sexism*, ed. Rosemary Radford Ruether, 150–83 [New York: Simon and Schuster, 1974].) For a different assessment of Gregory on gender, and a review of recent literature, see Sarah Coakley, ed., *Re-Thinking Gregory of Nyssa* (Oxford: Blackwell, 2003), especially chaps. 1 and 5.

44. John of the Cross, "The Spiritual Canticle," Stanza 39.3–4, in *The Collected Works of St. John of the Cross*, ed. K. Kavanaugh and O. Rodriguez (Washington, D.C.: I.C.S. Publications, 1991), 623.

45. See Moltmann, *Humanity in God*, 100–101, and Moltmann and Moltmann-Wendel, *God—His and Hers*, 8–9, 36–37, for the Moltmanns' support of Nazianzen's analogy of father, mother, and child for the Trinity (with which Augustine took issue).

46. See Moltmann, *History and the Triune God*, 70–79, at 77 (my emphasis).

12. God's Perfect Life

1. *Summa Theologiae* 1a.q4.a1 corpus.

2. *Contra* Aquinas (*Summa Theologiae* 1a.q4.a2 corpus): "Whatever perfection exists in an effect must be found in the effective cause. . . . Since therefore God is the first effective cause of things, the perfections of all things must pre-exist in God in a more eminent way." The companionability between Aquinas's theological claim and the procedures adopted by some kinds of *perfect being* philosophy of religion ought not to be overstated. See K. A. Rogers, *Perfect Being Theology* (Edinburgh: Edinburgh University Press, 2000).

3. Karl Barth, *Die Kirchliche Dogmatik* (Zurich: EVZ, 1946), II/1:362.

4. See Isaak A. Dorner, *A System of Christian Doctrine* (Edinburgh: T&T Clark, 1880), 1:230.

5. H. Gollwitzer, *The Existence of God as Confessed by Faith* (London: SCM, 1965).

6. The best account of the matter remains Eberhard Jüngel, *God's Being Is in Becoming: The Trinitarian Being of God in the Theology of Karl Barth: A Paraphrase* (Edinburgh: T&T Clark, 2001).

7. Robert W. Jenson, *Systematic Theology*, 2 vols. (Oxford: Oxford University Press, 1997–99), 1:63–161.

8. Ibid., 1:64.

9. Dorner, *A System of Christian Doctrine*, 1:454.

10. Karl Barth, *Church Dogmatics* (Edinburgh: T&T Clark, 1957), II/1:306.

11. Dorner, *A System of Christian Doctrine*, 1:252.

12. Ibid., 1:257.

13. Ibid., 1:258.

14. Ibid., 1:259.

15. Jenson envisages his presentation of the doctrine of the triune God, in which "the biblical narrative . . . is the final truth of God's own reality" (Jenson, *Systematic Theology*, 1:108), as "the final overcoming within the doctrine of the Trinity of pagan antiquity's interpretation of being as persistence" (1:159).

16. Criticism of the dominance of protological concerns in trinitarian doctrine is a major topic in Jenson's pneumatology. See Jenson, *Systematic Theology*, 1:156–59.

17. A representative account is that of Catherine M. Lacugna, *God for Us: The Trinity and Christian Life* (New York: HarperCollins, 1991). Lacugna proposes that "[d]ivine perfection is the antithesis of self-sufficiency, rather it is the absolute capacity to be who and what one is by being for and from another" (304). Paul D. Molnar gives a trenchant response to the trend in *Divine Freedom and the Doctrine of the Immanent Trinity: In Dialogue with Karl Barth and Contemporary Theology* (Edinburgh: T&T Clark, 2002).

18. *Summa Theologiae* 1a.q43.a1.ad1; see also 1a.q42.a1.

19. In this connection, Aquinas's insistence that the divine processions are *ad intra*, that is, "corresponding to the act remaining within the agent" (*Summa Theologiae* 1a.q27.a1) offers a significant block against any hint of divine contingency.

20. *Summa Theologiae* 1a.q4.a2.ad3.

21. *[Full reference needed]*

22. Jenson, *Systematic Theology*, 1:64.

23. Dorner, *A System of Christian Doctrine*, 1:343.

24. Ibid., 1:343.

25. Ibid.

26. Jonathan Edwards, "The Pure in Heart Blessed," in *Sermons and Discourses 1730–1733*, ed. Mark Valeri (New Haven, Conn.: Yale University Press, 1999), 64.

27. Jürgen Moltmann, *Theology of Hope: On the Ground and the Implications of a Christian Eschatology* (London: SCM, 1967), 33.

13. DIVINE PROVIDENCE AND ACTION

1. In Protestant dogmatics, the doctrine of providence is usually expounded under the general heading of creation. Whereas for much medieval theology it is treated as an aspect of the doctrine of God, its links with creation and world government remain explicit. For a recent exploration of the location of providence in Aquinas, see Michael A. Hoonhout, "Grounding Providence in the Theology of the Creator: The Exemplarity of Thomas Aquinas," *Heythrop Journal* 43 (2002): 1–19.

2. Karl Barth, *Church Dogmatics* (Edinburgh: T&T Clark, 1960), III/3:57.

3. Hendrikus Berkhof, *Christian Faith* (Grand Rapids, Mich.: Eerdmans, 1986), 220.

4. The expression is that of Walter Brueggemann, *Theology of the Old Testament* (Grand Rapids, Mich.: Eerdmans, 1997), 528. In much of what follows, I am indebted to Brueggemann's discussion of creation as Yahweh's partner.

5. In this regard, the later distinction between general and special providence is not obviously apparent in Scripture. It may also be ecologically problematic if it suggests that creation is merely the external stage upon which the divine-human drama is enacted.

6. Jon Levenson, *Creation and the Persistence of Evil: The Jewish Drama of Divine Omnipotence* (Princeton: Princeton University Press, 1988).

7. The presence of such themes late in the wisdom tradition is explored by A. P. Hayman, "The Survival of Mythology in the Wisdom of Solomon," *Journal for the Study of Judaism* 30 (1999): 125–39.

8. Frederik Lindström, *Suffering and Sin: Interpretation of Illness in the Individual Complaint Psalms* (Stockholm: Almqvist & Wiskell, 1994). This point is discussed by Brueggemann, *Theology of the Old Testament*, 537.

9. Cf. Richard Bauckham, *The Theology of the Book of Revelation* (Cambridge: Cambridge University Press, 1993), 51–53.

10. *Summa Theologiae*, 1a.22.1.

11. Ibid., 1a.22.2.

12. Ibid.

13. Ibid.

14. Ibid., 1a.22.3. Cf. *De Potentia* 3.7.

15. Aquinas's relationship to Stoicism and his medieval predecessors is discussed in Gerard Verbeke, *The Presence of Stoicism in Medieval Thought* (Washington, D.C.: Catholic University Press, 1983), 71–96.

16. E.g., *Summa Theologiae*, 3a.24.1.

17. Ibid., 1a.23.

18. Keith Ward, *Rational Theology and Creativity of God* (Oxford: Blackwell, 1982), 87.

19. This is argued, for example, by William C. Placher, *The Domestication of Transcendence* (Louisville, Ky.: Westminster John Knox, 1996), 21–36.

20. These themes are treated in the context of divine providence by Brian Davies, *The Thought of Thomas Aquinas* (Oxford: Oxford University Press, 1992), 169–70.

21. *Summa Theologiae*, 2a.2ae.23.1.

22. Ibid., 1a. 105.5. Cajetan glosses this text with the remark, "Impotentis est non posse facere alia cooperativa sibi—it is weakness not to be able to let others cooperate with you." I owe this reference to Fergus Kerr. For further discussion of this topic, see Davies, *The Thought of Thomas Aquinas*, 177.

23. *Summa Theologiae*, 2a.2ae.83.2.

24. *Institutes* 1.17.5.

25. *Institutes* 1.17.10.

26. Ibid., 1.17.8. This sense of the total control of all things becomes even more marked in the history of Reformed theology with its threefold distinction between preservation, concurrence, and government. Cf. Heinrich Heppe's compendium, *Reformed Dogmatics* (Grand Rapids, Mich.: Baker, 1978), 251–80.

27. John Calvin, *Commentary on the Psalms*, trans. James Anderson, vols. 1–5 (Edinburgh: 1847).

28. Alexandra Walsham, *Providence in Early Modern England* (Oxford: Oxford University Press, 1999), 3. This thesis is argued by an exploration of journals, diaries, letters, autobiographies, and private memorabilia.

29. I owe this insight to my colleague David F. Wright's study of Calvin on the Pentateuch: "Calvin's Pentateuchal Criticism: Equity, Hardness of Heart, and Divine Accommodation in the Mosaic Harmony Commentary," *Calvin Theological Journal* 21 (1986): 33–50. He comments, "The distinctive element in this presentation seems not the gracious condescension of God but his malleability, even his vulnerability, indeed even his captivity to the passions and lusts of his rude people" (46).

30. "God in his unwearied kindness did not cease to strive with them on account of their perverseness of spirit." Calvin, *Commentary on the Psalms*, 4:242.

31. D. W. Torrance and T. F. Torrance, eds., *A Harmony of the Gospels: Matthew, Mark and Luke* (Edinburgh: St. Andrew, 1972), 1:221.

32. John Leith, *John Calvin's Doctrine of the Christian Life* (Louisville, Ky.: Westminster John Knox, 1989), 112.

33. G. W. Leibniz, *Theodicy* (London: Routledge & Kegan Paul, 1951). Voltaire parodies this account in his *Candide*. In the face of multiple calamities, he asks what must the other worlds be like if this is the best possible one.

34. David Blumenfeld, "Perfection and Happiness in the Best Possible World," in *Cambridge Companion to Leibniz*, ed. Nicholas Jolley (Cambridge: Cambridge University Press, 1995), 410.

35. Paul Helm, *The Providence of God: Contours of Christian Theology* (Leicester: Inter-Varsity, 1993).

36. In this regard, David Hume's theory of free will might be regarded as a secular variant of a theological account of freedom that held sway in the Reformed tradition.

37. Although its limitations are also stressed, the analogy is employed by Placher, *The Domestication of Transcendence*, 125.

38. For recent criticism of double agency along similar lines, see Vincent Brümmer, *Speaking of a Personal God: An Essay in Philosophical Theology* (Cambridge: Cambridge University Press, 1992), 108–10; and Paul Fiddes, *Participating in God: A Pastoral Doctrine of the Trinity* (London: Darton, Longman & Todd, 2000), 116–20.

39. Using the model of a stage director, rather than a playwright, who presides over a cast of actors, Tim Gorringe offers an account that is less determinist in *God's Theatre: A Theology of Providence* (London: SCM, 1991), 77–82.

40. Daniel L. Migliore, *Faith Seeking Understanding: An Introduction to Christian Theology* (Grand Rapids, Mich.: Eerdmans, 1991), 112.

41. A good example is John Sanders, *The God Who Risks: A Theology of Providence* (Downer's Grove, Ill.: InterVarsity, 1998). Sanders's work draws on a range of resources from biblical criticism and philosophical theology.

42. Gorringe, *God's Theatre*, 12.

43. Cf. J. R. Lucas, "Foreknowledge and the Vulnerability of God," in *The Philosophy in Christianity*, ed., Godfrey Vesey, 119–28 (Cambridge: Cambridge University Press, 1989).

44. This is argued by Colin Gunton. *The Triune Creator* (Edinburgh: Edinburgh University Press, 1998), 179–80.

45. W. H. Vanstone's *Love, Endeavour: Love's Expense* (London: Darton, Longman and Todd, 1977). The influence of Vanstone is explicit in the recent collection edited by John Polkinghorne, *The Work of Love: Creation as Kenosis* (Grand Rapids, Mich.: Eerdmans, 2001).

46. E.g., Levenson points out that Israel is never given the freedom to decide not to be chosen by God. In this respect, the covenant is unilateral although it creates also the possibility of free, obedient response. "Those who stand under covenantal obligation by nature and necessity are continually called upon to adopt that relationship by free decision." *Creation and*

the Persistence, 148. Similar remarks could be made in the context of the Christian doctrine of baptism.

47. An earlier version of this paper was presented as the presidential address at the (British) Society for the Study of Theology, 2002.

---

14. SPIRIT-CHRISTOLOGY AS ACCESS TO TRINITARIAN THEOLOGY

1. Cf. Karl Rahner, *The Trinity*, trans. J. Donceel (New York: Crossroad, 1997), 100. In the present essay, the teleological dimension of Spirit-Christology is named its prospective function; and the etiological dimension, its retrospective function.

2. The present dialogue between Jews and Christians has influenced the main theme of this essay. Cf. D. Ansorge, "God between Mercy and Justice: The Challenge of Auschwitz and the Hope of Universal Reconciliation," in *Good and Evil after Auschwitz: Ethical Implications for Today*, Proceedings of the Extraordinary Symposium at the Vatican in 1998, ed. J. Bemporad, J. Pawlikowski, and J. Sievers, 77–90 (Hoboken, N.J.: KTAV Publishing, 2000).

3. The prospective dimension of the Spirit-Christology of the early church is emphasized at the beginning of this essay so that the future role of Christians at the universal judgment is considered at the very start. For this reason the closing phrases of the second and the third articles of the Apostles' Creed are placed in the foreground of this systematic and pastoral-ethical reflection.

4. Cf. E. Stauffer, "ἐγώ" ("I"), in *Theological Dictionary of the New Testament*, hereafter cited as *TDNT*, ed. G. Kittel and G. Friedrich, trans. G. W. Bromiley, 10 vols. (Grand Rapids, Mich.: Eerdmans, 1964–76), 2:351. Stauffer states that the letters in Revelation are unique in the New Testament since they claim to be epistles sent from heaven in which Christ addresses the early church "in admonition, warning and promise."

5. Ernst Lohmeyer states that the connection of ideas in Rev. 3:20-21 is perfectly parallel to that which is found in Luke 22:29-30. The common meal of friendship is bound with the highest dignity of sharing in the community around the judgment throne of Christ; cf. *Die Offenbarung des Johannes*, Handbuch zum Neuen Testament 16 (Tübingen: J. C. B. Mohr, 1970), 39.

6. K. Schneider, "κάθημαι" ("to sit"), *TDNT*, 3:442.

7. H. Kraft affirms that the words of Christ to those who have conquered with him promise them a participation in his heavenly kingship. The biblical concept of following Christ does not imply an external and formal similarity to him, but a similarity based on like-mindedness and common goals. Cf. *Die Offenbarung des Johannes*, Handbuch zum Neuen Testament, 16/a (Tubingen: J. C. B. Mohr, 1974), 86–87.

8. Cf. O. Schmitz, "θρόνος" ("throne"), *TDNT*, 3:165, n. 34: "The act of sitting on the throne, which is alluded to in other places, indicates entrance into a judging activity"; and on p. 166 the author maintains that "already in Rev. 3:21 Jesus shares the throne of his Father, and promises the fellowship of the throne to those who overcome."

9. These observations on the freedom of the triune God and of human beings mirror the thoughts of Jürgen Moltmann, *The Trinity and the Kingdom of God: The Doctrine of God* (New York: Harper & Row, 1981), 212–22, especially the subdivision entitled "The Trinitarian Doctrine of Freedom."

10. Cf. Jürgen Moltmann, *The Way of Jesus Christ: Christology in Messianic Dimensions* (Minneapolis: Fortress Press, 1993), 73–150, esp. chap. 3, "The Messianic Mission of Christ," which begins with the subdivision "Spirit Christology."

11. Cf. Joachim Jeremias, *The Parables of Jesus* (New York: Charles Schribner's Sons, 1963), 229: "The parable-like actions of Jesus are kerygmatic. They show that Jesus had not only announced the message of the parables, but also that he had lived it and incorporated it into his person."

12. Gerhard von Rad, *Old Testament Theology: The Theology of Israel's Prophetic Traditions* (New York; Harper & Row, 1965), 2:95–98. On p. 96, the author writes: "For antiquity, the sign, like the solemn word we have already discussed, could not only signify a datum but actually

embody it as well; this means that it can act creatively, and in earlier cultures it probably had an even greater power to do so than the word."

13. The description of these Lucan texts as prophetic actions is based on the two studies that von Rad cites in the pages mentioned above in n. 12 of this chapter: W. Robinson, "Prophetic Symbolism," in *Old Testament Essays*, 16 (Charles Griffin & Co., 1924), in which the author speaks of the "sacramental meaning" of the prophetic sign-actions in Israel; and Georg Fohrer, *Die symbolischen Handlungen der Propheten* (Zürich: Zwingli Verlag, 1953).

14. Cf. Morna Hooker, *The Signs of a Prophet: The Prophetic Actions of Jesus* (Harrisburg, Pa.: Trintiy Press International, 1997).

15. Most exegetes hold that the faith of the penitent woman brought about her previous conversion, of which her loving gestures toward Jesus are the signs of gratitude. Cf. H. Schür-mann, *Das Lukasevangelium*, 1. Teil, Kommentar zu Kap. 1.1–9.50 (Frieburg im Breisgau, Germany: Herder, 1969), 436–38, and Joseph A. Fitzmyer, *The Gospel according to Luke (i–ix)* (Garden City, N.Y.: Doubleday, 1981), 1:686–87, 691–92.

16. Cf. Joseph A. Fitzmyer, *The Gospel according to Luke (x–xxiv)* Anchor Bible 28 (Garden City, N.Y.: Doubleday, 1985), 2:1011–12, in which the author points out that Jesus, while upbraiding the lack of compassion on the part of the crowd and of the leader of the synagogue, was not rude to them, but employed rational and forceful arguments.

17. These considerations on the eternity of the triune God as different *moments*, such as preincarnational and post-kingdom, can be justified in that both the retrospective and the prospective functions of Spirit-Christology demand logical presuppositions of their possibility. Even if it is claimed that the economic Trinity and the immanent Trinity are one and the same, the eternity of God is a mystery of faith, which Christian theology can contemplate only from the different points of view that sacred Scripture provides.

18. These viewpoints on the divine eternity, which Spirit-Christology affords, attempt to clarify two important articles of the Apostles' Creed: the Son was made flesh by the power of the Holy Spirit (from the second article), and the Holy Spirit leads the baptized into eternal life (from the third article).

19. In this way, without denying that human sin only partially tainted the goodness of the original creation, the Christian theologian can speak about the mandate of the Re-creator to renew it objectively through justification, and about the mandate of the Trans-creator to lead it subjectively, through holiness, to the fullness of its re-creation. The advantage of Spirit Christology is its ability to explain the justification and the sanctification of creation in a unified fashion while it respects the specific dynamism of the mandates of the Son and of the Spirit.

20. It is usually affirmed that the Son is the image and the communication of the truth of the Father; yet, in light of the present reconciling mission of the church, Christian theology can claim that the truth of God can be characterized through nonviolence and benevolence.

21. These observations are influenced by the thought of J. Moltmann in *The Trinity and the Kingdom of God*; they mirror what he has proposed especially in the subdivisions on pp. 182–87 entitled "The Procession of the Spirit from the Father of the Son" and "What the Holy Spirit Receives from the Son."

22. The terms *Father-Creator*, *Son-Re-creator*, and *Spirit-Trans-creator* clearly entail an attempt to use the word *Creator* as a root, first without any prefix and then with two different prefixes so that both the unity of the three divine persons and their threeness can be emphasized. The Father-Creator is the ground of the eternal nonviolence and benevolence; the Son-Re-creator is its objective image in the form of kenosis; and the Spirit-Trans-creator is its subjective image in the form of the glorification of the kenosis of the Son and of the creative power of the Father.

23. Cf. Moltmann, *The Way of Jesus Christ*, 336–38, a section entitled "The Christian Dilemma." Here the author distinguishes between the apocalyptic and the eschatological understandings of the universal judgment and favors the eschatological one, which rests on the saving gospel of Jesus Christ, who brings justice to those who have never received it and makes the unjust just. This is also the preference of O. Schmitz who understands Jesus along

with the community gathered around his throne of judgment (cf. Rev. 3:21) in such a way that he has participants in his judging activity, which is not the case in Matt. 25:31–46. This image of Jesus as the judge along with the members of his community is in greater accord with his message of justification than is the apocalyptic understanding; cf. O. Schmitz, "θρόνος" ("Throne") in TDNT 3:165.

24. Cf. Moltmann, *The Way of Jesus Christ*, 324–25; here the author states that the coming of Jesus not only as the Lord of the Church and the Messiah of Israel, but also as the Son of Man can be understood in such a way that the expectations of all people, in their various religious traditions, can be realized, who live with earnest longing for the final arrival of the new creation marked by justice and freedom.

25. This conclusion depends on the insight that both Christian orthodoxy, which is oriented to the future of Christ, and Christian orthopraxy, which is inspired by this same reality, are possible only in the power of the Holy Spirit. In a short formula, it can be said that the Father-Creator is the source of orthodoxy and of orthopraxy, the Son-Re-creator is their substance, and the Holy Spirit-Trans-creator is their efficacy.

15. Is There Justice in the Trinity?

1. Oliver O'Donovan, *The Desire of the Nations: Rediscovering the Roots of Political Theology* (Cambridge: Cambridge University Press, 1996).

2. The passage is translated in the NRSV as follows: "Hate evil and love good, and establish justice in the gate."

3. The passage reads thus in the NRSV: "Cease to do evil, learn to do good; seek justice, rescue the oppressed, defend the orphan, plead for the widow."

4. O'Donovan, *The Desire of the Nations*, 39. The NRSV renders the last passage cited: "And I will restore your judges as at the first, and your counselors as at the beginning. Afterward you shall be called the city of righteousness, the faithful city. Zion shall be redeemed by justice, and those in her who repent, by righteousness."

5. Ibid.

6. The NRSV has "righteousness" instead of "rectitude."

7. Mic. 6:8.

8. O'Donovan, *The Desire of the Nations*, 38.

9. The argumentation will be offered in my forthcoming book, *Justice*.

10. Brian Tierney, *The Idea of Natural Rights: Studies on Natural Rights, Natural Law, and Church Law* (Atlanta: Scholars, 1997).

11. What Kant actually said was, always treat *humanity* in a person as an end, never merely as a means. It will not be necessary for my purposes here to explain why Kant inserted the reference to humanity.

16. Eschatology and Christology

1. Cappadocia is a mountainous region in central Asia Minor stretching from the Pontic mountains to the Taurus and from the Salt Lake to the Euphrates. The Cappadocian Fathers combated fourth-century Arianism and became theological authorities in the Orthodox world. For an introduction to their thought, with special attention to the doctrine of creation, see Jaroslav Pelikan, *Christianity and Classical Culture: The Metamorphosis of Natural Theology in the Christian Encounter with Hellenism* (New Haven, Conn.: Yale University Press, 1993).

2. Jürgen Moltmann, *The Trinity and the Kingdom of God: The Doctrine of God*, trans. Margaret Kohl (New York: Harper & Row, 1981), 175.

3. Jürgen Moltmann, *Experiences of God*, trans. Margaret Kohl (Philadelphia: Fortress Press, 1980), 7.

4. Specifically in the first and second of the *Theological Orations*, numbered 27 and 28 in Gregory's corpus. Cf. Gregoire de Nazianze, *Discours 27–31*, ed. Paul Gallay, SC 250 (Paris: Cerf, 1978).

5. Cf. Gregory of Nyssa, *On the Life of Moses* 249–55, ed. Jean Daniélou, SC 1 (Paris: Cerf, 2000), 278–82; St. Gregory of Nyssa, *The Life of Moses*, trans. Abraham Malherbe and Everett Ferguson (New York: Paulist, 1978), 118–20.

6. The Philippian notion of *epektasis* encapsulates Gregory of Nyssa's doctrine of perpetual ascent (or deepening) into divine infinity, detailed in his *On the Life of Moses* 5–10, ed. Daniélou, 48–50. See also Gregory of Nyssa, *Life of Moses* 5–10, trans. Malherbe and Ferguson, 30–31.

7. Jürgen Moltmann, *God in Creation: An Ecological Doctrine of Creation*, trans. Margaret Kohl, Gifford Lectures (San Francisco: Harper & Row, 1985).

8. On this subject, Moltmann's cosmology has many parallels with Dionysius the Areopagite, *On the Divine Names* 4.13 and 4.7.3 (cited below, nn. 17–18).

9. The Greek text used in this paper is the edition of Emmanuel Amand de Mendieta and Stig Y. Rudberg, *Basilius von Caesarea. Homilien zu Hexaemeron*, GCS, Neue Folge 2 (Berlin: Akademie Verlag, 1997). I have also consulted Stanislas Giet's earlier edition, *Basile de Césarée. Homélies sur l'Hexaéméron*, SC26 (Paris: Cerf, 1968). English translations are adapted from Agnes Clare Way's in *Saint Basil: Exegetic Homilies*, FC 46 (Washington, D.C.: Catholic University of America Press, 1963), 3–150.

10. Cf. Louis Swift, "Basil and Ambrose on the Six Days of Creation," *Augustinianum* 21 (1981): 317–28; Robert W. Thomson, *The Syriac Version of the* Hexaemeron *of Basil of Caesarea*, CSCO, vols. 550–51, Scriptores Syri (Louvain: Peeters, 1995); Robert Grosseteste, *Hexaëmeron*, ed. Richard C. Dales and Servus Gieben (London: Oxford University Press for the British Academy, 1990); Richard W. Southern, *Robert Grosseteste: The Growth of an English Mind in Medieval Europe* (Oxford: Clarendon, 1992); and Henry W. Norman, *The Anglo-Saxon Version of the* Hexaemeron *of St. Basil* (London: J. R. Smith, 1848).

11. Gregory Nazianzus, *Oration*, ed. Jean Bernardi, SC 384 (Paris: Cerf, 1992), 272.

12. Basil, *Hexaemeron*, ed. Alexis Smets and Michel van Esbroeck, SC 160 (Paris: Cerf, 1970), 166. Note that the authenticity of this tenth sermon remains under discussion; it may reasonably be ascribed to the school of Basil, if not to Basil himself.

13. For a discussion of this process, see Paul Blowers, *Exegesis and Spiritual Pedagogy in Maximus the Confessor: An Investigation of the Quaestiones ad Thalassium* (Notre Dame, Ind.: University of Notre Dame Press, 1991). See also Jaroslav Pelikan, "The 'Spiritual Sense' of Scripture: The Exegetical Basis for St. Basil's Doctrine of the Holy Spirit," in *Basil of Caesarea: Christian, Humanist, Ascetic*, ed. Paul J. Fedwick (Toronto: Pontifical Institute of Medieval Studies, 1981), 2:337–60; and Philip Rousseau, *Basil of Caesarea* (Berkeley: University of California Press, 1994), 318–49.

14. R. P. Lawson, *Origen: The Song of Songs, Commentary and Homilies*, ACW 26 (New York: Newman, 1956), 43–44; cf. Marguerite Harl, "Les trois livres de Salomon et les parties de la philosophie dans les Prologues des Commentaires sur le *Cantique des Cantiques* (d'Origène aux chaînes exégètiques grecques)," in *Texte und Textkritik: Eine Aufsatsammlung*, ed. Jürgen Dummer, 249–69 (Berlin: Akademie-Verlag, 1987).

15. Basil, *Hom.* 12.1, *On the Beginning of the Book of Proverbs*: "We know of three treatises by Solomon: Proverbs, Ecclesiastes, and the Song of Songs, each one composed for a particular purpose (*skopos*). Proverbs is for the correction and amendment of our vices, and for teaching a right manner of living. Ecclesiastes touches on the logic of nature (*physiologia*), and reveals to us the vanity of this world, so that we do not imagine that transient things are worthy of our attention, or that vain things are worthy of the soul's concern. The Song of Songs indicates the manner of the perfection of the soul, for it describes the intimacy of the soul with God as the union of a bride and groom" (PG 31.388AB).

16. For discussion, see Robert Lamberton, *Homer the Theologian: Neoplatonist Allegorical Reading and the Growth of the Epic Tradition* (Berkeley: University of California Press, 1986).

17. Dionysisus, *On the Divine Names*, ed. B. R. Suchla, *Corpus Dionysiacum* I (Berlin, 1990), 159, lines 9–14; cf. Eric Perl, "The Metaphysics of Love in Dionysius the Areopagite," *Journal of Neoplatonic Studies* 6, no. 1 (1997): 45–73.

18. Dionysius, *On the Divine Names*, 198, lines 8–9.

19. Cf. Basil, *Hexaemeron* 1.2: "Not knowing God, they (i.e., the philosophers) could not grasp the minded (*emphronos aitia*) cause of creation, but rather drew their conclusions in a manner consistent with their initial ignorance" (ed. GCS, 4, lines 4–6; trans. Way, 5).

20. Argued by Philip Rousseau, *Basil of Caesarea*, The Transformation of the Classical Heritage 20 (Berkeley, Calif.: University of Californa Press, 1998), 321.

21. The Greek text and English translation are in Basil, *The Letters*, trans. Roy J. Defarrari, (Cambridge, Mass.: Harvard University Press, 1970), 4:200.

22. *Hexaemeron* 3.10 (ed. GCS, 55, lines 7–18; trans. Way, 53); cf. *Hexaemeron*, 1.7, where all the arts are said to have their "proper purpose, aim, and end" (ed. GCS, 12, lines 6–15; trans. Way, 11–12).

23. Cf. Evagrius of Pontus, *Thoughts* 25: "Demonic thought in fact is an incomplete image of the sensible person constituted in the intellect," trans. Robert Sinkewicz, *Evagrius of Pontus: The Greek Ascetic Corpus* (Oxford: Oxford University Press, 2003), 171.

24. *Hexaemeron* 1.7 (ed. GCS, 12, lines 16–17; trans. Way, 12). Homilies 1 and 2 were delivered on the morning and evening of the same day ("before and after work"), and thus homily 3 was given on the following morning. Note that there may have been stone carvers among the "artisans" present in Basil's congregation; cf. *Hom.* 3.1 (ed. GCS, 39, lines 1–2; trans. Way, 37).

25. *Hexaemeron* 4.6 (ed. GCS, 66, lines 9–19; Way, 63–64).

26. Origen, *Commentary on the Song of Songs*, trans. Lawson, 44.

27. Cf. Lawson, *Origen*, 43–44; cf. Gregory of Nyssa, *Commentary on the Song of Songs*, *Hom.* 4, trans. Casimir McCambley (Brookline, Mass.: Holy Cross, 1987), 105; Evagrius of Pontus, *Commentary on Ecclesiastes* 1.2, ed. Paul Gehin, SC 397 (Paris: Cerf, 1993), 58: "To those who have entered the spiritual *ecclesia*, and who have contemplated the nature of created beings, this verse says, 'Do not think that this is the ultimate end that is set aside for you in the promises,' for all these things are 'vanity of vanities' with respect to the knowledge of God himself. For just as medicines are in vain after perfect health, so too the knowledge of the principles of the ages and of worlds is in vain after one has attained the knowledge of the Holy Trinity." See also Theodoret, *Commentary on the Song of Songs*: "Ecclesiastes interprets the nature of visible things, and teaches us about the vanity of the present life, so that we might learn how all things in the present are subject to death, and thus despise them, and desire the future things which last forever" (PG 81.48A).

28. As above, n. 24.

29. See the nearly 30 citations indexed in GCS, 22.

30. These terms occur in *Hexaemeron* 1.5 (ed. GCS, 9, line 12; trans. Way, 9), and again in 1.6 (ed. GCS, 11, lines 11–12; trans. Way, 11).

31. Ibid., 7.3–4 (ed. GCS, 118–20, lines 21–28; trans. Way, 111–12).

32. Ibid., 7.3 (ed. GCS, 116, lines 10–24; trans. Way, 109).

33. Ibid., 7.5 (ed. GCS, 121 line 25 and 122 line 1; trans. Way, 114).

34. *Hom.* 21, *On Detachment from the World* 5 (PG 31.549A).

---

17. JOHN DONNE ON THE TRINITY

1. *Theological Investigations* (London: Darton, Longman and Todd, 1967), 3:294–317, especially 294–302 (poets) and 302–7 (priests).

2. See Jürgen Moltmann, *The Crucified God: The Cross of Christ as the Foundation and Criticism of Christian Theology*, trans. R. A. Wilson and John Bowden (New York: Harper & Row, 1974); *The Trinity and the Kingdom: The Doctrine of God*, trans. Margaret Kohl (New York: Harper & Row, 1981); *History and the Triune God: Contributions to Trinitarian Theology* (New York: Crossroad, 1992).

3. See, most recently, John Donne, *The Complete English Poems*, ed. and intro. C. A. Patrides (New York: Knopf, 1991), for all the poems discussed herein.

4. See, for example, the wonderfully direct poem by George Herbert, "Trinity Sunday," in his collection *The Temple* (1633).

5. In Immanuel Kant, *Religion and Rational Theology*, trans. A. W. Wood and G. di Giovanni (Cambridge: Cambridge University Press, 1996), 264 (emphasis added).

6. See John Donne, *Sermons*, ed. George R. Potter and Evelyn M. Simpson (Berkeley: University of California Press, 1953–62).

7. Donne understood "litany" as supplication or humble and heartfelt petition.

8. See Thomas Aquinas in *In 2 Sent.* 35.1.2c: "*ubi amor, ibi oculus* (where there is love, here is vision)."

---

18. TRINITARIAN BELIEF AND WORSHIP

1. John Calvin, *Institutes* 1.13.2.

2. Philip W. Butin, *Revelation, Redemption, and Response: Calvin's Trinitarian Understanding of the Divine-Human Relationship* (New York: Oxford University Press, 1995).

3. Richard Muller, *The Unaccommodated Calvin: Studies in the Foundation of a Theological Tradition* (New York: Oxford University Press, 2000); Stephen Edmondson, *Calvin's Christology* (Cambridge: Cambridge University Press, 2004).

4. *Institutes* 1.13.19.

5. Stephen Hampton, "Reformed Scholasticism and the Battle for Orthodoxy in the Later Stuart Church" (D.Phil. diss., University of Oxford, 2002).

6. Philip Dixon, *Nice and Hot Disputes: The Doctrine of the Trinity in the Seventeenth Century* (New York: Continuum, 2003).

7. Bryan D. Spinks, "*Johannes Grabe's Response to William Whiston: Some Reflections on a Lutheran Convert's Contribution to 18th-Century Anglican Orthodoxy and Liturgy*," in *Lord Jesus Christ, Will You Not Stay: Essays in Honor of Ronald Feuerhahn on the Occasion of His Sixty-Fifth Birthday*, ed. Barth Day et al, 91–104 (St. Louis: Concordia, 2002).

8. James P. Ferguson, *Dr. Samuel Clarke: An Eighteenth Century Heretic* (Kineton: Roundwood, 1976), for fuller biographical details.

9. Ibid., 40–41.

10. Thomas Emlyn, *Works* (London, 1746), 2:479.

11. Samuel Clarke, *Scripture: Doctrine of the Trinity, In Three Parts* (London, 1712), viii.

12. Ibid., xi.

13. Here Clarke places together what for Nicenes were different issues, derivation and subordination.

14. Clarke, *Scripture: Doctrine of the Trinity*, 241.

15. Ibid., 243.

16. Ibid., 244.

17. Ibid., 245.

18. Ibid., 263, 265.

19. Ibid., 270.

20. Ibid., 304, 349, 290–92, 272.

21. Ibid., 354.

22. Ibid., 415–80.

23. British Library C.24.b.21. The book was printed by John Basketh, London. It was presented to the British Museum by Clarke's son. This should not be confused with *The Book of Common Prayer Reformed According to the Plan of the Late Dr. Samuel Clarke*, London, 1774, which bears little semblance to Clarke's manuscript suggestions.

24. Ibid.

25. Ibid.

26. Thomas C. Pfizenmaier, *The Trinitarian Theology of Dr. Samuel Clarke (1675–1729): Context, Sources, and Controversy* (Leiden: Brill, 1997), 136.

27. Ibid., 140.

28. Robert Gregg, ed., *Arianism: Historical and Theological Reassessments* (Philadelphia: Philadelphia Patristic Foundation, 1985); Rowan Williams, *Arius: Heresy and Tradition*, rev. ed. (Grand Rapids, Mich.: Eerdmans, 2002).

29. James E. Force and Richard H. Popkin, *Essays on the Context, Nature, and Influence of Isaac Newton's Theology* (Dordrecht: Kluwer Academic Publishers, 1990); Force and Popkin, eds., *Newton and Religion: Context, Nature, and Influence* (Dordrecht: Kluwer Academic Publishers, 1999).

30. Newton, Yahuda Ms 14, f.25, Hebrew University, Jerusalem. Cited by James E. Force, "Newton's God of Dominion," in Force and Popkin, *Essays on the Context*, 79.

31. Keynes Ms 10, "Paradoxical questions concerning the morals & actions of Athanasius & his followers."

32. Isaac Newton, *Principia*, trans. Andrew Motte, rev. Florian Cajori (Berkeley: University of California Press, 1960 [1729]), 546.

33. See Richard H. Popkin, "Newton as a Bible Scholar," in Force and Popkin, *Essays on the Context*, 103–5.

34. Samuel Clarke, *A Discourse Concerning the Unchangeable Obligations of Natural Religion* (London, 1706), 239–40.

35. Newton, *Principia*, 544.

36. James E. Force, "Newton's God of Dominion," in Force and Popkin *Essays on the Context*, 79.

37. Isaac Newton, *Opticks* (1730; New York: Dover Publications, 1952), 403–4.

38. Newton, *Principia*, 546.

39. Newton, Yahuda MS 15.1, Hebrew University, Jerusalem, cited in Force, "Newton's God of Dominion," 79.

40. Clarke, *Scripture Doctrine of the Trinity*, 332–33.

41. Thomas Hobbes, *Leviathan*, chapter 16: "A PERSON is he whose words or actions are considered, either as his own, or as representing the words or actions of an other man, or of any other thing to which they are attributed, whether Truly or by Fiction. When they are considered as his owne, then he is called a *Naturall Person*: And when considered as representing the words or actions of an other, then he is a Feigned or *Artificiall Person*."

42. John Locke, *An Essay Concerning Human Understanding*, ed. Peter H. Nidditch (Oxford: Oxford University Press, 1975), 2:27.9.

43. *Rationes* No. 7, cited by Pfizenmaier, *The Trinitarian Theology of Dr. Samuel Clarke*, 163.

44. R. Mayo, *A Plain Scripture-Argument against Dr. Clark's Doctrine Concerning the Ever-Blessed Trinity* (London, 1715), 8.

45. Ibid., 27.

46. Dixon, *Nice and Hot Disputes*, 194.

47. C. Kavin Rowe, "Luke and the Trinity: An Essay in Ecclesial Biblical Theology," *Scottish Journal of Theology* 56 (2003): 1–26, 13–14.

48. Margaret Barker, *The Great High Priest: The Temple Roots of Christian Liturgy* (London: Continuum, 2003). Even if Barker's argument that YHWH was originally the son of El'Elyon, this makes no difference to the equating of YHWH and Jesus.

49. See Christopher R. Seitz, "Our Help Is in the Name of the LORD, the Maker of Heaven and Earth," in *Nicene Christianity: The Future for a New Ecumenism*, ed. Christopher Seitz (Grand Rapids, Mich.: Brazos, 2001), 19–34.

50. Augustine, *De fide et symbolo* 9.6. Emphasis added.

51. Bryan D. Spinks, "Trinitarian Theology and the Eucharistic Prayer," *Studia Liturgica* 26 (1996): 209–24.

52. Though for symptoms of modernity, see Kathryn Greene-McCreight, *Feminist Reconstruction of Christian Doctrine* (New York: Oxford University Press, 2000).

53. Ruth C. Duck, *Gender and the Name of God: The Trinitarian Baptismal Formula* (New York: Pilgrim, 1991).

54. Ruth C. Duck and Patricia Wilson-Kastner, *Praising God: The Trinity in Christian Worship* (Louisville, Ky.: Westminster John Knox, 1999).

55. Ibid., 54.

56. Jürgen Motlmann has argued that the narrative context shows precisely the unique manner in which "Father" is used in the New Testament. "The Motherly Father," in *Faith and the Future*, ed. Johann-Baptist Metz and Jürgen Moltmann, 123–30 (Maryknoll, N.Y.: Orbis, 1995). It may be the case that contra both Duck and some of her critics, Father, Son, and Spirit are neither the proper name nor one among many metaphors for the Triune God; but, as R. Kendall Soulen urges, one indispensable inflexion of the YHWH who has done, does, and will do. R. Kendall Soulen, "Who Shall I Say Sent Me? The Name of God in Trinitarian Perspective," unpublished paper. See also his "Hallowed Be Thy Name! The Tetragrammaton and the Name of the Trinity," in *Jews and Christians: People of God*, ed. Carl E. Braaten and Robert W. Jenson, 14–40 (Grand Rapids, Mich.: Eerdmans 2003).

57. Karen B. Westerfield Tucker, "'Praise God from Whom All Blessings Flow': Trinitarian Euchology in the Churches of the Reformation," in *Source and Summit*, ed. Joanne M. Pierce and Michael Downey, 109–20 (Collegeville, Minn.: Liturgical, 1999).

58. Alexander E. Peaston, *The Prayer Book Reform Movement in the XVIIIth Century* (Oxford: Blackwell, 1940).

59. Thomas Marsh, *The Triune God: A Biblical, Historical and Theological Study* (Dublin, Ireland: Columba, 1994), 9.

Index

Available from Gütersloher Verlag—

Der lebendige Gott als Trinität

Edited by Michael Welker and Miroslav Volf

CONTENTS

416 pp.; paperback, €39,95, ISBN 3-479-05229-2
To order, visit www.gtvh.de.

DEDICATION

To Mom and Rodney here with me, and Dad in Heaven...

I love you.